MARCELLA M. MEALIA
Sales Representative
District Office
217 McKee
Willowdale, Ontario M2N 4C8
Telephone: 416-223-4759

WM. C. BROWN COMPANY PUBLISHERS
DUBUQUE, IOWA 52001

What Will We Do in the Morning?

The Exceptional Student in the Regular Classroom

What Will We Do

Senior Authors

Michael L. Hardman
University of Utah

M. Winston Egan
University of Utah

Elliott D. Landau
University of Utah

wcb
Wm. C. Brown Company Publishers
Dubuque, Iowa

in the Morning?

The Exceptional Student in the Regular Classroom

Backgrounds of Contributors

Hearing Impairment

Grant B. Bitter
University of Utah

Margot J. Butler
Extension Division of Utah School for the Deaf

Visual Impairment

Ruth Craig
Brigham Young University

Claudia Howard
SLC School District

Severe-Multiply Handicapped

Mary K. Dykes
University of Florida

Child Development

Elliott D. Landau
University of Utah

Mental Retardation

Michael L. Hardman
University of Utah

Joan Sebastian
*Educational Consultant
Salt Lake City, Utah*

Media Specialist

Joanne Gilles
Utah State Office of Education

Learning Disabilities

Mary Buchanan
University of Utah

Susan Ryberg
*Educational Consultant
Salt Lake City, Utah*

Joan Sebastian
*Educational Consultant
Salt Lake City, Utah*

Carol Weller
University of Utah

Joan Wolf
University of Utah

Behavior Disorders

M. Winston Egan
University of Utah

Jeannette Misaka
University of Utah

Bill R. Wagonseller
University of Nevada/Las Vegas

Gifted and Talented

Jeanette Misaka
University of Utah

Gloria Rupp
*Granite School District
Salt Lake City, Utah*

Joan Wolf
University of Utah

wcb group

Wm. C. Brown, Chairman of the Board
Mark C. Falb, Corporate Vice President/Operations

Book Team

William J. Fitzgerald and Susan J. Soley, Editors
Julia A. Scannell, Designer
Nicholas Murray, Production Editor
Mary M. Heller, Visual Research
Mavis M. Oeth, Permissions Editor

wcb

Wm. C. Brown Company Publishers, College Division
Lawrence E. Cremer, President
Raymond C. Deveaux, Vice President/Product Development
David Wm. Smith, Assistant Vice President/National Sales Manager
David A. Corona, Director of Production Development and Design
Matthew T. Coghlan, National Marketing Manager
Janis Machala, Director of Marketing Research
Marilyn A. Phelps, Manager of Design
William A. Moss, Production Editorial Manager
Mary M. Heller, Visual Research Manager

Photo Credits

Cover Photo
Bob Coyle

Part Opening Photos
Part 1   *Peter Karas*
Part 2   *Julie O'Neill*
Part 3   *Bob Coyle*
Part 4   *Jean-Claude Lejeune*

Chapter Opening Photos
Chapters 4 and 12   *Paul Conklin*
Chapter 10   *Peter Karas*
Chapters 1–3, 5–9, and 11   *John Telford*

Contents

Foreword

An outstanding feature of this book is that it provides regular teachers with concise and accurate information about two public laws exemplifying new directions in public policy: (1) Section 504 of the Vocational Rehabilitation Act, and (2) the Education of All Handicapped Children Act: Public Law 94–142. Intellectually, morally, educationally, and ethically, these recent acts of legislation mandating public schools to provide handicapped students with free and appropriate education in the least restrictive environment are fundamentally sound. How to implement them, however, is a nationwide challenge. Admittedly, "least restrictive environment" is not to be interpreted to mean that every handicapped child be placed even a portion of the day in a regular classroom; but for mild and moderately handicapped children, the regular classroom is usually the least restrictive environment.

Much of the resistance among regular educators to having handicapped children placed in their classrooms arises from lack of knowledge about handicapping conditions and their impact on learning and behavior, as well as from lack of skills essential for educating handicapped students in the mainstream. The better prepared regular teachers are to facilitate the integration and learning of handicapped children, the more likely they are to be successful. Thus, preservice training of prospective teachers must include in its course offerings and practicum experiences an understanding of handicapping conditions and strategies for facilitating the students' optimal learning and development in the regular classroom. This book should serve as a valuable reference in the training of regular teachers. Since mainstreaming is the accepted practice for educating the gifted and talented, the regular classroom teacher is also concerned about meeting the individual needs of these children. Children with outstanding gifts and talents need an appropriate educational program rather than just more of the same.

Regular teachers in service, who have completed their formal training, need additional training to acquire information that will enable them to understand and program for exceptional children placed in their regular classes. This book responds to the inservice needs of regular teachers who have or may have handicapped and gifted children in their classroom.

It is important for the regular teacher to understand the rationale for and role of each member of the multidisciplinary team. The chapter dealing with this subject handles the concepts superbly, and the example of a case involving multidisciplinary team action brings those concepts to life.

Parent involvement, the topic of one of the chapters, is an important area for regular teachers to consider, especially when they have an exceptional child enrolled in their classroom. The four methods of parent involvement—(1) parent conferences, (2) IEP conferences, (3) parent education, and (4) parent training—are covered in detail. Studying this chapter should encourage the regular teacher not only to read other literature in the field but also to try some of the suggestions with parents of nonhandicapped students.

Regular teachers should find it helpful to read the chapters on learner characteristics of the mildly handicapped and strategies for behavioral programming. Coping with behavior problems is often even more perplexing to the regular teacher than determining what and how to teach the handicapped. Specific examples of how to use various techniques facilitate understanding of concepts and their application in the classroom.

Help in programming for exceptional children is another need of regular teachers. The chapter dealing with this important topic is filled with suggestions for modifying the goals, materials, methods, and environment of the classroom to accommodate the exceptional child. These strategies supplement the teaching strategies the regular teacher uses.

The chapter that focuses on speech handicaps and their implications for programming provides the regular teacher with a wealth of information and suggestions for teaching these students.

The last two chapters, on teaching the gifted and talented, highlight learner characteristics and also give many specific suggestions for meeting the individual needs of these students.

Vignettes of exceptional individuals who have actualized their potential convey to the reader that handicapped individuals do have strengths and, if social barriers are removed, can make a contribution to society.

The appendixes have some valuable tools and forms that the regular teacher should find useful; for example, teaming effectiveness scales, forms for recording team meetings, summaries of student progress, and instructions for selection and integration of materials.

Every public school should consider obtaining at least one copy of this book for its library. Many regular teachers will find it such a valuable reference that they will want to own a copy for their personal library.

The contributors to this book are to be commended for sharing with regular teachers their knowledge of what various exceptional children are like and especially their suggestions as to how to meet their individual needs. Regular classroom teachers, after reading this book, will feel better prepared to educate the exceptional child, whether handicapped or gifted. In all probability, when regular classroom teachers use the knowledge and techniques offered in this book in teaching the exceptional children in their classrooms, they will upgrade the instructional program for all of their charges.

Merle B. Karnes
Professor of Special Education
Institute for Child Behavior and Development
University of Illinois
Urbana/Champaign Campus

Preface

This book has two main purposes: (1) to assist regular educators in understanding the learning and behavioral characteristics of exceptional children whose most appropriate educational placement is the regular classroom, and (2) to provide the classroom teacher with specific instructional strategies designed to facilitate the exceptional child's success in the regular classroom.

What will I do in the morning? Recent national legislation has affirmed the right of individuals with significant learning, sensory, physical, and emotional differences to a free and appropriate education. Does this legislation mandate that *every* handicapped individual be returned to the regular classroom for a significant portion of his or her educational program? The answer is no! However, sound educational practice does dictate that every individual, handicapped or not, be placed in an educational environment that meets individual needs—an environment that will not restrict learning potential. The national legislation is simply a commitment to this practice. It is true that, for many exceptional individuals, the most appropriate educational environment is the regular classroom with an adequate special education support system. For other exceptional individuals, the setting may need to be more restrictive. So, what does all of this talk of "mainstreaming" mean to the classroom teacher? In a recent field-based survey conducted by the Dean's Project at the University of Utah, elementary and secondary teachers consistently ranked the following as major needs: (1) empathy and general awareness of handicapping conditions, (2) educational planning and assessment of instructional materials, and (3) classroom organization and behavior management. The present volume intends to address these areas of need.

The book has been divided into four parts: (1) Educating the Exceptional Student: A Changing Focus, (2) Students with Mild Learning and Behavior Differences, (3) Students with Speech, Sensory and Orthopedic Differences, and (4) The Gifted and Talented.

The purpose of the introductory chapter in part 1 is to give the reader a brief historical overview of community and educational services for the handicapped. Two important pieces of recent national legislation (Public Law 94–142 and Section 504 of the Vocational Rehabilitation Act) are examined in order to give the classroom teacher some perspective on the necessity of special education services. The multidisciplinary team is introduced in the second chapter, and the roles and responsibilities of various professionals are examined as they relate to assessment and educational programming for exceptional students. An important component of the team process is the establishment of a positive parent and professional relationship. Chapter 3 focuses on specific methods to clarify and enhance the role of parents in their child's education program.

Part 2 is entitled "Teaching Students with Mild Learning and Behavior Differences." Chapter 4 of this part, which concentrates on the characteristics of students with learning and behavior problems, examines definitions of mental retardation, behavior disorders, and learning disabilities. The regular classroom teacher, as a member of the school's multidisciplinary team, must be able to distinguish students in each of these categories by their definitional descriptors. This chapter also examines the similarities among such students on the basis of the individual's actual performance in a classroom setting. The remaining two chapters in this section provide a sequence of academic and behavioral strategies that will facilitate the integration of students with mild learning and behavior differences into the regular classroom.

Part 3 is entitled "Teaching Students with Speech, Sensory and Orthopedic Differences." Each of the chapters in this part examines learner characteristics and provides specific instructional techniques to help the classroom teacher provide for the educational needs of students with speech and language deficiencies, hearing impairments, visual impairments, physical handicaps, and health problems.

An analysis of characteristics and teaching strategies for the gifted and talented is the focus of part 4. Although this population was excluded from Public Law 94–142, they too should have access to resources and personnel in order to meet their educational potential in the regular classroom. This part is intended to provide some concrete instructional suggestions to classroom teachers who are expected to educate students with extraordinary talents and cognitive abilities.

For their review and constructive criticism of the manuscript, our thanks are due to Michael D. Orlansky (University of Virginia, Charlottesville) and Nanci M. Bray (University of Texas at Dallas).

Michael L. Hardman
M. Winston Egan
Elliott D. Landau

Educating the Exceptional Student

A Changing Focus

part
1

1 Introduction

"What will I do in the morning? I don't have the necessary background, experience, or time for students who are physically, mentally, or emotionally different. What is my responsibility as an educator? What resources are available to help me provide for the needs of exceptional students in a regular classroom environment?"

These statements have been echoed by nearly every educator in this country. The comments do not reflect an antagonistic attitude toward the exceptional student; on the contrary, they are simply some realistic questions from concerned professionals. Students with intellectual, behavioral, sensory, and physical differences are being integrated (**mainstreamed**) into regular classrooms. Who are they? What can be done to facilitate the integration for exceptional children, their classroom peers, and their teachers? These questions relate directly to professional attitudes and practice, and responding to them will require practical knowledge, specific skills, and training. This volume is intended to provide the classroom teacher with a foundation for developing the necessary skills. Its focus is on understanding the characteristics of exceptional students and building a repertoire of strategies to facilitate the exceptional child's success in the regular classroom.

Initially, it is important to distinguish between *exceptional* and *handicapped*—two terms commonly used to describe individuals with differences. We prefer the term *exceptional*. Although these two terms are often used synonomously, we recognize an important distinction. *Exceptional* implies that the individual's differences are *not* necessarily below the norm or average, but may in fact exceed it. This term takes into account higher achievers as well as lower achievers; capability as well as disability. *Handicapped* has a narrower and more negative connotation. The term focuses only on disabilities, and excludes the gifted and talented. Although national legislation (e.g., Education for All Handicapped Children Act) has consistently ignored the extraordinary needs of the gifted and talented, educators are recognizing the necessity of meeting this population's educational potential by providing additional resources and personnel.

Reaffirming Educational Rights

This section is concerned with the rights of all handicapped individuals to a free and appropriate education. The term *exceptional* is not used in this section, because the legislation to be discussed is specific to handicapped individuals and does not address gifted and talented populations.

The 1970s have been characterized as the era for affirmation of civil rights for the handicapped. Historically, educational and social services for this population have been inconsistent and in many cases discriminatory. As an example, in 1970 The Bureau for the Education of the Handicapped (BEH) estimated that approximately 62 percent of all school-age children were not receiving appropriate educational services. As a result the seventies became a decade of litigation, and a number of civil cases prepared the groundwork for a fundamental change in our human service models. Two public laws were enacted that every educator should know, because they exemplify the new directions in public policy. The laws are (1) Section 504 of the Vocational Rehabilitation Act (U.S. Congress 1973), and (2) The Education of All Handicapped Children Act: Public Law 94–142 (U.S. Congress 1975). Section 504 makes it unlawful to discriminate against the handicapped in employment, housing, access to public facilities, and public education. The Education of All Handicapped Children Act clearly specifies the provisions of a free and appropriate education. These include educating handicapped and nonhandicapped children together to the maximum extent possible, providing appropriate and continuous diagnosis and evaluation in a nondiscriminatory way, providing appropriate educational options and placement, and due process, if necessary. The specific provisions of this legislation may be altered with time and experience, but the concepts of nondiscrimination and appropriate educational services for all children will be the standard of the 1980s.

The Vocational Rehabilitation Act (Section 504)

Section 504 of the Vocational Rehabilitation Act provides comprehensive protection to handicapped persons against the major forms of discrimination related to civil rights. The provisions of the law pertain as appropriate to all handicapped persons: children, youth, and adults. A portion of Section 504 includes the following assurance:

> No otherwise qualified handicapped individual in the United States shall, solely by reason of his handicap, be excluded from the participation in, be denied benefits of, or be subjected to discrimination under any program or activity receiving Federal financial assistance.

Discrimination manifests itself in varied configurations. Prior to the implementation of this legislation and ensuing litigation, significant numbers of handicapped children and youth were denied access to free and appropriate educational services from the public schools. These students were simply not allowed to begin school or participate in public school programs, nor were they given the privilege of benefiting from their learning potential.

From a closer perspective, one can easily imagine the plight of the physically handicapped student who cannot conveniently enjoy lunch with friends or use the library because there is no ramp to the cafeteria and no elevator large enough to accommodate a wheelchair. Easy access to classrooms, restrooms, and resource facilities is vital to the educational success of handicapped children. Of equal importance are the rights of parents to have educational programs available to their children in neighborhood elementary schools. Thus, the need to implement Section 504 of the Vocational Rehabilitation Act of 1973 is obvious.

The Education for All Handicapped Children Act has had and will continue to have a profound effect on America's public education system. The passage and implementation of this Act came as a result of the efforts of many individuals, organizations, and advocacy groups. The Act is very far-reaching in its impact. All levels of public education are affected, from the state education agency to each individual handicapped student. To receive additional funding for educating the handicapped, states and school districts must comply with the following provisions of the law. First, they must assure that they are making every effort to serve all handicapped students. Second, they must assure the federal government that they are using nonbiased assessment procedures to screen and identify students as handicapped. Third, they must assure that all students identified as handicapped are placed in educational settings that are the most suitable for their educational and social needs. Each student must be educated in the least restrictive environment. Fourth, each student who is placed in a special education program must have an individualized education program (IEP)—a written statement including an evaluation of strengths and weaknesses, current levels of educational functioning, and a statement of long-term goals. Fifth, each state education agency and local school district must submit a comprehensive plan for personnel development. These plans must identify the steps that will be taken to provide teachers, support personnel, and administrators with appropriate skills to educate the handicapped in a variety of educational settings. Sixth, each state education agency and local school district must assure the federal government that they have enacted procedural safeguards to protect the rights of both children and parents. Seventh, each local educational agency must provide for an annual review of each student's progress and placement. These seven provisions are discussed in some detail in the following sections.

The Education for All Handicapped Children Act (PL 94-142)

Free and appropriate public education.   What is meant by the term *free and appropriate education*? For a considerable period of time, significant numbers of handicapped children and youth did not receive public education. If they were involved in schooling, it was at their parents' expense. States that choose to secure federal funding through PL 94–142, must provide, at no expense to parents, special education and related services. Special education, as defined by this law, is specially designed instruction—personally tailored to the needs of each handicapped student. In order to fully personalize a program for a handicapped student, the law requires the provision of certain related services. These, too, are rendered without charge to the guardians or parents. Examples of such services include transportation to and from school, psychological assistance in testing and diagnosis, physical education, occupational and recreational therapy, and counseling. Developing individualized educational programs (IEPs) for exceptional students is a team endeavor. Everyone responsible for rendering services must participate in the careful development of each IEP.

Nonbiased assessment.   Historically, the screening and diagnostic procedures used to identify and place exceptional students have not been totally fair or just. Results drawn from tests measuring ability and achievement have not always given a complete and accurate picture of the culturally different student's ability. As a result many culturally different students in past years were inappropriately identified and labeled as retarded, learning-disabled, and so forth. One need only to consider the feelings of a Chicano family whose son appears to be very skilled in his own native language and home-related behaviors, but who is identified by school assessment as retarded. With the advent of new testing procedures and multidimensional evaluations, and the nonbiased assessment provision of PL 94–142, fewer culturally different children and youth will be identified as handicapped. Test creators, psychologists, and other diagnosticians have not totally solved the problems associated with "fair and just" assessment, but great strides have been made in rectifying the many dimensions of assessment problems.

Least restrictive environment.   What is meant by the terms *least restrictive environment* or *least restrictive alternative*? To answer this question, one must be familiar with the variety and number of service models that are currently available for educating exceptional students. For seriously emotionally disturbed youths, a residential unit may be a very restrictive and controlled environment. In such a unit, they are not free to go and come as they please, nor are they able to spend considerable time with their peers and families. In contrast, emotionally disturbed youths who can be successfully placed in a part-time resource room program in a regular high school, have considerably more latitude and freedom. The least restrictive environment may include placement in a **residential classroom,** a **special school,** a **self-contained special education class,** a **resource room,** or some combination of the preceding environments. The least restrictive alternative is that educational environment which balances needs for restriction or structure with individual needs for achievement and behavior change. In most instances the least restrictive alternative for the mildly handicapped student is placement in a resource room with significant involvement in the regular classroom environment.

Individualized education program (IEP). The IEP has several significant components. In addition to the usual student identification information, the IEP includes (1) a statement of annual goals with supporting short-term instructional objectives, (2) a delineation of specific educational services to be used in achieving the annual goals, (3) a specification of the initiation and projected duration of the specialized programming and services, and (4) a delineation of the evaluative procedures to be used in assessing placement and programming effectiveness.

The IEP process serves several purposes. It provides an opportunity for parents, special and regular educators, and other related professionals, to join together in problem solving. In some instances, it allows handicapped students to become involved in planning their own education. Once the IEP is in final form and adopted by all concerned, the work really begins. The regular class teacher may be responsible for implementing a self-instructional spelling program that is supported by peer-aged tutors and the special education teacher. The special education teacher may be responsible for implementing a specialized reading and math program that is particularly well suited for handicapped students. The counselor in a high school IEP meeting may be responsible for changing a class schedule and providing counseling on a regular basis. The IEP, under the direction of a team leader, becomes a management tool for initiating and evaluating the efficacy of specialized services.

Comprehensive plan for personnel development. Congress knew that many professionals would be ill-equipped to deal effectively with all or many of the provisions of the law. As a result, they provided monies for state and local school districts to provide in-service training. Such training should be tailored to the needs of those who are serving and will serve the handicapped. Professionals interested in reviewing their own district or state comprehensive plans for personnel development should consult with their local and state special education directors or administrators.

Procedural safeguards. Procedural safeguards are designed to protect students and their families from conditions and decisions that may adversely affect their present and future lives. Before a student can be tested for learning or behavioral problems, permission in writing must be secured from the student's parents or guardians. The same permission must be secured for labeling and placing a student in any kind of special public education. As required by the constitution, procedural safeguard features must include (1) proper notice in advance, (2) an opportunity for parents to be heard and to present evidence, and (3) a fair hearing for grievances. For instance, parents whose language may be different from that of the general school community have the right to be informed with notices in their own primary language. Likewise, deaf parents would be guaranteed access to an interpreter in an impartial hearing concerning their child. Procedural safeguards protect the rights of students and families to involve themselves only in those procedures and programs that seem valuable to them from both a present and a future perspective.

Annual review. On a yearly basis, all students who have received special education and related services must be evaluated. Progress toward each annual goal should be measured. If students are not making adequate progress, or have reached an achievement or behavioral level commensurate with their peers, their programming or placement or both should be changed. In instances where inadequate progress has been made, instructional materials and strategies should be re-examined, and perhaps new ones chosen. In some instances, students may be better served in other programs. For those who have managed to bring their achievement level up to a par with regular students, total integration into the regular school becomes a reality. Annual review serves several functions. It makes it possible for students to move from very restrictive to less restrictive programs. For those who plan and implement the IEPs, annual review provides valuable feedback regarding the appropriateness of goals chosen and the progress made relative to these goals.

Changing Public and Professional Attitudes

The national legislation of the 1970s has provided education with a vehicle for change. It is only a beginning, but it is a necessary first step towards making the integration of exceptional individuals into society a reality. Scientists from many fields are assisting in finding solutions to complex problems through research and practical experience. Humanitarians are shaping popular opinion; philanthropists are providing financial aid; the national government, assisted by state legislatures, is reflecting new attitudes through legislation. As a result, fatalistic attitudes about exceptional individuals are slowly disappearing. Gradually, communities are awakening to the value of all human beings. Slow, steady progress has begun towards helping all individuals with significant differences find their places, not only in appropriate educational programs, but in society as well—not on the basis of their disabilities, but on the basis of their value as human beings. The crucial issue relative to recent legislation goes far beyond maximum educational practices, funding, or mechanically moving children from one setting or another. It deals with attitudes. Problems created by the mind and heart have little to do with laws, institution, buildings, appropriations of money, or highly trained specialists. It is a basic question of how we conceptualize the worth of human beings, and our degree of commitment to the implementation of programs that consider their value. It begins with acceptance and respect for exceptional children as valued human beings, having the capacity for personal development, and the right to lead full, productive lives.

The implementation of an appropriate education will bring to the surface both human greatness and human weakness. Changing traditional educational and social practices requires hard work, since there is always risk and fear associated with conquering the unknown. The lure of the status quo and the apathy of administrative convenience are always present. However, as history tells us, unfortunate results accrue when human beings resist or reject new ways, or are slow to modify traditional approaches to enhance the achievement levels of those with differences.

Achieving success in mainstreaming the exceptional child depends upon the teamwork of at least three institutions: the family, the school, and the community.

The family.   This is where it all begins: the importance of self in relationship to others; learning to accept or reject, to love or hate, to aspire or despair, to serve or to command, to develop responsibility or irresponsibility. In this atmosphere, children have the opportunity to share in the fun, the pain, the laughter, the conversations, the responsibilities and confrontations of family give-and-take.

The school.   Involvement in the neighborhood school allows exceptional children to model after their nonhandicapped peers. It permits the exchange of social and educational experiences, which can enhance tolerance, acceptance, self-confidence, and meaningful development of skills. This environment helps to clarify values and erase negative stereotypes about disabilities. It emphasizes independence and minimizes dependence. The world of the regular classroom need not be frustrating if parents, educators, legislators, support personnel, and the community at large have done their homework.

The community. Active participation by exceptional children in neighborhood activities can minimize or prevent social isolation. It is from this miniworld that they may gain the poise, confidence, and skill needed to face the larger, competitive world around them. Through constant, positive, and meaningful interaction with the world, the limitations of disability are minimized or removed; the limitations that society imposes through stereotypes and labels are dispelled; and the limitations that individuals impose upon themselves, such as extreme guilt and self-pity, are eliminated. It should be readily apparent that the conservation of human and material resources can be effectively and efficiently accomplished when there is mutual cooperation of the family, the school, and the community.

Postlude: What Some Have Done in the Morning!

The records show that—

Mona, a vibrant five-year-old, skipped, ran, jumped, and loved life as any other child . . . until polio struck! Paralyzed from her neck down, she barely clung to life for what seemed to be an eternity, but she lived. Then there were countless, agonizing therapy sessions, hospitals, special schools. She learned to "run" again in her wheelchair. She completed a B.S. degree and decided to achieve a Master's degree. Leaving a familiar campus in the Midwest, she traveled across the country to an unfamiliar one. On a cold, wintry day during the Christmas recess, Mona wheeled into a professor's office and exclaimed, "I want to get a graduate degree in vocational counseling; will you help me?" "Impossible," the professor thought, but then Mona had already done the impossible—why stop now? A university community went into action. A nurse invited Mona to share her apartment. Transportation was successfully arranged. Professors and students alike were filled with admiration as, one day, she wheeled along in the commencement procession to receive the acclaim granted only to those of courage. Mona's thesis became a guide for many agencies in removing physical barriers. More than that, she helped conquer social, emotional, and psychological barriers.

Marianne is a skilled speech therapist, a competent legal secretary, a musician, a composer, and a singer. Presently, she is a member of a renowned choir. So what! Many people record such accomplishments! Marianne is blind. Six months after her birth, it was discovered that she failed to respond to objects held in front of her; long, anxious visits to the doctors confirmed that she was blind. Heartache became almost insurmountable for her parents as she was placed in school far from home. She became an honor student in high school and later received a scholarship to attend Perkins Institute for the Blind in Massachusetts. Later, with two Master's degrees in music and speech pathology/audiology, she was ready for the world of work. Because of the faith in the uniqueness of the human spirit of those who loved and respected Marianne, she, too, became a contributor. As a young girl, Marianne had asked her parents if they thought she could ever become a professional teacher, and they replied: "You'll never know unless you try!"

Colleen, born with a profound hearing loss, was declared by some to be unteachable—"deaf and dumb"—to be isolated all her life. But her family and teachers rejected that notion. Compelled by her fascination for sounds and things—life in all of its intriguing manifestations—Colleen learned to talk, sing, work, and love people. She played softball with her brothers and was a valued team member. Attending her own neighborhood high school, she excelled in drama. During her junior year, she won the role of Helen Keller in *The Miracle Worker* over 350 competitors. The cast loved every minute of working with her. During her senior year, the student body elected her as first attendant to the homecoming queen. Colleen's formula for living was not crying, "I'm deaf; I can't do it," but rather, "Here I am, world, I'm coming in!" At the honors assembly before graduation from high school, the drama club presented her with a beautiful plaque that reads:

To Colleen
For outstanding service to the drama club and school. She has filled our hearts with love and touched our lives with sunshine. She, too, is a miracle worker.

References

U.S. Congress. 1973. Section 504 of the vocational rehabilitation act (Public Law 93–112).
U.S. Congress. 1975. Education for all handicapped children act (Public Law 94–142).

2 The Multidisciplinary Team

In accordance with the Education for All Handicapped Children Act (Public Law 94–142), evaluation, placement, and educational planning for the exceptional child is to be carried out by a group of persons or "multidisciplinary" team drawing upon information from a variety of sources (section 121a.532 [d] and [e], section 121a.533 [a] [1] [2] and [3], and section 121a.344 [a] and [b]).

A team is a group of people joined together to plan and perform an action. The word *action* implies that something is going to happen as a result of their being together. *Multidisciplinary* means that team members are trained in different fields of study. In a school situation, the multidisciplinary team concept means that professionals whose skills are related to a particular student's needs coordinate their efforts in order to provide an appropriate total educational program.

The Multidisciplinary Team

Obviously, the team approach is not a new concept or unique to the field of education. People have always joined together to deal with situations in which individual efforts would not be fruitful in resolving problems. Communities, neighborhoods, and families have always survived in part because of a commitment to one another and to ongoing group effort.

Ideally, the team process should certainly occur in educational settings. Historically, group interaction with exceptional students has often been accidental or handled in a rather piecemeal fashion. Although educators usually recognized the importance of such processes, they have not pursued them in a systematic fashion for a variety of reasons. Today we no longer have the *option* of using teams when we are dealing with the exceptional student. We can no longer treat this issue casually when federal law (Public Law 94–142) *mandates* the use of a multidisciplinary team. It is now critical that professionals in the field begin a concerted, unified effort to ensure that the team approach not only occurs, but operates in a systematic manner that will lead to better educational programs for all students.

The Rationale for the Team Process

While we certainly recognize that the "normal" individual is a complex being, we have only started to unlock some of the mysteries surrounding human behavior. The multifaceted and diverse problems encountered by some exceptional students make the puzzle even more complex. It follows that a person would be at a grave disadvantage if assigned the task of addressing these problems single-handedly. Furthermore, such an isolated approach could often result in erroneous decisions regarding a student. The tale of the blind men of India who claimed to have "seen" the elephant can be likened to such a singular approach. In this fable, one blind man felt the elephant's leg and described it as a tree trunk; a second examined the tail and thought the elephant like a rope; a third touched the trunk and described the elephant as a snake; another felt the ear and believed the elephant was like a fan; the next explored the elephant's side and thought it like a wall; yet another touched the elephant's tusk and likened it to a spear (Lerner 1976). The elephant was assessed from several different perspectives, and each man arrived at a separate and inaccurate conclusion. This fragmented problem-solving approach clearly illustrates the potential consequences of the lack of a unified group effort.

Although there is a scarcity of available research on the issue of the multidisciplinary team, Woody (1969) states that research supports the view that multifactor and multidisciplinary diagnosis are much superior to any single-factor and single-discipline approaches. There are several other reasons that support the idea of team work. Taba (1962) notes that the group provides a dynamic atmosphere in which one person's insight triggers another's, one idea generates another. The circular interaction created in a group climate releases and magnifies intelligence. The broader the group's experience base, the greater the learning and range of perspectives that become available to all. The combined knowledge, competence and skill of a multidisciplinary group give it the potential to be a unique problem-solving body.

One can hardly argue with the concept of the multidisciplinary team, considering what we know about the efficacy of the group process. Why, then, is this model not being used more effectively in the educational system? Why do we see such defined professional boundaries, the unyielding preservation of territorial rights, and an "each to his own" attitude prevailing in educational arenas? Research has indicated that there are a variety of reasons for the difficulties encountered by multidisciplinary teams (Gross, Mason, and MacEachern 1958). Two major contributing factors are conflict and misunderstanding about the roles of team members. Other contributing factors may involve personality and communication problems among team members, and differences in goals, standards, orientations, and backgrounds (Barclay 1971; Rich and Bardon 1963).

We are considering a group of highly skilled and talented individuals possessing great potential. Provided the team consists of competent professionals, then the key ingredient to the optimum functioning of this group seems to be mutual cooperation. This certainly includes the use of good verbal and nonverbal communication skills along with an understanding of each member's contribution to the problem-solving process.

The multidisciplinary team includes professionals of varying educational backgrounds and experiences. The purpose of table 2.1 is to list potential members of such teams and provide an overview of suggested roles and responsibilities that may be performed by each member. For further information concerning individual team members' perceptions of their roles and responsibilities, see appendix A.

The Roles and Responsibilities of the Team

Table 2.1 Roles and responsibilities in the multidisciplinary team

Team Member	Suggested Roles/Responsibilities
*Principal/Vice-Principal/ Administrator	Team leader Determines team constellation Calls team meetings Guides and directs discussion; facilitates problem-solving process during meetings Establishes time lines Insures that team decisions are properly implemented Functions as a liaison between school and community (e.g., may interpret concept of multidisciplinary teaming to school faculty and parents) Ensures implementation of appropriate procedures for identification, placement, programming, and evaluation of exceptional students
*Classroom Teacher(s)	Is primarily responsible for designing student's educational program in the regular classroom Is responsible for initial referral of students, or will assist other referring agents Is able to identify and collect information on students in classroom who may be potential candidates for special education services Presents accurate and ongoing record of student's functioning levels in the regular classroom Ensures that any special programming for the student is realistically designed for the conditions present in the regular classroom Is accountable to the team for recommendations implemented in the regular classroom Maintains ongoing communication with other team members regarding a particular student's program Serves as an advocate for the student in the regular class
*Parents/Legal Guardian	Is the primary advocate for the child May initiate a referral for the child Ensures that the child receives an appropriate education Provides team with information regarding child's performance outside of school Maintains ongoing communication with the team regarding child's performance Provides input related to design of child's total educational program May implement and follow through with team recommendations in the home setting Must provide written consent for evaluations conducted by the team Must provide written consent for any changes in child's placement (e.g., resource rooms, special classes, etc.)

Table 2.1 (continued)

*Resource Teacher (Special Education Teacher, Educational Diagnostician)	Selects, administers, and interprets appropriate assessment instruments, including formal and informal measures of student performance May observe student in the regular classroom setting Compiles, organizes, and maintains files on students receiving special education services Designs programming alternatives for students, based on the assessment information collected May implement programs for the student Assists in coordination of student's total program Maintains ongoing records that reflect student's current performance levels Assists regular classroom teacher in modification and adaptation of curriculum May design and construct materials to meet the specific needs of exceptional students Can locate additional human and material resources that may be necessary for optimum functioning of team Maintains functional and current knowledge of curriculum materials Is accountable to the team for implementation of recommendations Maintains ongoing communication with other team members regarding a particular student's performance
Psychologist	Selects, administers, and interprets appropriate psychological, educational and behavioral assessment instruments May observe student's performance in the regular classroom Assists in design and implementation of behavioral management programs in school and home May consult and counsel with parents, teachers, and team members regarding student's cognitive, affective, and psychomotor development
Social Worker	Collects pertinent information from the home setting as well as other background data relevant to student's needs Locates resources and serves as a liaison between community agencies (i.e., mental health clinics, family services, etc.) and school team May select, administer, and interpret appropriate instruments designed to assess student's emotional and social behavior May design and implement behavioral therapy programs with individuals and groups of students May consult and counsel with parents, teachers, and other team members regarding student's emotional and social behavior May observe student's social interaction in a variety of school settings (i.e., playground, classroom, halls, etc.)
Communication Specialist/ Speech Therapist	Selects, administers, and interprets appropriate diagnostic instruments designed to assess student's speech development, language development, and auditory perceptual skills May assist in design and implementation of speech, language, and auditory perceptual programs with individuals and groups of students May consult with parents, teachers, and other team members regarding speech and language problems

School Counselor	May take responsibilities similar to those listed under Social Worker;
	Additional responsibilities (particularly at secondary level) may include the following:
	    May assist students in selection of classes and coordination of class schedules
	    May assist and counsel students regarding vocational decisions
	    May consult and counsel with students, parents, teachers, and other team members regarding such things as attendance, behavioral, and academic problems

School Nurse	Collects and interprets relevant medical information for team members regarding student's health (i.e., may screen for vision and hearing problems, confer with physicians, monitor medication, etc.) Assists in management of chronically ill students in school setting Consults with parents, students and other team members regarding short-term medical health needs of students (i.e., nutritional problems, childhood diseases, enuresis, etc.)

Table 2.1 (continued)

Media Coordinator	Assists in design and development of student's Individualized Education Program
	Selects and secures appropriate instructional materials for use in student's educational program
	Consults with teachers and parents regarding effective use of materials and media for exceptional students
	Assists in adaptation and modification of existing instructional materials
	Assists teachers with development, use, and management of instructional media and materials (i.e., learning centers, modules, etc.)
Other Team Members Paraprofessionals, Probation Officers, Juvenile Court Representatives, Physicians, Family Members, Community/ Agency Personnel, Occupational Therapists, Vocational Rehabilitation Specialists, etc.	The multidisciplinary team may request the expertise and participation of other individuals, depending upon the specific needs of a particular student. It should be noted that often (particularly at intermediate and secondary levels) the student can be a viable member of the team.

*These individuals constitute the primary or core members of the multidisciplinary team as suggested in section 121a.344 of the Education for All Handicapped Act (Public Law 94–142).

It should be noted here that although each team member has certain role-specific duties, there are many shared responsibilities or commonalities that should be emphasized. Each member of the group has the responsibility to maintain ongoing communication with other members, provide appropriate input, actively participate in problem-solving situations, and follow through with any assignments for which he or she is responsible.

The Team Process

There are many situations (both formal and informal) that may necessitate a team meeting to discuss a particular student. The action taken may range from as few as two members discussing a student's needs during recess to a more formal gathering involving several members. The latter situation may call for a rather structured meeting that could occur in the principal's office. This action may occur prior to a formal written referral of a student and continue until a student no longer requires any type of special services (other than what would be provided in a regular class situation).

The following flow chart provides a sequential outline of situations that may require action (both formal and informal) by the multidisciplinary team. It should be noted that at certain points throughout the entire process, the team should conduct several formal meetings. Subsequent action by the team (beyond what is required) is also suggested in the flow chart and should occur in order to ensure that ongoing communication is maintained. Two case examples are presented to illustrate how the process may operate at both the elementary and secondary levels. Additional forms designed to facilitate communication, record keeping, and the decision-making process may be found in appendix B.

Case Example: Elementary Level

1. Classroom teacher notices a student problem

Team Action Suggested
Classroom teacher meets informally with resource teacher

2. Classroom teacher formally refers student for special services

Team Action Suggested
Classroom teacher confers with parent regarding the student's referral

3. Principal screens referral and decides which team members should be involved at this point

Team Action Suggested
Core team members meet to brainstorm alternatives and decide on a possible course of action

Mary had tried several different techniques with Mark in her second-grade classroom to help him succeed in her low reading group. Her curriculum modifications had little success, and she was at a loss when trying to deal with his fighting and disruptive behavior. She soon realized that the low reading group was totally inappropriate for his needs. She discovered that he was unable to say any letter sounds or say more than three preprimer sight words after assessing him using the second-grade basic skill list.

Mary decided to seek help from Bob, the resource teacher, and they discussed Mark's problems at lunch the next day. The resource teacher and Mary explored some alternatives, and Mary, after consulting with Mark's parents, asked Bob to observe him during reading to validate her perceptions of Mark's academic and behavioral difficulties.

Bob observed Mark for a week and concurred with Mary's assessment of the situation. Bob recommended that Mary obtain a formal referral from the principal and complete the necessary information.

Mary called Mark's parents to further discuss her difficulties with him and went on to explain the steps she was going to initiate.

She assured them that they would be included throughout the entire process, functioning as team members, and that their input would be vital to any alternatives the team considered.

The principal reviewed the information on the referral form and decided to contact the classroom teacher, the parents, and the resource teacher in order to arrange a convenient time to meet and discuss Mark's current situation.

The meeting was held after school, and the team members shared their observations and concerns about Mark's academic and behavioral performance at school and at home. The parents provided additional information about Mark's resistance to reading at home, and were also concerned about fighting which had recently developed with his younger brother. The team determined that they needed further specific information about Mark's performance. Team members agreed to the following actions: (1) the parents were to keep track of the number of fights Mark initiated with his brother during a one-week period; (2) Mary and Bob were to maintain regular contact with Mark's parents in order to provide feedback and assistance during the one-week assessment period; (3) Mary was asked to count the number of fights Mark initiated in the classroom and on the playground for one week; (4) Bob was to administer a series of formal and informal tests to ascertain Mark's specific levels and skills in the academic areas, particularly reading; (5) the psychologist would complete a psychological evaluation to learn more about Mark's academic functioning and social behavior. The parents agreed with the decision to pursue this referral and gave written consent for the evaluations that were to occur. The principal then scheduled a follow-up meeting in ten days and notified the psychologist concerning the assigned responsibilities.

All team members were able to complete their assignments and reconvened at the next scheduled meeting. The following information was presented by each person. (1) The parents reported that a total of fifteen fights occurred over the seven-day period. (2) The classroom teacher had recorded twenty fights that involved Mark, but she was unable to determine exactly how many Mark initiated. During her observations, she also discovered that Mark seldom interacted positively with other students. Practically all of his interaction resulted in some disruption in the class. (3) The resource teacher determined that Mark was above grade level in math skills and confirmed initial data that Mark lacked the ability to say letter names, sounds, and sight words, which placed him at a preprimer reading skills level. (4) The psychologist reported that Mark had above-average intelligence and performed especially well on verbal tasks involving comprehension abilities. Other assessments by the psychologist appeared to indicate Mark's frustration and difficulties in social situations.

The principal summarized all the information and asked for alternatives to be presented by each team member regarding an appropriate educational placement for Mark. The group brainstormed different placement options (e.g., self-contained classroom, resource room, regular classroom). Based on their discussion, they decided upon the least restrictive setting for Mark that would (at the same time) best meet his needs. The group felt Mark could remain in the regular classroom for the major portion of the day, with curriculum modifications and assistance from the resource teacher. It was also decided that Mark would receive intensive reading instruction in the resource room for one hour each day. The parents agreed with the decision and gave written consent for the placement.

4. Student evaluation information is collected by the multidisciplinary team (required)

Team Action Required
Evaluation data interpreted and discussed

Team Action Required
Student placement and program alternatives discussed; decisions made by team

Team Action Required
Student placement decision is made

5. Team members design an Individualized Education Program

Team Action Suggested
Team members meet informally to brainstorm and write objectives

Team Action Required
Team members formulate and write the Individualized Education Program

Team members then received individual assignments to design separate components of Mark's total educational program, including specific goals, objectives, materials, and time lines for completion. This information was to be in final form at the team meeting scheduled for the following week.

Each team member developed a sequence of objectives for the area assigned. This included the materials to be used, methods and techniques, schedules, and a means for evaluating Mark's progress.

During the week, the resource teacher met with the regular classroom teacher and Mark's parents to coordinate objectives for Mark related to reading. Each decided to focus on letter names and consonant sounds.

Each team member came to the meeting with a rough draft of proposed objectives for Mark. These were presented, discussed, and summarized into four major goals. The team then transferred this information to the form that recorded the details of Mark's Individualized Education Program (IEP). Portions of this document are illustrated in figure 2.1. At the conclusion of this meeting, a date was set to review and evaluate Mark's progress as outlined on his Individualized Education Program.

Figure 2.1 Portions of information from Mark's Individual Education Program (IEP)

Measurable Annual Goals	People Responsible
1. Mark will correctly say all consonant, short vowel, long vowel, vowel plus *r*, vowel team, diagraph, and diphthong sounds when presented visually in random order at the rate of 120 per minute.	Resource teacher
2. Mark will correctly say all Dolch Sight Words up to and including the 3.1 level when presented visually in random order at the rate of 90 per minute.	Classroom teacher and resource teacher
3. Mark will correctly hear and write all Dolch Sight Words up to and including the 3.1 level.	Classroom teacher and resource teacher
4. Mark will interact appropriately with school peers on the playground or in the school building.	Classroom teacher and psychologist
5. Mark will interact appropriately with his brother in shared play activities.	Parents

Team Action Suggested
Team members meet informally
to discuss Mark's progress

One week after Mark's IEP was begun, Bob and the classroom teacher discussed the initial effectiveness of the new program. Bob enthusiastically reported that Mark had mastered ten sight words over a one-week period in the resource room. Mary had observed similar gains with Mark in her classroom. Part of her responsibility dealt with the spelling component, and Mark had passed the first mastery test covering the same words. Additionally, Mark's fighting had been reduced substantially. She had not observed this aggressive behavior for several days.

After more discussion of Mark's rapid progress, the two teachers realigned one of their long-term goals for Mark. The initial changes observed in Mark's performance were so significant that the teachers sent a note to the parents to tell them of Mark's success.

Additional formal and informal team meetings were held throughout the year to discuss Mark's performance. His progress was monitored closely at home and at school, and curricular decisions were made based on the evaluation data that were collected.

6. Team members conduct an annual formal reevaluation

Team Action Required
Individualized Education Program is reevaluated

The team conducted a final evaluation at the end of the year in order to assess Mark's progress toward his long-term goals and to determine future plans for him. The team members agreed that Mark would benefit from supportive special services. Tentative goals were formulated for Mark that were made final at the onset of the next academic year.

Case Example: Secondary Level

1. The English teacher notices a student problem

Ms. Grant was becoming concerned with several of the behaviors Jim was exhibiting in her second-period junior English class. His attendance was becoming increasingly worse, he rarely submitted his assignments, and he was very belligerent when approached on these issues. Ms. Grant felt confident that Jim had the ability to complete the class work, as the few assignments she had received were of high quality. Because these behaviors persisted, Ms. Grant decided to consult with Jim's counselor.

2. Additional information is collected to clarify the problem

Team Action Suggested
English teacher meets informally with school counselor

Ms. Grant described Jim's behavior to Mr. Barton, the counselor, during her free period. Mr. Barton pulled Jim's folder to seek additional information and recalled that Jim had transferred to East High School last term. Teacher comments and attendance records in Jim's cumulative file revealed that similar behavior patterns had existed throughout his school years. It was also noted that during sixth grade he was enrolled in a special class program for emotionally disturbed students. There were no details about this experience and no indication of other special services provided for Jim. The records also revealed that Jim's father had died when he was in the fifth grade. The counselor and Ms. Grant decided that a meeting with Jim would be helpful to clarify some of their concerns and to get input from Jim about his feelings.

The following day Mr. Barton arranged to have Jim excused from his homeroom period and asked him to attend a conference in the student lounge with him and Ms. Grant.

The counselor explained to Jim the purpose of the meeting and then asked Ms. Grant to discuss her concerns. Jim pleaded with them not to contact his mother. During the course of the discussion, Jim agreed that his behavior was not appropriate and offered some explanations for his attendance problems and poor work in English. He also indicated that his behavior was quite similar in all of his other classes, with the exception of auto mechanics. Ms. Grant, the counselor, and Jim then tried to suggest alternatives for dealing with this situation, including (1) a formal referral of Jim for special education services, (2) suspension, and (3) the use of a behavior management program in Ms. Grant's class. Jim was concerned about being referred and felt that his problem was not severe enough to warrant suspension.

The entire group then decided to try the last alternative on an experimental two-week basis. They agreed that Ms. Grant would write a contract with Jim designed to specify certain desirable behaviors (i.e., attendance in English class, completion and submission of assignments, and appropriate verbalizations in class). The contract would also include a statement of consequences that would occur depending upon how Jim complied with the contract. They all agreed that after the two-week trial period they would meet again to review Jim's progress.

Ms. Grant made an appointment with Ms. Dobson, the resource teacher, for the next day at lunch. Ms. Grant explained their plans with Jim and asked for some help in developing a contract. Ms. Dobson showed her several examples of behavioral contracts, and together they modified one that would be appropriate for Jim. The next day in English class Ms. Grant explained the final contract to Jim and obtained his signature (see figure 2.2).

Team Action Suggested
English teacher, student and counselor meet to discuss the situation

3. A programming change is made to deal with the situation within the regular classroom setting

Team Meeting Suggested
English teacher meets informally with resource teacher

Teacher to obtain programming assistance

Figure 2.2 Jim's contract in English

I_____agree to comply with the following:

  1. Attend English class at least nine out of ten days.

  2. Complete and submit on time 80 percent of the assignments given in the English class.

  3. Talk out no more than once per period in the English class.

If the requirements of this contract have been met by Jim on _____
then one of the following may be selected: Date

  1. Two free theater tickets

  2. One six-pack of soda pop

  3. One free period in auto mechanics

Signed by,   _____   _____
                        Student   Teacher

                _____   _____
                        Teacher   Date

4. School counselor collects additional information regarding student performance in other subject areas

Team Meeting Suggested
School counselor meets informally with other teachers

Mr. Barton contacted Jim's other teachers for information about his performance in their classes. They reported similar difficulties, and some asked for help. At this point Mr. Barton explained the contract used in the English class. He also suggested that they document specific occurrences of Jim's behavior for two weeks before making any changes in their approach. Mr. Barton said that he would check back with each of them in two weeks to discuss future plans based on their observations and Jim's performance.

The preceding section has illustrated what might be considered an optimal operational process involving a multidisciplinary team. Unfortunately, many professional preparation programs at the University level currently lack courses that are specifically designed to teach the multidisciplinary team process as it is now conceptualized. However, efforts are being made in this direction at universities across the country.

Until more sophisticated preservice training is developed in this area, local school districts will be faced with the primary responsibility of assisting and facilitating the multidisciplinary team effort. Regardless of where this training

Organizing the Multidisciplinary Team

occurs, it is well recognized that some type of preparatory experiences should be provided if we expect diverse individuals to work efficiently together. As stated previously, teams do not magically bond together in a productive way just because they exist in name only. A concerted effort and commitment on the part of all members, combined with an understanding of the team function and process, can only begin to guarantee the success of this multidisciplinary approach. Too often teams disintegrate at the beginning stages because of difficulties in role perceptions and communication skills. Table 2.2 has been developed to assist multidisciplinary teams as they begin their working relationships. Team needs have been identified and are coupled with training suggestions that should help to develop positive attitudes and mutual respect within the group. Additionally, these suggestions may serve as a catalyst for initiating effective channels of communication among group members.

Table 2.2 Team needs and in-service training suggestions

Team Needs	Training Suggestions
1. Understanding and respect for *each* team member's roles and responsibilities need to be developed.	a. During a preschool workshop, each team member is assigned the task of writing a job description that encompasses all of his/her responsibilities. Each job description is then shared with the total group, and a discussion focuses on the unique contributions of each member as related to the team process and programming for exceptional students. b. During a preschool workshop, each team member completes the Team Process Questionnaire (appendix A). A discussion follows that centers around real and ideal role perceptions. c. Team members should be cognizant of federal and state laws regarding the provision of services for handicapped students.
2. Group roles and responsibilities that are specific to the entire team need to be clearly defined.	a. Team members should develop a working paper that specifies the roles and responsibilities of team members and outlines the procedures that will be used during team meetings. This could include such factors as (1) dual responsibilities and areas of overlap between team members' roles (2) procedures for eliciting input from team members (3) procedures for recording and distributing the team meeting discussion (4) leadership roles (5) problem-solving and decision-making processes to be used (6) defining what constitutes a formal and informal team meeting
3. Effective communication skills and trust need to be developed among group members.	a. The entire team should participate in a social event outside of the school environment. This could provide an atmosphere where informal interactions could occur that were not particularly related to the educational arena. (e.g., a pot luck dinner party that occurs prior to the beginning of school and may be the culminating activity for a team workshop.) b. Team members could make a list of the professional jargon that is specific to their discipline. Following this activity, they could present their lists to the group and compare their perceptions with regard to what the terms mean to other disciplines. The eventual goal would be to agree upon lay language terminology and emphasize the use of specific behavioral descriptions when discussing a student's performance. c. The team could prepare a mock case study. Team roles could then be assigned in order to conduct a simulated team meeting for a student's placement or programming. This activity would be most helpful if the meeting could be videotaped and replayed for the group's evaluation and critique of the communication process being used.

Again, it is important to stress that certain activities should occur *prior* to the onset of the team process. The activities that have just been described are only examples of the types of training that might take place within a school setting. The need for this training cannot be overemphasized. Any team's effectiveness will most surely depend upon the atmosphere that is established early in the process. It should also be pointed out that these activities alone will not guarantee a team's success but will increase the probability of a more workable unit. Additional suggestions will be provided in the next section to illustrate the procedures a team might use to strengthen its effectiveness.

Previous sections in this chapter have discussed some rather ideal team situations. Certainly, anyone with some experience in a school setting knows that groups do not always work smoothly. Breakdowns can occur anywhere in the process and ruin a team's effectiveness. Many factors too numerous and complex to discuss can contribute to the difficulties encountered by a multidisciplinary team. However, most of them can be categorized into three major areas. These are (1) role perceptions and expectations, (2) verbal and nonverbal communication, and (3) professional skill or competence.

Remember that a significant component of the successful team process is the knowledge and use of a problem-solving process. Gordon (1970) provides a sequence of six steps that outline the process one should employ in the "no-lose" method of solving problems. These steps represent a widely recognized and accepted method for problem solving:

First Step: Clearly specify and define the problem.
Second Step: Brainstorm alternatives for solving the problem.
Third Step: Carefully evaluate each alternative.
Fourth Step: Select the most appropriate solution.
Fifth Step: Design feasible procedures for implementing the solution.
Sixth Step: Evaluate the effectiveness of the solution on an ongoing basis.

This procedure should be used not only when dealing with a student problem, but also when handling team difficulties that arise within the three main problem areas mentioned above.

The first step in Gordon's process is a critical one if the group is to move through the method effectively. It may not always be an easy task to clearly identify and define the conflict unless all members are comfortable and willing to share their perceptions of the difficulty. Each member of the team may see the problem in a slightly different way, but it is important that, as a group, they express their feelings openly and agree upon the problem. At this point, it is vital that team members employ good listening skills so that each person feels that he or she has been heard.

Table 2.3 Gordon's method as applied to the multidisciplinary team

Problem Area	Situation	First Step: Defining the Problem	Second Step: Brainstorming Alternatives (What can the team do?)
Role perceptions and expectations, and professional skill or competence	At the diagnosis team meeting the classroom teacher did not have samples of the student's work. She was also unable to present any informal test data to document and clarify the referred student's problem.	The classroom teacher did not understand her role in the data collection process for students being referred for special education services. Additionally, she was not trained in appropriate procedures for identifying and defining students' academic and behavioral problems.	1. Clarify the term *data collection* for the classroom teacher and other team members who may be uncertain about its implications. 2. Supply the teacher with appropriate informal tests. 3. Train the teacher in behavior-recording systems. 4. Ask the resource teacher to collect the necessary data. 5. Transfer the student to another teacher. 6. Present the teacher with examples of the type of information that needs to be collected.
Verbal and nonverbal communication	A diagnosis team meeting was held, and the parents, classroom teacher, principal, resource teacher, and psychologist attended. The purpose of the meeting was to discuss the results of the testing and decide upon an appropriate placement for the student. During this meeting the parents rapidly became confused by the "meaningless" terminology used to describe and label their child. Additionally, they began to feel angry and hostile, as they had not been asked to contribute information, and their few comments and questions were ignored by the team. The parents angrily walked out of the meeting commenting that "the meeting was totally useless and you obviously are not interested in what *we* have to say about *our* child."	Team members were using inappropriate procedures to communicate student test data to the parents. Lay language was not used by the team, parent input was not solicited, and parent concerns (both verbal and nonverbal) were not heard. In general, the team was not sending or receiving messages effectively, and there was no evidence of the use of a problem-solving process.	1. Team members could participate in training that would teach a problem-solving process including the use of active listening skills, and verbal and nonverbal communication. 2. A team meeting without the parents could be held in order to plan appropriate strategies for communicating with and involving parents in the discussion. 3. Apologize to the parents after recognizing their frustration and reschedule the same team meeting. 4. Begin team meetings with a climate that helps promote group participation—seating arrangement, location of the meeting, time, etc., are considerations. 5. Invite the parents to contribute relevant information about their child and let them know you heard their input. 6. Recognize that the parent is just as important as any other team member. 7. Videotape a real or simulated team meeting so that it can be analyzed later in terms of the communication processes being used.

Third Step: Evaluating each Alternative	Fourth Step: Selecting the Most Appropriate Solution	Fifth Step: Designing Procedures and Implementing the Solution	Sixth Step: Evaluating the Effectiveness of the Solution
The team discussed the advantages and disadvantages of each alternative and eliminated those that were not feasible. Numbers 4 and 5 were eliminated because this issue was the responsibility of the regular class teacher, and the problem needed to be dealt with rather than avoided by transferring the student.	The team agreed that alternatives 1, 2, 3, and 6 needed to be implemented to resolve this problem effectively.	The resource teacher and the psychologist clarified the term *data collection* for other team members. The resource teacher also conducted an after-school workshop for the entire team and school staff on informal diagnosis. All classroom teachers were given examples of informal diagnostic tools and were trained in their administration. Each teacher was assigned to collect information on one student.	At the next team meeting, the classroom teacher presented detailed information on her student that clearly documented her referral concerns. The resource teacher held a follow-up one-hour workshop for the other teachers to check their informal assessment assignment. Feedback was provided for each teacher.

Considering the disastrous team meeting that had occurred with the parents, the team knew that some action was necessary in order to rectify the situation. Each alternative was assessed, and it was concluded that all were important if the team was to improve its communication skills.

Since all of the alternatives were deemed appropriate, the team members decided that they should be sequenced in terms of priorities. Time lines for completion were also established. The team mapped out the sequence and projected time lines as follows:

Alternative	Time Line
3 and 6	immediately
2	1 week
4	next meeting
5	next meeting
1	2 weeks (ongoing)
7	1 month

Alternatives 1 and 7 required some planning for effective implementation. The principal was in charge of locating an appropriate resource person from the local university to conduct the training sessions. The district provided some in-service training money for this purpose.

The school media specialist was contacted to arrange for videotape equipment to implement alternative 7. This activity would also be tied in with the in-service training.

Parents were routinely asked to complete a brief evaluation form at the end of each team meeting to obtain feedback on the communication processes being used. Team members were also asked to complete a brief questionnaire after each meeting. The school secretary compiled this information periodically for the team to study.

Videotape sessions were also evaluated by the group with the in-service training consultant.

Once the problem has been identified and defined, the team is ready to move into the second stage of Gordon's no-lose method. Again, this is a group process, and each member should contribute possible alternatives for dealing with the situation. At this stage each alternative should be accepted in a nonjudgmental fashion; they will be evaluated later in the process. The brainstorming session that occurs in step 2 is an illustration of what Taba means by the "potent dynamic to rethinking" where one idea generates another; thus the circular interaction that is created in a group climate essentially releases intelligence (Taba 1962, p. 471). In this case, a variety of creative alternatives can be generated that may have potential for resolving problems.

Table 2.3 has been developed to illustrate the use of Gordon's method in an actual team setting. The general problem area and a brief description of the situation are presented in the first two columns. Subsequent columns describe the use of each of the six steps.

General Recommendations

Those who enter a multidisciplinary team situation do not face an easy task, particularly if they are to be productive members of the group process. The challenge must be met, however, since the multidisciplinary team process is guaranteed by law. As mentioned throughout this chapter, Public Law 94–142 makes team action a basic requirement for the evaluation and placement of exceptional students. The team process is a complex and complicated procedure involving many variables that are often difficult to control. The following list summarizes the most important points to remember when dealing with the multidisciplinary team:

1. All team members should know the roles and responsibilities of each member and respect the expertise of each member.
2. Team members should understand the reasons for meeting, including the mandates and implications of relevant federal and state laws.
3. Team members should be aware of different types of student problems and be able to judge when team meetings should occur.
4. Team members should have the necessary professional competence to perform their designated duties.
5. Team members should be knowledgeable in the use of verbal and nonverbal communication skills.
6. Team members should know how to use effective record keeping and tracking systems in order to facilitate and document the team's business.
7. Team members should use ongoing evaluation procedures to ascertain their effectiveness.

Barclay, J. R. 1971. Descriptive, theoretical, and behavioral characteristics of subdoctoral school psychologists. *American Psychologist* 26:257–80.

Gordon, Thomas. 1970. *P.E.T. Parent Effectiveness Training.* New York: Peter H. Wyden.

Gross, N. C., Mason, W. S., and MacEachern, A. W. 1958. *Explorations in role analysis.* New York: Wiley.

Lerner, J. W. 1976. *Children with learning disabilities.* 2d ed. Boston: Houghton Mifflin.

Rich J., and Bardon, J. I. 1963. The teacher and the school psychologist. *Elementary School Journal* 64:318–23.

Taba, H. 1962. *Curriculum development.* San Francisco: Harcourt, Brace, and World.

U.S. Congress. 1975. Education for all handicapped children act (Public Law 94–142).

Woody, R. H. 1969. *Behavioral problem children in the schools.* Englewood Cliffs, N.J.: Prentice-Hall.

3 The Parent/Professional Team

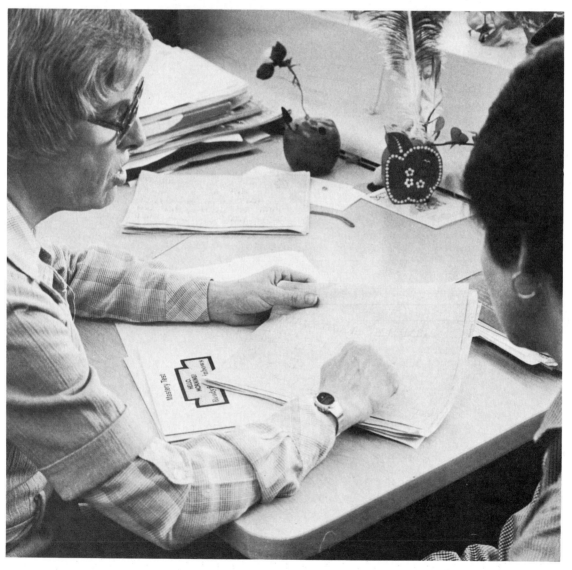

One of the major determinants of educational success for exceptional children is the quality of cooperation and teamwork that occurs between educators and parents. Many teachers have made and are continuing to make parents a significant part of educational programming. In fact, many teachers have carefully put into effect cooperative school/home programs that have emphasized a variety of educational, social, and behavioral goals. By working together, teachers and parents make it more likely that exceptional children will achieve their full potential.

Professional educators must change their perception of parents and increase parent participation in educational planning. The importance of teamwork between parents and teachers cannot be overemphasized. When school and home do not cooperate, communication breaks down, and children suffer. Many teachers attribute their success in educating exceptional students to parent involvement.

Becker (1971) states that parents are the first teachers of their child and also the most influential teachers in the child's life. Parents have turned over a portion of the teaching function to professional educators (approximately 6 hours a day for 185 days per year) but for the remainder of the time, education is primarily a parental responsibility. Educators must share with parents the skills learned in their professional training as well as the techniques used daily in the classroom. Helping parents to develop teaching skills will increase their effectiveness as teachers in the home.

Parents have been blamed for many of the learning and behavior problems exhibited by students, but few parents have been trained to meet the overwhelming responsibility of teaching children. They need systematic techniques that will allow them to meet this responsibility successfully. Lillie (1976) has suggested that parents who are informed about educational goals and expectations are better able to focus on these same goals in their homes. The consistency between school and home is thereby increased greatly, and exceptional children profit from this cooperation. Since parents have little opportunity to develop techniques or strategies, they need direction from the educator to increase their skills so they can help their children develop their full potential.

Current research overwhelmingly supports parental involvement in the instruction of all exceptional children. Teachers have sometimes forgotten that parents have been living with their child's exceptionality for many years and are open for meaningful suggestions or may have suggestions that might aid the teacher. Gorham (1975, p. 521) stated the feelings of many parents when she wrote:

> Although I have learned much, I am clearly one of the lost generation of parents of handicapped children. We are parents who are either intimidated by professionals or angry with them or both; parents who are unreasonably awed by them; parents who intuitively know that we know our children better than the experts of any discipline and yet we persistently assume that the professionals know best; parents who carry so much attitudinal and emotional baggage around with us that we are unable to engage in any real dialogue with professionals—teachers, principals, physicians, psychologists—about our children.

Teachers exposed to these kinds of emotions cannot help but reconsider or at least analyze their attempts to communicate with parents. It is important that parents care, but they also need skills and knowledge to work with exceptional children. Providing these is the role of the professional. Educators have been aware that parents, especially the parents of exceptional children, need supportive help and guidance in raising their children. However, a real problem arises because the majority of educators, who lack formal training in child management, remediation of learning problems, and counseling parents, feel inadequate to work with parents.

The Education of All Handicapped Children Act, discussed earlier in this volume, has provided the stimulus for schools to share educational decision making with parents. The implementation of this act will allow parents and professionals to share their feelings, perceptions, and insights. Some educators have received these laws with mixed reactions, but most know this new legislation has had a positive effect on parent/teacher relations.

> Parents have to be recognized as special educators, the true experts on their children; and professional people—teachers, pediatricians, psychologists, and others—have to learn to be consultants to parents (Hobbs, 1978, p. 496).

The remainder of this chapter is devoted to specifying four methods that educators should consider in working with the parents of exceptional children. They include (1) parent conferences, (2) IEP conferences, (3) parent education, and (4) parent training. Teachers should not be expected to conduct or supervise all of these services or programs, but they should be aware of their importance and encourage their application. Traditionally, teachers have said, "Parent involvement is essentially the responsibility of the classroom teacher, but I don't have the time or training to involve my parents." Considering the level of responsibility placed on classroom teachers, it is not difficult to understand why they are concerned. Only a minimum number of parents have had any formal training in parent involvement. Yet teachers have inherited the responsibility of working with parents because other professional staff in the school district who should assume it have cast it off. The four methods recommended in this chapter involve teachers, but also include other professional school district staff (i.e., counselors, school psychologists, administrators, nurses, and curriculum specialists). The parent-teacher conference and the IEP conference would essentially be the responsibility of the classroom teacher. However, parent training and education programs could be conducted by other members of the multidisciplinary team. School districts may also choose to employ an outside consultant to develop a comprehensive parent program.

The varying formats of the four methods presented in this chapter stress that it is the primary responsibility of the school and not the teacher to plan for parent involvement. A *multidisciplinary* team effort allows a district to provide a broad spectrum of parent services; administratively, it is a better division of labor and responsibilities. Teachers cannot be held responsible for being everything to everyone in the school setting. Parent education and training require a great deal of support and involvement from the administration and pupil personnel staff. The school district's parent involvement program should be a network of services—parent involvement is much more than having parents sign off on the IEP forms.

Parent Conferences

Parent conferences are conducted with two of the most significant people in the child's life—the teacher and the parent. Preliminary planning is important because without systematic preparation the conference becomes a conversation without direction or purpose.

Long (1976, pp. 84–85) lists some excellent conference guidelines for the professional educator:

1. Study the child's cumulative records, plan in advance to cover specific areas of the child's background or educational history that seem pertinent, and list the points to be covered for reference in case the meeting becomes sidetracked.
2. After beginning with a friendly or welcoming remark, outline at the outset which areas of the child's performance or background will most likely be covered so that the parents have an idea of what will be stressed and when and where to introduce topics they may wish to raise.
3. Have on hand representative samples of the child's best, worst, and most characteristic work, but engage the parents in positive discussion about the child before discussing the child's current work or problems.
4. Avoid professional jargon and try to communicate simply but accurately, in language appropriate to the parents' educational, social, and cultural background.

5. Reinforce and encourage the parents' continuing to take an active interest in their child's school experiences.
6. When discussing the child's current performance, try to "emphasize the child's strengths, assets, and positive accomplishments, making a limited number of realistic suggestions for their improvement."

Dembinski and Mauser (1977) conducted an in-depth study with parents who were members of the Association of Children with Learning Disabilities to find out what they want from professionals. The results indicated that parents want professionals to—

1. Be straightforward with parents; use language that they comprehend and omit professional jargon;
2. Include both parents when possible in conferences that involve the child.
3. Give parents reading material that is relevant to their child's problem and helps them understand their child better;
4. Share with parents all reports written about their child.
5. Engage in interdisciplinary communication with other professionals who are working with the child;
6. Give parents concrete and relevant advice on handling management and learning problems.

Kroth and Simpson (1977) suggest that the interviewer evaluate (1) the parents' perception of the problem, (2) the child's developmental history, (3) the parents' perception of the child's personality characterization, (4) the child's school history, (5) the parents' goals and expectations for the child, and (6) family and social information.

Gallagher (1979, pp. 286–87) stated some techniques that teachers can use to enhance an open communication network during classroom conferences:

1. Provide adult-sized chairs.
2. Arrange chairs informally.
3. Provide ashtrays.
4. Have coffee and tea available.
5. Serve refreshments at group meetings.
6. Offer several appointment options for conferences, including evening and before-school hours.
7. Be prepared for students and siblings who may accompany parents to the conferences. Arrange for activities the children can do independently while the adults are engaged in the discussion. Supervision of younger children also may need to be considered.
8. In teacher-initiated conferences, prepare an outline of the discussion topics.
9. Develop a parent conference form to record conference dates, names of individuals attending the conference, major topics covered, and plans, if any, that are to be followed through.
10. Be an active and responsive listener.
11. Assume a partnership role.

12. Be cognizant that as the teacher and parents discuss a student's behavior, the student is being described according to two different environments so, in a sense, you are talking about two different children. Some teachers and parents have a tendency to mistrust each other's behavioral descriptions, especially if discrepancies arise. For example, a student could be extremely quiet in a family setting and yet be an acting-out child in the classroom.
13. Keep the student in mind during the conference, as the focus of the meeting.
14. Be positive in the discussions. If the student's weaknesses are part of the discussion, make the wording positive, such as, "Susan needs to grow in . . ." rather than, "Susan has weakness in . . ."
15. Be honest, but use tact and diplomacy.
16. Remember that a teacher is not a therapist, although a conference could have therapeutic effects. If the student's parents need counseling, consider including carefully chosen additional staff personnel in a conference.
17. Have parents leave a note on their child's desk regarding something positive that occurred during the conference (for example, "Your teacher said you have tried hard in math," "I saw your neat science essay," "Your graph on sharing shows a lot of progress."
18. Compliment the parents for their efforts.
19. Encourage parents, guardians, or involved child-care workers to attend all conferences. If only one member attends a conference, do not assume that information emerging during the conference is shared with the absent persons.
20. Be sure to follow through on ideas, communication gains, goals, and plans evolving from the conferences.
21. Invite parents to observe their child's class in session.

The conference should begin by setting up a positive atmosphere to minimize the anxiety, shame, and guilt that parents might be feeling about attending a parent-teacher conference. The teacher should serve as the leader and outline what information will be discussed while conveying the importance of things that might be directly or indirectly related to the problem. The conference leader should carefully sensitize the parents to the responsibility that they share in facilitating the child's education. Once the rapport has been established, the teacher should discuss specific academic goals, the child's strengths and weaknesses, techniques for handling problems, and topics of mutual concern. Kroth and Simpson (1977) suggest that the educator should obtain the following information during the parent-teacher conference:

1. How does the child use free time at home?
2. What activities does the child do after school? Before bed time? Weekends?
3. Children whom the child plays with? Age? Sex? Siblings or neighbors?
4. Does the child pursue hobbies? Or are hobbies selected by parents?
5. What organizations or teams does the child belong to?
6. Does the child frequently select certain toys or playthings.
7. What amount of time does the child spend watching T.V.? And what are the child's favorite programs?
8. Does the child have a regular allowance? What activities does the child do for the allowance? How is the allowance used?

Finally, the teacher should make plans for future conferences. The conference should end with a brief review and a synthesis of the activities to be jointly pursued.

Information obtained during parent conferences should be shared by the special and regular educators. If communication breaks down between the special education teacher, regular education teacher, and parents, the child's education program will not reach optimal effectiveness. It is clear that, if parents are responsible for the child approximately eighteen hours per day, and the regular and special education teachers share the education responsibility for six hours, mutual trust and a good working relationship must be established between these parties. With appropriate communication, all concerned are in a position to assist the child with emotional and educational adjustment at school and at home.

Many special and regular education teachers use the telephone to develop cooperative parent-teacher interaction. Telephone calls are an excellent medium for daily reporting of home or school problems that need immediate attention. A call from the regular or special educator to the parents about a child's success is an excellent approach to assisting the child and building trust and rapport. Calls that communicate negative information soon turn parents off, and communication may be discontinued.

Individualized Education Program (IEP)

The parent is a crucial member of the IEP team and provides information that will assist the team in developing an appropriate education program. Parents have the the right to participate in planning for their child's education. The child may also be a member of the IEP team if deemed appropriate. The IEP is discussed extensively in chapter 1 of this volume, but it is important to remember that the regular education teacher working with exceptional children should also be included in the IEP process. The regular education teacher is a valuable information link between the home and special education services.

After completing an IEP, communication between home and classroom should continue regularly. Parent-teacher conferences should be scheduled periodically. Such conferences might be discussed in the original IEP meeting, in which one of the objectives is to involve parents in ongoing planning and placement for their exceptional child.

Parent Education and Parent Training

A clear distinction between parent education and parent training is necessary. Parent education is informing the parent of issues directly related to their child's learning or behavior problems. Any sessions using professional speakers to educate the parent on specific topics related to the child's psychological, emotional, or physical deficits would be considered parent education. The parent education session is intended to give parents of exceptional children understanding and information beyond what is generally provided by the traditional parent-teacher conference. Parent training, on the other hand, is specifically developing functional skills in parents through a variety of training techniques. This training might encompass such areas as communication skills between parent and child, managing and motivating appropriate behavior, and other related skills.

Parent education meetings should be designed to cover topics that would facilitate parents' work with school-related concerns (e.g., language development skills, conceptual skills, perceptual-motor skills, gross motor skills, and fine motor skills). The district should prearrange the topics to be included in these meetings and schedule them periodically throughout the school year. Teachers and administrators should know the dates and specific topics for each meeting so that they can recommend meetings that would be significant for particular parents. It would be impossible for teachers to cover curriculum and techniques that would be appropriate for each exceptional child during individual parent-teacher conferences or IEP meetings.

Parent Education Meetings

Susser (1974) indicates that parent-teacher discussion groups have three primary objectives: (1) to communicate practical theoretical information to parents, (2) to assist parents with problem solving relative to their child, and (3) to provide parents with an atmosphere of mutual support and understanding. Karnes and Zehrbach (1972) have recommended single-topic meetings between educators and parent groups. These groups are composed of a few parents with a common problem. The problems are often related to such content areas as math, reading, handwriting, or language.

The topics for parent education sessions may vary from a general discussion of community services to specific evaluation and remediation techniques designed to help parents work with their children's academic deficiencies. Parent education classes should also cover behavior management and communication skills.

To ensure that parent education classes actually meet the needs of parents, the school district should first organize a parent advisory committee to be responsible for assessing parent needs. The school and parent advisory board should write up a "menu" of topics that could be covered in parent education and send it to all the parents of exceptional children, asking them to rank their preferences. The choices might be presented and divided into three categories: (1) understanding your exceptional child, (2) the school curriculum, and (3) community services available. After an analysis of the parent needs assessment, the school district should assume responsibility for developing programs to meet the parents' expressed needs.

The selection of the parent education leader is critical. This person should be a professional who has a working knowledge of the parent education topics and can empathize well with parents. The session leader might be a district *reading consultant* who would have the skills needed to work with parents on their child's reading problems; a *school psychologist* to speak about working appropriately with motivation techniques; a *psychiatrist* to cover techniques for working with emotional problems; a *speech therapist* to present material that will enable parents to work effectively with speech and language problems.

There are many advantages of the parent education meetings. Parents are able to receive in-depth knowledge about particular topics of interest to them. Many parents can be reached at one time, and they can share information and common concerns. Finally, it allows the district to use the time of its professional staff most efficiently.

Parent Training Meetings

Kroth (1975) has suggested several purposes for conducting parent training meetings: (1) to communicate information to parents quickly and efficiently, (2) to facilitate parents' problem-solving efforts, and (3) to train parents in specific behavior management techniques.

Parent training programs usually follow a lecture-discussion format and often use commercially produced audiovisual kits to increase parents' interest in attending. Many educators want to provide parents and staff members with such programs but do not have the time to develop them. There are a number of commercial materials requiring a minimum amount of background to use that can help solve this problem. Usually the materials have guides and manuals for leaders as well as appropriate materials for participants. These materials require a tape recorder, phonograph, and slide or filmstrip projector. The following kits address various phases of parent training:

Systematic Training for Effective Parenting by Don Dinkmeyer and Gary D. McKay. American Guidance Service, Inc., Circle Pines, MN 55014, 1976.
Managing Behavior: A Parent Involvement Program by Richard L. McDowell, B. L. Winch and Associates, P.O. Box 1195, Torrance, CA 90505, 1974. Also distributed by Research Press, Champaign, IL.
Even Love Is Not Enough: Children with Handicaps. Parent Magazine Films, Inc., 52 Vanderbilt Ave., New York, NY 10017, 1975.
The Art of Parenting by Bill R. Wagonseller, Mary Burnett, Bernard Salzburg, and Joe Burnett. Research Press, Champaign, IL., 61820, 1977.
Keeping in Touch with Parents: The Teacher's Best Friends by Leatha Mae Bennett and Ferris O. Henson, p. 251. Learning Concepts, 2501 N. Lamar, Austin, TX 78705.

McDowell (1976) notes that in the past most parent training has been centered around two types of programs: (1) communication, and (2) involvement. The communication approaches focus on establishing direct communication between parent and child; the involvement approaches focus on promoting positive parent-child relationships.

More recently the behavior management strategy has been developed and used as an effective training method. Parents involved in behavior management training learn a variety of management techniques. They are taught to choose a target behavior and record the behavior they want to increase, decrease, or maintain. Then they are able to apply systematic techniques to designated target behaviors.

Galloway and Galloway (1971) taught behavior analysis techniques to parents so they would have a better knowledge of their children's behavior and what techniques they could use to change it. Behaviors taught in school were maintained or accelerated by the parents. The parents were taught simple observation techniques to identify appropriate responses and consequences that would have a positive or negative effect on the target behavior. Using this approach, the authors reported a positive change in parents' attitudes about children's handicaps; parents learned that they can be effective in changing their own children's behaviors.

Parent training programs have been conducted at mental health centers, child guidance centers, and juvenile court facilities. Parents view these programs as services that help them to deal with parent/child or school-related problems. Parents are requesting preventive types of parent training sessions where they can learn skills that will prevent future problems.

Parent training workshops are generally divided into two major activities: (1) the presentation of materials that increase parents' understanding of their children's behavior patterns, and (2) the discussion of techniques and methods for handling whatever problems arise. The prospective leader of the parent training session might be a school administrator, psychologist, social worker, counselor, teacher, trained parent, or consultant. The order mentioned above is irrelevant—any of these professionals could be very effective in leading a group. The leader should first assume the role of group facilitator by following some general guidelines:

1. Immediately establish that all questions are relevant and reinforce parents who ask questions. Make it clear that learning occurs with the asking of questions. Persons who ask questions should be immediately reinforced for doing so.
2. Identify the ground rules that will be used in conducting the sessions. Care should be taken to explain that the session is not a parent therapy program. Parents should be made aware of the problems that arise in

group work when one or a few persons dominate the discussions. Parents should be informed that problems specific to their child can be dealt with following the last parent training session.

3. Assist in stimulating discussion during the discussion session.
4. Use simulation activities as a basis for discussion. Simulations can provide tremendous practice for parents in dealing with interpersonal problems. The simulations should correlate closely with the material covered in the session.
5. Develop appropriate audiovisual materials and handouts that add to and reinforce the skills taught.

A typical three-session parent training program might emphasize the following skill areas: (1) communication, (2) behavior management theory and methods, and (3) behavior management: increasing, decreasing, extinguishing behavior. The following paragraphs outline a session on the development of appropriate communication techniques. For more specific information on behavior management programs, refer to chapter 5 of this volume.

Session: Communication.   Communication is the single most important aspect of childraising skills, but it is by far the most complicated skill that parents must learn and use consistently. The major problem in using effective communication skills is that emotions, moods, and environmental pressures for both parties are involved when attempting to communicate feelings and concerns. Many problems between parents and children could be avoided by using good communications skills to help settle difficulties before they turn into major confrontations.

Kroth (1975) outlines four steps to developing good listening skills:

1. *Be supportive, don't criticize.* Use words and actions which show children you like them as persons and you care about how they feel. This shows children they can trust you to listen and you will take time to hear what they are saying. Use appropriate nonverbal signals when listening, such as leaning forward, positive head nods, smiles, and other gestures. All of these let children know you're listening and it's okay to talk.
2. *Set a good example.* Keep your cool. Don't overreact if children attempt to shock you with a new word or idea. Many times children will be testing to see if the parent is comfortable in talking about certain topics, (e.g., sex and drugs). If you overreact at this time, children may stop talking.
3. *Listen, get involved.* Give children your full attention. Don't nod or mumble behind a newspaper. Listening requires effort to use all of your listening skills.
4. *Repeat key ideas.* "Mirror back" or restate what children say. This lets children know you are listening, and also that you are getting the same message that is being sent.

Anderson (1972) has also listed some suggestions that may help to avoid breakdowns in communication:

1. Avoid hasty or unduly critical responses. Weigh the message and the people involved to derive the correct meaning.
2. Don't rush the other person. Allow children time to be themselves and to reveal themselves before you make any judgments.
3. Communication breakdowns can be used as learning situations. They are inevitable, but we can learn from our mistakes.
4. When misunderstandings are corrected, relationships are strengthened, and the possibility of another misunderstanding is lessened.

To help parents become good listeners, Wagonseller and McDowell (1979) list the following steps to help parents create an atmosphere that will encourage communication:

1. Turn the television off or put the newspaper down when your child wants to converse.
2. Never take a telephone call when a child has something important to tell you. Be as courteous to your child as you would be to your best friend.
3. Never tower over your child. Get physically down to the child's level when talking.
4. Listen carefully and politely. Don't interrupt the child when he is trying to tell his story.
5. Don't ask "Why?" but "What happened?" Children don't know why.
6. If you have knowledge of the situation confront the child about the information that you know or have been told.
7. Assist the child in planning some specific steps to the solution.
8. Keep adult talking, preaching, and moralizing to a minimum, this is not an effective solution to getting communication open and remaining open.
9. Don't use "put-down" words—dumb, stupid, lazy, etc.
10. Let the child know that you are interested and involved and that you are there to assist when needed.
11. Don't be a "wipe-out artist" where you unravel minor threads of a story and never allow a theme to develop. This is the parent who reacts to the incidentals of a message while the main idea is lost, (i.e., The child starts to tell you about what happened and you say, "I don't care what they are doing, but you had better not be involved in anything like that.").
12. If you are very angry about some behavior or incident, don't attempt communication until you regain your cool, because you cannot be objective.

Communication is important not only between parent and child, but between parent and professional as well. Here are some pointers to help parents communicate with professionals:

1. Be positive in your communication (e.g., "I have a lot of respect for you as a professional.").
2. Write down the questions you want answered (e.g., "How do you handle insurance forms?").

3. Be direct and to the point with your questions. Don't give a double message and expect a direct answer.
4. Be a good listener (e.g., don't keep thinking about what you are going to say next while the professional is talking).
5. Be assertive and not passive or aggressive (e.g., the parent might say, "Since I have the long-range responsibility for my child, is there any long-range effect of this type of medication that I should be aware of before we make this decision?").

Parents should not be concerned with identifying where the problem started, but with how to change a poor relationship and restore positive relationships. One of the most common problems that comes up in parent training is that of power struggles. Such conflicts happen in most homes, and the "why" is not as important as the "how to handle" aspect of it. Wagonseller et al. (1977) discuss how power struggles develop and may be avoided. Power struggles develop when a parent confronts a child with a request that the child may reject or feel is unfair. The parent does not listen; the child feels threatened, reacts negatively, and will not give in. By now the parent is determined to establish "authority," even if it means overreacting. In the end, both parent and child lose. The parent may win by sheer size and authority, but also loses in terms of the child's negative feelings toward the parent. How can power struggles be avoided? The parent must use other techniques besides the club, parental authority, physical size, or the "inherent" right that goes with being a parent. Here are six specific steps, as described by Gordon (1970), for resolving conflicts:

1. Define the specific problem or behavior.
2. Suggest possible alternatives.
3. Evaluate and discuss each alternative.
4. Decide on a *mutually* acceptable plan.
5. Implement the plan.
6. Evaluate the plan.

Recommended topics that might be discussed in detail during the communication session follow:

1. Appropriate and effective ways for a child to express anger, aggression, and hostility without infringing on others' rights.
2. Importance of body language and other nonverbal interactions in communication between a parent and child.
3. Establishing ownership of problems in parent-child relationships. Ownership falls into three categories: *yours, mine,* and *ours* (Wagonseller and McDowell, 1979).

4. Deterrents to good listening: fatigue, anger, put-down, shock words, preaching, or moralizing.
5. Have parents discuss the word respect: Is it an "inherent" right that goes with being a parent? Is it something a parent must earn?
6. Statement of penalties to be imposed if specific behaviors are not performed as stipulated.

At the end of the three parent training sessions, the leader should leave time for open discussion. These parent training sessions might be followed up by professional speakers on such topics as:

1. Discipline vs. Punishment
2. Respect and Responsibility in Parenting
3. Consistency in Interaction
4. Professional Help Available

Involving parents in the education of their exceptional children has been a welcome trend during the past few years. Parent involvement has been strengthened by the passage of Section 504 of the Vocational Rehabilitation Act and the subsequent passage of Public Law 94–142. This new legislation has outlined parents' rights and responsibilities. In order to develop a comprehensive parent involvement program and not a fragmented effort, the parent and educator must make a concentrated effort to work as a team.

In order to have meaningful parent involvement, parents and the school district must develop a comprehensive model like those proposed in this chapter. Hobbs (1978, pp. 495–96) suggests that most parent involvement is at the teacher level. Some parents need more informative knowledge and skills, and school and other related professionals should be accountable for training these parents and helping them to acquire parenting skills. Parents can reciprocate by providing information, knowledge, and skills to professionals and other parents. At the same time professionals must acknowledge the parents' role as teachers and accept and use their information and skills. Only if parents and professionals work together and respect one another's influence on children's lives will children receive the most appropriate education available.

References

Abidin, R. R. 1976. *Parenting skills.* New York: Human Science Press.
Alberti, R. E., and Emmons, M. L. 1974. *Your perfect right.* San Luis Obispo, Calif.: Impact Press.
Alvord, J. 1973. *Home token economy: an incentive program for children and their parents.* Champaign, Ill.: Research Press.
Anderson, K. E. 1972. *Introduction to communication theory and practice.* Menlo Park, Calif.: Cummings Publishing Co.
Baker, B. L., Brightman, A. J., Heifetz, L. J., and Murphy, D. M. 1976. *Steps to independence: a skill training series for children with special needs.* Champaign, Ill.: Research Press.

Becker, W. C. 1971. *Parents are teachers.* Champaign, Ill.: Research Press.

Bornstein, M. R., Bellack, A. S., and Hersen, M. 1977. Social-skills training for unassertive children: A multiple baseline analysis. *Journal of Applied Behavior Analysis* 10:183–95.

Colletta, A. J. 1977. *Working together: a guide to parent involvement.* Atlanta, Ga.: Humanics Limited.

Cooper, J. O., and Edge, D. 1978. *Strategies and educational methods.* Columbus, Ohio: Charles E. Merrill.

Cotler, S. B., and Guerra, J. J. 1976. *Assertion training: a humanistic behavioral guide to self-dignity.* Champaign, Ill.: Research Press.

Creer, T. L., and Christian, W. P. 1976. *Chronically ill and handicapped children: their management and rehabilitation.* Champaign, Ill.: Research Press.

Croft, Doreen J. 1979. *Parents and teachers: a resource book for home, school, and community relation.* Belmont, Calif.: Wadsworth.

Dembinski, R. J., and Mauser, A. J. 1977. What parents of the learning disabled really want from professionals. *Journal of Learning Disabilities* 10:578–84.

Dobson, J. 1977. *Dare to discipline.* New York: Bantam Books.

Dodson, F. 1970. *How to parent.* New York: Signet Books.

Doernberg, N. L. 1978. Some negative effects on family integration of health and education services for young handicapped children. *Rehabilitation Literature* 39:107–10.

Donahue, A. T., and Nichten, S. 1964. *Teaching the troubled child.* New York: Grune and Stratton.

Dreikurs, R., and Soltz, V. 1964. *Children challenge.* New York: Hawthorn Books.

Education for All Handicapped Children Act (PL 94–142), *Federal Register.* Washington, D.C., August 23, 1977.

Eimers, R., and Aitchison, R. 1977. *Effective parents/responsible children.* New York: McGraw-Hill Book Co.

Eisler, R. M., Hersen, M., and Miller, P. M. 1973. Effects of modeling on components of assertive behavior. *Journal of Behavior Therapy and Experimental Psychiatry* 4:1–6.

Fast, J. 1971. *Body language.* New York: Pocket Books.

Gallagher, P. A. 1979. *Teaching students with behavior disorder: techniques for classroom instruction.* Denver: Love Publishing. List used with permission of the publisher.

Galloway, C., and Galloway, K. C. 1971. Parent classes in precise behavior management. *Teaching Exceptional Children* 3:120–28.

Gambrill, E. D., and Richey, C. A. 1976. *It's up to you: developing assertive social skills.* Millbrae, Calif.: Les Femmes.

Gardner, R. A. 1970. *The boys and girls book about divorce.* New York: Bantam Books.

Ginott, H. G. 1965. *Between parent and child.* New York: Macmillan and Co.
———. 1969. *Between parent and teenager.* New York: Macmillan and Co.

Gordon, T. 1970. *Parent effectiveness training.* New York: Wyden.

Gorham, K. A. A. 1975. *A lost generalism of parents. Exceptional Children* 41:521–25.

Gosciewski, F. W. 1976. *Effective child rearing: the behaviorally aware parent.* New York: Human Sciences Press.

Guerney, B. G., Jr. 1969. *Psychotherapeutic agents: new roles for non-professionals, parents, and teachers.* New York: Holt, Rinehart and Winston.

Heward, W. L., Dondig, J. C., Rossett, A. 1979. *Working with parents of handicapped children.* Columbus, Ohio: Charles E. Merrill.

Hobbs, N. 1978. Classification options: a conversation with Nicholas Hobbs. *Exceptional Children* 44:494–97.

Homme, L. et al. 1970. *How to use contingency contracting in the classroom.* Champaign, Ill.: Research Press.

Karnes, M. B., and Zehrbach, R. R. 1972. Flexibility in getting parents involved in the school. *Teaching Exceptional Children* 5:6–9.

Kroth, R. L. 1975. *Communicating with parents of exceptional children: improving parent-teacher relationships.* Denver: Love Publishing.

———. *Counseling and human development.* Denver: Love Publishing, forthcoming.

Kroth, R. L., and Scholl, G. 1978. *Getting schools involved with parents.* Reston, Va.: Council for Exceptional Children.

Kroth, R. L., and Simpson, Richard L. 1977. *Parent conferences as a teaching strategy.* Denver: Love Publishing.

Krumboltz, J. D., and Krumboltz, H. D. 1972. *Changing children's behavior.* Englewood Cliffs, N.J.: Prentice-Hall.

Lange, A. J., and Jakubowski, P. 1976. *Responsible assertive behavior.* Champaign, Ill.: Research Press.

Lazarus, A., and Foy, A. 1975. *I can if I want to.* New York: William Morrow.

Lillie, D. L. An overview to parent programs. 1976. In *Teaching parents to teach: a guide for working with the special child,* ed. E. L. Lillie and P. L. Trohanis. New York: Walker and Co.

Long, A. 1976. Easing the stress of parent-teacher conferences. *Today's Education* 64:84. Conference guidelines reprinted by permission of *Today's Education* and the author.

Madsen, C. K., and Madsen, C. H. 1970. *Parents-children-discipline: a positive approach.* Boston: Allyn and Bacon.

McDowell, R. L. 1978. *Managing behavior: a program for parent involvement.* 2d ed. Torrance, Calif.: B. L. Winch and Associates.

———. 1976. Parent counseling: the state of the art. *Journal of Learning Disabilities,* no. 10, 9:6–11.

McIntire, R. W. 1970. *For love of children: behavioral psychology for parents.* Del Mar, Calif.: CRM Books.

Miller, W. H. 1976. *Systematic parent training: procedures, cases and issues.* Champaign, Ill.: Research Press.

Norton, G. R. 1977. *Parenting.* Englewood Cliffs, N.J.: Prentice-Hall.

Patterson, G. R. 1975. *Families: applications of social learning to family life.* Champaign, Ill.: Research Press.

Patterson, G. R., and Gullian, M. E. 1971. *Living with children: new methods for parents and teachers.* Champaign, Ill.: Research Press.

Rettig, E. 1973. *ABC's for parents: an educational workshop in behavior modification.* Van Nuys, Calif.: Associates for Behavior Change.

Rinn, R. C., and Markle, A. 1977. *Positive parenting.* Cambridge, Mass.: Research Media.

Rogers-Warren, A., and Baer, D. M. 1976. Correspondence between saying and doing: Teaching children to share and praise. *Journal of Applied Behavior Analysis* 9:335–54.

Ross, A. O. 1964. *The exceptional child in the family.* New York: Grune & Stratton.

Rutherford, R. B., Jr., and Edgar, E. 1979. *Teachers and parents.* Boston: Allyn and Bacon.

Sarason, I. G., Lindner, K. C., and Crnic, K. 1976. *A guide for foster parents.* New York: Human Science Press.

Silberberg, N. E., and Silberberg, M. C. 1974. *Who speaks for the child?* Springfield, Ill.: Charles C. Thomas.

Smith, J. M., and Smith, D. E. P. 1976. *Child management: a program for parents and teachers.* Champaign, Ill.: Research Press.

Smith, M. J. 1975. *When I say no I feel guilty.* New York: Dial Press.

Susser, P. 1974. Parents are partners. *The Exceptional Parent,* no. 3, 4:41–47.

Turnbull, A. P., and Turnbull, H. R., III. 1978. *Parents speak out.* Columbus, Ohio: Charles E. Merrill.

Valett, R. E. 1970. *Prescriptions for learning: a parent's guide to remedial home training.* Belmont, Calif.: Fearon Publishers.

Wagonseller, B. R., Burnett, M., Salzberg, B., and Burnett, J. 1977. *The art of parenting.* Champaign, Ill.: Research Press.

Wagonseller, B. R., and McDowell, R. L. 1979. *You and your child.* Champaign, Ill.: Research Press.

Watson, D. L., and Tharp, R. G. 1972. *Self-directed behavior: self-modification for personal adjustment.* Monterey, Calif.: Brooks/Cole.

Weintraub, F. I. 1972. Recent influences of law regarding the identification and educational placement of children. *Focus on Exceptional Children,* no. 2, 4:1–10.

Wood, S., Bishop, R., and Cohen, D. 1978. *Parenting.* New York: Hart Publishing.

Zifferblatt, S. M. 1970. *Improving study and homework behavior.* Champaign, Ill.: Research Press.

Teaching Students with Mild Learning and Behavior Differences

part 2

4 Learner Characteristics

The primary focus of this volume is on strategies and techniques for educating the exceptional child in the regular classroom. The present section includes three chapters on students with mild learning and behavioral differences: (1) Learner Characteristics, (2) Strategies for Behavioral Programming, and (3) Strategies for Academic Programming.

The traditional approach to the education of students with mild learning and behavioral differences is generally one of separate and distinct categories including behavior disorders, mental retardation, and specific learning disabilities. The rationale for the present section's deviation from this categorical approach is based upon the authors' contention that these allegedly distinct populations are actually more alike than different in their academic and behavioral programming needs. This approach does not deny that differences do exist among categorical populations in such areas as ability, rate of learning, and attention to task. Rather, the approach stresses that the traditional categorical label is not functional in the development of educational programs for exceptional children with mild learning and behavior differences. Additionally, it is the authors' premise that separate categories are maintained more for administrative convenience than for effective educational programming for individual students. Therefore, in relationship to the format of the present volume, three separate chapters on educational strategies for each traditional category are not warranted. Academic and behavioral management strategies will be approached from a **cross-categorical** frame of reference.

Given the present administrative structure for funding of special education programs, the generic term "mild learning and behavior differences" has little meaning. Financial support for programs in special education continues to depend upon maintaining separate categories of exceptional children regardless of educational programming considerations. This has a great deal of significance for the regular educator, who must be knowledgeable about separate special education categories in order to be an effective member of a school placement team. These multidisciplinary teams are generally charged with the responsibility of determining the appropriate educational service delivery system for the individual child, based upon traditional categories. Thus, today's educator faces the dilemma of maintaining a working knowledge of special education categories for placement purposes, while remaining aware that programming considerations may not be as distinct and pure as the categories seem to imply.

The initial chapter in this trilogy specifically discusses definitions, classifications, and etiological factors associated with mild learning and behavioral differences. The traditional definitions associated with behavior disorders, mental retardation, and learning disabilities are carefully examined in order to place the discussion in a familiar context for the regular educator, who must know this terminology thoroughly. However, the major focus of the chapter is to analyze the attributes of these traditional categorical populations and present a case for adhering to the cross-categorical concept in the development of academic and behavioral strategies for direct classroom instruction.

Mild Behavior Disorders

One of the more widely discussed and controversial issues in today's public schools is behavioral deviance. Newspapers and periodicals are replete with articles addressing a variety of discipline problems in the classroom. Estimates of prevalence based upon several studies (Glidewell and Swallow 1968; Stennett 1966; Wickman 1928) indicate that anywhere from 10 to 42 percent of the school-age population will exhibit adjustment difficulties severe enough to warrant professional intervention. Every educator at one time or another is confronted with students whose actions fall outside the range of acceptable standards. Educational programming for these children depends upon the intensity and duration of these behavioral problems in the classroom.

Given the nature of this topic and its present impact on public education, it is not surprising to find a number of definitions as well as etiological theories associated with these problems. One position is that the school curriculum is unrelated to individual needs and personally unrewarding. Another theory is that parents and educators have created the situation by being far too lenient in handling discipline problems.

Etiological theories are extremely divergent and correlate directly with the perspective of the person describing the deviance. For example, medical personnel may seek organic causes, while sociologists attempt to identify adjustment disorders associated with the individual's social and cultural background. Attempts to incorporate etiological factors into a general, functional definition have been foiled by the inconsistent use of clinical terms (e.g., schizophrenia, disorder of the personality, emotional disturbance, mental illness, etc.) by a myriad of professional disciplines. Bakwin and Bakwin (1972, p. 198) point out that "It is important to keep in mind that many of the deviations in behavior commonly seen in children are inexplicable. . . . Disorders of thinking, feeling, and mobility . . . are generally dependent on multiple causes."

Any description of behavior disorders must be viewed in the context of the child's cultural or environmental norm. From a narrow educational perspective, this means adaptation to the regular education classroom. Pate (1963), discussing the educational concept of behavior disorders, suggests that the child's observable behavior is so inappropriate that regular class placement without additional support services (1) disrupts the child's peer group, (2) places undue pressure on the classroom teacher, and (3) contributes further to the disturbance of the child. However, Pate's description of the behaviorally different child overlooks several critical factors that must be considered in order to analyze accurately the severity of the child's behavior problems and determine the necessity for additional professional intervention. These factors include (1) teacher tolerance level, (2) impact on the child's academic achievement, (3) frequency and persistence of the behavior, and (4) long-range effect on classroom peers.

The behavior in the classroom must be understood in terms of its deviation from the acceptable standard, or what is "normal." Any behavior that violates expectations enough to evoke a disturbed reaction from the environment will be considered deviant. The greater the environmental reaction, the more severe the disturbance. Consequently, social prohibitions and sanctions, including segregation from normal peers, are also applied on the basis of the behavior's deviation from the standard. In order to understand the child's behavioral problems in the school setting, it is essential to determine the range of "normalcy" in the specific classroom environment. A child may be labeled as "disturbed" from the perspective of one classroom teacher and yet be well within the range of acceptable standards for another. Thus, what can be described as normal depends upon the individual teacher and the situation in which the behavior is observed. Clarizio and McCory (1976) suggest that, although there are no acceptable definitions of normalcy, there are specific components that every definition must include:

1. The child's developmental level (what is required as normal at one age might well be viewed as abnormal in another);
2. Consideration of the child's culture or subculture;
3. Allowances for individuality;
4. Any definition must be multidimensional (it must take into account how the child functions in various representative areas of development).

These components represent the basic focus of educational assessment for purposes of categorizing or labeling the child. Beyond this definitional framework, the educational diagnostic team must also attend to (1) how often the unacceptable behaviors occur in the classroom; (2) the number and intensity of behavioral symptoms that are exhibited; and (3) the manageability of the behaviors (e.g., the behaviors persist even after intervention strategies have been employed).

The problems of the behaviorally different child in the regular classroom can be viewed in terms of distinct patterns of conduct. The child, although at times conforming to the appropriate code of classroom behavior, cannot consistently relate to peers and authority figures (Haring and Philips 1962). These behavioral incongruencies can be classified as behavior excesses (acting out, aggression), behavior deficits (withdrawal), problems related to consistent attendance (high rates of absenteeism), and difficulties in interpersonal relationships (socialization skills, communication). The result of these behavioral problems is a "failure-orientation" toward school. There will be an inability to learn resulting in significant gaps between expected levels of achievement and actual performance. The child may develop fears about school and, therefore, seek to disrupt or avoid confronting things closely associated with it—specifically teachers and classroom peers.

The child's interaction and adaptation in the classroom will ultimately determine the degree of the problem and whether or not the child remains in the regular program. The task for the educational diagnostic team is to weigh as many factors as possible in making the placement determination. There are no absolute criteria for assessing whether or not the child can benefit from regular class placement with special education support services. However, from a definitional standpoint, Kelly, Bullock, and Dykes (1974, p. 10) suggest that children with mild behavior disorders "can be helped adequately by the regular classroom teacher and/or other school resource personnel through periodic counseling and/or short term individual attention and instruction." The critical factor is being able to assess accurately the level of deviance in relationship to the demands of the classroom situation.

Mild Mental Retardation

As a professional discipline aligned with special education, the field of mental retardation has a long history and a solid foundation of research and practice. Despite its historical roots, this discipline is plagued with definitional problems. These problems may be attributed to many factors, including the vast array of professions external to special education that have been concerned with the mentally retarded (psychologists, sociologists, anthropologists, social workers, and physicians). Many traditional definitions of mental retardation were founded upon the medical model and stressed "pathology" and "incurability." This physiological orientation served little productive purpose in the education of the mentally retarded and merely perpetuated the misconception that all mental retardation has a genetic origin. Additionally, the negative prognosis inherent in these definitions of incurability impugned the value of educational programming.

More recent definitions of mental retardation have emphasized intellectual functioning in conjunction with adaptation to societal norms of appropriate behavior. These concepts are incorporated in the definition of mental retardation put forward by the American Association on Mental Deficiency (AAMD) (Grossman 1973, 1977; Heber 1961). Presently the AAMD definition is the most widely used in the public schools' special education placement process. The definition states that:

> Mental retardation refers to *significantly sub-average general intellectual* functioning existing concurrently with deficits in *adaptive behavior,* and manifested during the *developmental period* (Grossman 1977, p. 5).

"Significantly sub-average general intellectual functioning" is assessed by an individual, standardized intelligence test indicating that the child falls more than two standard deviations below the mean (IQ below 70 on the *Wechsler Intelligence Scale for Children–Revised*). The developmental period is defined as birth to eighteen years of age, in order to distinguish mental retardation from other disorders. Deficits in adaptive behavior are determined by "the effectiveness or degree with which the individual meets the standards of personal independence and social responsibility expected of his age and cultural group" (Grossman 1977, p. 11).

Using the AAMD definition of sub-average intellectual functioning (two standard deviations below the mean on an intelligence test), general estimates show that approximately 2–3 percent of the total population is mentally retarded. Actual prevalence may be closer to 1 percent, as documented in a community survey of 100,000 individuals (Mercer 1973; Tarjan et al. 1973). Regardless of whether the total incidence is 1 or 3 percent, the fact is that nine out of ten individuals categorized as mentally retarded are within the classification range of mild mental retardation.

The term *mild mental retardation* has its origin in the AAMD *symptom severity* classification system, which includes mild, moderate, severe, and profound disorders. The classification of *mildly retarded* is synonymous with the historical term *moron* and the public school designation of *educable mentally retarded*. Mild mental retardation is generally characterized by an IQ level ranging from approximately 55–70 (AAMD definition). Adaptive behavior level is a function of the child's developmental age. Generally, the preschool-age mildly retarded child will develop socialization skills that are age-appropriate, but may exhibit minimal retardation in sensorimotor areas. The school-age mildly retarded child can function in basic academic content areas and will be able to use reading and mathematics as functional tools (MacMillan 1977). The mildly retarded adult who has been adequately trained in an educational program is capable of social and vocational independence.

The determination of **etiology** for the mentally retarded population has been an insurmountable task. There are over two hundred known causes of retardation, but this accounts for only about 25 percent of all recorded cases. This means that we are unable to determine the cause for 70–80 percent of this population. Concerning etiological factors associated with mild mental retardation, it has been well documented (Mercer 1973) that socioeconomic and cultural factors are direct correlates, although their precise role in causing mental retardation is unknown (MacMillan 1977). Mercer's eight-year, comprehensive epidemiology (in Riverside, California) compared the characteristics of persons labeled mentally retarded by members of their immediate community. Several important findings were reported:

1. The public schools were the primary labelers.
2. The public schools relied mainly on IQ test scores in making a diagnosis of mental retardation.
3. Black and Spanish-surname children . . . were more likely to score 79 or below on the IQ test than Anglo children.
4. Among those scoring below 79 on the test, children who were Spanish surnamed, who were from low socioeconomic levels, or who had been identified by the teacher as possibly mentally retarded were more likely to be placed in special classes.
5. Only 19 percent of the children placed in classes for the mentally retarded returned to the regular mainstream program of the school.
6. Black and Spanish-surnamed children were 'overlabeled' as mentally retarded, and Anglo children were 'underlabeled'.
7. Persons from lower socioeconomic backgrounds were 'overlabeled' and persons from higher socioeconomic backgrounds 'underlabeled' (Mercer and Lewis 1979, pp. 1–2).

These findings support the premise that the highest incidence of *mild* mental retardation occurs among children who are culturally different and from lower socioeconomic backgrounds. The data confirmed that such children were more likely to be "situationally retarded" and commonly referred to as "six-hour retardates" (i.e., the children were perceived as retarded only at school; people in their immediate community outside the school setting did not so label the children). Mercer's findings also clearly documented that, regardless of the AAMD definition emphasizing adaptive behavior level, the intelligence test was the sole criterion for labeling the child retarded.

The results of the Riverside study, in conjunction with the concepts advocated in Public Law 94–142, suggest several implications for the placement of mildly retarded children in the public schools. There is an obvious need for a strong multidisciplinary team in the assessment process, including regular and special educators, psychologists, social workers, medical personnel, and parents. Each team member contributes information concerning the child's school performance in order to eliminate the "single-score" orientation of intelligence tests. Teachers may informally assess the child's academic and social functioning level within the classroom environment; the psychologist provides a **normative-referenced assessment** of the child's general intellectual functioning, achievement, and adaptive behavior; the social worker may work directly with parents in order to determine cultural or socioeconomic factors that are relevant to the child's educational program; and the physician may screen for physiological conditions contributing to the child's educational problems. Based upon this multidisciplinary analysis, the school will generate significant information concerning the "total child" in relationship to the demands of the regular classroom. The educational focus is on the needs of the individual child and not the stigma associated with the label of mental retardation. Stereotyped misconceptions, such as "the retarded cannot learn," will not be applied to children on a wholesale basis. When expectations about the child's learning and social capabilities are based on a variety of input from professionals and parents, the mystique surrounding the education of these children will fall away.

Learning disabilities, an unknown educational category until the early 1960s, has become the largest area, and one of the most controversial, in the field of special education. The nature of the controversy focuses on the lack of an acceptable definition that is theoretically sound as well as functional for labeling and placing students in special education. Definitions associated with learning disabilities have not shown any consistency within or among professional disciplines.

Learning Disabilities

The evolution of this field is unique; it has not followed the same growth patterns as the fields of mental retardation and behavior disorders. Hallahan and Kauffman (1976, p. 2) explain that

> the field of learning disabilities, unlike other sectors of special education, lacked the advantage of developing within a unified framework of thinking. Instead, the concepts, ideas, and directions of this "new" field were, and continue to be, fostered almost exclusively within widely varied educational circles. . . . It is unfortunately true also that the educational profession of the early 1960s was not prepared to accept the challenge of developing this new area of exceptionality.

Several disciplines have been directly involved with the learning-disabled child, each advancing its own unique terminology. Psychology has contributed the terms *perceptual disorders* and *hyperkinetic activity;* medicine uses such descriptors as *brain damage, injury,* and *impairment;* and language specialists employ the terms *aphasia* and *dyslexia.* This widely diversified terminology emphasizes the theoretical and conceptual differences among the professional disciplines. This confusion can be exemplified by an analysis of two widely known theories associated with this area: (1) **perceptual-motor** theory and (2) language disability theory. The field of learning disabilities, as perceived by the perceptual motor theorists (Kephart 1971), "examines the normal sequential development of motor patterns and motor generalizations and compares the motor development of children with learning problems to that of normal children" (Lerner 1976, p. 142). The language disability theorists concentrate on the child's deficiency in language. They believe that language plays the critical role in learning and that "an intimate relationship exists between learning disabilities and deficits in language" (Lerner 1976, p. 205). The theoretical comparison presented here is shallow and not representative of the various philosophical positions within the learning disabilities field (e.g., developmentalists vs. behaviorists). However, on the basis of this single comparison, it is not difficult to understand the problems of formulating a single "totally acceptable" and "professionally practical" definition of learning disabilities.

Contemporary definitions of learning disabilities have their historical origin in the concepts or organic "brain injury" (Strauss and Lehtinen 1947) and "minimal brain dysfunction" (Clements 1966). The Strauss brain-injured child was perceived as suffering from an "infection of" or "injury to" the brain, resulting in disturbances in perception, thinking, and emotions. Clements' expanded definition of minimal brain dysfunction (MBD) included the Strauss child as well as children manifesting deviations in language and motor development. The Clements definition also sought to clearly distinguish MBD from mental retardation by limiting the population to only those children of "near average intelligence" (pp. 9–10). Kirk (1962) coined the phrase "specific learning disabilities," and even though the term was introduced four years prior to the MBD definition, it was not widely used until several years later.

> A learning disability refers to a retardation, disorder, or delayed development in one or more of the processes of speech, language, reading, spelling, writing, or arithmetic resulting from a possible cerebral dysfunction and/or emotional or behavioral disturbance and not from mental retardation, sensory deprivation, or cultural or instructional factors (Kirk 1962, p. 263).

The conceptual framework of Kirk's interpretation of learning disabilities was initially incorporated into the definition developed by the National Advisory Committee on Handicapped Children (1968) of the U.S. Office of Education, and later employed in Public Law 94–142. Although minor wording changes are evident, the intent of Kirk's original definition remains intact.

'Specific learning disability' means a disorder in one or more of the basic psychological processes involved in understanding or in using language, spoken or written, which may manifest itself in an imperfect ability to listen, think, speak, read, write, spell, or to do mathematical calculations. The term includes such conditions as perceptual handicaps, brain injury, minimal brain dysfunction, dyslexia, and developmental aphasia. The term does not include children who have learning problems which are primarily the result of visual, hearing, or motor handicaps, of mental retardation, of emotional disturbance, or of environmental, cultural, or economic disadvantage (Education of All Handicapped Children Act, PL 94-142 1975).

Several components of this definition have come under strong criticism for a number of reasons.

1. The definition's focus is on explaining what learning disabilities are not; traditional handicapping conditions (mental retardation and emotional disturbance) are excluded even though these populations could also exhibit one of the specific learning disabilities.
2. There is no differentiation made between expected learning capacity (intelligence) and actual achievement.
3. This open-minded definition could be interpreted so that as many as 40 percent of the school-age population would qualify for special education programs in learning disabilities.

These three areas of concern warrant further analysis in order to gain better understanding of this complicated definition.

Definition by Exclusion

The concepts incorporated into the definition given by Public Law 94-142 have been described as a "catch-all" for children previously excluded under the traditional categories. Hammill (1976) criticizes the exclusionary nature of the definition and suggests that present testing procedures are grossly inadequate for making clear-cut differential diagnoses. The assumption that only children within the normal range of intelligence can be identified as having a learning disability is not founded upon solid empirical evidence. Dunn (1973, p. 540) further explains that

while the primary disability of certain children may be emotional disturbance or mental retardation, the definition does not recognize that these pupils with traditional disability labels may also have a major specific learning disability such as reading.

Gearheart and Weishahn (1976) suggest that, given the theoretical diversity among professionals in the field, the definition-by-exclusion focus of PL 94-142 was the least "unacceptable" of several alternatives. The definition was necessary as a funding vehicle for a population excluded under other definitions and thereby deprived of the appropriate special services so desperately needed. Additionally, there has been no agreement between the professional disciplines as to etiological factors or remediational procedures; the present definition at least provides a compromise for this debate.

> The modern concept of learning disabilities has fused various categories as traditionally conceived, such as brain damage and developmental dyslexia, and eliminates the distinctions. As an educational concept, learning disabilities has focused attention on the remediation of learning problems of children, while allowing a continuance of the debate over etiology and more specific syndromes (Marsh, Gearheart, and Gearheart 1978, pp. 8–9).

Discrepancy Between Capacity and Achievement

Bateman (1965) first introduced the concept of assessing the discrepancy between capacity and achievement as an added dimension to the definition of learning disabilities.

> Children who have learning disorders are those who manifest an educationally significant discrepancy between their estimated intellectual potential and actual level of performance related to basic disorders in the learning process, which may or may not be accompanied by demonstrable central nervous system dysfunction, and which are not secondary to generalized mental retardation, educational or cultural deprivation, severe emotional disturbance, or sensory loss. (Bateman 1965, p. 220)

Although the discrepancy between capacity and achievement is not a definitional component of PL 94–142, it is an integral part of the Federal Rules and Regulations (1977). These rules and regulations are established to clarify the intent of the public law and to delineate procedural guidelines for its implementation. According to these guidelines, the determination for classification is based upon an already existing *severe* discrepancy between capacity and achievement:

> (1) whether a child does not achieve commensurate with his or her age and ability when provided with appropriate educational experiences, and (2) whether the child has a *severe* discrepancy between achievement and intellectual ability in one or more of seven areas relating to communication skills and mathematics abilities (*Federal Register* 42 [205] (1977):65083).

These concepts are interpreted on a case-by-case basis, and the discrepancy must exist in one or more of the following areas:

> (1) oral expression; (2) listening comprehension; (3) written expression; (4) basic reading skill; (5) reading comprehension; (6) mathematical calculation; or (7) mathematical reasoning (*Federal Register* 42 [205] (1977):65083).

The most common criterion for determining the significance of the discrepancy is performance one or two years below expected level of achievement. Johnson and Myklebust (1967, p. 18) point out that using this criterion presents some "serious limitation because one year below expectancy at eight years of age is not comparable to one year below expectancy at sixteen years of age." The exact meaning of the phrase "severe discrepancy" is a concept that certainly needs additional expansion and clarification.

Prevalence figures for children with learning disabilities range from 1.5 to 40 percent of the school-age population. Initially, under PL 94–142, the USOE recommended that 2 percent of the school-age population be included in the learning disability classification. This ceiling was later rescinded, and the issues surrounding prevalence left unresolved. This has important implications for the public schools as they attempt to put this definition into practice. There is an obvious paradox in attempting to comply with an open-ended definition that has no prevalence ceiling while restricting prevalence to the funds available. The determination of prevalence for learning disability programs will continue to be fraught with problems as the public schools attempt their own interpretations of definitional components and further contribute to the confusion.

An Open-Ended Definition

This chapter has attempted to examine the categorically oriented definitions associated with mild behavior disorders, mild mental retardation, and specific learning disabilities. These categorical definitions essentially maintain the purity of each population by focusing on discrepant attributes: unique or exclusive characteristics that distinguish the defined population from the other special education categories. As a case in point, the definition of learning disabilities in PL 94–142 seeks to distinguish the defined population by the explicit exclusion of mentally retarded and behavior-disordered populations. "The term [learning disabilities] does not include children who have learning problems which are primarily the result of . . . mental retardation, of emotional disturbance or of environmental, cultural or economic disadvantage" (Education of All Handicapped Children Act, PL 94–142 1975). The clause implies that children who are sub-average intellectually or whose behavior is not within acceptable standards cannot manifest any one of the several major learning disabilities (reading, mathematics, etc.). This exclusionary concept is not based upon empirical evidence nor is it supported by some of the prominent professionals within the field of learning disabilities (Dunn 1973; Hammill 1976).

Mild Learning and Behavior Differences

Although traditional definitions have attempted to preserve categorical purity, there appears to be considerable overlap when the *actual performance* of children is examined. This is particularly evident for mildly handicapped populations (Hallahan and Kauffman 1976). Special education's overemphasis of the discrepant attributes of categorical populations has left the classroom teacher with a rather narrow perspective on these children. Educational programming has been based upon *definitional expectations by label* instead of the individual child's task performance. Table 4.1 illustrates the comparison of definitional expectation and actual performance for each traditional category in general (individual characteristics may differ). The table analyzes shared and discrepant attributes in capacity (intelligence), achievement, and social skills. The following paragraphs expand and clarify the concepts addressed in table 4.1.

Table 4.1 Comparison of capacity, achievement, and social performance by special education categorical area

	Definitional Expectation	Actual Performance
Capacity (Intelligence)	*Mild Behavior Disorders:* Average or above-average performance on intelligence tests	*Mild Behavior Disorders:* Behavior problems occur in all ranges of intelligence, e.g., mentally retarded range.
	Learning Disabilities: Average or above-average performance on intelligence tests	*Learning Disabilities:* Specific learning disabilities occur in all ranges of intelligence, e.g., mentally retarded range.
	Mild Mental Retardation: Low potential— significantly sub-average (two standard deviations below the mean) performance on intelligence tests	*Mild Mental Retardation:* Mental retardation is limited by definition to IQ below 70. Definition excludes children whose IQ is *between* one and two standard deviations below the mean (IQ 70–85).
Achievement (Academic Learning)	*Mild Behavior Disorders:* Definitions do not generally include low achievement as a criterion.	*Mild Behavior Disorders:* Low achievement can be secondary effect of behavior disorders (behavior problems interfere with academic learning).
	Learning Disabilities: Low achievement is an integral part of LD definitional concept. Child will perform at least one or two years below grade level.	*Learning Disabilities:* Child performs at least one or two years below grade level.
	Mental Retardation: Low intelligence indicates poor academic potential.	*Mental Retardation:* Mildly retarded child performs at least one or two years below grade level.
Social Skills (Adaptive Behavior)	*Behavioral Disorders:* Child will be deficient in socialization and classroom adaptation skills.	*Behavioral Disorders:* Child is deficient in socialization and classroom adaptation skills.
	Learning Disabilities: Social deficits are not included in LD definitional structure.	*Learning Disabilities:* Poor performance in social and adaptive behavior may be secondary effect of learning problems.
	Mental Retardation: Adaptive behavior skills are an integral part of mental retardation definition.	*Mental Retardation:* IQ continues to be *major* factor for categorization. Social deficits are not necessarily correlated with poor performance on intelligence tests.

The most widely used definitions in the traditional categorical areas incorporate, either directly or indirectly, criteria related to the child's intellectual functioning. Generic definitions in learning disabilities typically indicate that the child's intelligence test score must fall within the "normal" range (Kirk 1962; Clements 1966; Education of All Handicapped Children Act 1975). Definitions associated with behavior disorders generally focus more on the level of emotional functioning than on intellectual capacity. However, intelligence tests are used as "disqualifiers" for placement decisions to ensure that the behavior-disordered child is within the "normal" range of intelligence. The mentally retarded are sub-average intellectually and, by traditional standards, have a low potential for school success. *Capacity*

Although definitional expectations mandate distinct intellectual differences between these categories, the actual performance of children suggests that learning and behavioral problems are not specific to any one level of intellectual functioning. For example, even though the retarded are excluded from the behavior disorders category, emotional problems are prevalent among this population (Chinn, Drew, and Logan 1979). The category of learning disabilities also excludes the retarded on the basis of intelligence, although there is no substantial evidence to support the contention that this population will not manifest major specific learning disabilities (Hammill 1976).

Another significant problem with the traditional approach to the placement of children with mild learning and behavior differences is the exclusion of those who need special education services but do not qualify under any of the three traditional categories. For example, a child whose IQ is below the "normal" range (under 85), but above the cutoff range for mental retardation (70–75), cannot receive special education services if the state rules and regulations rely solely on normal intelligence as a qualifier for programs in learning disabilities and behavior disorders.

The quality and quantity of a child's performance in the academic content areas can be described in terms of achievement. The child's performance may be compared to that of his or her peer group and is usually reported as a grade-level or percentile score. The concept of achievement is an important factor in the definitional structure of each category. *Achievement*

The learning-disabled child must exhibit a severe discrepancy between actual and expected achievement level—performance at least one or two years below expected grade level. The most widely used definition of mental retardation (Grossman 1973, 1977) does not directly mention achievement as a definitional criterion, but the implications are that the child's intellectual deficit will be a factor in poor academic performance. Definitions associated with behavior disorders are highly suggestive of a cause-and-effect relationship between behavioral problems and poor academic performance. The child's behavioral differences interfere with learning.

The actual performance of children in a classroom situation indicates that poor academic performance is characteristic of all children with mild learning and behavior differences. The etiology of the learning problem may differ from child to child, but the ultimate outcome (failure in the classroom) is the same.

Social Skills There is an obvious similarity between definitions of mental retardation and behavior disorders in regard to social skill or adaptive behavior development. Grossman included adaptive behavior deficits in the AAMD definition of mental retardation as significant criteria for categorization. Adaptive behavior is defined on the basis of personal independence and social responsibility expected of the age group. These two concepts are strikingly similar to Kauffman's (1977) description of the behavior-disordered child as one who responds to the environment in "socially unacceptable and/or personally unsatisfying ways" (Kauffman 1977, p. 23). Social immaturity and maladaptive behavior are integral concepts in definitions of mental retardation and behavior disorders. These concepts are not, however, generally included in definitions of learning disabilities.

The actual performance of children in the development of social skills suggests that maladaptive behavior is not specific to any one of the three traditional categories. The only real issue is again one of primary etiology, which is indistinct for this population. Social problems do exist for the learning-disabled as well as the retarded and behavior-disordered. Although it can be argued that, for the learning-disabled child, adjustment problems are a secondary effect of academic learning difficulties, the fact remains that these problems *do* exist, regardless of definitional exclusion or unknown etiology.

References Bakwin, H., and Bakwin, R. M. 1972. *Behavior disorders in children.* 4th ed. Philadelphia: W. B. Saunders.

Bateman, B. D. 1965. An educator's view of a diagnostic approach to learning disorders. In *Learning disorders,* vol. I, ed. J. Hellmuth. Seattle: Special Child Publications.

Chinn, P., Drew, C., and Logan, D. 1979. *Mental retardation: A life cycle approach.* 2d ed. St. Louis: C. V. Mosby.

Clarizio, H. F. and McCory, G. 1976. *Behavior disorders in children.* 2d ed. New York: Thomas Y. Crowell.

Clements, S. D., ed. 1966. Minimal brain dysfunction in children: terminology and identification: phase one of a three-phase project. NINDS Monography No. 3. (U.S. Public Health Service Publication No. 1415). Washington D.C.: U.S. Government Printing Office.

Dunn, L. M. 1973. Children with mild general learning disabilities. In *Exceptional children in the schools: special education in transition,* ed. L. M. Dunn, pp. 125–88. 2d ed. New York: Holt, Rinehart and Winston.

Gearheart, B. R., and Weishahn, M. W. 1976. *The handicapped child in the regular classroom.* St. Louis C. V. Mosby.

Glidewell, J., and Swallow, C. 1968. *The prevalence of maladjustment in elementary schools.* Chicago: University Park Press.

Grossman, H. J., ed. 1973. *Manual on terminology and classification in mental retardation.* Washington, D.C.: American Association on Mental Deficiency.

Grossman, H. J., ed. 1977. *Manual on terminology and classification in mental retardation.* Washington, D.C.: American Association on Mental Deficiency.

Hallahan, D. P., and Kauffman, J. P. 1976. *Introduction to learning disabilities: a psycho-behavioral approach.* Englewood Cliffs, N.J.: Prentice-Hall.

Hammill, D. D. 1976. Defining learning disabilities for programmatic purposes. *Academic Therapy* 12:29–37.

Haring, N., and Phillips, L. 1962. *Educating emotionally disturbed children.* New York: McGraw-Hill.

Heber, R. 1961. A manual on terminology and classification in mental retardation. 2d ed. *American Journal of Mental Deficiency, Monography Supplement.*

Johnson, D., and Myklebust, H. 1967. *Learning disabilities: educational principles and practices.* New York: Grune and Stratton.

Kauffman, J. M. 1977. *Characteristics of children's behavior disorders.* Columbus, Ohio: Charles E. Merrill.

Kelly, T., Bullock, L., and Dykes, M. 1974. *Teacher perceptions of behavioral disorders in children.* Florida Educational Research and Development Council.

Kephart, N. C. 1971. *The slow learner in the classroom.* 2d ed. Columbus, Ohio: Charles E. Merrill.

Kirk, S. A. 1962. *Educating exceptional children.* Boston: Houghton Mifflin.

Kirk, S. A. 1972. *Educating exceptional children.* 2d ed. Boston: Houghton Mifflin.

Lerner, J. W. 1976. *Children with learning disabilities.* 2d ed. Boston: Houghton Mifflin.

MacMillan, D. L. 1977. *Mental retardation in school and society.* Boston: Little, Brown.

Marsh, G. E., Gearheart, D. K., and Gearheart, B. R. 1978. *The learning disabled adolescent.* St. Louis: C. V. Mosby.

Mercer, J. R. 1973. *Labeling the mentally retarded.* Berkeley, Calif.: University of California Press.

Mercer, J. R., and Lewis, J. F. 1979. *System of multicultural pluralistic assessment: Technical Manual.* New York: The Psychological Corporation.

National Advisory Committee on Handicapped Children. 1968. *First Annual Report.* Washington D.C.: U.S. Office of Education.

Pate, J. E. 1963. Emotionally disturbed and social maladjusted children. In *Exceptional children in the schools,* ed. L. M. Dunn, pp. 239–83. New York: Holt, Rinehart and Winston.

Sloan, W., and Birch, J. 1955. A rationale for degrees of retardation. *American Journal of Mental Deficiency* 60:258–64.

Stennett, R. G. 1966. Emotional handicaps in the elementary years: phase or disease? *American Journal of Orthopsychiatry* 36:444–49.

Strauss, A. A., and Lehtinen, L. E. 1947. *Psychopathology and education of the brain-injured child,* vol. 1. New York: Grune and Stratton.

Tarjan, G., Wright, S. W., Eyman, R. K., and Keeran, C. V. 1973. Natural history of mental retardation: some aspects of epidemiology. *American Journal of Mental Deficiency* 77:369–79.

Wickman, E. K. 1928. *Children's behavior and teacher's attitudes.* New York: Commonwealth Fund.

5 Strategies for Behavioral Programming

Managing students at any age or grade level can be an extremely challenging task. In fact, the success achieved by teachers in educating students is often directly proportional to their ability to use appropriate management strategies to direct individuals, small groups, and large groups. Frequently their classes include students who have mild learning and behavior differences; they have been identified or classified, for example, as learning-disabled, emotionally disturbed, or educable mentally retarded, or hearing-impaired. Because of the mildness of these conditions, such students frequently spend the majority of their school time in regular classrooms. On the whole, students with mild learning and behavior differences are more like their peers than different from them. They are equally capable of misbehaving and requiring management from teachers.

Classroom management is a broad term, often synonymous with such words as *control, direction,* and *leadership.* In a technical sense, management is the judicious use of strategies and techniques to achieve certain specified goals. The goal of education, generally speaking, is to teach students new behaviors that are appropriate to successful participation in society. Optimal use of classroom management strategies, then, would permit educators to teach new, meaningful behaviors effectively and efficiently. Unfortunately, many if not most educators are not adequately prepared to deal with the challenges of managing regular students, let alone exceptional students.

Where does one learn how to manage students? In the main, most teachers manage students as they were managed during their school years. But in many instances the management strategies of the past are ineffective in dealing with problems of the present. Other teachers develop their management strategies by the "trial and error" method. This approach is often fraught with errors and punishment practices rather than positive control or leadership techniques. Still other teachers consult their colleagues as to what works with students in managing classroom behaviors. This approach is also limited. As a last resort, teachers eventually read a book or take a course about discipline, hoping that they will become more effective in managing students.

Using suitable management skills effectively takes both knowledge and active practice. The purpose of this chapter is to introduce a broad array of management strategies that have been effectively used with both exceptional and regular students. Knowledge alone about these management strategies will not make teachers effective managers. Effectiveness comes from actual practice. In some cases, additional in-service or university coursework may be necessary before teachers will feel comfortable using the strategies discussed in this chapter.

Another purpose of this chapter is to enlarge the fund of teacher techniques available for dealing with certain student behaviors. A limited inventory of management techniques limits a teacher's potential for success. By broadening the range of their alternatives, teachers can at least choose resources (techniques) that are specifically designed for the problematic behaviors at hand. The techniques offered here are designed to serve three functions: (1) to prevent certain maladaptive behaviors from occurring, (2) to eliminate negative behaviors exhibited by students, and (3) to maintain present, positive student behaviors. It is important to note here that these techniques do not necessarily make teaching easier, nor do they solve all the management problems associated with teaching exceptional and regular students. Knowledge and skill in using the techniques may, however, make teaching less frustrating and more enjoyable.

There are currently available many management techniques and strategies that can be easily employed in regular classrooms. When mastered, they are useful in dealing with a broad range of student behaviors ranging from inattentiveness to aggression. The strategies that are presented here vary in their potential strength. The strength of a particular management strategy often depends on the teacher's skill and commitment in using the strategy. In reviewing these strategies, teachers should be aware of their own teaching styles and personalities. Some of the strategies will be very appealing while others will be unappealing because of the factors of teaching style and personality. The strategies are not presented as ultimate answers, but rather as problem and tension reducers.

The strategies to be discussed are grouped according to four types: (1) relationship/communication, (2) behavior modification, (3) structure, and (4) combinational (see table 5.1). The strategies also vary according to the philosophical framework from which they are drawn. The greatest challenges in using them are: choosing the most appropriate strategy or set of strategies for the particular time and setting; choosing a strategy that blends well with the teacher's style; and gaining the ability, as a result of active practice and consultation, to apply the strategies effectively and efficiently with individuals or groups. Subsequent sections introduce each type of strategy

Table 5.1 Four types of classroom management strategies

Strategy Type	Specific Strategies
Relationship/communication strategies	Reality Therapy Strategies Teacher Effectiveness Strategies Strategies of Dreikurs, Grunwald, and Pepper
Behavior modification strategies	Strategies for Establishing Positive Standards Reinforcement Strategies The Strategy of Shaping Strategies for Terminating or Weakening Behaviors Contracting Strategies
Structure strategies	Classroom Design Strategies Rule and Routine Strategies
Combinational strategies	Surface Behavior Management Strategies Kounin's Strategies

and the techniques associated with it. The techniques that are outlined and reviewed for each strategy should be considered as condensed overviews rather than comprehensive descriptions. Teachers interested in the complete descriptions of techniques as described by their creators should refer to the reference section at the end of this chapter.

Relationship/Communication Strategies

Techniques associated with relationship/communication strategies are based on the premise that the quality of relationship and communication between student and teacher has a tremendous impact on student behavior. The techniques discussed in this section provide different ways of building relationships with and between students and various approaches to communicating with students.

Reality Therapy Strategies

Dr. William Glasser, the author and originator of *Reality Therapy* (Glasser 1965), feels that all students seek to fulfill their needs in various ways. According to Glasser all persons have two basic psychological needs: (1) the need to love and be loved, and (2) the need to feel worthwhile to others and to themselves. When these needs are met, students are generally happy and successful. When they are not met, students experience pain and unhappiness. Feeling worthwhile to others and having close, meaningful relationships with others are critical in Glasser's view to obtaining the level of self-respect so necessary for coping successfully with school and life in general. Students who are lacking in self-respect and overflowing with problems or irresponsible behaviors need involvement with a sensitive, caring, responsible teacher. The teacher serves as a personal catalyst helping and motivating the student to learn and choose new, more responsible ways to behave. The steps involved in implementing this relationship/communication strategy are as follows: (1) be personal, (2) deal with present behavior, (3) have the student make a value judgment about the problem behavior(s), (4) have the student develop a plan or develop one together, (5) secure a commitment from the student to implement the plan, (6) accept no excuses for not making the plan work, (7) administer no punishment, (8) don't give up, (9) if the plan does not work, recycle these steps until success is achieved.

Becoming personally acquainted with students does not imply that the teacher should be involved in their private activities. It merely implies that the teacher needs to develop a relationship with each student that is truly personal. The teacher needs to know students' names and call them by their first names at frequent intervals. An occasional telephone call or special note about a student's achievement goes a long way in creating the basis for successful reality therapy. The teacher needs to know something about the strengths and aspirations of students, particularly those students who may be presenting or developing problem behaviors. Students who know that teachers care by virtue of their teaching behaviors are much more likely to respond to the relationship/communication techniques involved in reality therapy.

Dealing with present behavior is not always easy to do. Basically, the teacher is encouraged to ask questions such as—

What are you doing right now?

What did you just do?

What were you doing just then?

Please tell me what you were doing.

Describe for me what you were doing.

These questions often put students on the defensive. Their defensiveness is manifested by interrogative, declarative, or exclamatory statements like these:

Why are you asking me? I wasn't here when this happened.

It wasn't my fault. I just happened to be walking by when . . .

It wasn't me. I was just sitting here when . . .

Who me? I didn't touch him!

The focus on present behavior forces the students to examine not attitudes or feelings necessarily, but what they were actually doing. The feelings and attitudes of students are important, but generally speaking, behaviors get students in trouble with teachers, not thoughts and feelings. Therefore, it is present behavior(s) that receives the emphasis.

Having the students make value judgments about the appropriateness or rightness of their behavior is very challenging to say the least. Reality therapy is based on the premise that children and youth, with rare exceptions, are capable of evaluating their own behavior and making accurate judgments as to its appropriateness. This step in the reality therapy process begins with questions that relate the present behavior to the individual student. Subsequent questions are expanded to relate the present behavior to peers, the teacher, the school, the society, or other appropriate levels of potential human interaction. The value judgment questions take the following form and sequence:

Is what you're doing helping you?

Is what you're doing helping you accomplish what you want to in this course, this class, this life?

Is what you're doing responsible behavior?

Is what you're doing helping anyone else?

Is what you're doing helping me, your teacher and friend?

Is what you're doing helping the class?

Is what you're doing helping the school?

Is what you're doing helping the community in which you live?

Obviously, these questions could be expanded to include behaviors that affect national and international events and relationships. The reason for this line of questioning is directly tied in with the concept of personal responsibility so stressed by Glasser. This questioning also emphasizes the importance of the interrelationships that are shared by individuals who must for their very survival be cognizant of the helpful and hindering effects their behaviors have on others. The questions are designed to assist both students and teachers to focus their attention on the responsibility they have for themselves and others in any learning environment. Negative responses to these questions should be dealt with according to the established classroom rules (see the sections on Strategies for Establishing Positive Standards and Rule and Routine Strategies).

Having the students develop a plan of action assumes that the students are capable of choosing other behaviors that are more responsible. Glasser believes that students, for the most part, are capable of developing plans. If a student is incapable of developing a plan, the teacher and student must develop one together in a mini-conference—during recess, lunch, an assembly, or during a consultation/preparation period. Frequently, students respond to the plan-making step by indicating that they just "won't do that (behavior) anymore." This response is insufficient and should not be accepted. Choosing not to do or exhibit a certain behavior only tells the student what *not* to do. Negative behaviors must be replaced with responsible, *positive* behaviors in order for the plan to receive the approval of both the student and the teacher.

Plan-making—either as a cooperative activity with a lot of teacher/student interaction or as an individual activity, with the major responsibility for planning resting with the student—should be done very carefully. "By the inch it's a cinch and by the yard it's hard" is an adage that can be readily applied to planning. Plans that involve tremendous changes in student or teacher behavior are not likely to be accomplished. Therefore, teachers helping students to formalize their plans should realistically ask themselves these or similar questions: How much change is really possible? What amount of change would be realistic in light of the student's past behavior? Gradual increments of behavior change should be sought rather than gigantic increments.

Students and teachers can create many varieties of plans. The plans themselves often take the form of contracts: written agreements that detail the behaviors to be performed by people who are interested in exchanging some commodity or service. The subject of contracting will be fully developed in the section on behavior modification strategies.

Securing a commitment for the plan of action or contract can take place in a variety of ways. Handshakes or some other agreed upon signals, verbal or nonverbal, are often very effective in obtaining the level of commitment necessary for change. In contracting, signatures are required from both the teacher and the student to conclude the agreement. In some cases the level of commitment is enhanced by the presence of witnesses or notaries (peers or other teachers) who provide additional support and reasons for complying with the behavior change plan. Again, it is important to mention that commitment in any interpersonal endeavor is based on the quality of the relationship. Teachers who are uninvolved with their students or who have been unable to become learning partners or friends with students will have tremendous difficulty in securing valid commitment.

Accepting no excuse for failing to comply with an agreement or achieve the planned goals is extremely difficult. Questions that begin with *why* are taboo in reality therapy. Asking such questions removes the responsibility for failure from the student to someone else or some situation or event. If a student has been unsuccessful, the teacher and student should negotiate another plan. Renegotiation of plans, as was mentioned earlier in the plan-making phase, can frequently be prevented with intelligent effort and realistic goal setting. When renegotiation becomes necessary, the student should again be encouraged to ask the question, Is what I'm doing helping me? If the answer to the question is again no, then the teacher and student need to brainstorm ways in which they can cooperatively attack the problem behavior(s) using different methods for achieving success in more gradual degrees. Techniques presented later in this chapter under other types of strategies will assist the teacher in helping the student develop new plans.

Administering no punishment should not be misinterpreted. According to Glasser (1969, p. 27), "pain follows an act that someone else disapproves of, and that someone else usually provides the pain." Punishment only shifts the responsibility from the student to the punisher (the teacher). Punishment is viewed by many students as the payment for misbehavior which permits them to misbehave again. Restated, punishment is an excuse for students to be bad again. The natural or logical consequences which come from misbehavior should be applied rather than punishment.

Not giving up when a student has failed or been unsuccessful is one of the true tests of teacher endurance. In fact, in times of failure, being able to "hang in there" and endure is particularly critical for students with learning and behavior problems. They are accustomed to having persons give up on them and "throw in the towel." Being able to start again with renewed hope and effort on the part of the teacher helps the student to believe that trying counts. The "starting over" or renegotiation period frequently forces both the student and teacher to look for the "bugs" in the program or planning which make success difficult to achieve. Often with slight modifications, the student can be off and running again in a positive direction rather than wallowing in self-defeat and pain.

Classroom Meetings. William Glasser (1969) is also responsible for creating a class get-together called a classroom meeting. The major purpose of classroom meetings is to provide students with a forum to discuss activities or problems that have some meaning or worth to them in a nonjudgmental atmosphere. Glasser has identified three types of meetings: (1) problem-solving meetings, (2) open-ended meetings, and (3) educational-diagnostic meetings. Each type is designed to provide students with different discussion topics and emphases. The problem-solving meeting is particularly well suited to dealing with student behavior problems. Glasser has developed some excellent guidelines for conducting problem-solving meetings:

> All problems relative to the class as a group and to any individual in the class are eligible for discussion.
> The discussion itself should always be directed toward solving the problem: the solution should never include punishment or fault finding.
> Meetings should always be conducted with the teacher and all the students seated in a tight circle. (Glasser 1969, pp. 128, 129, 132)

It is also important to mention here that if the meetings are to be effective, they must be short. For young elementary students, the meetings should not exceed thirty minutes; for older students, thirty- to forty-minute meetings are appropriate.

Becoming proficient at directing problem-solving meetings takes time and practice. The practice comes first by teaming with someone who is familiar with the technique: the principal, a fellow teacher, or a school counselor. Often training is available through a university or special in-service workshop.

Both exceptional and regular students profit from the opportunity to be involved with real classroom problems, which are really nothing more than societal problems on a miniature scale. The class meeting approach has been used successfully by many regular and special teachers. It is not designed to remedy all social or interpersonal problems, but with appropriate judgment and skill, teachers can use this approach to help students achieve pleasant social relations in the classroom.

Teacher Effectiveness Strategies

Since the publication of *Parent Effectiveness Training* (Gordon 1970), Thomas Gordon and others have developed a variety of effectiveness programs to assist people who are interested in influencing and helping others. Shortly after 1970, Gordon and Burch wrote a book for teachers entitled *Teacher Effectiveness Training* (TET) (Gordon and Burch 1974). TET provides three distinct techniques that teachers can apply in classroom management: (1) Active Listening, (2) I Messages, and (3) Method III Problem Solving. Each technique is used for distinctively different purposes; likewise, each technique is used for different types of relationship problems and relationship activities.

When students exhibit problems, the teacher, according to Gordon and Burch (1974), must be able to determine "problem ownership" by asking "Is this student's behavior bothering me, or is it primarily bothering the student?" A student who has just failed a test may be experiencing some real, emotional pain. The teacher who has the student the next hour may notice the emotional problem and empathize somewhat, but the real problem, in terms of owner-ship, lies with the student. However, when a student is exhibiting a behavior such as talking-out excessively, and this particular behavior bothers the teacher a great deal, or even slightly, the problem in terms of ownership lies with the teacher. The student exhibiting the behavior feels no emotional pain and may actually enjoy the laughter caused by comical remarks. Another kind of relationship problem occurs when both teacher and student share joint ownership of the problem or problems; that is, both teacher and student suffer emotional and sometimes physical pain. In summary, problem ownership may reside with the student primarily, the teacher primarily, or with both.

After teachers become skilled in identifying problem ownership, they have a basis for choosing one of the techniques for resolving or at least alleviating the problem. Table 5.2 illustrates briefly some typical problems, the types of ownership involved in each problem, and the technique suggested by Gordon and Burch (1974) in resolving the problem.

Active Listening is an extremely valuable technique, particularly for use with students who tend to have negative feelings about themselves or their accomplishments. Many exceptional students experience situations and inter-personal events that cause them discomfort. Active Listening helps them to identify the exact nature of their feelings. Active Listening on the part of the teacher tells all students that it is all right to have and express feelings. The teacher who correctly uses Active Listening also helps students to begin to name and understand the various kinds of feelings they are experiencing. Often by knowing types of feelings, students can, in concert with the teacher, begin to understand which situations and events cause certain repeated feelings. Gradually, the students will be able to anticipate or even prevent the situations or events that make them feel uncomfortable. Likewise, the student who has had a lot of involvement with Active Listening will begin to use it with friends and possibly teachers. In summary, Active Listening promotes the building of teacher-student relationships, helps students to become less afraid of expressing negative feelings, fosters problem-solving activities between teachers and students, and enhances the probability of students listening to each other.

Table 5.2 Gordon/Burch techniques for typical problems

Typical Problem	Problem Ownership	Suggested Technique for Resolving the Problem
The student is extremely angry when he or she enters the room and shows it with verbal and non-verbal behaviors.	Student owns the problem	Active Listening
The student talks out continually when the teacher is trying to teach the class a new math concept.	Teacher owns the problem	I Message
The student butts into a lunch line in front of a timid, non-assertive classmate.	Teacher owns the problem	I Message
The teacher has asked the students to listen and refrain from any talk or conversation while he or she presents new material. The students, however, have a tremendous need to talk to each other and continue to do so even when I messages are used.	Both students and teacher own the problem	Method III Problem Solving
The student tries but cannot put together egg cartons effectively in a new art activity and decides to chuck the whole mess into the garbage can adjacent to the teacher's desk.	Student owns the problem	Active Listening

Reprinted with permission from *T. E. T. Teacher Effectiveness Training,* by Thomas Gordon and N. Burch, copyright © 1974. Published by David McKay, Inc.

Many teachers, in attempts to resolve student-owned problems, choose verbal responses that seriously impair teacher-student communication. Gordon and Burch (1974) describe such responses as "communication roadblocks" (see table 5.3). These roadblocks include such verbal responses as ordering, warning, moralizing, advising, lecturing, judging, stereotyping, and being sarcastic. Each of these roadblock responses communicates various messages to the student.

Communication roadblocks should be avoided, for they lessen the chances that students will be able to resolve their own problems. As shown in table 5.3, roadblocks deter the student from the problem at hand to other behaviors or feelings that may compound the present problem or create new problems for the student.

In Active Listening the teacher should attempt to understand what feeling(s) the students are broadcasting with their words and nonverbal behaviors. After receiving the broadcast, the teacher should attempt to transmit back to the students in words a reflection of the student's feelings. As Gordon and Burch (1974) indicate, many teachers reflect the student's feelings inaccurately because they (1) add to the message sent, (2) parrot the message back to the student, (3) rush the student's description of his or her feelings, or (4) over- or underinterpret the message sent. All of these teacher responses interfere with effective communication.

Table 5.3 Examples of communication roadblocks

Types of Roadblock Responses	Actual Verbal Response	Message the Student Might Receive
Ordering	Get that sad look off your face and get started on your math.	The teacher really doesn't care about my feelings or what makes me sad.
Warning	Get that spelling assignment done immediately or I'll really give you something to complain about.	The teacher probably doesn't know how I feel today. She thinks that I need more work to feel differently or get my spelling work done.
Moralizing	You shouldn't have done that. How stupid can you be?	I guess I am kind of stupid. I really don't know what the right thing to do is.
Advising	You should be able to remember to take off your boots when you come in the class in the morning.	Perhaps, I really don't have the ability to take care of myself. I should probably always check with the teacher.
Lecturing	If you would just do your assignments at home as I told you to, you wouldn't be feeling so bad right now.	I guess I just have to sit here and listen to him babble on. "I told you so! I told you so!" I'm so sick of hearing that! I'm not feeling bad. I'm feeling mad! I'll get even somehow.
Judging	You are always the one who misbehaves and ruins it for the rest of the class. Can't you behave yourself and act a little grown up?	When I hear her talk to me that way, I'd like to say to her, "You're not such a good teacher either!" I'm always the one who gets in trouble. I guess that's the way I'll always be!
Stereotyping	I thought you knew how to handle yourself! You are just like the rest of them.	He really thinks that I'm just like the rest of 'em. I'll show him.
Being Sarcastic	You are such a good student, I just can't believe it. Maybe we should nominate you for the honor roll.	Guess I can't talk to her about my problems. I really thought I'd be able to talk to her.

Teachers can effectively initiate Active Listening on the part of students with simple "door openers" (Gordon and Burch, 1974). These statements tell the student that the listener (the teacher) has the time to listen and wants to listen to the student-owned problems. Gordon (1970, p. 48) has provided the following prototype "door openers."

I see . . .
Oh . . .
Mm hmmmmm . . .
How about that . . .
Interesting . . .
Really?
You don't say.
No fooling.
You did, huh.
Is that so?
Tell me about it.
I'd like to hear about it.
Tell me more.
I'd be interested in your point of view.
Would you like to talk about it?
Let's hear what you have to say.
Let's discuss it.
Tell me the whole story.
Shoot, I'm listening.
Sounds like you have something to say about this.
This seems like something important to you.

Once students have responded to these invitations to express their thoughts and feelings, the teacher has the obligation to listen with interest and acceptance. In order for the student to know that the teacher is accurately receiving the student-owned problems and feelings, teachers are encouraged to show their reception and understanding by comments like the following:

You're really feeling quite guilty about what you did to John.
You wish you had the same athletic ability as Susan—right?
Let me see if I have this right.
You feel skeptical about your ability to succeed on this upcoming test.
You're feeling kind of empty and maybe a little bit lonely.
You'd like this friendship relationship to go away?
You're worried about your brother and how his operation will work out.
You've been thinking about moving to another school, and this really bothers you, I'll bet.

Responding with statements like these takes a lot of practice. Many teachers discover that they, like their students, have a limited vocabulary for describing feelings. They also discover the importance of being able to label and describe their own feelings. With some intensive practice in an in-service workshop or university course, and with additional practice at school with students, teachers can become comfortable in using the "language of acceptance" (Gordon and Burch 1974) and understanding. All students, including those with learning and behavior problems, benefit from having opportunities to express their feelings of disappointment, frustration, and anger. Active Listening on the part of the teacher allows students to believe that feelings are important and should be expressed at suitable times. Although Active Listening has been identified for use with unpleasant feelings, the technique can also be used to help students express feelings of accomplishment and success. The following list of feeling words is provided to assist teachers to enhance, if necessary, their ability to describe the broad spectrum of both unpleasant and pleasant feelings that may come as a result of student-owned problems and successes.

Unpleasant		Pleasant	
Angry	Odd	Befriended	Helpful
Annoyed	Overwhelmed	Bold	High
Bored	Petrified	Calm	Honored
Cheated	Pressured	Capable	Important
Cold	Rejected	Caring	Impressed
Confused	Restless	Challenged	Infatuated
Crushed	Sad	Charmed	Inspired
Defeated	Skeptical	Cheerful	Joyful
Empty	Startled	Clever	Kind
Exasperated	Stupid	Comforting	Loving
Exhausted	Threatened	Confident	Peaceful
Fearful	Trapped	Content	Pleasant
Flustered	Troubled	Delighted	Pleased
Foolish	Uneasy	Determined	Proud
Frantic	Unsettled	Eager	Refreshed
Frightened	Weak	Energetic	Relaxed
Frustrated	Worried	Enjoy	Relieved
Guilty		Excited	Rewarded
Irritated		Fascinated	Safe
Left out		Fearless	Satisfied
Lonely		Free	Secure
Longing		Fulfilled	Settled
Mean		Generous	Sure
Miserable		Glad	Warm
Nervous		Happy	

Through the process of Active Listening, teachers are able to receive and interpret accurately the messages students send. Students, in turn, are able to respond to the verbal reflections of their feelings in such a way as to tell their teachers, "Yes, you did understand me." Teachers who are unaccustomed to using this technique will be surprised at the students' reactions. Some students have been known to say: "Wow, I wondered what happened to her." "I can't believe it, he actually listened to me without giving me his story about when he was a student." "I think she actually understands me now. That's never happened before!"

Here is an example of an Active Listening session in which a student with learning problems was able to come to a resolution of his feelings as a result of the teacher's reflective listening skills.

Student: Are we going to have to finish our written reports this week?

Teacher: You must be a little anxious about having to get your report written before the end of this week.

Student: Yes, it takes me a long time to write up my reports and I'm not very good at handwriting.

Teacher: I see, you'd feel better if you had a little more time.

Student: Yes, I always panic when I don't have the weekend to finish reports like this one.

Teacher: That's not a problem for me. Just get your report to me early Monday morning.

Student: Wow, I feel much better now. I'll have it done for sure on Monday. Thanks!

It would be improper to infer from this example that exceptional students always need more time to complete assignments. This may be true in many activities, but more than deadline modifications, these students need to be able to share their negative or unpleasant feelings with others. Many of the academic tasks that come so easily to regular students are only accomplished with a great deal of endurance on the part of students with learning and behavior problems. Having a teacher who understands the effort and exertion required in attaining the ability to write between the lines or to divide a two-digit number into a four-digit number or to master a driver's license exam can really make a difference. This difference is generally conveyed not in lowered expectations, but in expectations that are harmonious with the student's ability and strengths. Active Listening can be used for both trying times and exhilarating times for all students. Teacher responses such as the following characterize these two types of Active Listening.

It's a challenge to have to wait so long, but together I think we can make it.

Today you were able to control your temper without any reminders and you even got fifty bonus points which Miss Jones, your resource teacher, will give you. I can tell by your smile that you feel like you have really accomplished something.

You feel like you got cheated, right?

You're really feeling relaxed now! What an accomplishment. I remember when you couldn't even think about the times tables without getting frustrated.

I can tell that you're really feeling confident.

What John said made you feel very hurt.

You're really feeling frustrated.

It sounds as if you are feeling very pressured about this program.

When they call you names, I'm sure that you feel almost crushed.

Feeling lonely is tough to deal with, isn't it?

Active Listening is not always effective. Frequently students will want to wait for awhile before they are willing to talk through a problem-provoking situation. More often than not, teachers may not have the time to fully focus their listening efforts to a student whose behavior says "I've got a problem!" In addition, some students may want active help rather than Active Listening. They may be requesting some specific information or physical assistance. When this is the case, Active Listening should not be used.

Active Listening is a valuable management technique that can be used for a variety of purposes. It is primarily effective in assisting students who have problems that they themselves own. Active Listening promotes positive teacher-student relationships, helps students express negative feelings, and provides them with a means for identifying self-selected solutions rather than teacher-imposed solutions.

The second technique that was developed by Gordon (1970) to deal with problem behaviors is called an *I Message*. Whereas Active Listening is used for student-owned problems, I Messages are used for teacher-owned problems. In order for teachers to actually own a problem, they must be feeling some discomfort or pain as a result of a certain student behavior(s). The feelings may be those of irritation, exasperation, defeat, or frustration. Headaches, stomachaches, and other psychosomatic problems are representative of the pains experienced when a teacher owns a problem. As Gordon and Burch put it, "Teachers are human; teachers have their legitimate needs . . ." (Gordon and Burch 1974, p. 127), and these needs must be met if the teacher is to function adequately.

Here are some examples of typical behaviors (that both exceptional and regular students might perform) that might bother or even provoke teachers:

A student teases another student persistently.

A student tips over a desk intentionally.

Several students are involved in a heated argument at recess on one of the four square areas.

A student regularly interferes with other students by kicking or taking away their game ball.

One student continually bothers other students when they are lined up and waiting to go to lunch.

A student breaks another student's pencil maliciously.

A student frequently threatens other students with objects like paint brushes or scissors.

A student continually makes sarcastic remarks about another student in the class.

A student consistently cheats on examinations and quizzes.

A student frequently distracts others and acts like a clown during instructional sessions presented by the teacher.

A student is physically and verbally aggressive when confronted with problems either academic or social.

A student frequently talks about the teacher under his or her breath, making comments about the teacher or other teachers in the building.

These behaviors would prompt most teachers to take some action. Generally speaking, these are not behaviors that a teacher can ignore or pass off. They must be dealt with in some fashion—but how? Gordon and Burch (1974) have suggested that teachers have one of three options when they are confronted with student behaviors that bother them. They can modify the student's behavior, the learning environment, or their own behavior. I Messages are used in an attempt to modify the student's behavior rather than the learning environment or the teacher's behavior. I Messages are basically confrontation statements in which teachers take responsibility for the feelings they have as a result of certain student behaviors. Teachers not only own the feelings in the sense that they feel them and are aware of the feelings, but they also let the student know how they are feeling. Teachers do this by making statements such as—

When you tease John, I feel very upset . . .

When you tip over your desk, I feel very annoyed . . .

When you argue and are unable to play cooperatively, I really get irritated . . .

When you make sarcastic comments about Steve, I really get angry . . .

When you talk under your breath about me or others, I feel extremely uneasy . . .

When you look at others' papers or work during exams, I feel very uncomfortable and a little disappointed . . .

When you use the baseball bat to scare or threaten other students, I become very nervous and anxious . . .

When teachers make such statements, they are really revealing a part of themselves. Self-disclosure on the part of teachers is a risky endeavor. In fact, most students are unaccustomed to hearing about how their behaviors affect teachers. If students know how their misbehavior makes teachers feel, they may be more likely to cease behaviors that cause teachers emotional pain. In contrast to You Messages (Gordon 1970)—e.g., You get in line! You stop that fighting! Sit in your seat! You are so sarcastic! You bully!—I Messages place the responsibility for choosing a better or more appropriate decision on the shoulders of the student. Thus the students, rather than conforming to or battling with a *you* confrontation, must decide whether they will behave differently if they know how the teacher is really feeling inside. I Messages, according to Gordon and Burch (1974, p. 140), have three major advantages in comparison to You Messages:

1. They have a high probability of promoting a willingness to change.
2. They contain minimum evaluation of the student.
3. They do not injure the relationship.

In addition to these advantages, I Messages keep open the lines of communication, maintain the students' self-concept, and preserve the teacher-student relationship. When I Messages are used regularly and appropriately in classrooms, both teachers and students are more likely to have their emotional needs met. They are also more able to communicate with each other regarding the ways in which their teaching and learning behaviors interact.

Technically, I Messages contain the following important elements:

1. A nonblameful description of the student behavior or class behavior that affects the teacher significantly.
2. The concrete or tangible effect that the student or class behavior has on the teacher's work.
3. A description of the feelings caused by student or class misbehavior.

Incorporating element number two into the I Message is often extremely challenging because many student misbehaviors violate only the teacher's values about behavior rather than having some direct, concrete, or tangible effect on the teacher. Teachers often find it difficult to mention effects other than feelings caused by certain behaviors or conditions. However, in order for an I Message to have its greatest impact on student behavior, it should be as complete as possible—that is, it should contain all of the elements outlined by Gordon and Burch (1974).

I Messages generally begin with the word *when* followed by a description of some negative or inappropriate student or class behavior or a condition created by some misbehavior(s). These *when* descriptions should be emphasized as nonjudgmental and nonblameful statements. Next follows the teacher's description of the specific, concrete effect that the behaviors or conditions have on the teacher as an individual. Lastly, the teacher describes the feeling(s) caused by the behaviors or conditions. Here are some typical, complete I Messages that could be used in response to behaviors of both exceptional and regular students:

When you tease John, I can't effectively teach this reading group, and I get very upset.

When you tip over your desk, it disrupts my teaching activities and the learning of others, and I feel very annoyed. You must be very angry about something (an I Message combined with Active Listening).

When you argue and are unable to play cooperatively, it really interferes with my relaxing a bit during the noon hour, and I really get irritated.

When you make sarcastic comments about Steve, I really get angry. It makes me want to be unkind to you, and I really don't like to have thoughts like that.

When you talk under your breath about me or others, I think you are making fun of me or criticizing me, and I feel extremely uneasy. Are you feeling a little angry about something I have done or said to you? (Again, an I Message combined with a little Active Listening.)

When you look at others' papers or work during exams, I feel that I haven't effectively taught you or motivated you to learn, and I feel very uncomfortable and a little disappointed.

When you use the baseball bat to scare or threaten others, I must immediately leave what I am doing for fear you might accidentally or even purposely hurt someone. Each time you do this I become very anxious and nervous. If someone really got hurt, I might lose my job, too.

I Messages from teachers frequently shift the ownership of the problem from the teacher back to the student. When this happens, the teacher must be able to "shift gears" (Gordon and Burch, 1974) from giving I Messages to Active Listening. Several of the I Message examples cited previously were followed with Active Listening statements. When students find that their behavior has had some negative physical or emotional impact on a teacher, they may feel bad, upset, or any number of other feelings. When these feelings surface as a result of I Messages, teachers need to be prepared to provide some time for Active Listening.

The third technique that was developed by Gordon (1970) to deal with problem behaviors is called *Method III Problem Solving.* This technique is designed to help teachers and students resolve relationship problems—problems that are owned by both the teacher and student. Method III Problem Solving involves six discrete steps:

1. Defining the problem
2. Generating possible solutions
3. Evaluating the solutions
4. Deciding which solution is best
5. Determining how to implement the decision
6. Assessing how well the solution solved the problem (Gordon and Burch 1974, p. 228).

When teachers and students become involved in defining the problem, care should be taken to define it in terms of personal and collective needs. The I Message format is often useful for describing the feelings or needs of each individual.

In generating possible solutions, everyone involved should have the opportunity to participate. As ideas are generated, they should be recorded on the blackboard for all to see and ponder. Evaluation of these ideas should be postponed until both the students and teacher have fully exhausted their idea-generating potential.

Steps three and four in the Method III Problem Solving are closely interrelated: step four occurs as a natural outcome of step three. In evaluating each idea, it is wise to ask the following questions before a final decision is reached:

Docs this idea solve the problem?

Does this idea hurt anyone?

Can everyone be involved in this solution?

Can I (the teacher) accept this solution?

As this solution was evaluated, did I use Active Listening to be sure that I fully understood the comments of the other person?

In determining how to implement the solutions selected, Gordon and Burch (1974, p. 233) recommend the asking of the following questions: "What do we need in order to get started? Who is going to be responsible for what? And by when?" The answering of these questions provides teachers and students with the confidence that something will actually happen that may change the nature of the relationship in a positive way. Each decision to be implemented should be recorded in written form. In this manner, the efficacy of the solutions can be assessed after a period of time. If at step six the teacher and students agree that the solutions chosen were ineffective in helping them meet their needs, they can return to the beginning of the problem-solving process or to one of the other appropriate steps.

In summary, the Teacher Effectiveness strategies pioneered and developed by Gordon (1970) and Gordon and Burch (1974) are effective in dealing with three types of problems: student-owned, teacher-owned, and teacher/student-owned (relationship problems). Each type suggests the use of one of three techniques or a combination of these techniques. Active Listening, I Messages, and Method III Problem Solving can be effectively used to assist both exceptional and regular students. For in-depth elaboration of these and other Gordon techniques, teachers are encouraged to become involved with one or all of the following: publications that have been cited in this chapter, workshops offered by colleges or private agencies, and in-service trainers in a school or district who are qualified or certified in Teacher Effectiveness Training.

Dreikurs, Grunwald, and Pepper (1971) have developed a framework for understanding the motives and behaviors of students. According to Dreikurs, Grunwald, and Pepper, all behaviors are goal directed; that is, students, by virtue of their behaviors, are seeking goals that are generally worthwhile and sensible. Often, however, students are unable to achieve their goals through appropriate behaviors, and they resort to misbehaviors. Both exceptional and regular students frequently seek goals in ways that are inappropriate or irresponsible. Such inappropriate and irresponsible behaviors must be dealt with and rectified unless teachers are willing to accept them.

Strategies of Dreikurs, Grunwald, and Pepper

Four goals of misbehavior have been identified by Dreikurs, Grunwald, and Pepper: (1) attention, (2) power, (3) revenge, and (4) disability. Each goal also motivates students to exhibit certain kinds of behaviors in order to achieve a place in life or a place in the class, school, or home. By understanding the motivations and intentions of students, teachers can help both exceptional and regular students to achieve worthwhile goals through appropriate behaviors rather than negative or maladaptive behaviors.

For purposes of clarification, we will briefly describe the four goals of misbehavior. The goal of attention is initially pursued with positive behaviors. However, when students are unable to achieve the attention level needed with their best efforts at positive behavior, they resort to negative behavior. Rather than be ignored or forgotten, these students, though often reprimanded or punished sharply, continue to seek recognition and attention.

The goal of power is closely related to the goal of attention, in that each goal is pursued by students in order to achieve recognition or a place of esteem. Teachers who choose to accept power struggles with students will discover that they have very little to gain that is beneficial to them or to students, and a great deal to lose. Power as used in this context is synonymous with such terms as *defiance, daring, resistance,* and *opposition.* The student who refuses to stop pencil engraving after reasonable appeals from the teacher, and persists even when the teacher threatens harsh action, is an example of a student who is seeking power and possibly revenge.

Again, the goals of misbehavior are essentially pursued for the same reasons as are the goals of positive behavior. Students are seeking ways of becoming significant to themselves and others. The misbehavior goal of revenge is an attempt to gain this significance through hurting others or getting even with others. Revenge is used after attempts at obtaining attention and power have been thwarted. Victory in achieving revenge is shown by students who exult in being known by other students as the bully, the fighter, the hard guy, or the tough girl.

The last of the misbehavior goals deals with the display of a disability, which allows the students to protect themselves from trying or actively participating in growth-producing activities, while still remaining members of a class or group. Rather than risk the possibility of failure, such students ease themselves into a self-imposed, protective disability that allows them some social contact and participation without the attendant responsibilities of doing daily assignments, responding in class discussions, or completing reports or term projects.

Dreikurs, Grunwald, and Pepper have provided a very simple method for identifying the type of misbehavior goal sought by students in their attempts to become significant. Teachers are encouraged to monitor closely the immediate response of a student to corrective efforts (e.g., "Will you sit down, John?" "Please do not bother John!" "Please get busy and complete your assignment, Robert!"). The student's response to the corrective effort provides the diagnostic information necessary for identifying the student's misbehavior goal. Teachers are also encouraged to analyze their own immediate response to a student's negative behavior (e.g., "Do I feel annoyed with this behavior?" "Do I feel threatened?" "Do I feel that I really can't even ask this student to perform?" "Do I feel like I have been hurt?"). Teachers frequently discover that they are, in effect, encouraging the pursuit of misbehavior goals by their response patterns. In addition, students are often unaware or unconscious of the goals of their misbehavior. When teachers become effective in revealing to students the intents or purposes of their misbehavior, students often show what Dreikurs, Grunwald, and Pepper describe as a *recognition reflex.* The recognition reflex is nothing more than a form of communication: a smile, a nod, or a verbal statement. These verbal or nonverbal forms of communication let the teacher know that students now understand their motives for misbehaving.

One first asks the child why he misbehaves. We know that the child does not know the reason and, therefore, will either say he doesn't know or give a rationalization. But this question is necessary as a preparation for the next question: "May I tell you what I think?" And then after the child agrees, one has to present the goal as a hypothesis. "Could it be that . . ." Then follows the reference to the specific goal: " . . . to keep the teacher busy with you; to show her that you can do what you want to and she can't stop you; to punish and hurt her because of what she did to you; to be left alone because you can't do anything." The recognition reflex may not come immediately because the child may have to think it over first. Therefore, one has to wait for his reaction. It is most dramatic to watch the child, how he first considers it, and then the corners of his mouth begin to expand in a knowing smile and a gleam appears in his eyes. He begins to recognize what he was up to." (Dreikurs, Grunwald, and Pepper 1971, p. 41.)

Helping students to identify their reasons for misbehaving does not make the misbehaviors go away or disappear, but it does help students and teachers to be clear about why certain behaviors are occurring and possibly what must be done to help students choose positive approaches to achieving personal significance.

In addition to the "Could it be that you . . ." method of confronting students, Dreikurs and his associates have identified a number of "democratic methods" for assisting students to choose positive approaches to self-fulfillment and success. Basically these methods deal with the effective use of (1) encouragement, (2) natural and logical consequences, (3) group discussions, and (4) role-playing. All of these methods will be useless unless the teachers have been successful in "winning" their students and in achieving positive teacher/student relationships. These positive relationships come as a result of hard work, knowledge of students' successes and interests, and time spent in relationship-building activities. Teachers who are interested in pursuing these methods in depth should refer to the bibliography following this chapter.

In summary, Dreikurs, Grunwald, and Pepper have created a framework for analyzing and dealing with the misbehavior of students. In their framework, the student is the actor and the teacher serves as a reactor. In order to change the nature and quality of the interactions between student and teacher, one or both of them must change. Teachers, as a result of their experience and understanding, are most capable of modifying the interactions that occur. They can do this by changing their reactions to certain identified misbehaviors of students (see table 5.4). In addition to the strategies identified in table 5.4, this approach involves the use of special forms of encouragement, natural and logical consequences, group discussions, and role-playing. All of the strategies are designed to help the student obtain self-significance or a positive place in the classroom, home, and community. By understanding students' intentions and motivations, teachers using the strategies of Dreikurs, Grunwald, and Pepper have the opportunity of changing the misbehaviors of both exceptional and regular students to positive behaviors.

Table 5.4 The strategies of Dreikurs, Grunwald, and Pepper

Student (Actor) Misbehavior Goals	Teacher (Reactor) Strategies for Establishing New Patterns of Behavior
Attention	1. The teacher should ignore attention-getting behaviors. 2. The teacher should give students encouragement for appropriate substitute behaviors.
Power	1. The teacher should withdraw from attempts by the students to involve him or her in a conflict or power struggle. 2. The teacher should realize that the power on the part of students is only effective when it is contested. 3. The teacher should assist the student to find other more appropriate ways to use his or her energies.
Revenge	1. The teacher should attempt to establish a positive relationship with the student so that the student has no reason to hurt or get even with the teacher. 2. The teacher should use group and peer activities which help the student to realize that he or she can be liked and is liked by others.
Disability	1. The teacher should seek to provide the student with appropriate amounts of encouragement particularly when he or she makes a mistake. 2. The teacher should provide the student with tasks which he or she is capable of completing. 3. The teacher should seek to identify strengths in other areas which can be utilized to assist the student in gradually changing his or her self-perceptions regarding ability adequacy.

Data from "The Four Goals of Misbehavior," in *Maintaining Sanity in the Classroom: Illustrated Teaching Techniques,* by Rudolf Dreikurs, M.D., Bernice Bronia Grunwald, and Floy C. Pepper. Copyright © 1971 by Rudolf Dreikurs, Bernice Bronia Grunwald, and Floy C. Pepper. Reprinted by permission of Harper and Row Publishers, Inc.

Behavior Modification Strategies

Behavior modification strategies are designed to do one or all of the following: (1) decrease or eliminate negative student behaviors, (2) increase certain positive student behaviors, (3) initiate or teach new student behaviors, and (4) to refine or improve presently occurring behaviors. In determining what constitutes negative or positive behaviors, Fagen and Hill (1977) recommend a system for exploring human values with which teachers are able to establish "positive standards" and "limits."

Strategies for Establishing Positive Standards

According to Fagen and Hill (1977, p. 36), "Human values for school environments may be thought of as learner rights and responsibilities, which become the basis for establishing behavior standards and limits." In reviewing or establishing rights and responsibilities, they suggest using the sentence completion form shown in figure 5.1 to stimulate teachers to think about their values for classroom environments and interaction. A similar form (fig. 5.2) could be developed for students to aid them in establishing values for the classroom.

Figure 5.1 Sentence completion form. (From S. A. Fagen and J. M. Hill, *Behavior Management*, p. 35. Copyright 1977 by Psychoeducational Resources, Inc. Used with permission of the publisher.)

1. I really get angry when students _____ _____ .

2. It unnerves me when _____ _____ .

3. I really like it when a student _____ _____ .

4. It doesn't bother me when students _____ _____ .

5. It disturbs me when other teachers _____ _____ .

6. I appreciate it when other teachers _____ _____ .

7. It makes me feel good when the administration_____ _____ .

8. It upsets me when the administration _____ _____ .

Figure 5.2 Sentence completion form. (Adapted from Fagen and Hill.)

1. I really get angry when my classmates _____
   _____ .

2. I really get angry when my teacher _____
   _____ .

3. I really get anxious when my classmates _____
   _____ .

4. I really get anxious when my teacher _____
   _____ .

5. It disturbs me when my classmates _____
   _____ .

6. It disturbs me when my teacher _____
   _____ .

7. I appreciate it when my classmates _____
   _____ .

8. I appreciate it when my teacher _____
   _____ .

9. It makes me feel good when my classmates _____
   _____ .

10. It makes me feel good when my teacher _____
    _____ .

11. It upsets me when my classmates _____
    _____ .

12. It upsets me when my teacher _____
    _____ .

Together teachers and students should develop a set of values or rights and responsibilities, and positive standards and limits that they can jointly adhere to. This gives both exceptional and regular students a frame of reference from which to judge their actions. The following are some typical rights and responsibilities.

The right to learn without undue distraction and noise

The right to feel safe

The right to have your personal possessions safe from being taken or damaged

The responsibility to follow agreed-upon standards

The responsibility to make an effort to learn with appropriate incentives, materials, and conditions

Fagen and Hill have developed the form shown in figure 5.3 for analyzing values, rights and responsibilities. In completing this form, teachers and students have an opportunity to define desirable behavior standards. They also have the opportunity to review the consequences which come from adhering or not adhering to the standards which have been identified. Figure 5.4 is an example of a completed form.

Figure 5.3 Establishing behavior standards and limits. (From S. A. Fagen and J. M. Hill, *Behavior Management*, p. 46. Copyright 1977 by Psychoeducational Resources, Inc. Used with permission of the publisher.)

Values (Rights and Responsibilities)	Positive Standards (Desirable Behavior)	Limits (Behavior Violations)

Likely Consequences of Adhering to Positive Standards		Likely Consequences of Not Adhering to Positive Standards	
Within School	Outside School	Within School	Outside School

Figure 5.4 Establishing behavior standards and limits—completed form. (From S. A. Fagen and J. M. Hill, *Behavior Management.* Copyright 1977 by Psychoeducational Resources, Inc. Used with permission of the publisher.)

Values (Rights and Responsibilities)	Positive Standards (Desirable Behavior)	Limits (Behavior Violations)
Example A: Right to learn	1. Pays attention 2. Asks questions or requests help when uncertain 3. Uses materials properly	1. Disrupts teacher presentation 2. Withdraws or disturbs others 3. Misuses material or takes materials from others

Likely Consequences of Adhering to Positive Standards		Likely Consequences of Not Adhering to Positive Standards	
Within School	Outside School	Within School	Outside School
1. Develops positive relationships		1. Develops poor relationships	
2. Gains in self-direction		2. Often executes tasks incorrectly	
3. Gains in group and self-organizational skills		3. Is unorganized and unable to find information	

Another useful form for selecting behaviors for modification has been developed by Buckholdt, Sloan, Ferritor, and Della-Piana (1972). This form helps teachers to focus on behaviors that they would like to see changed (only a part of the actual form is represented in figure 5.5).

This form is helpful to teachers in several ways. In addition to identifying negative behaviors and behaviors that the teacher would like to see, it gives a picture of the frequency of certain behaviors and what teacher or peer actions maintain or support the behaviors identified. All behaviors identified on the form must be observable behaviors that one can actually see or measure. Some examples of behaviors that might be entered on this form are given below.

I wish—
1. my students would do more of their math assignments;
2. my students would not talk so much during our spelling tests;
3. I could reduce fighting or arguing among students at recess;

4. I could reduce the number of negative comments students make about themselves and others in the class;

5. the majority of the class would pay attention during our social studies period.

I wish—

1. my students would use more polite language in asking each other for assistance and materials;

2. my students would arrive on time for the beginning of each period;

3. my students were able to start working immediately when an assignment is given;

4. my students would make more positive comments about my teaching efforts;

5. my students would work more rapidly in completing English assignments.

Figure 5.5 Behavior observation form. (From D. R. Buckholdt, H. N. Sloane, D. E. Ferritor, and G. M. Della-Piana, *Classroom and Instructional Management Program*, p. 9. Copyright 1972 by Cemrel, Inc. Used with permission of the publisher.)

Behaviors	Who Actually Does or Does Not Engage in This Behavior?	How Often Does It Occur?	Maintenance
Five things students do I wish they would not do. 1. 2. 3. 4. 5.			
Five things students do not do I wish they would do. 1. 2. 3. 4. 5.			

Many of the behaviors identified on the previous list are observable and countable. Teachers using various observation techniques can, in fact (with simple devices such as golf counters, wrist counters, watches, or timers), keep track of the number of occurrences or the duration of a certain behavior. The observations made can be graphed on a daily basis. This graphing allows the teacher to make comparisons with other students in the class or school, and it also serves as an evaluation tool for monitoring the effects of specific behavioral interventions.

Reinforcement Strategies

In the words of Krumboltz and Krumboltz (1972, p. 2), "Good behavior must pay off." Behavior modification is based on the idea that the behavior of students and teachers is greatly influenced by the environment of the school and by the consequences that follow certain behaviors. If teachers want to initiate or increase positive behaviors, they should use appropriate amounts or types of positive reinforcement. A **positive reinforcer,** by definition, increases the frequency or strength of the behavior that it follows. The Krumboltzes provide the following illustrative examples of positive reinforcement.

> Gary had developed a habit of rushing into American History class just after the bell stopped ringing every day, collapsing in his seat, and frequently missing the beginning instructions of the teacher. One day, for some unaccountable reason, he appeared early. The teacher, wishing to strengthen this change in Gary's time of arrival, immediately approached his desk, quietly thanked him for getting to class before the bell rang, and asked if he would take roll, a prestige job exchanged among the earlier arriving class members. Following this incident Gary began arriving at class on time and more frequently (Krumboltz and Krumboltz 1972, p. 9).

> Rita seemed to have little desire to succeed in fifth-grade arithmetic. She frequently put down anything on her paper just to have something there. At the blackboard she stood looking sullen or, if possible, copied from another student. She did poorly on tests. Her IQ was only slightly below average.
>
> Her new teacher began by trying to eliminate all sources of pressure, punishment, and failure. This task was not completely possible, but she always tried to find something praiseworthy about Rita's work.
>
> When she was certain Rita could succeed, the teacher would send her to the blackboard, praising her after the successful performance. She would also correct Rita's papers and tests as soon as possible, adding some comments of praise or encouragement in response to the best parts of Rita's work.

In this particular school district the policy was that only the accurate, neat papers could be displayed on the bulletin board. Since Rita's papers were seldom perfect, there was a danger that her parents would come to the open house and not find any of her work. The teacher devised an easy test on which Rita was able to make a perfect score, and this paper was displayed at the open house.

Along with the individual encouragement, the teacher also arranged for another pupil to assist her. As Rita's work began to improve, the teacher asked her to help another classmate who had been having difficulty.

Conferring with Rita's parents, the teacher told them what she was trying to do. They discussed ways they could all show an interest in Rita's work and praise her improvements. Prior to this time the parents had been pressuring their daughter to do well and had been extremely critical of failures. Now they began to take more interest in her homework papers and emphasized the problems that she had solved correctly. Even her classmates noticed and commented spontaneously on the change in Rita.

Successful performance combined with recognition from teacher, parents, and classmates changed Rita's previous attitude of inferiority. Motivated to succeed, she now viewed her mistakes as challenges to overcome instead of as glaring evidences of failure. Both her daily homework and her test scores improved (Krumboltz and Krumboltz 1972, pp. 20–21).

As indicated, positive reinforcement increases the frequency of behaviors that it follows. In both of the examples, the behaviors reinforced were positive and valued by the teachers involved. How does one select appropriate reinforcers? Buckholdt et al. (1972, pp. 15–18) have delineated three procedures for selecting positive reinforcers: (1) "ask the students" strategy, (2) "ask other teachers" strategy, and (3) "try and see" strategy. Each of these strategies is self-explanatory. There are many types of reinforcers—social, activity, material, edible, and token reinforcers. The particular advantages and disadvantages of each type become readily apparent with use. Like other educational techniques and strategies, reinforcers must be tailored to the individual or group. Following is a representative list of a broad spectrum of potential reinforcers according to type (Buckholdt et al. 1972, pp. 22–23).

Social Reinforcers	Activity Reinforcers	Material Reinforcers	Edible Reinforcers
hugging	stringing beads	penny candy	badges
nodding	field trip	apples	make-up kits
tickling	puppet show	raisins	records
applause	leading discussions	peanuts	marbles
	watering plants	gum	ribbons
	marking papers	crackers	stickers
	extra swim period		posters

Reinforcement Menus. The preceding list of reinforcers could also be identified as a **reinforcement menu.** A reinforcement menu is simply a collection of potential reinforcers for rewarding certain student or group behaviors that the teachers or students collectively value. Clarizio (1976) has developed the exemplary elementary and secondary reinforcement menus shown in figures 5.6 and 5.7.

Figure 5.6 Reinforcement menu: elementary class. (Reprinted, by permission, from H. F. Clarizio, *Toward Positive Classroom Discipline*, 3d ed. Copyright © 1980 by John Wiley and Sons, Inc.)

---

1. Go to the library to work on a special project relating to the unit being studied.

2. Arrange the game shelf and be permitted to pick out a game to play.

3. Listen to the reading stories on the phonograph with earphones (up to four at a time).

4. Use the electric and flannel boards to work on exercises found in the science corner.

5. Work in the art corner—take out plain paper and draw any kind of pictures at desk.

6. Record favorite story on the tape recorder making sure that it is read with expression and clarity.

7. Work on scrapbook on history project—can use the magazines in the room.

8. Leave five minutes early for lunch.

9. Be line captain.

10. Be in charge of taking attendance.

11. Get a drink at any time without asking permission.

12. Be in charge of passing out papers and other class materials.

13. Be excused fifteen minutes before the end of the school day to clean the erasers and blackboard.

14. Let teams of students wad up spitballs, throw them at the wastebasket, and see which has the best record.

15. Permit students to draw on steamed-up windows with their fingers.

Daily Specials

Monday	Listen to the transistor radio via earphones.
Tuesday	Use the viewmaster to look at pictures of the country being studied in geography.
Wednesday	Be group leader for the social studies group.
Thursday	Add another piece to the classroom puzzle or mural.
Friday	Plan for the Friday afternoon group activity—help the teacher pick out the group game to be played.

Figure 5.7 Reinforcement menu: high school geometry class. (Reprinted, by permission, from H. F. Clarizio, *Toward Positive Classroom Discipline*, 3d ed. Copyright © 1980 by John Wiley and Sons, Inc.)

1. Challenge teacher or another student to a game of chess.

2. Use the portable computer.

3. Do extra credit problems and see how they can raise grade.

4. Make up a geometry quiz and give it to the class.

5. Sit at the teacher's desk while doing homework problems.

6. Prepare the bulletin board using a display of the student's choice.

7. Write letters.

8. Play chess.

9. Read.

10. Play charades.

11. Talk over past or forthcoming athletic or social events.

12. Have a creative exhibit period (a grown-up version of show and tell).

13. Compare a 1902 Sears Roebuck catalogue with the current one, discussing changes in style, price, and the like, and trying to discover why the changes occurred.

Daily Specials

Monday	Appear as guest lecturer in the other math classes.
Tuesday	Do the special crossword puzzles involving geometry concepts learned.
Wednesday	Take time to play a math game with another student.
Thursday	Construct special paper models using geometrical figures to complete.
Friday	Do mystery problems involving mathematical solutions.

The Strategy of Shaping All of the activities mentioned in the elementary reinforcement menu are designed to strengthen or increase the frequency of valued behaviors. However, teachers often seek to change certain levels of student behaviors from poor to excellent overnight. Students rarely change the nature of their behaviors that rapidly. A more suitable approach to changing behaviors is called **shaping**. Shaping is defined as a process whereby the teacher gradually rewards improvements in behavior in a stepwise fashion until the student's behavior is complete or the student has accomplished the level of behavior desired. The following is an excellent example of the use of shaping to improve a student's cursive writing.

> Doug was a ten-year-old whose handwriting was fast but illegible. His primary fault was that he did not close the letters *d* or *a* so the *d* looked like *cl* and the *a* resembled *u*. His teacher felt he needed help and told how she gave it to him:
>
> One day when I returned an assignment to Doug, I circled the best *a* he had written. It was not good, but I said to him, "Doug, here is the best *a* you have written on this paper. Your *a* still looks a little bit like a *u*, but I'm sure you know that it ought to look more like this (demonstrating a closed *a*). Here's how the *d* should look. See how both are completely closed." Whenever I saw on Doug's papers an *a* or a *d* that was closer to the standard, I circled it and wrote "better" beside it. One time I asked Doug to look over one of his own papers and tell me which *a* he thought was best and which *d* best. I did not comment on the poorly written letters.
>
> After three weeks his handwriting had improved markedly. I retrieved one of the papers he had written a month earlier, and we compared it with his current handwriting. He was impressed with the difference and could see how much he had improved (Krumboltz & Krumboltz 1972, p. 42).

Strategies for Terminating or Weakening Behaviors Often it is necessary to use procedures to weaken or decrease student behaviors. Response-weakening procedures that are associated with behavior modification are extinction, response cost, time out, and punishment. **Extinction** is the withholding of positive reinforcement following behaviors. Extinction, as used by teachers, generally takes the form of ignoring or not attending to behaviors that teachers are seeking to reduce or weaken. Few teachers realize the degree to which they reinforce disruptive individual or group behaviors. In order for extinction (ignoring) procedures to be maximally effective, teachers should reinforce positive, substitute behaviors that can gradually or ultimately replace the negative behaviors. It is important to note here that extinction cannot be used for all behaviors; some behaviors cannot be ignored because of their potential impact on others or on the students themselves.

Response cost is the loss of privileges or points as a result of a behavior violation. Response cost does not occur without prior preparation and planning on the part of the teachers and students. As a rule, response cost procedures are only effective in grading or management systems in which points are accumulated for a specific grade or special activity. Some teachers have effectively used response cost procedures with rule systems. Violations of certain rules carry with them certain penalties or fines. Clarizio (1976) has prepared lists of logical and natural consequences that can be used effectively with response cost procedures. Several representative types of each are listed below.

Logical Consequences

If you push or shove in line, you go to the end of the line.

If you vandalize you must make restitution.

If you act immature (baby talk), the teachers and others won't listen. (Clarizio 1976, p. 148)

Natural Consequences

If you develop a reputation for stealing, no one will trust you and you will be the first one blamed.

If you goof off as a group leader, you will not be picked by peers as a leader again.

If you use a straight chair as a rocker, you may fall on the floor. (Clarizio 1976, p. 150)

Time out is a procedure whereby students are removed from learning activities that are reinforcing to them or learning materials are withdrawn. In a technical sense, time out means time out from reinforcement. In other words, during the time out period the students are not able to receive reinforcement nor are they able to earn reinforcement. Time out is achieved by several means: (1) students are often removed from the class itself and isolated from their peer group or class, (2) students may be asked to go to a specific carrel in the classroom that faces the wall, (3) students may have their learning materials removed for a time until they are able to demonstrate appropriate behaviors, or (4) the students may be sent to a hall, the principal's office, or another designated area where they are able to "cool off" or regain composure. Like other response-weakening procedures, time out cannot be used effectively without advanced planning and preparation. Both teachers and students must be clear as to the behavior violations that are serious enough to merit the use of time out. Cooperation and planning with parents and other school personnel (other teachers, the principal, school counselors, and the custodian) cannot be overemphasized. Each person must be clear as to the reasons for time out, the procedures for removing or secluding a student, the verbal components involved in timing out a student, the actual amount of time to be spent in time out, and the procedures for having the student return to the classroom or ongoing activities. Generally, time out involving the use of the principal's office or other designated area is used only for serious rule or standard violations involving very aggressive or destructive behaviors. Lesser forms of rule violations incur milder forms of time out procedures identified earlier in this section. The actual duration of time out need not be long. Often students are given the option to return when they have been able to get control of themselves. In removing students or asking students to remove themselves, the teacher should not lecture the students, but simply and calmly indicate why they are being timed out. In returning the students to the classroom or ongoing teaching activities, the teacher should integrate them without excessive attention or comments. In order for time out to be effective, it must truly be a time out from reinforcing activities and events of the classroom. If the classroom is devoid of reinforcing activities and events, the time out procedures will serve as a reprieve from a nonstimulating, boring environment. Buckholdt et al. have provided the following example illustrating time out.

Barney was a fourth grader who constantly disrupted class by shouting obscene words. Although the behavior was not dangerous, a time out procedure was considered as this shouting tended to completely upset the class. In addition, it was felt that the hilarious reactions of the entire class reinforced this behavior, in addition to the attention it did produce from the teacher.

Before starting the procedure, the behavior was carefully defined as Barney's audible [use] to the teacher of any one of three undesirable words which he used. A four-day baseline record of this behavior indicated a rate of about five times a day. Before the time out procedure was used, a week of teacher non-attention was tried, with no change in rate.

A chair and a screen were placed in a L-shaped corner of the room, completely isolating this area visually, and partially isolating it from classroom noise. The teacher told Barney that if he used bad language in class anymore, he would be separated from the other students and not allowed to take part in classroom activities for a while. When Barney asked the teacher what she meant, in a matter-of-fact manner she named for him the words he used which were prohibited. The teacher also told Barney that she could not allow these words in the classroom because they created a lot of laughing and other remarks, and disrupted work. All of this was done *before* the procedure was started.

A sheet of paper with columns marked "start time," and "end time," and "for language only" was taped on the wall next to the screen. In addition, at the top of the paper were written "two minutes only" and "extend for 30 seconds after noise audible in class."

The first time Barney said one of his words the teacher took him to the chair by the hand, saying, "You can't stay in class if you use that language." After Barney had been in the time-out area for a little under the two minute period, he shouted one of his words, and repeated this at frequent intervals so that his first period in time out lasted nearly seven minutes (all recorded on the sheet). The second time the teacher placed Barney in time out, she also verbalized the reason to him. This time out lasted a bit over four minutes, again extended by bad language plus a loud kick on the screen. After this, the teacher did not verbalize the reasons for Barney going to time out.

The teacher always ended the time out period by saying, "Barney, please return to your seat and _____," naming the classroom activity in the last part of the sentence. For instance, in one case, she added ". . . join us in our spelling game." In one instance Barney did not come out when so requested. The teacher casually mentioned that he should return to his seat "when he was ready," and he did after a few moments.

By the end of the second week, Barney was going to time-out zero to twice per day, and usually staying in time-out for the two minute period only.

While in the time out period, Barney could not engage in any classroom activities. No materials were available for him in that area. If he did not finish some work due to spending time in the time out area, he used recess time or time in some other activity to complete the work. This was rare, and usually when it did occur, it took only a minute or so. The teacher required this, however, so time out could not be used as a way of avoiding work. While Barney was in time out, the teacher avoided doing things such as reading a story in a loud voice, which could provide some reinforcement in the time out area (Buckholdt et al. 1972, pp. 14–16).

Using punishment to weaken or remove a behavior must be done very cautiously, if at all. Many school systems have rules prohibiting certain forms of punishment, and other schools allow for the use of physical punishment with specific guidelines. **Punishment**, in the terms of behavior modification, is the presentation of events or conditions that terminate the behaviors they follow or greatly reduce their future occurrence.

Why should punishment be used cautiously or avoided if possible? Punishment produces some very negative side effects in students. In the main, punishment procedures teach students avoidance behaviors. In order to avoid being punished, students learn to sneak, to lie, to cheat, to "cut" classes, or other similar actions. Teachers who use physical punishment as a means of reducing or terminating behaviors also serve as aggressive models for students. In turn, students learn that they, too, if they choose to imitate their teachers, can use aggressive or physical forms of behavior to deal with interpersonal problems with other classmates or their own siblings. Punishment also interferes with the relationship between the teacher and the student. Students with teachers who use primarily punitive approaches to classroom problems produce less and are not as willing to risk participation in new learning activities for fear of punishment or reprimands. According to Buckholdt et al., teachers who use punishment "may acquire punishing characteristics" (1972, p. 3).

Another interesting sideline related to punishment is that often punishment procedures do not deal with or eliminate the reinforcers that maintain the behaviors. If and when punishment must be used, Becker, Engelmann and Thomas (1975, pp. 259–60) suggest the following rules:

1. *The punishment should be immediate.* Take away the points or start the time out when the punishable behavior begins.
2. *When reinforcers are taken away, be sure to define a way to earn them back.* "You may rejoin the group after you are quiet for five minutes." "You may go to gym tomorrow if there is no fighting between now and then."
3. *Use one warning only.* The first time a punishable behavior occurs, give a warning. The next time, back up your warning signal with a cost contingency or time out.
4. *Stay calm* and matter-of-fact when administering a punishment. Don't fuel the fire with personal anger. You are trying to teach responsible behavior. Show that behavior yourself.
5. *Be consistent.* Be sure the undesired behavior is not reinforced now and then.

Contracting Strategies

"I'll make you an offer you can't refuse!" Contracting is another behavior modification strategy that can be used for a variety of problems. Simply speaking, a **contract** is an agreement (written or verbal) between two or more persons that stipulates responsibilities of the persons involved concerning an item or an activity. There are some basic assumptions (Polsgrove 1977, pp. 29–55) upon which contracting as a strategy is built. Contracting heightens communication. With written contracts especially, both teacher and student can be very clear as to what each is expected to do in order to accomplish some educational or social/emotional goal. Contracting also makes communication between teacher and student more reciprocal. Not only must students agree to what they will do, but the teacher must clearly identify what teaching support will be rendered in the contractual agreement. Contracting clarifies the nature of the interpersonal rewards and privileges that will come to both the teacher and the student as a result of their cooperative endeavor. Contracting also insures the fair exchange of rewards for tasks and activities that have been successfully mastered or completed.

Why should contracts be used? There are many answers to this question. From a programmatic point of view, contracting has been used successfully by many clinicians, therapists, and teachers (Becker, Engelmann, and Thomas 1975; Buckholdt et al. 1972; Clarizio 1976; De Risi and Butz 1975; Fagan and Hill 1977; Homme et al. 1970; Walker and Shea 1976; and Zifferblatt 1970). Contracts are particularly well suited for older students (preadolescents and adolescents). They perceive contracting as an adult or mature activity. Contracts have also been successfully used with many exceptional students as a part of their involvement in a resource room or with an itinerant teacher.

The actual act of signing a personalized contract is a powerful means for helping a student to take an agreement or contract seriously. In the latter stages of completing contracts, students become capable of generating their own contracts for change and thereby increase their own power for self-control. Certainly not the last reason for using contracts is that contracting emphasizes the responsibilities to be assumed by the signees, namely the teacher and the student. Neither exceptional nor regular students can place blame for failure to achieve a contract goal(s) if the teacher has complied with the stipulations of the agreement. Particularly in the latter stages of contracting, when students begin to create their own learning goals and dates for completion, students can no longer blame the teacher for uncomfortable due dates for assignments or exams. Contracting finally allows for student input into the learning process. Students are encouraged to provide feedback about the teacher's effectiveness in helping them to reach their contractual goals. Each participant in the contracting process is encouraged to express feelings about why the contract worked or did not work. Such feedback sessions also insure the development of good interpersonal relationships, problem-solving skills, and student self-control.

In creating a contract, one must follow some very simple steps. First, one must specify in clear language the amount and quantity of behaviors or products to be produced. Secondly, the contracting parties should identify appropriate reinforcers. Thirdly, the entire contracting process should be approached in a spirit of fair negotiation, tempered frequently by compromise. Finally, explicit agreement on the terms of the contract must be achieved before the contract is finalized with a handshake or signatures. Walker and Shea (1976) have developed a Contract Work Sheet, shown in figure 5.8, which more fully and formally details the steps to be followed in creating contracts. Figure 5.9 is a sample contract created by Walker and Shea (1976).

There are many types of contracts (Homme et al. 1970). Generally speaking, the first contract initiated by a teacher is teacher controlled; that is, the teacher plays the greatest role in determining the behaviors or activities to be pursued. Gradually, the teacher moves from the teacher-dominated contract to transitional contracts in which the student or group gradually assumes greater responsibility for choosing goals and rewards. With success on both the teacher-controlled and transitional contracts, students can begin to develop self-contracts. In addition to the types of contracts briefly discussed above, there are verbal contracts, three-party contracts, and total-class contracts. Each of these types of contracts can also be taken through the process outlined above, in which the teacher gradually assumes less of a directive role in controlling the contracting process.

Figure 5.8 Contract worksheet. (From James E. Walker and Thomas M. Shea, *Behavior Modification: A Practical Approach for Educators*, pp. 53–54. St. Louis: The C. V. Mosby Co., 1976.)

(X)	Tasks	Comments
( )	1. Establish and maintain rapport.	
( )	2. Explain the purpose of the meeting.	
( )	3. Explain a contract.	
( )	4. Give an example of a contract.	
( )	5. Ask the child to give an example of a contract; if there is no response, give another example.	
( )	6. Discuss possible tasks.	
( )	7. Child-suggested tasks: _____ _____	
( )	8. Teacher-suggested tasks: _____ _____	
( )	9. Agree on the task.	
( )	10. Ask the child what activities he or she enjoys and what items he or she wishes to possess.	
( )	11. Record child-suggested reinforcers.	
( )	12. Negotiate the ratio of the task to the reinforcer.	
( )	13. Identify the time allotted for the task.	
( )	14. Identify the criterion or achievement level.	
( )	15. Discuss methods of evaluation.	
( )	16. Agree on the method of evaluation.	
( )	17. Restate and clarify the method of evaluation.	
( )	18. Negotiate the delivery of the reinforcer.	
( )	19. Set the date for renegotiation.	
( )	20. Write two copies of the contract.	
( )	21. Read the contract to the child.	
( )	22. Elicit the child's verbal affirmation and give your own affirmation.	
( )	23. Sign the contract and have the child sign it.	
( )	24. Congratulate the child (and yourself).	

Teaching Students with Mild Learning and Behavior Differences

Figure 5.9 Contract. (From James E. Walker and Thomas M. Shea, *Behavior Modification: A Practical Approach for Educators*, p. 129. St. Louis: The C. V. Mosby Co., 1976.)

Date _____

Contract

This is an agreement between _____

Child's Name

and _____ . The contract begins on

Teacher's Name

_____ and ends on _____ . It will be

Date   Date

reviewed on _____ .

Date

The terms of the agreement are:

Child will _____

_____

_____

_____

Teacher will _____

_____

_____

_____

If the child fulfills his part of the contract, he will receive the agreed-on reward from the teacher. However, if the child fails to fulfill his part of the contract, the rewards will be withheld.

Child's signature _____

Teacher's signature _____

Homme et al. (1970, pp. 18–21) have developed ten basic rules for contracting. In creating contracts for the first several times, these rules would be helpful to anyone new to the contracting process.

Rule 1.   The contract payoff (reward) should be immediate.
Rule 2.   Initial contracts should call for and reward small approximations.
Rule 3.   Reward frequently with small amounts.
Rule 4.   The contract should call for and reward accomplishment rather than obedience.
Rule 5.   Reward performance after it occurs.
Rule 6.   The contract must be fair.
Rule 7.   The terms of the contract must be clear.
Rule 8.   The contract must be honest.
Rule 9.   The contract must be positive.
Rule 10.   Contracting as a method must be used systematically.

Buckholdt et al. (1972, pp. 12–14) have created some very helpful ideas in contracting for schoolwork, homework, study skills, and social skills. The prospective contract writer would do well to examine carefully these instructive ideas.

Contracting for Schoolwork

1. For a student whose major problem is that he does little work, each contract might require a slightly greater amount of work than the last one.
2. For a slow student who does work regularly, each contract might require that a set amount of work be done in a smaller amount of time than the last contract required.
3. For a sloppy or inaccurate student, each contract might require a slightly higher degree of accuracy, a higher grade, or less errors than the previous one.

Contracting for Homework

1. For a student whose main problem is that he does little homework, each contract can require a slightly larger amount to be done than the last contract did.
2. For a student who does not get his homework in on time, each contract can specify a deadline, and the deadlines can be made shorter and shorter in successive contracts until they are the same as the deadlines given students who perform well.
3. For a student who puts things off to the last minute, and then does a sloppy rush job, contracts can break the work down into smaller amounts with a due date for each portion of the project or assignment. Each later contract can then break the work down a little less finely.
4. Again, for sloppy or inaccurate students each contract can require a slightly more accurate paper, a lower error rate, or a higher grade than previous contracts.

Contracting for Study Skills

1. For the procrastinator, contracts can be written for starting classwork within a certain amount of time. Each contract can require a faster start.
2. For the poor scheduler as far as homework, contracts can be written to start homework at a set time and place at home each day. Successive contracts can require that this be met more and more strictly.
3. For the student who "forgets" books, materials or supplies, contracts can be written to require that these be in the correct place at the correct time. In each successive contract more and more items can be included.

Contracting for Social Skills

A sequence of contracts for social skills requires expert use of shaping procedures and of correct progressions. Some general strategies are listed below, but must be considered only suggestive.

1. Each contract can require a slightly better approximation than the previous one. For instance, one contract might require an isolate student to score another student's quiz, while the next contract might also require him to go over the scoring with the other student.
2. Each successive contract can require a slightly higher or lower frequency of some behavior. For instance, if a student has excessive "talk-outs" at inappropriate times, each contract might require a slightly smaller number of such behaviors than the last.
3. Each new contract can require some desired behavior to occur in more situations than the last one did, or require that an undesired behavior occur in less situations.

In implementing or experimenting with contracting strategies, teachers frequently do not experience the success they are seeking, often for a variety of reasons. De Risi and Butz (1975) have developed a guide for evaluating contract failures. Teachers who are interested in analyzing contract strategies that were not effective in changing student behaviors should consult this excellent guide.

In summary, contracting with both exceptional and regular students has many advantages. As a strategy, contracting is an excellent means for helping students, either individually or in groups, to assume responsibility for their own academic and social/emotional behaviors. Contracting promotes the development of self-control and self-management and enhances teacher/student communications. Contracts can be cooperatively used by resource teachers, regular class teachers, and parents of both exceptional and regular students in planning and implementing educational programs. As with all strategies identified in this chapter, contracting must be used with careful teacher judgment and planning.

Structure Strategies

Providing structure for a group or class of students can occur in a number of significant ways. Classroom furniture can often be rearranged in order to create new traffic patterns in a room. Some teachers use "strategic seating" arrangements in order to enhance or decrease certain types of student interaction, both verbal and physical. More often than not, experienced teachers structure the environment with clear cut expectations and rules. Another means for providing structure in the classroom is the establishment of healthy routines. Such routines make the sequence of teaching events and activities predictable, thereby allowing students to anticipate and prepare for upcoming assignments or instructional sessions. By modifying the classroom environment, teachers can often prevent problems (Gordon and Burch 1974). This section elaborates on some of the strategies teachers might employ in structuring the classroom environment to prevent problem behaviors and encourage positive learning behaviors for both the exceptional and regular students.

Classroom Design Strategies

The physical features of a classroom can be arranged so as to increase, maintain, or even reduce certain types of student movement and communication. Student movement can be modified by rearranging seating patterns, by designating certain task areas, by establishing group instruction areas, and by reducing open spaces that encourage running or similar behaviors. A room with maze characteristics will often stimulate investigative behaviors. Students of all ages enjoy exploring shopping centers and malls that have a lot of different "nooks and crannies" or behavior settings. A classroom that allows a number of student behaviors to occur simultaneously has greater potential for meeting a broad variety of learning and behavior needs. However, the "mall" approach to classroom design can often be overstimulating to students. Teachers should obviously use their best judgment in arranging classrooms to suit the needs of both the students and the teacher.

With regard to communication and student interaction, spatial relationships in the classroom have a tremendous effect on both the nature and the amount of communication that takes place. Students who are working in a circular seating arrangement are much more likely to participate in a group discussion than if they are seated in rows, with some of them seeing nothing but the back of their classmates' heads. Exceptional students who are shy or generally non-participative are much more likely to become involved in both verbal and nonverbal communications when they are placed in seating arrangements that promote communication rather than discourage it.

In a similar vein, teachers who are interested in changing the patterns of student interaction ought to become familiar with classroom assessment techniques that help them to identify students who are popular or sought after because of their attributes. A student who is capable and confident can often be used very effectively to provide peer tutoring or peer support in areas that are challenging to the exceptional student. One such tool for assessing social interactions in a classroom or group instruction setting is a sociogram. A **sociogram** is nothing more than a map of the tabulated results of a verbal or written questionnaire. The following questionnaire is an excellent example of a collection of predominately positive questions that could be administered in an elementary classroom.

Whom would you choose in this classroom—
1. for a boss _____
2. to send an important message _____
3. to discuss a new idea with _____
4. as a buddy to play with _____
5. to ask for help if you were in serious trouble _____

6. to be marooned with on a tropical island _____

7. to invite you to go on a trip with him/her _____

(San Diego County Department of Education 1975, p. 58)

Gordon (1966), Dreikurs, Grunwald, and Pepper (1971), and Brown (1978) provide excellent guidelines for the optimal use of sociometric techniques. The data drawn from sociograms can be effectively used in a variety of ways. For the exceptional or regular student who is unskilled in relating, the teacher can arrange seating assignments that encourage relationship-building activities. The teacher may also be able to foster events that pair the socially skilled with the socially unskilled so that their abilities are complementary. Another very unique use of the sociogram procedure is asking questions that allow teachers to learn about students' communicative actions in class. Brown (1978) has suggested the following request for inclusion in the typical questionnaire: "Write the name of the class member whom Ms. Jones likes best," or "Write the name of a class member whom Ms. Jones does not like." As is apparent from the type of information gathered through a sociogram, teachers must treat such information with great care and confidentiality.

Experienced teachers know of the benefits derived from "strategic seating" assignments. The exceptional or regular student who is likely to induce others to misbehave can be seated with students who are capable of ignoring negative behavior while at the same time encouraging positive learning behaviors. Often students must be separated, placed close to the teacher's desk, or placed in a carrel or office free of distractions. Room dividers or partitions are also effective in reducing certain types of excessive communication or noise.

Rule and Routine Strategies

Another way of helping both exceptional and regular students to develop responsible behaviors is the process of creating and implementing rules and routines. According to Charles (1976, p. 125), "Students need the assurance of boundaries. . . . They need to know what things are acceptable and what are not." Rules provide a guide or framework for student behavior in both learning and social activities. In order for rules to be effective they must be definable, reasonable, and enforceable (Smith and Smith 1966). When students are capable, they should be involved in the rule-making and enforcing process. Madsen, Becker, and Thomas (1968, pp. 143–44) have developed some excellent recommendations for formulating and enforcing rules: The rules should be formulated with the class and posted in a conspicuous location (a chart in front of the room or a special place on the chalkboard where they will not be erased). Go over the rules three or four times asking the class to repeat them back to you when they are initially formulated and use the following guidelines:

(a) Make the rules short and to the point so they can be easily memorized.
(b) Five or six rules are adequate. Special instructions for specific occasions are best given when the occasion arises. Children will not remember long lists of rules.
(c) Where possible phrase the rules in a positive not a negative manner (for example, "Sit quietly while working," rather than, "Don't talk to your neighbors"). We want to emphasize positive actions.
(d) Keep a sheet on your desk and record the number of times you review the rules with the class (strive for at least four to six repetitions per day). Remember that young children do not have the retention span of an adult and frequent reminders are necessary. Let the children recite the rules as you ask them, rather than always enumerating them yourself.
(e) Remind the class of the rules at times other than when someone has misbehaved.
(f) Try to change no other aspects of your classroom conduct except for the presentation of the rules at appropriate times.

In addition to these recommendations, Madsen and Madsen (1974, p. 181) have also developed some guidelines for creating rules:

1. Involve the class in making up the rules.
2. Keep the rules short and to the point.
3. Phrase rules, where possible, in a positive way. ("Sit quietly while working" instead of "Don't talk to your neighbors.")
4. Remind the class of the rules at times *other* than when someone has misbehaved.
5. Make different sets of rules for varied activities.
6. Let children know when different rules apply (work-play).
7. Post rules in a conspicuous place and review regularly.
8. Keep a sheet on your desk and record the number of times you review rules with class.

Various age groups and settings will require different rules. The guidelines provided by both Madsen, Becker, and Thomas (1968) and Madsen and Madsen (1974) provide an excellent framework from which teacher and students together can generate a workable set of appropriate rules.

Here are some typical lists of rules generated by teachers for the purpose of establishing clear-cut expectations for both exceptional and regular students. These lists of rules should be reviewed in light of some of the guidelines presented earlier in this section.

1. Raise your hand if you wish to talk.
2. Wait to be called on.
3. Listen while others talk.

(Becker, Engelmann, and Thomas 1975, p. 28)

1. Raise your hand when you wish to talk.
2. Walk in the room and halls.
3. Keep your hands and feet to yourself.
4. Be polite.
5. When you finish your work you may find something to do from the back of the room.

The children were reminded of the rules by—

1. Having the children read them each morning.
2. Making praise comments contingent on the following specific rules and making references to the rule in the praise comment: "Johnny, I like the way you walk in our room"; "I called on Johnny because he raised his hand."
3. Only attending to behavior within the limits of the rules.

(Becker, Engelmann, and Thomas 1975, pp. 117–18)

Reading and Math Periods

1. Keep your eyes on the teacher while directions are being given.
2. Keep working quietly until you finish.
3. Raise your hand for help and to talk.
4. Take turns during discussion.
5. Stay in your seat when teacher is giving directions.
6. When work is finished, do a free time activity.

(Greenwood et al. 1974, p. 185)

Rules are sets of standards that enhance the likelihood that learning will take place. They also provide bounds for the types of interaction that will be accepted and appreciated by both students and teachers. If and when rule breaking does occur, Clarizio (1976, p. 43) suggests that the following questions be asked about the student who chooses to break the rules:

1. Does he know what is expected of him; that is, does he clearly understand what the rules are?
2. If the student knows the rules but still misbehaves, . . . does he have the skills and abilities to do what I asked him to accomplish?
3. When the student knows what the rules are and when he has the competencies to perform in an acceptable way and yet continues to misbehave . . . is he motivated to do what is expected of him?

By asking these questions, teachers may modify the rules or seek additional motivation for helping the students to respond positively to rules that they helped to create. Glasser (1969) recommends the use of "classroom meetings" that emphasize problem-solving in dealing with rule violations or rule-amending activities. Routines, as compared to rules, are a form of scheduling, which provides firm expectations so that students can plan for and anticipate upcoming events. Students need to know how the day will flow. Students who are accustomed to established routines also require less active direction from the teacher. If they know what comes next, students can often begin the next activity without teacher direction.

Well-planned routines allow for the mixing of learning activities with appropriate rest and recuperation periods. Short intervals of movement can also be incorporated to help relieve tension or restlessness following academic work periods. On the elementary level, work periods can be followed by activities that might be naturally reinforcing, such as recess, gym, art, or related activities. On the secondary level, work periods might be followed by a time for discussing an upcoming athletic event, special musical group performance, or other appropriate activities.

In establishing routines, teachers are encouraged to follow many of the recommendations for establishing rules. The schedules or routines should be discussed and generated by both the teacher and students. The routines should be concise and understandable, and when they prove to be ineffective, they should be amended. In establishing routines, teachers are encouraged to post them in a conspicuous location in the classroom. When students, both exceptional and regular, are aware of an established schedule and have had an opportunity to participate in the planning and implementation of the schedule, their behavior is much more likely to be positive and organized rather than negative and disorganized.

Combinational Strategies

A great number of strategies could be discussed in this section. However, as a result of space limitations, only two strategies will be discussed. These strategies do not fall nicely into any of the other categories; they overlap and draw from the types of strategies discussed in the three preceding sections.

Surface Behavior Management Strategies

The first combinational strategy to be discussed in this section is drawn from an article written by Long and Newman for a publication entitled *Conflict in the Classroom*. Their article outlines twelve "influence techniques" that could be used to manage inappropriate or "surface" behaviors (Long, Morse, and Newman 1976, pp. 311–15):

1. Planned ignoring
2. Signal interference
3. Proximity control
4. Interest boosting
5. Tension decontamination through humor
6. Hurdle lessons
7. Restructuring the classroom program
8. Support from routine
9. Direct appeal to value areas
10. Removing seductive objects
11. Antiseptic bouncing
12. Physical restraint

Planned ignoring was discussed earlier in the section on behavior modification. Ignoring is used particularly when a student's behavior is reinforced by the teacher's attention. If the behavior is ignorable and not dangerous or "contagious," planned ignoring is a very powerful technique.

Signal interference describes nonverbal techniques that teachers employ. The "laser-beam look" of a teacher has prompted many a student to return to more suitable learning activities. Signals such as eye contacts, facial expressions, throat clearings, and various body postures can all effectively cause both exceptional and regular students to refrain from continuing or even escalating their current level of maladaptive behavior. According to Long and Newman, signal interference is most effective in dealing with the "beginning stages of misbehavior."

Proximity control is self-explanatory. Students who find themselves working in close proximity to their teacher are often more industrious than those who are in the back row or who are not under the direct purview of the teacher. Often by just taking a few steps in the classroom, the teacher can quickly prevent a behavior problem from occurring or neutralize a potentially volatile situation. The three techniques reviewed thus far do not interfere greatly with the teacher's ability to carry on other instructional functions, nor do they draw undue attention to the potential misbehaviors in the form of embarrassment or sarcasm.

Interest boosting is a teacher behavior aimed at sparking renewed student attention and motivation for pursuing a learning activity. The behavior can be nothing more than a question or a comment about the student's work. In fact, interest boosting comes as a result of the teacher's taking a few seconds to show personal concern for a student.

Tension decontamination through humor occurs in a variety of ways. All teachers know the value of humor in relaxing students, or making a tense situation more bearable. Long and Newman (1976, p. 312) provide an example to illustrate this influence technique:

> I walked into my room after lunch period to find several pictures on the chalk board with "teacher" written under each one. I went to the board and picked up a piece of chalk, first looking at the pictures and then at the class. You could have heard a pin drop! Then I walked over to one of the pictures and said that this one looked the most like me but needed some more hair, which I added. Then I went to the next one and said that they had forgotten my glasses so I added them, on the next one I suggested adding a big nose, and on the last one a longer neck. By this time the class was almost in hysterics. Then, seeing that the children were having such a good time and that I could not get them settled easily, I passed out drawing paper and suggested that they draw a picture of the funniest person they could make. It is amazing how original these pictures were.

Hurdle lessons or *hurdle helps* are teacher behaviors that help students to deal with a learning activity that is about to culminate in behaviors synonymous with "tossing in the towel," or tantrum responses. In hurdle help, the teacher, through assignment modification or actual tutoring, makes it possible for students to jump the assignment "hurdle" (problem) without resorting to pencil rolling, bothering neighboring students, drawing on their desks, or other more severe behaviors.

Restructuring the classroom program allows for a change in classroom routine according to the emotional or physical climate or other factors. Another term that might be associated with this influence technique is *flexibility*. For some teachers, choosing to vary from an established classroom routine is an extremely difficult (if not impossible) task. Often by taking just ten minutes to allow students to vent their feelings, or to relax, or to resolve a problem-provoking situation, the class can be returned to the established activity in accordance with the routine. Long and Newman (1976, p. 314) state:

> The children were just returning to the room after the recess period. Most of them were flushed and hot from exercise, and were a little irritable. They were complaining of the heat in the room, and many of them asked permission to get a drink of water as soon as the final recess bell rang. I felt it would be useless to begin our history study as scheduled. So I told all of the children to lay their heads upon their desks. I asked them to be very silent for one minute and to think of the coolest thing they could imagine during that time. The whole procedure lasted roughly ten minutes, and I felt that it was time well spent. The history period afterward went smoothly, the atmosphere within the room relaxed, and the children were receptive.

Support from routine as a management strategy was discussed in the previous section dealing with structure strategies. By way of review, routines help students to anticipate and prepare for the events of the day. Routines minimize the guesswork that often occurs in classrooms. Students generally feel less threatened and anxious when they are aware of the flow and sequence of curricular activities. Most of all, routines provide a certain level of security for both exceptional and regular students in that they make classroom life reasonably predictable and stable. It is generally best to post schedules so that all students have an opportunity to inform themselves about the activities and pursuits of any given school day or week.

Direct appeal to value areas as a technique takes a great deal of practice and teacher "savvy." According to Long and Newman (1976), teachers are often tempted to bombard the behavior code offender with severe and drastic interventions rather than trying to appeal to weak but present value areas that the student is gradually developing. These value appeals can take many forms. Long and Newman have identified four types of appeals: (1) a teacher/child relationship appeal, (2) a reality/consequence appeal, (3) an appeal based on peer standards for behavior, and (4) an appeal based on the teacher's authority. Each of these types are illustrated in table 5.5

Table 5.5 Four types of direct appeal to value areas.

Appeal Type	Teacher Response
1	"You are treating me as if I did something bad to you! Do you think that I have been unfair to you?"
2	"If you continue to talk, we will not have time to plan our party." "If you continue with this behavior, these are the things that will probably happen."
3	"If you continue to spoil their fun, you can't expect the other boys and girls to like you."
4	"I cannot allow you to continue this behavior, it must stop. I care about you, but I cannot permit you to behave the way you are."

Developed from Nicholas J. Long and Ruth G. Newman, "A Differential Approach to Management of Surface Behavior of Children in School," pp. 47–61, in *The Teacher's Handling of Children in Conflict,* Bulletin of the School of Education, Indiana University, July, 1961.

Removing seductive objects is a very simple technique to apply. Experienced teachers know the drawing power of certain toys and manipulatives such as small cars, flashlights, trinkets, balls, and so forth. In order to reduce the attraction of these objects and their use by students who are trying to do math problems or complete an English assignment, teachers are encouraged to secure such objects for return at a later time during the day or period. Teachers who are familiar with the Premack Principle (Premack 1959) would probably use such trinkets and toys as a contingency or reward activity for students who have completed an assignment or learning activity. The **Premack Principle,** simply stated, is the use of very probable behaviors to reinforce less probable behaviors. For instance, one teacher discovered that her exceptional student immensely enjoyed an opportunity to play chess during recess periods. In fact, playing chess with the teacher or a fellow student occurred with little, if any, prodding at a high rate. Observing this student's great liking for chess, this clever teacher decided to use the "chess playing behavior" as a reward for completing a specified number of academic tasks with specified levels of correctness. Seductive objects should be removed from students, but these objects can also provide effective free-time activities for students, both exceptional and regular, who have completed assignments or learning tasks.

Antiseptic bouncing is a technique in which the teacher makes it possible for a student to be removed briefly from a group situation that is of particular concern to the teacher or the student. Long and Newman (1976, p. 315) describe antiseptic bouncing in this manner: "In antiseptic bouncing there is no intent of punishing the child but simply to protect and help him and/or the group to get over feelings of anger, disappointment, uncontrollable laughter, hiccups, etc." Antiseptic bouncing is difficult because it is often very challenging to remove students from a classroom to another area in the school without making them feel that they are being chastized. The "antiseptic" part of the removal of students is difficult to achieve, but with some faculty brainstorming, most schools are able to create ways to implement antiseptic bouncing without hurting students.

Physical restraint as a technique should be used only when students may cause injury to themselves or others. The manner of the restraint should convey to the students that you are interested in protecting others as well as the offending students. Generally, the first impulse of teachers is to respond in punishing ways. Such punishment only adds to the behavioral fire and the problems of the students. In restraining an elementary student, Long and Newman suggest that the teacher stand behind the student while at the same time holding the wrists of the student, whose arms have been crossed across his or her chest.

Kounin's Strategies Kounin, Friesen, and Norton (1966) conducted a study dealing with emotionally disturbed children in regular classrooms. In this study, Kounin et al. used the concepts drawn from his previous research on classroom management to determine whether teachers whom he had identified as effective managers for regular classroom students would also be effective in managing students labeled emotionally disturbed. Their findings confirmed that teachers who successfully managed regular students were also successful in managing students with emotional problems.

Just exactly what constitutes successful management strategies? According to Kounin and Obradovic (1968, p. 135):

> . . . the business of running a classroom is based upon a complicated technology directed towards developing a non-satiating learning program; programming for progress, challenge, and variety in learning activities; initiating and maintaining group and individual movement in classroom tasks; observing and eliciting feedback for many different events, coping with more than one event simultaneously; directing actions at appropriate targets; and doubtless others yet to be determined.

Those teachers who were found to be successful excelled in the following areas: (1) Smoothness, the ability to initiate and sustain group movement; (2) group alerting, the ability to focus on all the students in a group during transition and recitation periods; (3) accountability, the ability to communicate to students that the teacher knows what students are doing relative to the designated learning activity(ies); (4) seatwork variety-challenge, the ability to provide a broad range of learning activities that are challenging and often novel; (5) with-it-ness, the ability to use "eyes behind one's head" or to demonstrate that the teacher is aware or "with it" in terms of what is happening in the classroom; and (6) overlappingness, the ability to attend to many teacher-directed and student-directed activities at one time. Kounin's ideas are not new, but his research does stress the importance of certain teacher behaviors. In order to run a classroom effectively, teachers should be concerned about behaviors that they regularly exhibit that slow down the learning process.

Such behaviors as excessive instruction giving, talking, or nagging only serve to slow the initiation of meaningful learning, whereas short, clear instructions, appropriate amounts of teacher talking, and the elimination of nagging promote immediate student involvement with learning activities.

Group alerting keeps students on their toes. They realize that the teacher does know what they are doing and expects them to perform. Kounin and Obradovic (1968, p. 133) have identified six behaviors that greatly facilitate appropriate group behavior:

1. creating suspense in the classroom by pausing after a question and looking around before selecting a child to recite
2. selecting reciters at random rather than in a predictable order
3. alerting the children that they might be called upon to evaluate a reciter's performance
4. circulating or deliberately looking around at the group during a child's recitation
5. presenting a challenging issue to the group during the recitation
6. acting in other ways indicating that the group is being kept alert and stimulated

Accountability behaviors make it clear to the students that the teacher will call upon them to demonstrate that they have been involved in a learning activity and mastered many of the concepts taught. Likewise, accountability behaviors let each student know that the teacher is aware of the student's level of involvement in pursuing a learning task. One teacher, in reviewing work completed during a math period, quickly notes the exact time of the last completed math problem on a student's worksheet and then returns a few minutes later to see what progress has been made.

Seatwork variety-challenge as an area has many dimensions. The variety portion of this concept is self-explanatory. Sameness is often synonymous with boredom. By mixing academics with nonacademics, arduous work with naturally enjoyable activities, deep-concentration activities with light-concentration work, and teacher-directed with student-directed tasks, boredom and lack of student interest and motivation disappear. The use of unusual or novel teaching props, materials, or game formats facilitates the holding of student interest and directed attention. Changing the location or the type of group involved in the learning activity is an additional means for maintaining motivation for student learning.

The ability to *overlap*, or keep in touch with two or more student learning activities at the same time, is a tremendous challenge. The teacher who is able to answer individual student questions while at the same time monitoring a reading or math skills group has achieved great prowess. Many of the structure strategies earlier outlined in this chapter make it possible for teachers to handle the chore of monitoring many students, since the students have been reinforced and rewarded for active compliance with scheduling times and classroom rules.

This chapter was designed to expose educators involved with both exceptional and regular students to a broad spectrum of techniques for dealing with typical behavior problems in regular classroom settings. The techniques were arranged according to strategy types: relationship/communication strategies, behavior-modification strategies, structure strategies and combinational strategies. These strategies vary in their strength potential for changing, eliminating, or maintaining behaviors. The strength potential of each is intimately tied to the teacher's commitment, teaching style, and skill in using each strategy. The strategies were not presented as solutions for all discipline and management problems, but rather as problem reducers. Teachers interested in truly mastering the strategies discussed in this chapter are encouraged to seek additional individual instruction and supervision from people trained in each strategy area, to complete additional reading, and (most importantly) to actively practice the skills and techniques reviewed and discussed.

References

Becker, W. C., Engelmann, S., and Thomas, D. R. 1975. *Teaching 1, classroom management.* Chicago: Science Research Associates.

Brown, L. 1978. Teacher strategies for managing classroom behaviors. In *Teaching children with learning & behavior problems,* ed. D. D. Hammill and N. R. Bartel. Boston: Allyn & Bacon.

Buckholdt, D. R., Sloane, H. N., Ferritor, D. E., and Della-Piana, G. M. 1972. *Classroom & instructional management program.* St. Ann, Missouri: Cemrel, Inc. The extracts in the text are reprinted with permission of the publisher. Copyright 1972 by Cemrel, Inc.

Charles, C. M. 1976. *Individualizing instruction.* St. Louis: C. V. Mosby.

Clarizio, H. F. 1976. *Toward positive classroom discipline.* 2d ed. New York: John Wiley & Sons.

DeRisi, W. J., and Butz, G. 1975. *Writing behavioral contracts.* Champaign, Illinois: Research Press.

Dreikurs, R., Grunwald, B. R., and Pepper, F. C. 1971. *Maintaining sanity in the classroom.* New York: Harper & Row.

Fagen, S. A., and Hill, J. M. 1977. *Behavior management.* Washington, D.C.: Psychoeducational Resources Inc.

Glasser, W. 1965. *Reality therapy.* New York: Harper & Row.

Glasser, W. 1969. *Schools without failure.* New York: Harper & Row.

Gordon, I. J. 1966. *Studying the child in school.* New York: John Wiley & Sons.

Gordon, T. 1970. *P.E.T. Parent effectiveness training.* New York: Peter H. Wyden.

Gordon, T., and Burch, N. 1974. *T.E.T. Teacher effectiveness training.* New York: David McKay Company.

Greenwood, C. R., Delquadri, J., Hops, H., and Walker, H. M. 1974. *PASS, Program for academic survival skills.* Eugene, Oregon: Center at Oregon for Research in the Behavioral Education of the Handicapped, Center on Human Development.

Homme, L., Csanyi, A. P., Gonzales, M. A., and Rechs, J. R. 1970. *How to use contingency contracting in the classroom.* Champaign, Illinois: Research Press.

Kounin, J. S., Friesen, W. V., and Norton, A. E. 1966. Managing emotionally disturbed children in regular classrooms. *Journal of Educational Psychology* 57:1–13.

Kounin, J. S., and Obradovic, S. 1968. Managing emotionally disturbed children in regular classrooms: a replication and extension. *Journal of Special Education, 2,* 129–35.

Krumboltz, John D., and Krumboltz, Helen Brandhorst. 1972. *Changing children's behavior.* Englewood Cliffs, New Jersey: Prentice-Hall. The extracts on pp. 92–94 are from this text (© 1972, pp. 9, 20–21, 42) and reprinted by permission of Prentice-Hall, Inc.

Long, N. J., and Newman, R. G. 1976. Managing surface behavior of children in school. In *Conflict in the classroom,* 3d ed. N. J. Long, W. C. Morse, and R. G. Newman. Belmont, California: Wadsworth.

Madsen, C. H., Jr., Becker, W. C., and Thomas, D. R. 1968. Rules, praise, and ignoring: elements of elementary classroom control. *Journal of Applied Behavior Analysis* 1:139–50. The extract on p. 108 is reprinted by permission. Copyright 1968 by the Society for the Experimental Analysis of Behavior, Inc.

Madsen, C., and Madsen, C. 1974. *Teaching/discipline.* 2d ed. Boston: Allyn & Bacon.

Polsgrove, L. 1977. Self-control: an overview of concepts and methods for child training. *Proceedings of a conference on preparing teachers to foster personal growth in emotionally disturbed students.* Minneapolis Minnesota: Advanced Institute for Trainers of Teachers for Seriously Emotionally Disturbed Children.

Premack, D. 1959. Toward empirical laws: I positive reinforcement. *Psychological Review* 66:219–33.

San Diego County Department of Education. 1975. *Teaching interpersonal social skills.* San Diego, California: San Diego County Department of Education.

Smith, J. M., and Smith, D. 1966. *Child management: a program for parents.* Ann Arbor: Ann Arbor Publishers.

Walker, J. E., and Shea, T. M. 1976. *Behavior modification.* St. Louis: C. V. Mosby.

Zifferblatt, S. M. 1970. *Improving study and homework behaviors.* Champaign, Illinois: Research Press.

6 Strategies for Academic Programming

Most youngsters have successful, positive learning experiences in school. Their attitudes toward the school environment are healthy and constructive. Whether we use a reading series with a visual or auditory approach does not seem to matter—they can learn with both or with either. Success builds upon success, and they gain skills, new knowledge, and a positive attitude about themselves and school. They develop academically, physically, socially, and emotionally in a nurturing environment.

Chapter 4 has reviewed the evolving definitions and the range of students with learning and behavioral differences. These students are in need of both programmatic and environmental modifications in order to succeed in school. Primary responsibility rests with the regular teacher, who is challenged to find ways to enhance the learning environment in order to accommodate their learning differences. These youngsters may need special attention because of limited ability, poor motivation, or specific learning disability. Frequently, their difficulties are related to a combination of or interaction among these factors. They often stand out because of characteristics such as inappropriate behavior, performance below grade level, or negative attitudes toward school.

Imagine what it would be like to be in an environment that gives you nothing but **negative feedback** most of the time—a place you hate, activities that are difficult and at which you frequently fail, people who emphasize your negative qualities (your inability to do something or your lack of knowledge). How would you feel about being in that environment six hours a day, five days a week, approximately 180 days a year for many years to come? Some children's perceptions about school are similar to this description. Because of a variety of factors—limited ability, poor motivation, specific learning disability—they have a high probability of experiencing school failures. How can we, as regular educators, often harassed by the needs and demands of all children, best meet the needs of students who need an extra support system in order to succeed in school?

Principles of Effective Support

An effective support system implies a program built on sound teaching principles. Strategies that match learning needs and styles with instructional practices increase the chance of success for these children. The application of these systematic teaching principles involves consistent practice, the use of successive approximation, and adjustment of the task demands.

For children with learning handicaps, the need for consistency is very high. Students need to know what to expect of their teacher, what is expected of them, and what the consequences are for success and failure. Because many children with learning and behavior differences are performing below grade level, a teacher may decide to use the principle of "successive approximation." This means scaling down the demands or requirements of a task based on a child's present performance in order to increase chances of success (Haring 1978). Gradually the criteria are increased until the goal is achieved. For example, a child who has not been handing in seatwork papers may initially receive credit for handing in papers regardless of quality or accuracy. Increased accuracy or neatness might be imposed and reinforced as each step is accomplished. Such a system requires frequent feedback so that the student has specific information concerning his or her performance and knows exactly what steps to take to improve.

Sometimes the teacher can find alternative methods of providing feedback to the student. The use of peer tutors or an older student might be feasible. Some students can be taught to record data on their own performance and can be involved in the decision-making process (Lovitt 1977). Examples of ways to use these strategies will be presented later in the chapter.

It is occasionally necessary to allow students alternative methods of displaying their knowledge of specific materials. A youngster may be able to write a list of spelling words accurately if given extra time or if placed in a corner of the room with few distractions. On the other hand, the child may need to spell the words orally into a tape recorder or with another student. If the purpose of the test is to ascertain a child's mastery of a given task, then some flexibility in the method of evaluating performance may be necessary.

The choice of various methods to promote a child's learning will depend not only on the task but on a student's particular learning style. Most children have intact **auditory and visual modalities,** and thus can be successful with tasks requiring either channel. However, some youngsters have deficits or "short circuits" in one channel or both. They may have difficulty *processing information* that they receive aurally or visually. Thus, they need some accommodation in methods of presenting new material and in ways of demonstrating their knowledge or understanding.

The teaching-learning act should focus on the individual learning styles of exceptional children (Lerner 1976). Often we say "Show me, don't tell me"; "Slow down, you're going too fast"; "I can only attend to one thing at a time." Repeatedly students are admonished for not listening, goofing off, or being unmotivated when the underlying problem may be, at least in part, that the demands made by the teacher are inappropriate to the learning style and the needs of the exceptional student.

If efficient learning is to occur, careful attention must be given to planning appropriate, well-structured teaching situations. Two questions are basic to planning educational programs for exceptional children: What do we want to teach? and how can we do it best? What to teach involves, first, the process of selecting appropriate goals based on the student's or parents' and teachers' judgments. This selection may be based on interests, levels of performance, ability levels, survival skills, and so forth. The second step is to determine the student's existing knowledge and skill levels as they relate to the long-range goals that have been selected. After it has been determined what the child already knows, appropriate short-term goals and instructional objectives can be set (Lowenbraun and Affleck 1976).

How best to teach involves fitting the task demands to the individual learning styles of students. Some students learn best by what they hear; others by what they see. Some students can respond best verbally; others prefer to respond in writing. The preferred learning style coupled with what the student needs to learn dictates instructional methods, materials, the setting, the mode of presentation, and the mode of response. Once the teacher understands the interaction of the task demands and the learning style, the sequence of teaching steps needed to achieve an objective can be developed.

Juanita may tell the teacher that she hates reading—that it's boring. She may attend class sporadically and have no friends in the classroom. She wishes she knew how to read better but appears to have little motivation to do so. The teacher and Juanita agree that she can read the stories but doesn't understand what she reads. The group reading tests she took in grades five and nine seem to support this observation. Her comprehension skills are poor; however, her **word attack skills** and **sight word skills** are strong. Together, teacher and student generate several alternatives. Juanita indicates that she would be willing to try something different, so the teacher decides to proceed by rechecking her programming. In order to pinpoint her level of performance, the teacher can design classroom tasks that become informal assessment tools (Stephens 1970). If these tasks are completed under teacher observation, then additional data will be available concerning how Juanita learns.

Following is a sample classroom task that may be used to assess reading comprehension informally. It is a multiple-choice exercise that the student completes after reading an assigned selection.

1. The baseball game was played on—

    (a) Monday   (b) Tuesday   (c) Saturday

2. The main idea of the story was—

    (a) good sportsmanship prevails
    (b) the problems of coaching
    (c) how to win a ballgame

3. After Bob made the home run—

    (a) the rain started
    (b) his best friend struck out
    (c) the pitcher was replaced

4. Bob played for the—

    (a) Royals   (b) Owls   (c) Cardinals

5. If Billy had made the home run with bases loaded—

    (a) his team would have won the game
    (b) the game would have been tied
    (c) his team would have won the championship

In this task, the input is visual (the student reads the exercise silently) and the output is motor (circling the correct response). The cognitive demand is attaching meaning to what is read. The same task can be varied so that the input is the teacher's oral reading, and the output task remains motor (Junkala 1972, 1973).

The teacher may observe over time that Juanita misses 50–80 percent of the responses on such multiple-choice tasks. Several questions surface. Does she miss more responses when the input is oral (teacher reading aloud) and the output is motor or when the input is visual (silent reading) and the output is motor? What are the cognitive demands of the task? For example, what kind of comprehension is being demanded: reading for detail, sequencing, finding the main idea, drawing inferences, cause and effect? An analysis of multiple-choice questions reveals that a mixture of comprehension skills are being tapped. Thus, the teacher is using clinical skills in order to diagnose the student's performance (Lerner 1976).

Perhaps the teacher will decide to delineate the various comprehension tasks and devise multiple-choice worksheets that assess one comprehension skill at a time. The teacher may decide to collect Juanita's responses over time and conduct an error analysis to determine the types of comprehension problems she exhibits. Through the process of observation, measurement, readjustment of the task demands, and reteaching, an efficient learning method can be determined for a student.

Through **error analysis** (Gearheart 1976), the teacher may conclude, for example, that Juanita performs best when reading the exercise silently and circling correct responses. The teacher may further note that she makes fewer errors in comprehension questions requiring **simple recall** and **sequencing.** Juanita misses the most items when the teacher reads orally and she responds motorically to items that demand **inferential skills** or **cause-and-effect comprehension skills.**

With this additional information about how Juanita learns, the teacher can begin to define clearly some specific goals and objectives to help her make progress in reading. Such information may be shared with Juanita to give insight into how she learns best.

Error analysis is often extremely helpful in providing information as to next steps to be taken. Let us look at a segment of the math seatwork done by Robert:

$$\begin{array}{cccccc} 47 & 64 & 37 & 68 & 29 & 37 \\ +32 & -11 & +58 & -43 & +41 & -11 \\ \hline 79 & 72 & 815 & \varsigma 5 & 610 & \varsigma 8 \end{array}$$

Several hypotheses or questions emerge from an examination of Robert's math work:

1. Is Robert attending to the operation signs?
2. Does he know what these signs mean?
3. Does he have concept mastery of *tens* and *ones?*
4. What is the basis for reversals of fives and twos?

Each of these questions must be answered if we are to improve Robert's math performance; remediation in each area must take place. Strategies may involve lessons to give Robert practice in forming twos and fives as an initial procedure. Fading techniques can be used (Sulzer and Mayer 1972), followed by a great deal of practice. The next step may involve the presentation of either addition *or* subtraction, instead of both together. If Robert demonstrates mastery of addition problems that do not require carrying, then the teacher might introduce addition with carrying, using concrete materials such as Cuisenaire rods, or an abacus. Only after this is mastered will subtraction be introduced, perhaps with extra cues when addition problems are presented on the same page—e.g., color coding the operational symbols (Gattegno 1962). Thus, we have used an analysis of Robert's own errors to determine the next steps for teaching and to decide which strategies may be appropriate.

Following are four vignettes of students who exhibit some of the problems described in the previous section. These problems may be related to differences in the way the child processes new information, to somewhat decreased learning capability, or to motivational problems. In every case, it is necessary to analyze the given task, determine the specific objectives to be accomplished, and move ahead with strategies to ensure that these objectives are accomplished.

Janie   Janie has many characteristics typical of the learning-disabled child. Her learning through visual input is much stronger than through the auditory mode. Task demands that depend heavily upon auditory input are difficult for Janie, and she tends to miss information needed for satisfactory *task completion* because of this **auditory deficit.** Janie has a short attention span and is highly distractible—a situation that creates difficulties for her and for her teacher. These characteristics are often present in the hyperactive child (Wender 1973). This hyperactivity is being reinforced by teacher and student attention, and Janie uses it to avoid difficult or unpleasant tasks. Thus we have a cycle of poor performance, high frustration, *acting out behavior,* and excessive amounts of attention leading to continued poor performance. Notice this cycle as we present Janie in vignette.

> Storytelling time is a restless time for Janie, a first-grader. She prefers show and tell, when she can do some of the talking. When required to listen, she squirms and wiggles and seldom pays attention. In fact, the teacher finds herself repeating directions to Janie on every task given her during the day. In spite of this added attention, Janie's assignments are often misunderstood and incorrectly completed. She has been struggling with readiness skills and reading. She is having particular difficulty with rhyming, identifying words that begin alike and end alike, and letter and sound association. She is also performing poorly in math seatwork, though when worked with individually she demonstrates mastery of basic addition and subtraction skills.
>
> When given math seatwork, Janie exhibits behavior that is characterized by excessive movement, talking out, and responding to extraneous stimuli. She is an expert at task avoidance. She is more out of her seat than in, disrupts the class during seatwork, and has several habits that irritate the teacher, such as twitching and leaning back in her chair.

For Janie, successful intervention will involve identification of a support system that can be used in the regular classroom without major disruption.

Janie's problems are exhibited in situations requiring listening skills, and in performance of both reading and math seatwork. The deficit in listening skills due to some weakness in the auditory mode of learning is hindering Janie's performance in the academic areas.

Let's take each of these problems and consider some strategies that might help Janie.

Strategies for Improving Janie's Listening Skills

Give one verbal instruction at a time. Limit verbal instruction to simple sentences presented briefly and logically.

Use visual aids when giving verbal instructions; give demonstration of the task whenever possible; pair instructions with gestures.

Include the student in the instruction—ask her to repeat the directions, give her an opportunity to ask questions.

Use a three-by-five card on which simple instructions are written. After verbal instructions are given, tape cards to Janie's desk so she can refer to them if necessary. Use simple language, pictures, uncluttered format for written directions.

Strategies for Improving Reading Skills

The hints on developing listening skills are applicable to working with Janie in reading. Janie may respond to a program that is heavily visual in its approach. At the same time, however, we want to work with Janie in strengthening her auditory skills (Ring 1975; Vance and Hankins 1975).

Play verbal direction games. Begin with one instruction, increase to two instructions, and so forth. For example, find the word that begins with *th*. Make the sound *th*.

Give the child an activity that involves identifying like or different sounds of words: bell-jar; box-toy, etc. Increase the similarity of the words: bell-bill; toy-boy; jar-far.

Verify whether Janie can tell the difference between gross sounds, such as those of a bell and a piano. Use a tape recorder for this activity and a game format.

Check the ability to rhyme words and teach the skill with instruction, demonstration, and imitation. Games and activities can be incorporated into small and large group sessions.

Involve Janie in storytelling activities. Balance listening and participating. Have Janie retell a short story or verse that you have just recited. Start by having her listen for certain words or sounds and raise her hand when she hears them. Encourage her to listen for the answer to a specific question you raise.

Strategies for Improving Math Skills

In addition to having trouble with some reading readiness tasks, Janie is not succeeding in her math seatwork. On daily papers of one-digit addition and subtraction facts with no borrowing, the number of problems done correctly during the last week has been:

3/20   1/20   2/20   2/20   3/20
(highest number of problems attempted: five)

When tested in a one-to-one situation, Janie demonstrates mastery of all combinations of one-digit addition and subtraction facts. She has developed the basic prerequisites for writing all numbers. Her distractibility and restlessness seem to be factors contributing to her failure in a group seatwork situation in which there is no individual monitoring. Following are some strategies that might be tried:

Reduce complexity of assignment. Present one type of problem on each page or in each seatwork assignment—addition *or* subtraction.

Set task based on present performance. Since the highest score Janie attained was 3/20, start by requiring four, then five problems done correctly in a given period of time, gradually working up to twenty problems according to Janie's performance.

Present the problems five at a time, possibly one row at a time. Give feedback at end of five problems, gradually increasing the task to the point where Janie does twenty problems at 90 percent accuracy.

Some support for keeping Janie *on task* might be built into the seatwork assignment. This might be done in the form of—

messages placed in a box on the window sill that Janie is allowed to fetch after doing five problems. The message would have some positive comment, like "keep going" or "good working." This would allow Janie to get out of her seat for a legitimate purpose, give her a needed break, and keep her on task.

a token system in which Janie is reinforced on a random basis for on-task behavior. Start delivery of tokens after four correct problems and gradually increase criteria.

a self-check in which, after five problems are done, Janie can check her answers against a key, correct errors, and move on to the next problems. Such a system builds in more frequent feedback, which may help keep Janie on task. If a self-check is not feasible, the assignment of another student to check Janie's answers and to respond to questions might be used.

Students like Janie can be found in every classroom. Learning for them can be a frustrating experience. However, a teacher who directs the learning in a purposeful manner can provide the successful experiences these students need. By designing reading and math tasks that focus on visual input, decrease the level of difficulty and length, and provide appropriate reinforcement, the teacher has made some major first steps in individualizing learning. Many of the strategies discussed in this section can be used in small or large group activities and benefit all students.

We are suggesting techniques that address the need for building Janie's auditory skills as well as methods to control her inappropriate seatwork behavior. The teacher will do well to "catch Janie when she is good" so that she will be receiving attention for appropriate behavior. Otherwise, the teacher runs the risk of conveying messages to Janie that will set up even more inappropriate behavior. Chances are reasonable that with increased **attending behavior,** Janie's performance will improve and her listening skills will be strengthened. By working directly on improving auditory skills, we will increase Janie's success with daily academic tasks. At the same time, we need to provide help to reduce the undesirable activity that Janie displays. Providing legitimate outlets for this activity and giving attention for appropriate behavior may help to deal with this problem.

The student whom you will meet next has experienced a great deal of failure **Craig** in school over the years. He may be described as a student with limited capacity who needs more than average time to master concepts. His difficulties are most apparent in reading-related tasks. Craig is typical of the poorly motivated student with limited abilities and, unfortunately, is well entrenched in a syndrome of failure and negativism.

Craig has had a history of learning difficulties and has severe problems in reading and writing. He is extremely restless when involved in reading and writing, and seems to tire easily. He frequently loses his place in the book and tends to follow words with his fingers. He still reverses letters or words when reading aloud. His grammar is poor, and logical sentence construction is difficult for him. Because of his trouble with sequencing the reading material and gaining meaning from visually presented material, his reading comprehension is very poor—assessed to be at a third-grade level. His poor comprehension is a severe impediment to any success in social studies and science, both of which he is failing. Yet, he is interested in some current events and often quotes information gained from a TV program, especially in regard to sports figures. He can remember discrete data, such as game scores, or boxing records.

Craig has an extremely negative attitude about school. He has experienced so much failure that he views himself as "a dummy." He is counting the days until he can quit school and get a full-time job. He is not a disruptive youngster, but is discouraged, turned off, and merely going through the motions until the day he can escape.

Identifying the Problem

Often by the time they reach junior high school, students like Craig are extremely frustrated by continuous failure and develop negative attitudes toward the environment in which this failure occurs. They are tired of trying without success, their motivation is very low, and they look forward to the day they can leave school.

Craig's problem is further compounded by the fact that in junior high school he has many teachers to face each day and a variety of tasks to which he must respond. There are demands for independent behavior in academic areas that he cannot begin to fulfill because he can neither read nor write well.

Craig will need much support in learning how to survive in the regular classroom. Aides, peers, resource teachers, and parents can assist the regular teacher in giving him the help he needs.

Craig is strong in some areas: he remembers what he hears and is able to quote detailed information about sports and current events that he picks up on television. His interest in current events and sports and his ability to retain information he hears as well as sees can be the key for reviving motivation and getting learning started. To provide additional motivation the teacher could capitalize on his interest in getting a job by working on basic skills through a study of careers and career opportunities. Let's consider these strengths in proposing strategies that may increase school success for Craig.

Strategies for Improving Reading

Since Craig appears to learn best by what he hears, provide him with assignments on audio tapes. These can be recorded by an aide, another student, or a parent. If a reading from his text book is recorded, have Craig follow in his book as he listens to the tape.

Provide oral reading experiences whenever possible by having student readers read aloud to Craig and a few other students who would prefer to listen rather than read on any given day.

Provide reading assignments that are geared to Craig's interests (hobbies, careers, or sports) to stimulate and sustain his interest. Introduce reading activities with motivating openers as activities. For example, relate an experience you have had or read about that touches on the theme of a story or stories you are about to introduce (winning against great odds, being cut from the school team). Involve the group in a discussion that allows them to share personal experiences orally.

Select materials that Craig can read and comprehend when he is given a silent reading assignment. Have him read for a specific purpose, such as the main idea, a specific detail, or an outcome.

Avoid assignments that require Craig to read aloud in front of his peers.

Use the language-experience approach to reading. Allow him to dictate stories that an aide or tutor can type. He can then read these stories in order to build his reading vocabulary.

Provide a variety of reading selections at his ability level. Observe to determine what is motivating for him. For example, if his interests are in sports, ask him to help you plan a unit, select some books, or develop a bulletin board. The unit may focus on a recent sporting event that he could report to the class, or it could contain a section on learning a sport (e.g., soccer or baseball). Craig could be responsible for organizing teams and teaching the game. For example, have him explain how batting averages are determined or how team rankings are figured.

Strategies for Other Academic Areas

Utilize public or network television. Look for programs Craig may watch and report to you about later in order to fulfill assignments in science and social studies, which he is failing.

Since Craig is looking forward to getting a job, study careers for young people. Plan an activity in which students may interview people in various careers. Plan the questions they would ask and have them return to class for small group discussions about what they have learned.

Allow the assignments Craig submits to be verbal (on tape or direct) whenever possible. Because reading and writing are frustrating, he will probably perform better on tests that are read to him and to which he can respond orally.

Written assignments should be brief and easily comprehended. Outline formats help students who have difficulty with writing and organizing. The length of assignments may be overwhelming. Start with brief ones and increase their length as student performance improves.

To help Craig with spelling, give him a few basic spelling rules, printed on cards, to which he can refer as needed. Initiate his spelling list from his own vocabulary. Cut the list in half. Teach him to study words using a multisensory approach—tracing a word with his finger as he spells it aloud. Have him write his words on small cards and keep them in a file box.

If Craig is allowed to type, it will help him with any reversals and handwriting problems he displays.

Build in strong reinforcement procedures for Craig's performance. Their selection can be based on what is motivating for Craig. Reward conscientious effort no matter how small. Let him know that oral reports are acceptable and five spelling words correct is great! Make positive comments on his writing assignments. Let his parents know that Craig is working and succeeding.

The goals for Craig need to be pragmatic and related to his present performance. We will not make Craig the class valedictorian, but with clearly defined objectives for the major academic areas and some exposure to specific career opportunities, we can keep him in school. By setting up the classroom so that Craig can experience success and see progress, we can build for him some much-needed basic skills. By relating reading tasks to his interest areas, we may increase his motivation to read. By giving him opportunities to explore various careers, we give him a purpose for coming to school and relate the school activities to goals he holds for himself. Pursuing such a route may add to Craig's feelings of self-esteem as well as give him some needed tools for the future.

Eric   The following vignette highlights some characteristics of youngsters whose inappropriate behavior interferes with academic performance. Poor **impulse control**, immature responses to other children and to authority, and a high degree of activity combined with a high rate of absenteeism all contribute to the problems of Eric and students like him. These characteristics are typical of many children who need an extra support system.

Eric is ten years old. He enrolled in the fourth grade at his present school in January. School records indicate that he had an extremely high rate of absenteeism at his previous school, approximately 30 percent since the beginning of the school year. A pattern of high absenteeism has been typical throughout his school years. Despite this situation, Eric is nearly at grade level in both reading and math as indicated by the **Wide Range Achievement Test (WRAT):** he scored 3.7 in spelling, 4.0 in math, and 4.1 in word recognition.[1] His reading comprehension is also at grade level, although he exhibits some undesirable habits related to poor *impulse control,* and lack of *self-correction skills.*

His difficulties in class manifest themselves in inattention and inappropriate behavior, such as talking out and roaming around the room at will. Messy and incomplete papers and an inability to participate in group discussion without being disruptive are also characteristic of Eric's behavior. In addition, he seems to waft in and out of group activities. He is tuned in one minute, and disruptive the next—bringing in unrelated comments, poking another student, laughing inappropriately, or moving excessively.

Eric has difficulty following any task to completion. He also has difficulty keeping track of his materials and has been found taking other children's supplies. According to test data, Eric is capable of excelling in academic work. However, he is severely impeded by his poor impulse control and immature behavior as well as his inability to relate appropriately in a group.

Before any improvement in Eric's academic performance can be realized, it will be necessary to help Eric gain better control of his behavior. The following strategies are designed to help Eric attend to tasks and exhibit appropriate behavior.

Identifying the Problem

Strategies for Improving Behavior

Initially, it is necessary to determine the length of time Eric stays on task. Measures of in-seat behavior, attending, and time on task need to be obtained (Cooper, 1974). Once the data are gathered related to specific behaviors, the teacher can determine the order in which behaviors will be targeted for change. Let us graph Eric's out of seat behavior for the past five days during reading and math (figure 6.1).

Figure 6.1 Eric's out-of-seat behavior

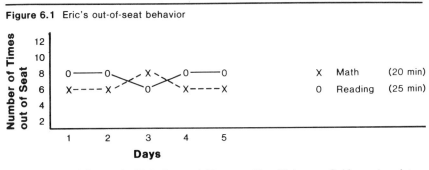

1. J. Jastak, and S. Jastak, *Wide Range Achievement Test* (Delaware: Guidance Associates, (1965).

The longest period of attending or on-task behavior that Eric exhibited in the last five days was six minutes. This period occurred in a reading session when in-seat work was to be done. After several starts, Eric remained on task for six minutes and completed one-half of the assignment.

Eric is obviously not exhibiting the behavior required to complete his in-seat work. He needs opportunities for active learning while still being held responsible for academic outcomes. An early goal would be to extend Eric's attending behavior. He might be required to work independently for a ten-minute period following which he is given an active task — moving from one room to another to carry a message, completing a task at an interest corner, charting his progress, or other activities of five to ten minutes in length. Such an activity will give Eric some respite from the requirements of in-seat behavior and at the same time provide an alternative for him that is acceptable to the teacher.

Eric's in-seat and attending behavior might be improved by giving him a voice in the sequencing of his activities. By giving him a choice of the order in which he can accomplish his tasks, we can build in a commitment to their completion.

Eric needs opportunities for *modeling* appropriate behavior. His high rate of absenteeism and the negative feedback regarding his behavior have started him on the road to extremely bad habits. He may need contrived situations in which he sees others *reinforced* for appropriate behavior. It is also important to obtain information concerning parent support for Eric. Are his parents aware of Eric's high rate of absenteeism? What are their feelings about it?

A "buddy" system in which Eric is paired with a student who exhibits many appropriate behaviors might help to reduce Eric's inappropriate behavior and would provide an appropriate model. Such a step will also give Eric an opportunity to establish a positive social relationship, a task that has been difficult because of his high rate of absenteeism and the frequent moves in the middle of the school year. A feeling of acceptance, first by another student, and gradually by other children who can respond more to his acceptable behavior, may reduce Eric's need to gain attention in inappropriate ways.

It is apparent that Eric has received a great deal of reinforcement from his teachers for his inappropriate behavior. This trend can be reversed by providing much more praise and support for appropriate behavior. Eric needs an image of himself that conveys positive messages (I am capable of good work, I can learn quickly, I am appreciated when I behave well).

Positive comments, a hand on the shoulder, a pat on the back, or simply standing near Eric may be effective ways of controlling his behavior. The use of charting for appropriate behavior, such as work completed or the length of time in seat, may also provide Eric with needed support.

Providing opportunities for Eric to earn some reinforcement for both himself and a friend may be an effective strategy. Attempts to work with key students who are taught methods of delivering positive reinforcement to Eric might also be considered.

Once Eric's behavior is under better control, it would be helpful to analyze his academic performance so that this, too, might be improved. Because of his high rate of absenteeism, Eric is likely to be missing some crucial skills that create gaps in his performance. He should be able to succeed at fourth-grade work in reading and math, but he is not working up to potential.

Strategies for Academic Improvement

The first step is an analysis of gaps in specific academic areas. This can be done by informal observation and teacher-developed assessment.

Units for development and practice of specific skills can be used—for example, a teaching package on division of two-digit numbers. Eric can go through this package individually and then check his understanding with another student—either another classmate or an older student.

Opportunities might be provided for Eric to help another student who is having difficulty with a specific skill, such as spelling. Not only would this be helpful to the other student, but it would provide potential benefits for Eric. These benefits would include the opportunity to review the words for a specific purpose, to build a positive self-image (Eric would see himself in a helping role), and to enhance the possibility that other students would begin to see Eric in a positive light.

Eric is only ten years old, and he has already learned many behaviors that will not only make him unpopular with other students but will also impede his progress in school. This student has high learning potential, but his prognosis for achievement is poor unless the teacher can initiate strategies in the classroom to help Eric deal with his inappropriate behavior. The strategies discussed in this section are based on sound principles of behavior management and can be incorporated into a teacher's management repertoire.

The last vignette deals with an elementary-age youngster who, because her **Lisa** ability is somewhat limited, is not progressing through the academic program at the same rate as other children. Lisa, like many children with mild learning handicaps, learns at a slower rate than the average child and has difficulty mastering academic tasks. Learning is not spontaneous as it is for many other children. Lisa has to labor very hard with her school work. She learns best on concrete rather than abstract levels. Her self-concept is not enhanced by her poor school performance.

Lisa is in the third grade but is working in a first-grade reading program with an emphasis on phonics. Her performance is very inconsistent in remembering her reading sounds from one day to the next. She does well in **blending** and **visual sequencing tasks;** however, her inability to remember sounds is holding her back. She knows the letters of the alphabet and a few sight words.

In math Lisa can successfully complete simple addition and subtraction problems if she has her counters on her desk.

Lisa is not accepted by her peers and is constantly the victim of teasing and physical abuse. Her frustration seems to build up, and she frequently throws temper tantrums after a particularly bad day. Lisa receives some help from the **resource program** but needs continued support in the regular classroom.

Identifying the Problem Students such as Lisa can be a puzzle to teachers in the regular classroom. It is difficult to manage time so that such a child can receive the individual help she needs. Lisa learns at a slower rate than other children; she needs more practice to help her remember things, and frequent review is essential. Her attention span is short, and her tolerance for frustration is exceedingly low. She shows an inability to learn abstractly, as evidenced by her low skills in math and reading. In addition, Lisa has developed many unacceptable behaviors.

Strategies for Improving Behavior

It would be wise to confer first with the resource teacher to determine what help Lisa is getting in the resource room. The resource teacher may be using a method of teaching reading that is effective for Lisa. Also the regular classroom programs can be coordinated with activities in the resource room.

Lisa needs help with her behaviors immediately. Information that can be obtained from the resource teacher, the parents, the school psychologist, or other support personnel relative to Lisa's behavior pattern may be of assistance.

Strategies for Improving Academic Performance

Lower the level of academic tasks for Lisa. Start where she can enjoy a measure of success. Perhaps a starting point would be the sight words she already knows. Let her use word cards to form sentences that she can then read aloud. Add a new word and, as Lisa learns it, she can add it to her word box, which contains all the learned words.

Allow Lisa to record her own progress on a visual chart. Make the chart attractive and rewarding so it can serve as an incentive to study words.

The **language-experience approach** to reading would allow Lisa to use her own vocabulary in writing stories. She could dictate a simple story based on an experience. This could be typed by an aide or older students and made into her own book of stories.

Build in time every day for review of learned concepts, since Lisa may have trouble remembering things. This practice can take the form of partner games that involve her classmates.

Use "Proud Notes" to send home to Lisa's parents announcing good days, and special accomplishments.

Observe Lisa carefully in the classroom to learn what she does well. Provide reinforcement for these behaviors through praise, privileges, free time, and so forth.

Lowering expectations for Lisa's academic performance while at the same time working to get her behavior under control are the core of the strategies suggested. Rewarding appropriate behavior through successive approximations for both academic and social behaviors is a key to reversing the negative feedback Lisa is receiving for most activities associated with school. Because Lisa is far behind in academic skills, it will be necessary to simplify tasks, provide many opportunities for practice, and emphasize gains made. As Lisa begins to see progress, she will have more reason for exerting herself and will learn to gain attention through appropriate behavior. This behavior will then have a positive effect on her learning environment.

We have been discussing strategies for students with specific individual needs who are in regular classrooms. Suggestions have included modifying the goals, materials, methods, and environment in such a way that the regular teacher can continue to accommodate the needs of all students in the classroom. It is assumed that the regular teacher has available the support system to aid in mainstreaming students with problems. Resource help, special teachers, reading specialists, psychologists, speech and language professionals, parents, and administrators may be part of the support system in the district. These people will assist in developing total programs and monitoring their effectiveness. The strategies suggested in this chapter are intended to supplement the repertoire of teaching strategies already in use. Several writers presented a variety of suggestions and teaching techniques to use with students as an extra support system (Gearheart 1976; Bush and Giles 1977; Gearheart 1977; Gearheart and Weishahn 1976; Kirk, Kleibhan, and Lerner 1978). In summary, several basic principles for successful learning experiences for all students and particularly for students with special needs have been presented.

Setting Goals and Objectives

Involve students in planning their own learning goals. Frequently objectives must be simplified for students with special needs in order to be realistic. They need goals broken down into smaller steps and require more time to reach each objective.

Programming

Simplify goals by teaching in step-by-step tasks. We must be certain that the student has the necessary skills to do the task assigned. For example, can the student attend to a task for the required length of time? If sixty addition facts must be done in one minute, is the student physically able to write the required numerals in one minute?

Introduce one new concept at a time in a simple and consistent manner.

Involve the child in the instructional process, and use visual as well as auditory stimuli. Teach the concept before practice is begun independently.

Limit task and response demands for the student. For example, one worksheet with a single type of task and a single task response, such as simple addition facts requiring a written response $(3+2=\ )$, is much less confusing than a page of mixed addition and subtraction facts presented in a variety of ways (missing addends, and so forth).

Once a child has mastered a concept under your direct supervision, allow the child to practice the newly acquired skill in a variety of ways (drill, partner practice, or games). Use the cycle of *teach, practice* and *review*.

Evaluation

Design an ongoing evaluation plan so that progress of all students can be monitored. In this way, the effectiveness of a certain program, method, or technique can be ascertained for a specific student. Evaluation is the indicator by which decisions are made to modify programs and environments.

Involve students in evaluating their own progress. This can be done through self-recording, use of charts, interviews, and questionnaires on specific program goals.

Allow for alternative methods of evaluating progress. If students can opt for oral or written tests, essay or multiple-choice items, a variety of reporting systems, performance based on contractual arrangements, then students will not only be involved in their own learning, but they will also have opportunities to make commitments to proving mastery and proficiency of such learning.

Accept a variety of styles of providing a nurturing, positive environment for learning. Consciously acquire modes of reinforcing progress. Build in child-child support systems as a way of using the environment.

Learn to use the whole system in teaching exceptional students. Become familiar with the role of various personnel in the district, such as the psychologist, resource teacher, or medical specialist. Determine the kind of support available to provide service for children with special needs. Plan an efficient use of paraprofessionals, parents and peer tutors in the classroom.

Acquire a variety of alternate materials for exceptional students, such as tape recorders, language masters, and other audiovisual materials. Begin to develop a card file of resource ideas, games, and motivators, that work especially well in your classroom. Over a period of time you will have a rich fund of ideas to keep learning stimulating.

These are only a few general ideas to assist you in teaching exceptional students. As a creative teacher, you will be able to add many of your own strategies.

Our goal must be kept clearly before us—that of providing free, *appropriate* public education for all children in the least restrictive environment. The challenge implied in this charge rests squarely on the shoulders of regular educators who must provide for children with special needs so that they, too, might succeed.

References

Buchanan, C. 1963. *Programmed instruction.* New York: McGraw-Hill.
Bush, W. J., and Giles, M. T. 1977. *Aids to psycholinguistics teaching.* Columbus: Charles E. Merrill.
Cooper, J. 1974. *Measurement and analysis of behavioral techniques.* Columbus: Charles E. Merrill.
Gattegno, C. 1962. *Words in color.* Chicago: Learning Materials.
Gearheart, B. R. 1976. *Teaching the learning disabled.* St. Louis: C.V. Mosby.
———. 1977. *Learning disabilities educational strategies.* St. Louis: C.V. Mosby.
Gearheart, B. R., and Weishahn, M.W. 1977. *The handicapped child in the regular classroom.* St. Louis: C.V. Mosby.

Haring, N., ed. *Behavior of exceptional children.* 2d ed. Columbus: Charles E. Merrill.

Junkala, J. 1972. Task analysis and instructional alternatives. *Academic Therapy* 8:36.

———. 1973. Task analysis: the processing dimension. *Academic Therapy* 8:401–9.

Kirk, S. A., Kliebhan, J. M., and Lerner, J. W. 1978. *Teaching reading to slow and disabled learners.* Boston: Houghton Mifflin.

Lerner, J. 1976. *Children with learning disabilities.* Boston: Houghton Mifflin.

Lovitt, T. C. 1977. *In spite of my resistance—I've learned from children.* Columbus: Charles E. Merrill.

Lowenbraun, S., and Affleck, James. 1976. *Teaching mildly handicapped children in regular classrooms.* Columbus: Charles E. Merrill.

Ring, B. 1975. Memory processes and children with learning problems. *Academic Therapy* 11:111–16.

Stephens, T. M. 1970. *Directive teaching of children with learning and behavioral handicaps.* Columbus: Charles E. Merrill.

Sulzer, B., and Mayer, G. 1972. *Behavior modification procedures for school personnel.* Hinsdale, Ill.: Dryden Press.

Vance, H. B., and Hankins, W. E. 1975. Teaching interventions for defective auditory perception. *Academic Therapy* 11:69–78.

Wender, P. 1973. *The hyperactive child.* New York: Crown.

Teaching Students with Speech, Sensory, and Orthopedic Differences

part

3

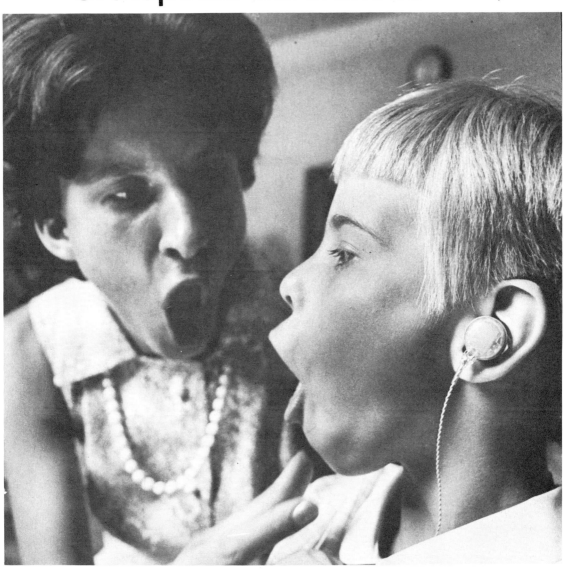

7 Teaching Students with Speech and Language Disorders

Students with speech and language disorders constitute the largest portion of the exceptional population in the public schools. According to recent estimates, some 3.5 percent of the students being served in educational programs today need some form of speech or language training. Public Law 94–142 specifies that these students must have their needs met in the least restrictive, most appropriate environment. For many, this environment is the regular classroom with special instruction from a speech and language clinician or a resource room teacher. However, for children whose speech and language problems are minimal, or for whom no service is available, speech and language training may become the instructional responsibility of the regular class teacher.

Before teachers can understand their role in the training of students with speech and language disorders, it is first necessary to become aware of the nature of such disorders and the role of professionals who specialize in this area. Therefore, it is necessary that teachers be able to identify and differentiate speech disorders from language disorders. Otherwise, referrals to professionals will be inadequate and unclear. Finally, it is important for teachers to become aware of what they can and should do in order to develop speech and language skills in students. Teachers must constantly balance the needs of students with restrictions imposed by time and training.

It is the purpose of this chapter to provide teachers with the information necessary to provide service to speech- and language-disordered students. The first section includes a brief description of the various speech disorders, information about the role of the speech clinician, and guidelines for enhancing speech. The second section contains a brief description of language disorders, information about the roles of the multidisciplinary team members in dealing with language disorders, and guidelines for enhancing language.

Differences in Speech and Language

Language problems and speech problems are inherently very different. Language deals with the understanding and formulation of thought, ideas, and meaning. Speech deals with the production of sounds and inflections. Language and speech differ as to the nervous systems primarily responsible for them. Language is a function of the **central nervous system**, while speech is a function of the **peripheral nervous system**. While both limit communication ability, perfect speech without meaningful thought is no more than parroting. On the other hand, without adequate speech, ideas and thoughts cannot be orally produced.

Perhaps differences in speech and language abilities can best be illustrated by the following summary, which shows how these various systems formulate a response.

1. Teacher asks, "Will you clean the chalkboard when you finish your math?"
2. Teacher's words become vibratory impulses, which are picked up by the hearing mechanism of the peripheral nervous system and transmitted to the brain.
3. Stimuli are received in the **temporal lobe** of the brain and the *language process is begun.*
4. The auditory analyzer in the temporal lobe separates the teacher's words from background noise.
5. Key words such as *clean, chalkboard, when, finish*, and *math* are retained while insignificant fillers such as *will, the*, and *you* are rejected.
6. The inflection pattern is interpreted as a question.
7. The key words are associated with their known equivalents.
   a. Chalkboard—something you write on, behind teacher's desk, green, perpendicular to floor, hanging on wall.
   b. Clean—erasers, water buckets, washing.
   c. When—after, must do something else first.
   d. Finish—complete, end of page.
   e. Math—assignments, numbers, addition.
8. Visual components are added to the words. Images of teacher's facial cues, locations of objects, etc., become involved.
9. Emotional components are associated to words, and inflection patterns.
   a. Clean—Me? I must be good, oh boy!
   b. Math—Difficult for me, I'll never get done.
   c. Inflections—Teacher's happy today.
10. Memory of past experiences is initiated. Past chalkboard cleaning and math finishing are remembered.
11. Key words, visual components, emotional reactions, and memories are synthesized in the brain and into the thought, "Yes, I will."
12. Thought is sent through an internal monitoring system to be re-analyzed for correctness.
13. Thought is sent by the brain to the peripheral nervous system and the *speech process is begun.*

14. Vocal cords adjust to appropriate tension or relaxation to make sounds.
15. Lungs force air into the breath stream.
16. Teeth, lips, and tongue form the sounds of the words.
17. The response has been made.

Teachers with speech- and language-disordered students in their classrooms should understand the differences in these disorders for two major reasons. First, since disorders of speech and disorders of language are functionally different, students with either of these problems will require different intervention strategies. Second, some students will have a combination of speech and language disorders and will need interventions for both problems simultaneously. Teachers must be able to differentiate speech disorders from language disorders in order to deliver the most appropriate interventions.

Speech Disorders

Speech is defined as the production of the sounds and rhythmic patterns that convey a person's ideas to others. Speech is considered disordered when its use in communicating those ideas is "conspicuous, unintelligible, or unpleasant" (Van Riper 1972). Although the speaker of English is given some latitude in speech production differences, neither the teacher nor the child will tolerate deviancies which are too great. Unintelligibility is not "cute," and if compounded with other problems of learning, such as lowered intelligence or achievement, it creates a negative impression.

Definitions of Speech Disorders

The most easily recognizable and most often referred speech problems are disorders of articulation. These disorders are related to the substitution, distortion, omission, or insertion of a sound in speech. For example, substitutions are found if a "thound ith thometimeth" interchanged with another "thound." Distortions may take many forms, including slushy or mushy consonant production ("pode pa" for "forest park"). Omissions are characterized by sounds that are missing for reasons other than dialect. Many sounds thought to be omitted may actually be pronounced, but their production is too weak to be heard by the listener. A child who says "'ky is b'ue," for "sky is blue," may be understood quite well in a quiet setting, but may become unintelligible among classroom noise. The final type of articulation disorder, that of insertions, involves additions of sounds to the standard patterns of words. "TSusie, look at that treehee," involves two such additions.

Young children show articulation deficiencies in varying degrees. Speech to them is like a new toy that can bring them praise for saying something "cute." By school age, however, misarticulations are no longer praiseworthy, but are often punished by both peers and adults. Students with articulation disorders find it difficult to be understood not only in factual communication, but in emotional communication as well. Tantrums, screaming, and loss of control are often the result. Such behaviors are seen in the case of Joe.

> Joe is a second-grade student with severe articulation disorders. Joe not only substitutes *w* for *r*, *f* for *th*, and other consonants, but he also exhibits such mushy speech that he is often misunderstood by the teacher and other students. The teacher has observed that Joe often throws a tantrum when other students cannot understand him. When the teacher asks him to repeat himself, Joe either refuses or bursts into tears. Joe's articulation is worst when another student has bullied him or made fun of him and he tries to report it to the teacher.

A second type of speech disorder that is typical of the young child is the time disorder called stuttering. Conversational speech for all but the most precisely fluent speaker is filled with hesitations, *huhs, uhms, you knows*, and repetition. Students whose timing problems go beyond the bounds of normal dysfluency are considered to have stuttering disorders.

Stuttering is a rather mysterious speech disorder; its causative factors and the training procedures for dealing with it are not universally agreed upon. The limits of stuttering versus those of normal dysfluency are not clearly defined. The age at which a child becomes a stutterer rather than a trial-and-error user of speech is also debated. What *is* agreed upon is that stuttering is an interrupted flow of speech production. In some cases it appears only in speech, but not in song. In other cases it is evident in stressful situations, but not in relaxed ones. It is characterized by oscillations, fixations, repetitions, and prolongations of sounds and syllables. Embarrassment for both speaker and listener may occur with stuttering speech.

The reactions to stuttering by the stuttering student may take a variety of forms. Such students may "block" or pause prior to certain words, use superstitious, nonverbal gestures such as finger-snapping to get speech patterns started, employ routinized sentence beginnings such as *well* or *uhm*, or stop speaking altogether. These reactions vary from student to student, and are often found in combinations. Tom is a student who stutters. His case study illustrates some of his frustrations with his problem.

Tom is a student of high-school age. He has been called a "stutterer" since he entered school. Although Tom knows he has a speech problem, he hates to be called "stutterer" as he feels it calls more attention to his problem than is necessary. Tom tells of a recent experience with a female student in his class. "One d-d-day I w-w-was t-t-t-talking to this really pretty g-g-girl. S-S-S-She acted like she m-m-might go out with m-m-me. Th-Th-This b-b-b-boy in the cl-cl-class came up to us and s-s-s-s-said, 'don't talk to him he st-st-st-stutters.' I was really m-m-m-mad. N-N-Now nobody will e-e-e-ever go out with m-m-m-me."

The third type of speech problem, called voice disorder, consists of three distinct categories of disorders related to speech tone. These disorders—-intensity, pitch, and quality—are often the most difficult of all speech problems to remediate. If the vocal tone varies too far from an acceptable level, the social stigma may be intense. This particular disorder must be treated in conjunction with self-concept enhancement.

The voice disorder of intensity includes problems of vocal loudness, weakness, and tremor. These disorders are often caused by vocal or emotional stress, or by habituated patterns of speech. Students with intensity problems who speak too loudly or too softly catch the attention of teachers, but attention is usually given in a negative manner.

Disorders of pitch are related to age and sex and carry connotations of more than vocal deviancies. While it would be expected that a boy of five would speak in a high-pitched voice, a man of thirty-five would be expected to speak in low tones. Women of thirty-five, however, would be conspicuous with a similar bass voice. Consistent monotone is not an expected vocal tone at any age in either sex. Pitch breaks or sudden upward or downward tonal shifts are tolerated under extreme stress or tension, but in the absence of tension, embarrassment may result.

Voice disorders of quality include hoarse, breathy, falsetto, strident or harsh, denasal, and hypernasal voices. These disorders are extremely difficult to retrain. Unless a physiological cause, such as nodules on the vocal cords or palate abnormalities, can be found, therapists are often at a loss for correction procedures. Teachers should be careful to rule out dialectical differences, temporary colds, or vocal strain before referring a student for voice quality disorders.

In order to select appropriate intervention strategies for articulation problems, stuttering, or voice disorders, teachers must understand the nature of the underlying problems. The following section discusses the types of speech problems that are often found in the school-age student.

The Nature of Speech Problems

Speech is composed of two basic elements, each of which must be mastered for verbal production of thoughts. These elements, phonology and prosody, should be understood by teachers of speech-disordered students.

The first element, phonology, consists of the sounds of speech in isolation without meaning. Sounds are combined into patterns called syllables or words. Users of English phonology employ thirty-six different sounds in speech, including both consonants and vowels. Vowels are formed with a minimal modification of the breath stream by selective placement of the tongue. Consonants, on the other hand, involve major modifications of the breath stream by the lips, teeth, or tongue.

It is most important for students with phonology problems to *feel* the production of their speech. Experts in speech pathology often deemphasize the role of self-hearing or external monitoring and emphasize the role of tactile and kinesthetic cues. The lack of such cues is illustrated by a completely numbed mouth, teeth, and tongue after an appointment with the dentist. Speech production is far more difficult under these conditions than under those so noisy that self-monitoring cannot take place.

The second element of speech is prosody. It involves the music, rhythm, and cadence of speech. In English, speech is communicated not only through sounds, but also through inflections. Higher pitch or ascending inflections are used at the end of questions, to add emphasis to words, and in exclamatory remarks. Lower pitch or descending inflections are found in statements, and many emotional comments. Inflection patterns give speech a musical quality. Students whose first language is not English use inflections and rhythms that are different from the standard. Students whose cadence of speech is broken or dysrhythmic are often called "stutterers."

Teachers of students with phonology and prosody problems can help them in several ways. Suggestions for enhancing the speech environment, providing practice, and providing reinforcement are included later in this section.

Roles of Professionals in Speech Disorders

Treatment of speech disorders is primarily the domain of the speech clinician. These professionals should assume responsibility for several aspects of speech training. Their tasks include—

Helping students to become aware of speech errors.

Focusing attention on the correct production of speech.

Helping students with correct production of sounds in isolation, in syllables, in words, and in sentences.

Providing feedback and reinforcement for both correct and incorrect speech productions.

Providing a nonthreatening environment where students can practice their new speech patterns.

Communicating to classroom teachers the type of speech therapy being done, and the techniques that may be useful in generalizing the new skill to the environment.

Although the speech clinician is responsible for the majority of speech therapy with a child, the teacher shares some of the responsibility. Initially, referrals must come to the clinician from classroom teachers. Later, practice and reduction of environmental tension become major responsibilities of the classroom teacher. Teachers should not assume, nor be expected to assume, the clinician's role, but should use techniques that enhance the student's speech performance.

Because some of the techniques discussed here may not be applicable to all speech-disordered students, teachers must follow this basic rule: *When in doubt, ask the clinician.*

Guidelines for Enhancing Speech

Referral of problems. The primary responsibility for referral of speech problems falls on classroom teachers. The following suggestions should be helpful in making an appropriate referral.

1. Ask the question, "Does the problem involve the production of sounds or rhythms rather than the use of thoughts and ideas?"
2. Note any specific errors of speech production that have been observed.
3. Supply any emotional or medical histories that are pertinent.
4. Do not refer dialectical differences unless these are causing problems for the student.
5. Consider the conspicuousness, unintelligibility, and unpleasantness of the speech as the criteria for referral.

Enhancing the speech environment. With minimal effort, teachers can do a great deal to enhance the speech environment for a speech-disordered student. The following suggestions could be used for all types of speech disorders.

1. Serve as a good speech model, using well-articulated sounds and inflection patterns.
2. Face the student when talking, to provide visual pronunciation cues.
3. Keep classroom noise to a minimum so the student can hear the sounds of speech.
4. Encourage other students to speak clearly and not to ridicule.
5. Do not over-emphasize speech patterns or raise the level of intensity when speaking to a student. Speak in a normal tone of voice.

6. Refrain from announcing the time of speech therapy to the entire class. Allow the student to exit and enter class as inconspicuously as possible.
7. Reduce pressures to speak without errors. Establish a classroom atmosphere that is relaxed and pleasant.
8. Reduce the requirements of oral reading, especially during the initial phases of therapy.
9. During early therapy, do not attempt to correct or call attention to speech errors. Practice and correction should be saved for later.
10. Do not expect overnight changes. A speech pattern that has been practiced incorrectly for years will take some time to change.

Providing practice.   After students master speech patterns in the therapy situation, they should begin to practice them in the classroom. After consulting with the clinician, initiate any of the following that are appropriate for the student's particular problem.

1. Have students use a tape recorder to practice speech. Allow them to play back the tape to listen for correct and incorrect productions.
2. When students make mistakes in speech, correct the errors by asking them to *feel* the correct sound.
3. When students are speaking of events or emotions particularly important to them, ignore speech errors. Never correct a joyous or excited student.
4. Provide books or stories that accentuate difficult sounds. For example, use "Sammy and Susie Snake."
5. Do not answer for the students if they become inarticulate or dys-rhythmic—this deprives them of necessary practice.
6. Use flashcard words containing the difficult sounds for reading.
7. Try the **neurological impress** or shadow-reading technique. In this technique, the teacher reads orally with the student and serves as a model.
8. Practice the difficult sounds in phonics drills.
9. Use puppet shows or plays that involve the students as actors.
10. Include words in practice that have the difficult sound in initial, medial, and final positions.
11. Do not equate practice with threat. Relax the tension. If students become overanxious or frustrated, stop the practice.

Providing reinforcement

1. Liberally use sincere social praise for correct speech production.
2. Avoid anger when a student misproduces speech.
3. Do not judge a student as intellectually inferior due to faulty speech production.

4. Ask parents to follow through with class techniques.
5. Use sincere social praise for noteworthy achievements other than speech.
6. Encourage other students to recognize the advances made in correct speech. Reinforce them for doing so.

These suggestions for enhancing speech do not assume that the regular teacher should become the primary therapist for a speech-disordered student. They do, however, provide the regular educator with some practical guidelines for helping students improve their speech in the regular classroom setting.

Language is defined as the formulation of thoughts and ideas and their synthesis into patterns that can be communicated in either verbal or nonverbal form. Language is considered disordered when thoughts are incoherent or inappropriate. Language disorders are characterized by two problems: (1) the inability to understand or interpret what is heard and seen, and (2) the inability to synthesize and express information in an appropriate communicative response. Language is a function of the central nervous system and involves the brain's interpretation of cues from the hearing, visual, tactile, kinesthetic, olfactory and gustatory senses. It must be present before meaningful speech, writing, gesturing, or body movement can take place. **Language Disorders**

Language disorders can be divided into three basic categories—different, delayed, and deviant language. The first, different language, is not a disorder at all; it is only perceived as such by some people. This type of language is characteristic of cultures or segments of the population who speak nonstandard English. While different language may handicap its users in some situations, not using it would certainly handicap them in others. Students who have a language difference are often taught standard English as a second language, thus protecting the integrity and usefulness of their difference. Language difference can be seen in the case of Annie. *Definitions of Language Disorders*

> Annie is a black student sixteen years old. She asks for "two paper," has "three pencil," and is "runnin" and "datin" around. Annie asks "whatsurename?" and "whereyagoin?" Her language difference is quite acceptable in the neighborhood in which she lives, but not so acceptable in other neighborhoods. There, her language makes her stand out and accentuates her difference.

The second category of language disorders is that of delayed language. Delayed language is characterized by lack of quantity among various parts of speech. Although all parts of speech are present and are found to be ordered correctly, some parts of speech are not present in the abundance necessary for adequate communication (Blount 1968). Whereas a normally speaking six- or seven-year-old may describe a dog as *big*, an elephant as *huge*, a skyscraper as *gigantic*, King Kong as *colossal*, and the earth as *stupendous*, a language-delayed student of the same age might call them all *big*. Other descriptive words, especially those with abstract referents or degrees of quality may be insufficient. Older students and many adults use profanity in place of descriptions in which they have delayed language.

Delayed language is attributable to several possible causes. Lowered intellectual ability, such as retardation, is a primary cause. Environmental deprivation, lack of early language stimulation, isolation, illness, abuse, and neglect can also be factors. Teachers should take care, however, not to confuse language delay with language difference, as some very rich language environments may be different from the standard. Glenna is illustrative of a student with language delay.

> Glenna is a ten-year-old student with a language delay. Glenna described a recent trip to the zoo as follows: "One day we went to the zoo. We saw lots of animals. They were real pretty. I ate lots of stuff and got sick. I want to go back."
>
> Glenna's sister, a nine-year-old without language delay, described the same trip somewhat more graphically. "Last week the whole family went on a trip to the zoo. We saw lions, tigers, elephants, and crawley snakes. I really liked the wild animals the best. I was most impressed with their fur and gigantic teeth. Glenna ate too much cotton candy and peanuts and got too ill to stay. I certainly hope we can go back to the zoo next month. If we can, it won't be too soon for me."

The last category of language disorders, deviant language, includes a wide variety of problems. The intensity of these disorders ranges from mild to severe. The following is a list of deviant language disorders found in the school-age student:

Telegraphic speech.   The student with this disorder speaks with as few words as possible, as if saving words on a telegram. Nouns and verbs are the primary components. When asked why you use bandages, the response might be "hurt," or "hurt finger," or "Mommy fix," or "better." This type of disorder is characterized by lack of descriptive words and functional fillers.

Jargon speech.   Jargon speech is much like telegraphic speech with the inflection pattern of English added to some true words. Nonsense words, syllables, or sounds are interspersed with nouns and verbs to give rhythm and cadence to speech. Typical of very young children of nine to eighteen months, jargon is considered deviant in the school-age student (Berry 1969).

A student with jargon speech might describe a meal at a restaurant in the following manner: "De ate da do um e table. E a ume," instead of "We ate the food at a table. It was yummy." Notice the preservation of the inflection patterns and rhythms of speech despite the use of only nouns and verbs.

Echoing. Consistent echolalia is the meaningless repetition of the words of others. If asked, "What is your name?," an echolalic student will answer, "What is your name?" One thing a teacher of an echolalic can count on is a response, albeit an inappropriate one.

Perseveration. Perseverative speech is also a repetitive deviancy but differs from echolalia. Perseverative students repeat the same word or phrase over and over as if it were new to them each time. Such a student might call every animal in a deck of animal pictures "racoon" or "chicken" or the name of whatever picture came up first.

Circumlocutions and anomias. These language deviancies involve the inability to use the name of something (anomia). Instead, the student will describe the needed word (circumlocution). Such a student might give a response for the word *snow*, as "that white stuff that's cold."

Word-sequencing problems or word salads. Word salad speech is a jumbled non-sequential form of speech resembling a tossed salad of English. A student with this deviancy does not use the standard constructions of the language, but places verbs before nouns, adjectives after verbs, articles after nouns, and so on. Even if the words themselves are correct, the order is so impaired that thought patterns cannot be appropriately communicated.

Internal feedback problem. In the process of thought formulation there appears to be a feedback system through which people can monitor what they are about to say. This system saves us from many social faux pas and lost friends. In students with internal feedback problems, the results can be socially disastrous even if grammatically correct. If students blurt out the first thought that occurs to them, they may unintentionally tell friends with whom they are angry that they hate them or never want to see them again. A teacher who can imagine saying the first thing that comes to mind when he or she is angry with the principal can empathize with the problem of this student.

Slow-motion processing. While the language interpretation and synthesis processes move at an incredible pace in most individuals, there are some in whom it appears to move in slow motion. Such students may stare blankly with an open mouth for several seconds, or even minutes, when asked a question. They respond with an appropriate answer at an inappropriate time. Because of their slowness, they are often viewed as retarded even when they are not. Without undue pressure, these students will eventually respond with a correct answer.

It will be noted that problems of language such as elective mutism, shyness, twinisms, and psychotic speech, have been omitted from the list of language deviancies. These problems are not actually language problems, but emotional ones. If such problems are present, a teacher would be wise to seek psychological assistance for the student.

Language deviancies, then, are characterized by a disturbance in the elements of language. Language-deviant students have great difficulty in processing thoughts and information. As a result, they often miss portions of important class discussions or presentations. In these students, appropriate appreciation of humor, nuance, and the social implications of language is drastically impaired. Their use of abstractions and reasoning skills is also faulty.

Just as it is important for teachers to understand the underlying causes of speech disorders, it is important for them to understand the underlying causes of language disorders. The following section will discuss three elements of language: morphology, syntax, and conceptualization. Each element of language must be understood before appropriate intervention strategies can be selected.

The Nature of Language Problems   Language is composed of three basic elements, each of which must be understood and used correctly for meaningful communication. These elements— morphology, syntax, and conceptualization—should be understood by teachers who work with language-disordered students.

The first of these elements, morphology, consists of the smallest units of language that have meaning. Morphemes are the roots of language structure. Often called root words in language arts, they serve to expand vocabulary, give quality and quantity to thoughts, and enhance reading and other academic abilities. However, morphology, or meaning of isolated thoughts, is not sufficient for appropriate communication. Students with telegraphic or jargon speech have command of morphology, but their language is far from standard communication patterns. In order to become more efficient language users, students must incorporate morphemes into orderly patterns of language called syntax. Frankie is an example of a student with a morphology problem. Note the limited use of all parts of speech, especially description words.

Frankie is a fifth-grade student with morphology problems. The speech and language clinician has termed him language delayed, his teacher thinks he might be retarded, and his peers have labeled him dumb. Recently Frankie told his teacher "I read the books badder than anybody. I get gooder soon. I like the book 'bout horse. It real good." Needless to say, Frankie reads much like he speaks. His teacher realizes that if words are absent from his speaking vocabulary, they will also be absent from his reading vocabulary.

Syntax (more commonly called grammar) consists of a multitude of patterns and constructions used by speakers of English. English syntax is based on the elaboration of a primary noun-verb sentence pattern such as *John went*. By elaborating the pattern with the addition of phrases, clauses, and other parts of speech, it could become, "*John*, who was a lovely boy, *went* to the town over the hill." The same basic pattern could also become, "The *john*, which everyone in the campsite used, suddenly *went* out of order." Syntactic elaboration can change the meaning of morphemes as well as the order of words.

Deficiencies in syntactical skills result in sequencing and order problems. When the deficiency affects the understanding of syntax, the abilities of following directions, repeating stimulus sentences, and formulating correct answers will be impaired. The student may show signs of slow-motion processing or word-order problems. When the syntactical deficits are related more to the use of syntax rather than its understanding, the student will be able to comprehend correctly, but may use output of the word salad variety.

There is much controversy among professionals in language pathology as to the age at which a child should become a fluent user of syntax. While developmentalists maintain that some constructions and elaborations do not enter the language structure until age six or after (Barrie-Blackley 1973; Jensen and Rohvner 1965), **psycholinguists** cite studies showing all constructions and elaborations present on command by age four (McCabe, Levin, and Wolff 1974). For the school-age student, syntactical deficits should be considered serious ones and training should be begun as early as possible. Tony is a student with a syntax disorder. The lack of grammatical sequencing is apparent when he tries to communicate even the simplest ideas.

Tony is an eight-year-old boy with grammatical sequencing problems. Tony's teacher reports that his descriptions of events are usually out of order, making him difficult to understand in even routine conversation. Tony tells the other students that "Wrong is it to line the break to lunch," and "Play students on swings at playground." Even when his syntax is most fluent, he reverses many parts of speech in every sentence.

Although syntax is a more advanced element of language than is morphology, the third element, conceptualization, is the ultimate requirement for efficient use of language. Conceptualization involves the incorporation of meaning and order with the use of language in social situations. Interpretation and use of subtlety, humor, **divergent thinking**, **convergent thinking**, logic, and reasoning, are necessary processes.

Students with deficits in conceptualization are often ridiculed for their inappropriate responses to social situations. Often literalists in their use of language, they interpret language subtleties such as, "He's all tied up at the office," as a man tied in his chair with a rope. In the academic area, such students often call words far better than they comprehend them, compute without understanding the mathematical processes involved, and memorize facts in social studies and science rather than generalizing relationships of events. Socially, their laughter is often inappropriate, they do not respond to rebuff or affection, their social reinforcers are concrete, and their lack of friends is a teacher's nightmare. Such students often excel in subjects that require little or no language; they tend to prefer art, music, mechanical arts, and physical activities over the more academic subjects. They are often viewed as hostile or aggressive students who use physical strength or bullying techniques to gain attention. Ava is a student with a conceptual language problem. The overlap of her language disability to other academic subjects is apparent in the following case study.

> Ava is an eighth-grade student with conceptual language disorders. Although Ava can read orally fairly well, her comprehension of what is read is very poor. Further, Ava does not generalize much of what she reads or hears to "real life" situations. Once someone told Ava that pregnant women ate a lot. Ava did not eat for a week for fear she would get pregnant. Another time Ava was read a story about a little girl who got lost in the woods. Now Ava thinks everyone who goes to the woods will get lost.
>
> Ava's teacher describes her as quiet and shy. She rarely participates in class discussion and appears to dread any classes in which she must verbally participate. She enjoys music and art classes, but is developing a fear of the science labs in which she must apply the concepts she has supposedly learned in class.

Roles of Professionals in Language Disorders

Whereas treatment of speech disorders is primarily the responsibility of the speech clinician, the treatment of language disorders requires a team effort of regular education teachers, special education teachers, and speech clinicians. Each professional should be responsible in varying degrees for the diagnosis and training of these students.

The speech clinician, by training, should be the primary professional responsible for language remediation; however, the itinerant service delivery system used by most clinicians makes this impossible. One or two hours of instruction per week are simply not sufficient for language training. Therefore, the clinician's primary role is in assessment and consultation. Major tasks for the clinician include—

Determining the type of problem through the use of standardized test instruments.

Determining the severity of the problem and the amount of treatment necessary.

Communicating the problem to teachers who will be training the student.

Serving as a member of the team that will recommend placement, write IEP's, and evaluate the student's progress.

Conducting yearly evaluations of the student's language growth.

Consulting on a continuing basis with regular and special education teachers who are involved with the student.

If the language problem is of a moderate to severe nature, the special education teacher will, in all probability, become the primary trainer. In some school districts, the service delivery system is the resource room; others use self-contained, full-time, or part-time models. Often the certification of the special education teacher will be in either mental retardation or learning disabilities or both. Sadly, when this is the case, the child may be labeled as mentally retarded or learning disabled to qualify for the program. Despite their inabilities in communication, however, language-disordered students are often of normal intelligence. Although their disorders may cause them to perform poorly on psychological and achievement tests, teachers should exercise caution in labeling them as intellectually inferior.

When language-disordered students become the responsibility of special education teachers, their goals include the following:

Selecting a training method that is most appropriate for meeting the particular language needs of the students

Conducting any further assessment necessary to determine the best training method

Recording data to illustrate the student's progress in language skills

Evaluating the data to determine the success of the training

Serving on the team during initial placement, IEP development, and reevaluation

Returning the student to the regular classroom for increasing amounts of time as soon as possible

Helping the regular teacher to carry out a language program with the student

Helping the regular teacher with techniques that will enhance the language environment

Consulting with the speech clinician for techniques and reevaluations

Helping the parents of the student to select ancillary services (tutors, private therapists, summer programs, etc.) and to continue the language training in the home

Serving as a public relations person among regular teachers, involving them to the fullest extent in language enhancement programs

In no way, however, should special education teachers be solely responsible for the training of language-disordered students. Regular classroom teachers should retain a major role in treatment. It will be the regular education teacher who initiates a referral for the student and, later, carries out much of the required training through incorporation of language into academic subject matter. The following guidelines for enhancing language provide suggestions to the regular teacher for fulfilling this role.

Guidelines for Enhancing Language

Because some of the techniques discussed here may not be applicable to every language-disordered student, teachers should consult with either the speech clinician or special education teacher before using them.

Making the Placement Decision

Referral.   The first responsibility of the classroom teacher in the placement decision is the initiation of a referral. This referral will be sent to speech services, special education, psychological services, or a combination thereof. In preparing an adequate referral for a language-disordered student, the teacher should state the effect of the problem on the student's (1) academic tasks, (2) social interactions, and (3) communication abilities. If a language problem is suspected, details of the type of problem, the behavioral characteristics, severity, and nature of the disorder should be stated.

Team membership.   The second role of the regular teacher in placement decisions involves service as a team member after evaluation. The team should include the regular education teacher, special education teacher, speech clinician, a representative of psychological services, principal, and parents. The student may be included when appropriate. This team is charged with the responsibility of determining placement and formulating the IEP for the student. It also sets a date for reevaluation of the student's progress.

Mainstreaming. The third responsibility of the regular teacher is to work closely with the special education teacher or speech clinician to insure that the student will remain in the regular class as much as possible. Regular teachers should take it upon themselves to weigh the amount of time they can spend with the student in language skills to assure that productive and appropriate education can occur.

On-going assessment. The final decision-making role of the regular education teacher is that of on-going assessment. Teachers should be prepared to monitor the progress of the student in their classroom. Progress or lack of it, should be reported to the teacher or clinician who is working intensively with the student.

Many of the techniques used for enhancing a speech environment are also useful in enhancing a language environment. For example, the teacher should—

Enhancing the Language Environment

Serve as a model for appropriate use of language

Encourage other students not to ridicule the student

De-emphasize pressures to use language fluently

Keep classroom noise to a minimum

In addition, the following techniques should prove beneficial for the student:

1. Provide language-stimulation activities that are appropriate by encouraging the students to relate events and emotions that have meaning. Further, provide in-class situations that are interesting and exciting, and discuss them with the students.
2. Explain new concepts clearly yet briefly. Do not overwhelm the student; make sure one concept is understood before moving to the next.
3. Use visual illustrations whenever possible. Demonstrations, experiments, visual aids, or drawings can often be more beneficial than words.
4. Be aware of the limits of the student's understanding. For example, it will be difficult to understand the nature of absorption if a student does not know what a sponge is.
5. Accept slow-motion processing problems of language. Do not exert undue pressures on students to respond to new information quickly.
6. Ignore inappropriate statements or questions generated by the students; give sincere praise for appropriate responses.
7. Inform parents of ways in which they can enhance language use in the home. Plan the strategy of home intervention with the help of the special education teacher or speech clinician.

The majority of the language training carried out by the regular education teacher should be in conjunction with the academic subjects being taught. Reading, language arts, mathematics, social studies, art, music, and movement, each lend themselves particularly well to the training of language skills.

Reading and language arts

1. When working with word attack skills, use grossly different sound patterns such as *dog* and *map*. Later move to finer discriminations such as *map* and *mat*.
2. Associate new words in reading with an object or concept. Do not assume that a student knows the meaning of a word just by "word calling" it.
3. Ask students to define words they read. For example:

   > the—specific one
   >
   > dog—animal that barks
   >
   > ran—moved in fast motion
   >
   > up—a direction of climbing
   >
   > a—nonspecific one
   >
   > street—a road that goes from one place to another

4. Ask students to define entire sentences. The previous sentence defines as: "A specific animal that barks moved in fast motion in a direction of climbing a non-specified road that goes from one place to another."
5. Use sentences with omitted words for the student to fill in. Omit words or parts of speech with which the student has difficulty.
6. Use rapid naming drills such as "As quickly as you can, name all the things you would find on a farm,"(in the city, etc.).
7. Use guessing games as reading stories. For example, try a story that describes something, then ask the student what that something is.
8. Ask a student to describe another student in class. Use this as an experience story. Then ask another student to read the story and draw a picture of the student who was described. Check the accuracy of the picture from the story.
9. Use short true-false statements for reading material. For example: "A horse can fly." Ask the child to describe the absurdity.
10. Ask children to find the absurdities in stories such as, "In June, Mary and Susan were playing. They went to the pool to build a snowman."
11. Write telegrams to friends conveying ideas in the fewest possible words. Try telegrams to convey the meanings of stories read or events seen.
12. Use short paragraphs followed by multiple-choice questions that require language and logical thought. For example: "If you have passed a gas station three miles back and now you see the gas gauge reads empty, what will happen?"

You should go straight and hope for another station.

You should turn around to go to the station you passed.

You will run out of gas.

You may run out of gas.

13. Have students watch a TV show, such as a daytime serial. Have them tell or write possible endings or next episodes.

14. Copy a story and cut it into sentence-length strips. Have students arrange strips to form a sequenced, coherent story.

15. Use newspaper stories without the headlines. Have students make headlines or choose correct headlines for each story.

16. Select untitled stories for reading. Have the students create appropriate titles.

17. Use many types of stories for reading. Include those with serious intents. Ask students what words the author uses to convey the mood of the story.

18. Use "how to" stories about certain projects (cooking, building, etc.). Have students do the projects after reading the stories.

19. Even with young children, use directions as a part of reading. Assemble different toys, equipment, etc., using written directions.

20. Use reading treasure hunts so that the prize may only be found by reading the clues.

Social studies

1. Convert any ideas given in the reading section to appropriate social studies lessons.

2. Have students respond to "What famous *people* might say" questions. For example, Columbus might say, "I need three ships to discover America."

3. Use real people or fictitious characters as persons of social interest. Make sure students understand the difference in the two.

4. When studying various states and countries, have students act out plays, speaking about the states or countries as they feel that someone from that place might speak.

5. Use a radio in a variety of ways. This simple language aid can provide—

    a. News for—
        1) current events
        2) setting up a classroom newsroom
        3) practicing interview techniques
        4) formats for classroom broadcasting

b. Music for—
　　1) movement activities
　　2) listening activities for remembering words to songs
　　3) pantomime to songs
　　4) acting activities to illustrate songs
c. Commercials for—
　　1) finding addresses on a city map
　　2) consumer studies
　　3) simple jingles to use as stories
　　4) humorous situations
d. Public service announcements
6. Write a story as the cavemen or Egyptians would write it using pictures or rebuses.

Mathematics

1. Convert any ideas given in the reading or social studies sections to appropriate math lessons.
2. Use story problems liberally.
3. Use verbal mediation in approaching new mathematical procedures. In this approach the teacher—
　　a. talks through the problem in the simplest terms (example: "First, I move the decimal, then, I . . .");
　　b. has the student say the talk-through with him or her;
　　c. introduces the actual problem, which they talk through together;
　　d. has the student talk through the problem alone, orally;
　　e. has the student talk through the problem alone, whispering;
　　f. has the student talk through the problem alone, silently;
　　g. has the student work the problem;
　　h. goes back to *a* if the problem is incorrect;
　　i. introduces a different problem with exactly the same talk-through if the problem is correct.
4. Ask the student to explain both *what* is being done and *why* it is being done as math problems are learned.
5. Capitalize on consumer problems. These will be very important for the language-disordered student. Particularly stress the concepts of—
　　a. money
　　b. time
　　c. space
　　d. distance
　　e. greater/lesser than
　　f. measurement
　　g. estimation

6. Do not expect drill on math facts to generalize to mathematical concepts. Concepts, as well as practical uses of mathematical processes, should be taught.
7. Use problems that require logic and reasoning skills. Be careful, however, to—
   a. present the problem-solving skills needed in a sequencing strategy;
   b. present sufficient examples (often as many as fifteen to twenty) employing the same type of logic strategy;
   c. reserve exceptions to the logic strategy until the strategy has been thoroughly mastered.
8. Include demonstrations and visual cues with verbal skills. Allow students to demonstrate knowledge through visual as well as verbal explanations.
9. View mnemonic devices such as finger counting as essential crutches for language-disordered students. Do not attempt to eliminate them, but encourage students to become efficient and effective in their use.
10. Keep in mind that the language problems of the students will cause future limitations. Gear the selection of the mathematical curriculum to the needs imposed by these limitations.
11. Encourage students to ask questions every time they do not understand a concept. Only by asking questions will a language-disordered student perceive the logic of mathematics.

The arts: music, movement, arts

1. Convert any ideas given in the reading, social studies, or math sections to appropriate activities in these areas.
2. Use the verbal mediation approach described in the mathematics activities, when appropriate.
3. Use study carrels for students whose language becomes confused in noisy or large-group situations.
4. Encourage students to "copy" other students' projects initially. Just be certain that the students they copy from are good models.
5. Go over directions individually with students *before* a project or activity is begun.
6. Put directions on a tape recording. Allow students to replay the directions as often as needed in order to follow them correctly. Use the tape for self-correcting when the project or activity is finished.
7. Pantomime parts of speech. For example, each student could act out a different part of speech. These become a sentence play.
8. Act out a story in mime. Have other students write the script down.
9. Ad lib a familiar story with puppets doing the talking. Later use a totally original extemporaneous story.

10. Tell a story without words, using cartoon art sketches.
11. Make a "Me" collage to describe self.
    a. life history through pictures
    b. emotions through color or texture
12. Make an abstract collage from tissue or other material. Have students describe what they see in the abstract forms.
13. Bring in an abstract print or a famous painting. Have students discuss its meaning to them.
14. Take a common object, such as a crayon. Have students draw the object as they see it and then describe everything that can be done with it in dance or mime.
15. Use cards with different emotions pictured. Select a musical instrument to fit that emotion. Compose a dance to the music of that instrument, i.e., happy—drum—fast movements.
16. Using a voice rhythm given by the teacher, have students draw a continuous line, stopping, starting, and accenting the line according to the inflection of the teacher's voice.
17. In any singing or musical activity, concentrate less on the perfection of word and note and more on rhythm and feeling.
18. Adapt familiar phrases in songs to teach new language constructions. In "Old McDonald," "on his farm," could become "in the field," "on the roof," etc.
19. Sing an opera with one word such as *Oh* that has various nuance patterns. Sing the word in as many ways as possible to convey many different meanings. Examples: disgust, flirtation, fear, etc.
20. Have the students make up hand or body movements to match with words in a song. This can be done as a round or without the words as students become proficient.
21. After a song has been learned well, have the students sing only every third word, in rhythm, retaining the rest of the words in their memory.
22. Have students photograph things or events in the environment that they do not fully understand or have the concept of. Discuss the photographs with them individually or in a show-and-tell session with other students, describing the photographs.

These suggestions for enhancing language should provide a teacher with some ways to help the language-disordered student through the regular curriculum. Many of the suggestions could be used with all students, while others would be more appropriately used on an individual basis. While regular classroom teachers should not be expected to provide the bulk of language services to language-disordered students, they should augment and supplement these services whenever possible. Through the combined efforts of speech and language clinicians, special education teachers, and regular education teachers, both speech- and language-disordered students can receive a communication program appropriate to their needs.

References

Barrie-Blackley, S. 1973. Six-year-old children's understanding of sentences adjoined with time adverbs. *Journal of Psycholinguistic Research* 2:153–65.

Berry, M.F. 1969. *Language disorders of children: the bases and diagnosis.* New York: Appleton-Century-Crofts.

Blount, W.R. 1968. Language and the more severely retarded: a review. *American Journal of Mental Deficiency* 73:21–29.

Hammill, D.D., and Bartel, N.R. 1975. *Teaching children with learning and behavior problems.* Boston: Allyn and Bacon.

Jensen, A.R., and Rohvner, W.D., Jr. 1965. Syntactical mediation of serial and paired-association learning as a function of age. *Child Development* 36:601–608.

McCabe, A.E., Levin, J.R., and Wolff, P. 1974. The role of overt activity in children's sentence production. *Journal of Experimental Child Psychology* 17:107–14.

Van Riper, C. 1972. *Speech correction: Principles and methods.* Englewood Cliffs, N.J.: Prentice-Hall.

8 Teaching Students with Hearing Impairments

Someone with a hearing impairment lacks the sense of hearing in quality and quantity, wholly or in part. The term *hearing impaired* is being used instead of *deaf* because not all people with hearing losses are deaf, just as not all people with vision problems are blind. Some people habitually call the hearing impaired *deaf and dumb*—a term that originally referred to the fact that the hearing impaired were not taught to speak, or were unable to speak. If a person has a very severe loss, *deaf* or *profoundly deaf* are preferred over the term *deaf and dumb*.

The classroom teacher should overcome any tendency to group everyone with a hearing loss into a general category. People with hearing losses cannot be stereotyped into one group any more than people *without* hearing losses can be stereotyped into one group.

Hearing is a continuum along which we have established labels. A hearing test is recorded in units of sound called **decibels** (dB) and the **audiogram** is the graph upon which the test is recorded. The audiogram shows the point at which the student can *first detect that any sound is present*—but that is *all*. It does not tell *what* the student hears or the quality of the hearing. Different frequencies (or pitches) are tested and the child will hear some louder than others, and some not at all. The audiogram is helpful in telling what sound a student can respond to, but two students with identical audiograms may, in fact, respond very differently to sound. This means that, although the audiogram is helpful, the final analysis must focus on the behavior of the individual student. Audiologists and teachers of the hearing impaired will often refer to students as "hard-of-hearing" because of the way in which they use hearing. However, hard-of-hearing students are able to learn and use language and speech much easier than a profoundly deaf student who often has the labored speech and difficulty with sentence sense that are traditionally associated with deafness.

Degrees of Hearing Impairment

The labels for the gradations of hearing impairment are described below.

1. The *normal range of hearing* is graphed anywhere from 0 dB to 20 dB.
2. The *mildly hard-of-hearing* are those whose loss is approximately from 20 dB to 40 dB. For such students the problem is slight (unless there are other multiplying handicaps). They may have a problem when the speech being listened to is faint or when the speaker is relatively distant. Mildly hearing-impaired students need favorable seating in the classroom and may need some help in speech and lip-reading (older students will have long since learned to compensate). Such students may have trouble hearing in a noisy classroom; with extra help, however, they will learn to function well both academically and socially in their peer group. They may or may not need hearing aids.
3. The *moderately hard of hearing* are those whose loss is anywhere from 40 dB to 60 dB. They will wear an aid, perhaps in both ears, and should benefit from it. Such students also need favorable seating, and will function in normal conversation to about five feet without difficulty. Communication becomes more difficult as the number of people increases or the background noises become louder. These students will have difficulty in understanding if the teacher's face is not visible or when his or her voice is faint or distant. They will need a moderate amount of extra work (both at school and at home) to build vocabulary and language structure. Their speech may have some slushiness, especially in high frequency sounds like *s, z, sh, ch, j,* and *zh.*
4. The *severely hard-of-hearing* are those whose audiograms show a loss from 60 dB to about 90 dB. Such students could respond to a loud voice at about a foot even without a hearing aid, although the voice may be unintelligible to them. They can hear some vowels and environmental sounds, but have trouble with consonants. This is especially true of breath sounds (*p, t, k, f*) and high-frequency consonants (*s, sh, ch, z*). These students will get a great deal of help from hearing aids. The severely hard-of-hearing need extra help in vocabulary and sentence structure. They also need favorable seating, which should be flexible for different situations or classes. Such students will probably have difficulty in large groups and discussions. Conversations will be understood only if they are directed right at them. Some students who fall into this range may be best-served in self-contained special education classes or resource rooms at least part of the day. Some may be placed in such classes through the early years to get basic skills in language, reading, and speech in more concentrated doses. These students will need extra help in other subjects when reading and language are involved.

5. The *profoundly deaf* have such severe hearing impairments that they are limited in processing language, and thus in educational performance. Those who are born profoundly deaf are called *congenitally* deaf. They may have severe reading problems and limited language. If the hearing loss is profound, support and cooperation from both school and home will be necessary if these students are to succeed. Those who become deaf through accident or illness after having heard normally are called *adventitiously* deaf or *deafened*. These students, having previously learned language, may not present the same teaching problems as the congenitally deaf. If the hearing loss has been gradually getting worse and comes after the student can already read, the language and reading problems will probably be minimal. If the hearing loss has been recent and sudden, you should be aware of the traumatic nature of such an experience. One student likened it to life's suddenly becoming a silent movie with no words, no sound, no sense of association, and a real sense of separateness resulting in a sense of unreality and great frustration. The student often lashes out from this frustration. The anger and sense of loss may show itself in social behavior and academic work until adjustment has been made. The support and reinforcement needed by the student during this time cannot be overemphasized. The person who is born deaf does not have to go through this sudden adjustment period, although in some respects one could say that the person's whole life is an adjustment period.

There are records available on which the sound has been filtered to simulate different hearing losses. Listen to one. It will amaze you how soft and unclear the sound is, and you will wonder how the student makes any sense out of it at all. No matter how loud you turn it up, some sounds are not heard. One such record is "How They Hear" (1966).

Hearing Aids

Almost every hearing-impaired student will be wearing hearing aids. If the student wears one aid, it is fitted monaurally; if two are worn it is fitted binaurally. From kindergarten, a hearing-impaired student will be able to put in the aids without help. The students should wear them all day unless some physical reason (a sore ear, swimming, excessive noise, etc.) interferes.

The hearing aid is like a personal public address system. It makes the sound louder, but the student does not hear *all* sounds even with the aid. Glasses correct most people's vision, but hearing aids do *not* correct people's hearing. Aids have made great strides in the space age, and early identification of the hearing loss allows more and more students with moderate and severe losses to function fairly normally. The aids allow many with severe and profound losses to function more as hard-of-hearing children than ever before.

To support the student who wears a hearing aid, classroom teachers should be fully aware of the components and characteristics of this device. *Feedback* is that squealing sound you hear when amplified sound from the hearing aid is picked up by the hearing aid microphone and goes through the system again. This will occur if one of the earmolds is not sitting in the ear properly. The hearing-impaired student will probably not be aware of the sound as it is so high-pitched, but it may cause you and the other students to climb the wall. There is no problem if the earmold is not properly in place; the student can simply wiggle the mold into place. However, if the earmold does not fit tightly because of poor design or because the ear has grown, the only thing to do is turn the aid down. Of course, this defeats its purpose, and you should inform the parents immediately that their child needs new earmolds as soon as possible.

Hearing aids come in two main types: (1) the body aid (named so because it is worn strapped to the body) and (2) behind-the-ear (BTE) aids. Cords and batteries are the parts of the aid that wear out most often. Ask the parents for spares to keep in the classroom. Even young children can take care of their own, but you may wish to store them in your desk for safekeeping. If anything else goes wrong with the aid, there is nothing you can do except refer it to the audiologist or the hearing-aid dealer.

The primary purpose of sound amplification is to bring a desired signal within the child's residual hearing capacity. This is referred to as an appropriate signal-to-noise ratio. This means that the signal (the sound you want the child to listen to) would be clearly distinguished auditorily from background sounds or noise. In a quiet situation the hearing-impaired student may respond to some sounds that would not be responded to in a noisy environment. This is because so much noise is being fed into the aid that the student cannot discriminate among all the sounds.

You do not have to shout or raise your voice to the child at close range, because the microphone makes the sound loud enough. In fact, shouting may distort the sound and make it painful enough that the student will turn the aid off. On the other hand, the further you get away from the aid, the less effective it is in picking up the sound of your voice. You may be drowned out by the students around the child who are shuffling feet or tapping pencils. The simplest way to improve the signal-to-noise ratio is to reduce the distance between the person who is speaking and the microphone of the hearing aid.

There are a number of teaching methodologies used in teaching the hearing impaired. Hirsh (1966) indicates that for normal children language is learned, for deaf children language is taught. This underlines the importance of quality teaching for hearing-impaired children. Teaching such children is a great responsibility and a great opportunity. Hearing-impaired students who succeed in school have two things in common: involved parents and excellent teachers. No one teaching *method* is best for *all* children. Individual differences must be recognized.

Three common approaches used in teaching hearing impaired children are described below.

1. *The auditory approach* presents material aurally to use what hearing the students have (residual hearing). This makes students aware of verbal language and their environment as a basis for education. **Lipreading** may or may not be stressed depending upon the student and the system used. **Sign language** is excluded, though gestures used naturally are acceptable.
2. *The oral approaches* (aural/oral) stress speech and lipreading as the primary mode of communication, using residual hearing whenever possible. Sign language is excluded, though gestures used naturally are acceptable.
3. *Total Communication* makes extensive use of a sign system or sign language and **fingerspelling** to supplement speech, lipreading, and auditory skills. There are various schools of thought within each of these main categories, and more detailed definitions are available from other sources (Caccamise and Drury 1976).

Your first adjustment may be to realize that you are involved with a team of people who share the responsibility for educating the student. This may require some adjustments in your schedule for meetings and consultation. Many school personnel are willing to help you in this adjustment process.

1. *The audiologist.* You will need close contact with this person for advice on the student's hearing and the maintenance of the hearing aid.
2. *The teacher of the hearing-impaired.* This resource is a necessity. The teacher of the hearing-impaired can give you advice, show you how to simplify materials, and give suggestions for parent follow-up. The itinerant teacher of the hearing-impaired will not have time to be a full-time tutor or interpreter if the student needs extensive help in communication. If the student needs this service, check with the principal. The classroom teacher may desire to learn sign language. This will be helpful for students who use it, but usually only students with severe and profound losses will

Teaching Methodologies for the Hearing-Impaired Student

Resource Personnel Available to the Classroom Teacher

have to rely on it. Students who need signing as a primary mode of communication may be best served by trained personnel. Most of the material in this chapter is oriented to the student who can function in the regular classroom using speech and lipreading.

3. *The resource teacher.* Most of the testing materials and special teaching materials published for students with exceptional needs will be available in the resource room and can be adapted for the hearing impaired.

4. *The speech and hearing therapist.* Most students with a hearing loss will need help with speech. Ling (1976) is an excellent text for a speech teacher to have on hand when working with the hearing-impaired, as is Calvert and Silverman (1975).

5. *An involved parent.* The parent is the most fundamental member of the team. To build a thinking, reasoning, and positive student, the school and home have to work hand-in-hand.

Hearing-Impaired Students and Their Classroom Peers

Helping students prepare for the presence of a hearing-impaired classmate takes time and sensitivity, but the effort can be rewarding. One student in junior high school who worked as an aide tutoring a hearing-impaired student said she had not realized how much her friend had overcome. This made her appreciate both her own opportunities and the abilities of her classmate and had a positive influence on her attitude and her behavior afterwards. A high school student, who was asked to take lecture notes for his hearing-impaired classmate, said at the end of the year that he was grateful for having had the assignment. This had taught him more than it taught his hearing-impaired classmate. He used to take sloppily written snatches of things, which didn't really deserve to be called notes. When he got home, if he did look at them, he could neither remember nor read what he had written. After receiving the assignment to take notes for the hearing-impaired student, he knew that his notes were really important, so he was careful in their preparation. He wrote carefully and legibly; he began looking for the organization of the teacher's lecture so that he could outline more easily as he wrote; he wrote sentences instead of snatches so that the transition from topic to topic was clear. He had been getting B's and C's in class but his grades improved and the discipline he learned carried over into his other classes. He reviewed his notes briefly before he went home to make sure his classmate could understand them; this was an important review for him, too.

An elementary student, when responding to a parent's criticism that the hearing-impaired student may have taken away time from her own child, commented, "We're glad Kevin is in the class. We are all better because he *was.*" The teachers of these classes had created a positive atmosphere, and it was a pleasure to see the other students grow and rise to the occasion.

There will be some physical adjustments in the classroom (e.g., modifying seating arrangements) to help the student lip-read, and to allow other students to give assistance. Will these changes be a help or a hindrance to other students? Will they make the class more difficult to handle? Will I have to make curricular changes in the class? How will this effect other teachers and programs that we have in the school? What can I expect of the student? Will, in fact, the whole thing be possible?

Every task that is adapted and improved for the hearing-impaired student's involvement in activities will be more useful for the other students in the class. Your teaching will have more focus and refinement in relation to smaller increments of improvement. Other students will also benefit.

The hearing-impaired student faces the same problems and adjustments in the classroom that every other student faces. Hearing-impaired students bring the same strengths and weaknesses and the same creativity; they also bring an added dimension that makes the classroom more interesting.

The hearing-impaired student may face the frustration of inconsistent goals, sometimes set too high and sometimes not set high enough. These children feel the stresses of isolation if they cannot communicate easily. If the hearing loss is severe, they may lack manners and social niceties because they do not understand what is being said. Even if the child understands the words, they have missed the meaning carried in the tone of voice. Hearing-impaired children make blunders because they miss not only the noises of life, but its silences as well. They don't hurry because they don't hear the quiet that would tell them that class has already begun. Additionally, participation in class will be minimal if they think someone will make fun of their response.

Some hearing-impaired students may have to make the adjustment of moving from a small self-contained class of six, where everyone is tuned to their specific needs and all the classwork is geared to them; where the teacher is able to give positive reinforcement more often than you will be able to; and where the teacher checks to make sure every instruction is understood. One kindergarten child, who had preschool work on a tutorial basis, said that the kindergarten had no teacher. When questioned, she admitted that there was a nice lady who walked around talking to the class, "but no one sat down with me."

The student may face emotional stress from being singled out. No one likes to be singled out at school for being different. These individuals may face emotional stress when they don't hear what the other students are laughing at. It is very easy to think, "Maybe they are laughing at me"—especially if someone glances in their direction.

Regular classrooms, very often, do not have enough opportunities for the repetition in language practice that the hearing-impaired so sorely need. So much school work can be answered with only one word or by simply circling the answer. These children will need whole-phrase and sentence practice.

Hearing-impaired children may face vocabulary and reading deficits that will defeat them when they receive an instruction like "Read chapter 5 and answer the questions at the end." For a nonreader just the first *page* of chapter 5 looks like a foreign language.

Language Deficits

Language deficits are a fundamental problem of the hearing-impaired. Because they cannot hear, they do not learn language automatically. You can expect them to have trouble with the kinds of words described below.

1. *Small words* that don't carry much meaning in and of themselves:

> He walked to the front door.
> He walked *up* to the front door.
> I saw it on TV.
> I saw it on *the* TV.

There are no adequate methods for explaining to a first grader the inclusion or the deletion of the word *up*. It just *is*. The inclusion of *the* in the fourth sentence can change the meaning of the sentence quite a bit.

2. *Abstract words* (e.g., "dependable"). Words like this have such broad and abstract meanings, that defining them quickly as they come up in a particular situation will not give a student its perspective. Analytically *explaining* or defining will not help the young hearing-impaired student who has few language skills. *Frequent use* of such words in appropriate situations is the best way for the child to see their varieties of meaning.

3. *Long or difficult words* (e.g., "antiestablishment"). It is not enough just to define such words. Remember that hearing children have heard a word many times even if they don't use it or read it. The hearing-impaired student does not have a storehouse of heard words to draw upon. The child may not even know the word exists. Give worksheets on which words have to be written in sentences in a variety of ways. Checking off a correct definition will not mean that the child can use the word or even understand it correctly.

4. *Words with multiple meanings and idiomatic expressions.* Asking, "What does *run* mean?" usually elicits an answer like "move fast." Unfortunately, if that is all the hearing-impaired student is exposed to, he or she will have a very peculiar idea of a man who *runs* for president, telephone poles that *run* along the side of the road, or anything that is *run* of the mill. When you explain that *water down* means to make easier, just enjoy the logic if he or she asks if *water up* means to make harder.

Language samples.   Here are three samples of the uncorrected written language of eleven-year-old hearing-impaired students of normal intelligence, typed exactly as they wrote them. Look for the skills the child *does* have.

Sample A

"Tom & Puppy"

Once upon a time Tom walk along street. He found a cute puppy. Tom took the puppy home. Tom loves puppy. He thinks is a girl dog. "It is" he said to his dog. Tom say to his dog "Your name will be fluffy." He keep hold the puppy for long time. He don't have girl friend. So he have puppy to be a girl friend.

"The End"

This child shows good thought processes, sensitivity to feelings, a sense of sequence, an appropriate title, a sense of closure even without "The End" typed at the end. There are no spelling mistakes. The child is at the point where he should be encouraged and taught to use complex sentences. The child uses only the present and past tenses in this piece and mixes them up, but not badly.

There are a number of words left out, but the child has such a good sentence sense that these mistakes can easily be rectified by discussing them as you would with any child, telling what is right, not what is wrong, and then giving ample opportunity to write again and again. The child is at the point where his skills could be expanded much as you would for any child. This is excellent for a hearing-impaired student.

Sample B

Woman put it litter bug. America is not beauful. Please don't litter. When need pick up the litter. America is beauful. Never do again. If do again get trouble.

This child also has sentence sense, even to the point of two complex sentences, but it doesn't come easily, and the output is only half as much as the other student's. The child is not able to use the infinitive as does the first student. Some of the language of this piece may come from posters—*litter bug* and *Please don't litter.*

The child also shows thought and an awareness of cause and effect three or four times. "If you do it again, you'll get into trouble." is a very firm closing statement to say the very least. There is only one spelling mistake, and it's a long word. Draw attention to it and have the child spell it to you verbally a number of times. Spelling is usually not a problem for the hearing-impaired as they focus on the visual so much. If a hearing-impaired student does have many spelling mistakes, look for causes other than deafness.

Sample C

No smoking to in heast Dead no smoking and Black in smoking and no Dead yes Dead. they No smoking more more more smoking and in Black Yes Dead and smoking an smoking and more more more and Store and smoking am Black and More Store is smoking. the no smoking More more and Black in smoking and Store More and More and More More. Yes Dead more Black Smoking more and more Yes Dead.

the end!

This student has some ideas but no sentence sense even though four periods were used. The capitalization of *No Smoking* makes one wonder if that comes from seeing No Smoking signs. The words *black* and *dead* apparently refer to a science lesson the class had on smoking, which pointed out that the lungs go black and finally you die. *Store* may mean you buy cigarettes at the store. *Heast* may be *heart* misspelled. The vocabulary is only about thirteen words, although the total output is more than either of the other two, which shows that the student has something to say and is eager to say it. The exclamation point is certainly appropriate to the topic. The student should be encouraged to continue writing, but at other times to work on with the question "Who is Doing What?"—to start building some sentences.

This student needs much individual help and reinforcement; so much so, in fact, that a small group would be appropriate.

Involving the Regular Education Student

Students can be mobilized in a variety of ways to help the hearing-impaired student both in and out of the classroom. This can be done in a natural manner, which neither condescends nor overprotects. If students learn that a hearing loss is a fact of life to be approached sensibly and optimistically, they will help the hearing-impaired student to compensate without sentimentality and with practical support. They will learn an important lesson from this individual. Try the following:

1. Use the buddy system. Choose a buddy to sit by the child and keep him or her aware of what is going on in class. The buddy can check to see whether the assignment was understood and properly completed.

2. Choose notetakers. Older students can be supplied with carbon paper when taking notes, so that the hearing-impaired student can attend to the lesson and still have the notes to take home and study. A few students could be given this assignment so that there are two sets of notes to compare and at least one set when one of the notetakers is absent.

3. Expect the other students to give presentations geared to the understanding of the hearing-impaired student, just as you adjust your own presentations. When a class member has to give a report, suggest a written outline for the hearing-impaired student to read. Use posters or visual presentations that are easy to read and understand. This should be required of the hearing-impaired student as well. If the class has the hearing-impaired student's outline, they know what kind of vocabulary to expect. If the speech is a little difficult to understand, the outline will help them follow the presentation.

4. Assign students various subjects to read and review with the hearing-impaired student and to assist in tutoring situations.

5. Train students to gain the attention of the hearing-impaired student by staying in his or her line of vision if the individual's hearing is not good enough to respond to sound. Classmates should be discouraged from hitting or touching any more than is necessary. The student may be in an unreceptive mood, or the touch may be harder than it needs to be and lead to a free-for-all. The answer, "I didn't *hit* him, I was just getting his attention," has been the postlude to many a fracas. No one likes to be grabbed or physically interrupted. It is a good idea to instruct students to be verbal and visual with the hearing-impaired student whenever possible. If the student does not respond to sound, attempt to stand in the line of vision. This will not always be possible, especially in emergency situations, but it is a good general rule for classmates.

6. Have students get into the habit of using full sentences when asking or answering questions. This will greatly aid the hearing-impaired student's use of language. Whole sentences will be easier to lip-read.

7. Help the hearing-impaired student to strive for independence. A visiting specialist, who had come to talk on hearing impairment to a class, was asked to discuss the following topic: Hearing-impaired students can do their own work. Regular students, in their eagerness to aid a hearing-impaired student, would attempt to help at the first sign of a frown on his forehead. Assistance was provided to the point of doing the work. Eventually, he sat back like a king while the other students vied to do the work for him.

8. Use the other students' excellent ideas for teaching. In schools where sixth-graders have been used as tutors for younger students, the ingenuity and creativity of their approach and materials have been an eye-opener for the teachers. The self-image of less academically able students is enhanced when they are asked to help, and they can do so in many other areas (e.g., sports, social, etc.).

9. Ask the students to stand when answering questions—the moment it takes for a student to stand allows the hearing-impaired student to make eye contact and lip-read more easily. If the person answering the question is seated, by the time the lip-reader finds out who is speaking and turns to see around the heads of other students, the answer has come and gone. The teacher should ask students to face the hearing-impaired student so it is possible to "see" the answer while everyone else can hear it. The teacher can also rephrase answers so that if the student had not lip-read it from the speaker, there would be another opportunity.

Involving Parents

Parents need to feel that they are helping, and this applies especially to parents of exceptional children. Give parents this opportunity, even if not all of them accept. Use the suggestions below to involve parents.

1. Keep them informed of activities by providing material from class to help their children. Give specific, practical suggestions. Avoid educational jargon.

2. Arrange for their participation in parent groups involved with hearing handicaps.

3. Use them as a resource—they see a side of the child at home that may not be apparent at school.

4. Find out from them the signs that show the beginning of frustration in their children so that you can be on the look-out for them in school.

5. Include them in formulating programs and goals for their children. The IEP may involve only one meeting, but it will be reinforcing for both you and the parents if these meetings continue throughout the year.

6. Give them various things to do—not all students react alike, and neither do parents. Have some alternative activities for them when you offer suggestions.

7. Let them help—some parents work well as aides in the classroom; others work better as room mothers.

8. Have them educate the other parents. They can be involved through parent and civic groups in obtaining better equipment, facilities, and so forth.

Remember that every hearing-impaired person is a *person first*. Hearing-impaired students are just as bright, slow, able, naughty, energetic, or rebellious as any others—only maybe more so because of frustration with the inconvenience of the handicap.

1. Outline the day's work and put it on the board so the student can see it.
2. Outline the day's (or week's) work assignments and send home copies so that parents and tutors can help.
3. Require all seatwork to be answered in complete sentences. Hearing-impaired students need all the practice they can get in using language. Even if they understand the question, they may not be able to put the answer in a "straight" sentence.
4. When explaining materials, write complete phrases or sentences on the board—don't write just one word. The hearing-impaired student doesn't always know how words fit together to make a sensible English sentence. Language is the great problem of the deaf and the lack of it stifles the ability to read and to reason.
5. Seat the student so that the rest of the class may be viewed as easily as possible. A semicircle is good if the class is small enough. If the class is mostly lecture, the student needs to be close to the place you spend most of your time. If there is a lot of interaction, you may wish to seat this student in the middle, a little toward a window, so it won't be necessary to squint into the light.
6. Give all spelling words and tests in sentences. Single words are hard to lip-read and easy to misunderstand.
7. Say it again if the student doesn't understand, as the student may not have been following closely enough. If the student still doesn't understand, rephrase it. There may have been a word that was causing difficulty. If you still are not understood, act it out, draw a picture—go back to the beginning. This is not always possible to do in class past the rephrasing or simplifying step, but you can have one of the other students help with it later in the day.
8. Do not be surprised at great gaps in learning. Do not show disgust or amazement that might make the students feel it is their fault.
9. Model correct language so that students can practice correct usage. Accept what they say and reinforce them by praising their effort. Give them the correct language, without criticism, then have them say it. This should not be a long, drawn-out event; it should be quick, purposeful, and matter-of-fact. If the child answers a question with "George Washington president first," praise the child for the correct answer and then respond with the correct model: "Say, 'George Washington was the first president.'" The child repeats that. "Yes, that's right."

10. Be certain the students know what is going on all the time so that they don't feel left out. We *hear* what is going on whether or not it effects us, and we gain a knowledge of our environment almost automatically. This gives us a storehouse of information to catalogue and use at a later time as needed. Hearing-impaired students do not. If there is an announcement over the loudspeaker about a meeting of the camera club, don't assume that they don't belong to the club and don't need to know about it. Tell them—or have an assigned student tell them. Chances are that they don't even know a camera club exists or what it does. If they did, they might want to join.

11. Check continually with other personnel to see how you are doing. Walking the line between expecting too much and not expecting enough is a difficult job.

12. Give hearing-impaired students enough experience with new vocabulary so that they really remember it; have them use it in a variety of ways. Relate it to words and concepts they already know. Use pictures and secure the objects themselves when possible. Create opportunities to *say* the word. Create opportunities to *write* the word. Act out experiences using the word.

13. Encourage all students to answer in full sentences to facilitate lipreading, speak clearly, not too rapidly (but not just word-by-word), without exaggeration or too much nodding of the head. All the students, not just you, need to feel comfortable communicating with hearing-impaired students. Ask hearing-impaired students if they understood an answer. If they didn't, ask the speaker to repeat it.

14. Remember that lipreading requires light on the face of the speaker and not in the reader's eyes. Lipreading is not easy at the best of times, and with the movement of the speaker and other distractions, not every word will be understood. It is best not to be over ten feet away if possible, although it is possible to lip-read from further away. Don't chew on pencils or gum. It is best to lip-read from the front or slightly to the side, but it is impossible to lip-read through your head when you face the blackboard and talk at the same time. Don't walk around the room giving instructions—a moving target is hard to hit. Very bright or striped or patterned shirts are hard to lip-read over.

15. Give short, concise instructions, then check to see that the students understood them by having them repeat the instructions before having to follow them. Alternate this with calling on other students so that the exceptional student is not singled out all the time.

16. Check on whether or not the hearing-impaired student knows the names of other students in the class. Names are hard to catch and often slip by. The student will often recognize someone but not know the name.

17. Don't expect hearing-impaired students to read if they don't have the vocabulary. Some people think that if a student doesn't understand, you should provide a book so that it can be read. This is fairly similar to having you read German if you can't speak it. Your reaction would be, "But I don't *understand* German." The hearing-impaired student not only needs the vocabulary (single words), but also needs the language (the influence words have on each other) to get meaning from the words themselves.

18. Ask the school district for inservice training, adequate staff, and equipment.

19. Type scripts for movies, filmstrips, and tapes used in class. Allow exceptional students to read them beforehand and leave sufficient light for checking the script and seeing the teacher during the film or tape.

20. Use diagrams, graphs, and visual representations to reinforce ideas where possible—but don't go overboard and think it is necessary to have a poster for everything.

21. Ask the school district to begin a professional library for you and other professionals working with the exceptional student.

22. Check to make sure the school library has books on hearing impairment for students to read—for example, *Ann's Silent World* (Wolf, 1977).

23. Don't allow exceptional students special privileges because you feel sorry for them. Require the same behavior from them as you do from other students in the class and assign them the same responsibilities. It will be a pleasure for you as well as the hearing-impaired student.

24. Enjoy the new experience. Don't be put off by the initial extra effort. Increased chalkboard use, increased overhead use, typed handouts, and outlined lessons will pay off in the long run and may improve your teaching skills. You'll be better organized and better prepared.

References

Caccamise, F. C., and Drury, A. M. 1976. A review of the current terminology in education of the deaf. *The Deaf American* 19:7–10.

Calvert, D., and Silverman, S. R. 1975. *Speech and deafness.* Washington, D. C.: Alexander Graham Bell Association for the Deaf.

How they hear. 1966. Northbrook, Ill.: George N. Stowe and Associates.

Hirsh, I. J. 1966. Teaching the child to speak. In *The genesis of language*, ed. F. Smith and G. Miller. Cambridge, Mass.: M. I. T.

Ling, D. 1976. *Speech and the hearing impaired child: theory and practice.* Washington, D. C.: Alexander Graham Bell Association for the Deaf.

Wolf, B. 1977. *Ann's Silent World.* Philadelphia: J. B. Lippincott.

9 Teaching Students with Visual Impairments

Jenny reads with her face almost touching the book; Mike often moves up the aisle from his seat to get a closer look at the chalkboard or a movie; Maria moves her head from side to side or up and down as she tries to copy from the board; Steven reads print books using a magnifier, while Laura only reads books with enlarged print; Tony reads and writes braille, but sees enough to walk comfortably alone through the halls and out-of-doors; Sylvia has no vision at all and depends largely on listening and touch for information in the classroom, and on her skill with a cane for independent travel. Each of these children, and any other whose imperfect vision seems a problem in school, may properly be called *visually impaired* or *visually handicapped* according to the all-inclusive definition of those terms used in this chapter.

> A visually handicapped child is one whose visual impairment interferes with his optimal learning and achievement, unless adaptations are made in the methods of presenting learning experiences, the nature of the materials used, and/or in the learning environment (Barraga 1976, p. 16).

The two subgroups of visually impaired individuals, *the partially seeing* and *the blind* are here defined according to Taylor (1973, p. 157).

> Visually handicapped children who use sight as their chief avenue of learning are referred to as "partially seeing" when it is necessary to differentiate between them and those who rely chiefly upon touch and hearing, the "educationally blind."

The very simplest distinction states that the child who must read braille is blind; the child who can read print is partially seeing. This statement considers only the reading medium, while Taylor's broader definition reflects the *sensory avenues* upon which the child depends for all concept development.[1]

The teacher familiar with school vision-screening using the Snellen Chart, and with the term *twenty-twenty vision* used to describe normal vision measured with that chart, may wonder how the sight of a visually impaired student compares with this norm. The vision specialist who works with the child as a resource teacher will know the actual measurement of the child's visual

---

1. In the literature, *visually handicapped* may be used instead of *visually impaired,* and either term is sometimes used to include only those called *partially seeing* in the definitions given here. In that case, *blind* has a separate meaning.

Figure 9.1 Field of vision in legal blindness

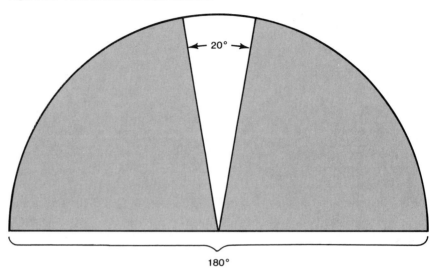

acuity[2] and whether it is sufficiently limited to fall within the definition of *legal blindness*. A person is considered legally blind if the measured visual acuity is 20/200 or less in the better eye with the best possible correction. This means that the person can read from 20 feet away only the top letter on the Snellen Chart—the letter which a person with normal vision can read from 200 feet—or can read nothing on the chart from 20 feet. The person may have some degree of vision between 20/200 and total blindness. Only 20–25 percent of those legally blind are totally without sight. An individual is also legally blind if the field of vision is so limited that its widest diameter subtends an angle of 20° or less. (The normal field of vision, shown in figure 9.1, encompasses 180°.) In this condition it is as if the person were looking through a pinhole or narrow tube; there is almost no side vision, even though the central vision may be better than 20/200. Such a restricted visual field imposes severe limitations on reading, physical activities, mobility, and many other tasks.

If a child is legally blind, the resource teacher will be able to order special school materials from the American Printing House for the Blind at no cost to the child or the school, and the child will be eligible for the services of the Library of Congress, Division for the Blind and Physically Handicapped and its regional libraries, and later for assistance from other government agencies. Both the resource teacher and the classroom teacher, however, need to be

2. " 'Acuity' refers to a clinical measurement of ability to discriminate clearly the fine details of objects or symbols at a specified distance" (Barraga 1976, p. 14).

Teaching Students with Speech, Sensory, and Orthopedic Differences primarily concerned with the degree of usefulness of the child's sight as demonstrated by his or her behavior in school.

The teacher working with a visually limited child who has some vision needs to understand what type of residual vision it is. Generally dim vision is only one of the principal categories. Cataracts produce that type of vision which gives the effect of looking through frosted glass. The *pinhole* or *tubular* vision resulting from severe limitation of the visual field may provide a fairly clear (though subnormal) view within the very restricted field, while *peripheral* vision is the opposite, with clear central vision gone, leaving a blank in the center of every image and dim edges. In *patchy* vision, another category, irregular blind spots make it difficult to get an object into clear focus. Not only each type, but each case within each type of residual vision has individual educational significance.

Both doctors and educators are aware of environmental and psychological influences on the effectiveness of a person's limited vision. James Boswell, in his famous biography of Samuel Johnson, discusses that great writer's defective vision and says that in spite of it "the force of his (Dr. Johnson's) attention and perceptive quickness made him see and distinguish all manner of objects, whether of nature or of art, with a nicety that is rarely to be found. . . . When I found that he saw the romantick beauties of Islam in Derbyshire, much better than I did, I told him that he resembled an able performer upon a bad instrument" (Boswell 1904, pp. 48–49). Every experienced teacher of visually impaired children or adults has known individuals who perform well visually on "bad instruments" and others who perform poorly. Many legally blind people read print and function essentially as sighted people; others who could do not, but live almost as if sight were totally lacking.

It is important for classroom teachers to realize that the old philosophy of sight-saving or sight conservation, in which the use of the eyes was restricted, has been abandoned. Medical opinion now holds that residual vision is not damaged by use but, on the contrary, should be used as fully as possible. Pupils are encouraged to read print if they can. If necessary, the material may be placed barely beyond nose length. *Low vision aids*—magnifiers for clarifying near-point visual tasks and small telescopic aids for increasing distance vision—are recommended where effective. As a result of these changes, "the trend in defining visually limited children *for educational purposes* has been toward utilizing criteria based on how the children *function* in school rather than how they perform and are measured on clinical tests" (Ashcroft 1963, p. 419).

Placement without specialized assistance. *Mainstreaming* is a new term but hardly a new concept in education of the visually impaired. Both partially seeing and blind pupils have been integrated into day school classes for many years. There is great concern in the field at present because, "mainstreaming is being interpreted by some educators as placement of visually handicapped children in regular classes without specialized assistance or with assistance from a consultant trained in another area of special education but not in the specific educational needs of the visually handicapped pupil" (Scholl 1978a, p. 3).

A consultant without specific training in education of the visually handicapped not only cannot meet the obvious needs of a blind child for instruction in braille reading and writing, but is also lacking in many other skills and understandings essential to the successful teaching of children with limited vision. The consultant might well, for example, assume that all children with poor vision need bright lighting. Actually, if a child's nearsightedness is the result of *albinism,* bright light will only make it harder to see. Ability to translate the eye doctor's diagnosis of a child's eye problem into meaningful assessment of the educational adaptations that should be instituted is just one of the skills in which the vision specialist is trained.

The education of visually handicapped pupils in regular classes has a long history of success. That success, however, has been due in large measure to the help given to such pupils by people specifically trained to work with them. For most visually handicapped pupils successful mainstreaming/integration cannot be effected without such supportive services (Scholl 1978b, p. 91).

Role of the vision specialist. A related issue concerns the role of the resource room or itinerant (traveling) teacher of the visually impaired, who works with pupils in day school programs.[3] When some visually impaired children first began attending regular day-school classes instead of segregated residential schools, the great desire of the educators promoting this arrangement was to prove that these children could succeed academically. The vision specialist, besides providing the necessary special materials and services, did a great deal of tutoring in academic subjects to help the visually impaired pupil keep up with the rest and sometimes the best of the class.

3. *Vision specialist* is the term used in the remainder of this chapter to indicate a person who holds professional certification as a trained teacher of visually handicapped students. Although recognizing that men also perform these functions, we will refer to the vision specialist and the classroom teacher as *she* and to the student as *he* to avoid constant use of *he/she.* The vision specialist will sometimes be called simply *the specialist.* As used in this chapter, the term does not refer to the doctor who is a specialist in diagnosing and treating eye diseases, and/or in examining the eyes and prescribing corrective lenses.

Over the years since that time, however, various devices have been developed that provide learning opportunities that the visually impaired child did not formerly have. One example is the *Cranmer abacus,* which greatly simplifies arithmetical computation for the child who is blind or has very low vision. New areas of curriculum have also been added to the schedule, such as instruction in making the best possible use of residual vision. These highly specialized skills will have lifelong value for the visually handicapped child, as well as immediate value in helping him succeed in the regular classroom. Time for learning and practicing these skills must come out of the period the pupil spends with the itinerant or resource room vision specialist, which is usually not more than one hour a day. Obviously, this reduces the time for academic tutoring during that period, thereby increasing the responsibility of the classroom teacher for the nonspecialized academic skills. One supervisor of an itinerant program asserts, "If we are to develop a real skills program we must get the regular classroom teacher to take more control over the academics" (Miller 1976, p. 15). The classroom teacher may use aides, other pupils, or family members to assist with tutoring when it seems necessary, realizing that the vision specialist must use her time to develop the special skills that each visually impaired pupil needs, for which the regular teacher is not trained.

Flexible school placement.   Related to the interpretation of "least restrictive environment" is the possibility of inflexible placement of visually impaired children in day-school programs. Josephine L. Taylor, coordinator of programs for the visually handicapped in the Bureau of Education of the Handicapped, U.S. Office of Education, reminds us that P.L. 94-142 "does *not* state that *all* children shall be educated in the mainstream" (Taylor 1976, p. 15). She stresses

> the need for flexibility in selecting facilities. That facility should be selected which fulfills a particular need, at the time of the need, and for only as long as . . . it is fulfilling this need. Switching from one facility to another should not necessarily be considered as a failure of the first facility but rather as a success in having solved the problem for which it was selected (Taylor 1976, p. 18).

Walker (1977a) suggests that a child of six might start school in a residential facility, transfer after several months to a local school, but later need placement in a residential school again long enough to establish desired special skills.

> If there is no flexibility for the child to move to the appropriate setting when his educational needs demand it, then any setting, even a regular, local, public school classroom can be too restrictive (Walker, 1977a, p. 32).

Services to preschool and multihandicapped blind children. Provision of educational services to preschool visually impaired children and support services to their parents was proceeding in some states well before the passage of P.L. 94-142, but must be greatly accelerated. Residential schools have been handling most of the training of multihandicapped blind children, but under the current law many of these children are attending local day facilities for multihandicapped children. Decisions must be made as to what administrative arrangements and types of programs will best serve these two groups of the approximately 35,000 visually impaired children in the nation who are unserved.

Teacher preparation. Hatlin (1978, p. 12) stresses the need for teachers to "be sophisticated in the use of formal and informal assessment procedures and above all to be good observers." He further suggests that many teachers are not prepared in these areas. This is but one voice expressing the spreading conviction that teacher preparation centers in the field must do a better job of effectively preparing teachers for the situations that actually exist. New emphasis is needed in such areas as assessment and evaluation, individualized program design; subject areas such as the teaching of daily living skills, human sexuality, and career planning; and especially the development of interpersonal communication skills so that the vision specialist can effectively "be the child's most important . . . advocate with regular school administrators, classroom teachers, parents, siblings, ancillary personnel, or rehabilitation personnel" (Walker 1977b, p. 62).

Vocational and prevocational training. The need for prevocational and vocational programs to prepare young people for the job market has been recognized, and to some extent met, as far as normal individuals are concerned. For visually impaired youngsters such programs are woefully lacking, as are leaders trained in conducting them. The need for this type of program and for such leaders is recognized as urgent throughout the field of education of the visually handicapped. The extension of school responsibility to include young people with impairments through age twenty-one increases the urgency of establishing more effective vocational programs in all areas of exceptionality.

Braille: the code and its teaching. Many sighted people do not realize that the braille code is not just a raised form of the familiar letters of the alphabet, but is an entirely different alphabet formed by combinations of raised dots. They do not know, further, that the code employs many contractions, so that even the beginning reader is decoding an elaborate shorthand system, making reading considerably more difficult than it is for sighted children. Because of its relative difficulty, and the possibility of "reading" by listening to records, tapes, or one of the marvelous electronic machines that read aloud directly from the printed page, some educators feel that braille has no future—that auditory aids and the new machines will replace it altogether. Others consider it still the blind person's most independent mode of reading, with no total replacement foreseeable. In the United States and abroad, work is being done to determine the feasibility of simplifying the braille code for ease of reader and computer transcription. The need for basal materials for the beginning braille reader has been recognized, and a reading series designed specifically for the blind child and for contracted braille as the reading medium is now available.

It should be encouraging to the classroom teacher to know that "many of the same methods are practicable with both normally seeing and visually handicapped children" (Napier 1973, p. 224), and that most of the differences in teaching approaches occasioned by the presence of a visually impaired child in a regular class are obvious. Visual approaches must either be changed to auditory or tactual approaches or supplemented through the other senses. This is true even for the partially seeing pupil, whose limited visual impressions should be reinforced through auditory or tactual channels. Providing the actual object to examine at close range visually and by touch is ideal, and a model is next best. Raised line drawings are useful to a limited degree, and the specialist in teaching the visually impaired will provide or arrange for these when appropriate. Sometimes a careful explanation of a picture or other visual aid is all that is possible. In making such explanations it is important to relate the new concept to one that is known to be in the pupil's realm of experience.

Strategies for the Classroom Teacher

Field trips that are good learning experiences for sighted pupils may provide only a jumble of unrelated bits of information and experience for the blind classmate or one with very low vision. An extra adult or a capable pupil assigned to help with the exploration of objects or to give needed explanations will make the trip more meaningful. It is well to keep in mind that

> if the visually handicapped child can hear it, handle it, pace it off with hands or feet, smell it, taste it when feasible, and generally involve his total being, he can learn from it. *When a teacher deliberately tries to teach more meaningfully because of the visually handicapped child in her group, she is usually teaching more meaningfully for the seeing children as well* (Napier 1973, p. 227. Italics added).

Actually stepping off the perimeter of an area rather than being given the measurements provides a more meaningful mathematical experience for any young child, for example. Even as simple a strategy as the teacher's saying aloud for the benefit of a visually impaired child what she is writing on the chalkboard for the rest of the class will give the sighted pupils valuable auditory reinforcement for their visual learning.

Although most school districts require vision-screening of pupils, some vision-screening programs are inadequate, and not all children with visual limitations are detected. The classroom teacher, who has the opportunity for daily observation of pupils, can often notice symptoms of visual disorders and request investigation by the school nurse. Observable symptoms fall into three categories: (1) appearance, (2) behavior, and (3) complaints.

Appearance

Crossed eyes or eyes not functioning together

Swollen eyelids

Red-rimmed, crusted eyelids

Frequent sties

Bloodshot eyes

Pupils of different sizes

Eyes in constant motion

Behavior

Walks with extreme caution

Blinks constantly

Trips or stumbles frequently

Rubs eyes frequently

Is overly sensitive to light

Tilts head; shuts or covers one eye when reading

Frowns when trying to see distant objects

Is unable to distinguish colors

Fails to see objects in his peripheral (side) vision

Holds reading material at an abnormal distance—either very close or at a great distance

Distorts face when using concentrated vision

Complaints of

Dizziness

Frequent headaches

Pain in the eyes

Blurry letters or objects

Double vision

Burning or itching eyelids

Teachers of primary grades should be aware that children in this age-range are often farsighted to some degree. However, their eyes adjust readily to close work in almost all cases. Children who consistently become restless or inattentive during near-vision tasks should be given a specific test for farsightedness, which the standard Snellen test does not detect. If extreme farsightedness is suspected, the child should be referred for professional examination.

Any child in whom a visual difficulty has been identified should go to an eye specialist for a thorough eye examination. The vision specialist does not have the training to diagnose or treat visual disorders. All formal testing, medication, surgery, and prescription of corrective lenses demand the expertise of the eye specialist. The vision specialist should, however, be competent in interpreting the eye specialist's report and knowledgeable of its educational implications. This teacher or the school nurse may take the responsibility for follow-up on the referral, making sure that the child receives the needed examination and that the school receives information on the results.

The Visually Impaired Child in the Classroom

Even an experienced, capable teacher may feel threatened when a visually impaired child joins the class for the first time. It may be reassuring to remember that such children have been successfully integrated into regular day-school classes for many years. The worried teacher needs to recall and accept that truism of special education: these children are more similar to than different from their fully sighted classmates. After all, visually impaired children can listen, speak, think, and participate in many physical activities. Most of them can even see, though not as clearly as the other pupils. Their needs, in most instances, can be met in the regular day schools.

It is true that the methods of meeting some of the visually impaired child's needs differ to some extent from those used with sighted children, and that the regular teacher's professional preparation may not have been oriented to those needs. Fortunately, the pupil's special needs are primarily the concern of the trained teacher of the visually impaired. Since the child's basic needs parallel those of sighted peers, the classroom teacher is capable of meeting them. Because one important avenue of sensory input is weak or absent, the mode of presentation of lessons must be altered occasionally, but not the content or the goal. The academic curriculum of the visually impaired child should match that of the sighted child; the academic involvement of each is the responsibility of the regular teacher.

The vision specialist may function in a vision resource room in a school that primarily serves sighted pupils, with the visually impaired pupils in the school usually spending an hour a day or less in the resource room, depending on their needs. The teacher may be itinerant, traveling throughout a school district and spending perhaps an hour a day with one of the visually impaired children on the case load, an hour a week with an older, more independent one. A teacher with the title of *consultant* may be responsible for such a large geographical area that there is little time for direct work with the children. Such a teacher consults with the regular teachers on problems that have arisen since the last visit and makes sure that the children have the special materials they need.

Whichever type of program has been instituted in a given area, cooperation between the classroom teacher and the vision specialist is essential. Each should appreciate the contributions of the other; the contributions of both are necessary for the visually impaired child to achieve full potential. The responsibility of each must be clearly defined and understood by both. Some problems will be the main or total responsibility of the classroom teacher, others the responsibility of the vision specialist. Both teachers will work on some of the problems, hopefully in a spirit of willingness to do all in their power to minimize the limitations that visual impairment imposes on a child.

One of the first responsibilities of the regular teacher is to examine her attitude toward blindness and visual impairment in general and then toward the particular child who has joined the class. Many adults think of blindness as synonymous with eternal sadness, helplessness, and hopelessness. If these terms describe the teacher's feelings, her attitude toward the child will be negative and will be conveyed to the other children and probably shared by them. She needs to realize that, though there are blind beggars, many blind people support themselves and their families, function as respected independent members of their communities, and live happy lives, successful by the same standards used to judge sighted people. As individuals, they are as different from each other as from their sighted friends, exhibiting all the various personality traits of the general population.

Blind children, too, are individuals: some venturesome, some fearful; some curious about the world, some apathetic; some conscientious, some lazy. Like the average child, the visually impaired pupil may be attentive sometimes, surreptitiously sharing secrets with a friend at another time; obedient most of the time, but planning mischief now and then. The teacher must discover the unique qualities of the visually impaired child as she does those of her other pupils. What are his strengths, his weaknesses? What positive contributions can he make to the class? What special problems does he have?

In each case, the nature of the visual deviation and the child's adjustment to it will determine the extent of educational adaptations necessary. The vision specialist is well acquainted with these concerns and should work closely with the classroom teacher to decide what modifications of the normal classroom procedures are necessary. Together they can evaluate the effectiveness of conventional methods before making multiple changes. Generally, the fewer changes the better.

The remainder of this chapter outlines specific problems that may arise, suggests where adaptations will be necessary, and offers possible solutions to the problems. The classroom teacher must remember that no single visually impaired pupil will have all of the problems presented. They are possible, not inevitable. Some pupils will have few of them. Although categorization always results in some overlap and some gaps, the most common problems and the suggestions for their solution are presented in the following pages grouped under five general headings: environmental problems, academic problems, developmental problems, social/emotional problems, and additional teacher concerns.

Orientation and mobility. The student may be unable to see clearly, if at all, hallways, stairs, desks, aisles, wastebaskets, and temporary furnishings such as rolling chalkboards and media carts. Location of rooms frequently used, such as the library, auditorium, restroom, and lunchroom requires at least a minimum of mobility skills. The problem can be accentuated in rooms where there is unassigned seating.

Environmental Problems

Instruction in cane travel or other specific mobility techniques should be given by a mobility specialist. Formal building and classroom orientation for the blind child are the responsibility of the vision specialist, who should also instruct the classroom teacher and sighted pupils in the basic techniques of leading and seating a blind person. There are several things a classroom teacher can do on a less formal basis to help:

1. Eliminate unnecessary obstacles; inform student of changes in room arrangement or of any temporary obstacles, such as a portable movie screen.
2. Keep doors completely closed or completely open to eliminate the possibility of the student running into a partially open door.
3. Initially, allow the student to travel with a companion to frequently used rooms, such as the library, restroom, and auditorium. Discuss the route, pointing out right and left turns and any distinguishing landmarks.
4. Allow the student to move about freely until he has familiarized himself with the room or route.
5. Discourage reliance upon sighted quides once the student has demonstrated the ability to travel independently.
6. If necessary, make provisions for a sighted guide for fire drills, field trips, assemblies, and seating in rooms that ordinarily have unassigned seating.

Illumination.   The student's seating arrangement may not satisfy illumination needs; the desirable amount of illumination varies with the particular disability. As already mentioned, in some visual impairments the eyes are sensitive to high levels of illumination and the child cannot perform well near a strong source of light or glare. Other eye conditions make extra lighting essential.

The vision specialist will know the student's lighting requirements. Consult this teacher to determine the best seating arrangement. Some general suggestions for the classroom teacher follow.

1. Avoid standing with your back to the windows; looking directly toward a light source is uncomfortable for all students and reduces visual efficiency.
2. Eliminate glare from highly polished desks and tables by moving them away from the direct light source. Cover the glass on cabinet doors. Avoid high-gloss surfaces on visual aids.
3. Adjust light to suit daily weather conditions.
4. Keep chalkboards clean and use a wide chalk stroke.
5. Use both natural and artificial illumination. Allow the visually impaired student to use a special lamp if prescribed by the vision specialist.
6. Permit the partially seeing student to move as close as necessary to the chalkboard, movie screen, or demonstration and to sit at the front during programs in the auditorium.

Work and storage space.   Educational materials frequently used by the visually impaired, such as talking books (record players), braillers, cassette players, large print books, and *tactile maps* are too cumbersome for use or storage on an average classroom desk. It is essential to provide a large work area to accommodate such bulky items, and arrange adequate storage space close to the work area. If necessary, the teacher should help the student organize materials for efficient use and care of equipment.

Isolation within the classroom.   Feelings of isolation may develop if the student's need for extra work space is resolved by separation from sighted classmates. Using talking books and tape recorders with earphones instead of reading from books also separates the child from other pupils. If the child brailles the assignments and the teacher cannot read braille, his interaction with that teacher is limited, contributing further to feelings of isolation.

The visually impaired child's table should be kept near other children's desks, close enough for conversation in informal moments. An excellent idea is to obtain an extra set of earphones so other children can listen with the visually impaired child to records and tapes. This provides good additional help for slow readers, who can listen while following in their books, thus receiving information through two sensory channels at once. The vision specialist can interline braille with print so the classroom teacher can read and grade the visually impaired pupil's papers, and someone can read the teacher's written comments to the pupil. However, the classroom teacher should make a point of speaking to the child often about his work.

Inefficient use of residual vision.   Doctors who inform parents that their child has a serious visual loss may give them the impression that there is no use in encouraging the child to look at anything. Since vision develops during childhood only if used, low vision will remain very inefficient unless deliberate efforts are made to foster its use.

Academic Problems

Parents and all teachers should encourage the child with the slightest residual vision to look at everything, regardless of how close to his face the object must be in order for him to see it at all, or how imperfect his visual impressions may be at first. The visual centers of the brain can learn to fill in details of incomplete visual impressions. In addition, the vision specialist should provide a regular training program to improve the pupil's visual efficiency. Training and practice can improve the visual perceptive process so that many children who originally could read only large print can learn to read normal print quite comfortably, thus gaining access to more educational materials. Children who could not distinguish any letters can learn to read and write large print well enough to understand memos left for them, to write down a message, and to read street signs and addresses on homes and businesses with a telescopic aid, even though braille or recordings may always be their primary reading medium. They may also learn to recognize broad outlines in pictures and often some details. This is helpful in developing concepts that cannot be conveyed by sound or touch. Training in the use of residual vision can improve visual-motor coordination as well.

Availability of educational materials.   There are not as many materials designed specifically for the visually impaired child's needs as there are for sighted children. Some assignments, especially research projects, may have to be modified if reference materials are not available in large print or braille. Lifelike models of animals, tactile maps, and other special materials may not be available either. It is often possible to overcome this problem by pairing the visually limited pupil with a sighted classmate. The vision specialist will try to provide materials and equipment to substitute for regular classroom materials that are inappropriate and will give training in their use. Some of the most frequently used tools are

1. Cassette tapes and talking books
2. Low-vision aids
3. Braillewriters and braille textbooks
4. Braille slate and stylus
5. Cranmer abacus
6. Large-print books
7. Tactile and auditory science materials
8. Tactile maps for the blind; enlarged and/or simplified maps for the partially seeing
9. Dark pens and pencils and dark-lined writing paper

Visual presentations. Many classroom presentations rely heavily upon visual perception: films, pictures, experiments, and other demonstrations. The low-vision child obviously cannot learn readily from such presentations unless adaptations are made. The teacher should

1. Sit beside the child during film presentations to describe action not made clear by the sound track. In upper grades, another student can do this.
2. Use rear-screen projection, which allows the visually impaired child to sit close to the screen without interfering with the projection. If possible, arrange an individual showing on a small screen at eye level. (See your school instructional materials specialist or librarian about these possibilities.)
3. Have the partially seeing child view a filmstrip on an individual projector rather than on the large screen with the entire class.
4. Use real objects or models in place of, or to supplement, pictures. Give the visually impaired student ample time to examine them thoroughly, pointing out explicitly relationships that might be obvious to sighted students. When models are not available, describe the picture or have other students describe it. Pass it to the partially seeing student to examine at close range after showing it to the class. Similarly, allow the blind and partially seeing student to feel demonstration and experimental materials when possible. Give careful explanations when tactual examination is not feasible, relating new concepts to known ones.
5. Adapt written assignments to oral presentations when practical. Assign a classmate to read the assignment to the blind student and record the responses.

6. Provide one-to-one instruction in cursive writing and other concepts that are generally taught from the chalkboard but are difficult for the partially seeing student to perceive. The vision specialist will help with handwriting skills and provide braille copies for the blind student if given the material ahead of time. For the partially seeing student, dictate or copy chalkboard assignments and provide a clear copy of dittoed assignments. If a class-mate does the transposing, be sure the copy is correct and legible before giving it to the visually impaired child.

Indefinite vocabulary.   Demonstrations and chalkboard presentations that include terms such as *this one* or *these* are confusing to those who cannot see the board or demonstration materials. Avoid words that require visual perception for understanding. When using the chalkboard, verbalize what is being written so the student can hear what is missed visually. For example, when demonstrating the proper placement of the apostrophe in possessive nouns, avoid saying "Place the apostrophe right here." Instead, say "Place the apostrophe after the root word and before adding the *s* as in S-a-l-l-y's bicycle (spell the example). When communication is this specific, the entire class benefits.

Lengthy assignments and timed tests.   The partially seeing child may find lengthy assignments or tests especially difficult because of eye fatigue or because his narrow visual span makes reading slow. The slowness of reading and writing braille as compared to print creates similar problems for the blind child. Time restrictions may increase the difficulty of a task for both groups. If necessary, allow additional time to finish assignments, or eliminate parts of them when the student has demonstrated understanding of the concept.

Teacher feedback.   The braille student receives no written feedback on his papers, such as "Good paper" or "Is this your best effort?" when the teacher has no knowledge of braille. Comment frequently to the visually impaired child about daily work. Grade honestly; do not overpraise, but recognize genuine achievement. If the child brailles assigned papers and the vision specialist corrects them, allow counseling time to receive feedback on student progress.

Spelling skills.   Although some blind students are proficient in spelling, some may not be, since "the braille reader has fewer contacts with the graphic forms of words than does the sighted reader . . . therefore, he may not have the mental image of the graphic form to aid him in his spelling" (Henderson 1973, p. 214). The sighted child often retains a visual memory of the way a word looks and can tell when he writes it if it does not "look" right. Besides, the braille reader seldom sees a word fully spelled out—most of them are at least partially contracted, and some are represented by only one letter. The letter *p*, for example, when standing alone represents the whole word *people*. To increase proficiency in spelling, use these suggestions:

1. Require frequent oral spelling.
2. Require complete spelling of words on spelling tests, omitting braille contractions.
3. Give training in auditory discrimination.
4. Spell out new vocabulary words encountered in social studies, science, current events, etc.
5. Make the child aware of trade names that sighted children generally observe incidentally, for example, "Kleenex" (not "Cleanex").
6. Emphasize personal spelling preferences in names of people, such as Kathy, Cathy, Cathe.

Math concepts and materials. Blind students have difficulty conceptualizing abstract mathematical principles. The traditional slow and tedious means of computing on the brailler or math slate add to their difficulties.

Visually impaired children need much practice in handling, counting, and sorting objects to master the number facts. Teachers should use tactual and manipulative materials whenever teaching a new concept and as needed for reinforcement later. Setting up and working math problems on the brailler is a slow and tedious process. All blind children and many partially seeing ones should learn to use the Cranmer abacus, which is an adaptation of an ancient Japanese calculating device. After learning to use it well, the blind student may be able to complete arithmetic problems as rapidly as sighted children, who would benefit from learning to use it too. A blind student might teach those who are interested. A much more expensive but very efficient device is the electronic "talking calculator," which speaks the entries and answers aloud in synthetic speech.

Reading. The blind pupil will usually read braille, and at first will use books different from his classmates'. Touch is a less efficient sensory mode for reading than sight, and braille is a complicated shorthand system, so the average blind child does not progress as rapidly in the reading program as the average sighted child, nor does he develop equal reading speed. The child who is partially seeing by educational definition reads print, but some differences in his mode of reading are possible. He is usually a relatively slow reader, too, because of his limited visual acuity or visual field. Both of these visually impaired children may read by listening to recorded books or to a live reader.

This is generally the fastest form of reading for either child, and very useful to them, but they also need to have an independent mode of reading.

An older, recently blinded child, or one with deteriorating vision, may face the problem of learning to read braille as a second mode. The vision specialist will be an advisor on the adaptations necessary to help the partially seeing child read as efficiently as possible. She may arrange for a lamp for extra illumination directly on the book or suggest that a desk be moved to avoid light that is too bright for certain eye conditions. The teacher may also provide markers to help the child keep his place on the page, and a bookstand to put the book at a comfortable reading angle, closer to the child's eyes than the desk top. It is important for this teacher to be sure that the child has been evaluated at a low-vision clinic to determine whether a magnifier or other low-vision aid, in addition to the regular glasses, will help with near-vision tasks. The specialist may provide large-type editions of books, but some partially seeing students are able to read standard print, either with or without a low-vision aid.

The classroom teacher should remember that the child may need to hold reading material very close to the face, and may hold it to one side because only one eye is able to see the words. Appreciating these difficulties, the teacher may allow the child to rest the eyes briefly at intervals, but should encourage him to read and to move along as quickly as possible. Some individuals with low vision have responded well to rapid reading instruction. The vision specialist may be able to motivate the student to increase reading speed.

The beginning braille reader will receive instruction from the vision specialist, who should realize that the child is learning not just the braille code, but *learning to read* as well, and should assess reading readiness carefully and use readiness materials similar to those used with sighted students. A reading series and language arts curriculum prepared with the peculiarities of the braille system and the blind child's special needs in mind is available and should be used in the early grades to make the blind child's reading experiences appropriate and meaningful. This will mean that the stories the blind child reads will be different from those in classmates' books, but it is possible to have the child trade storytelling with some of the sighted students. This will be a good language exercise for both, and will keep the blind child involved in the class interests. The child will soon be able to use braille copies of the books the class is reading, and by second or third grade should be able to join one of the regular reading groups even though still receiving some instruction in braille.

Children or youth who had already learned to read print and then lost their vision will also need individual instruction in braille from the vision specialist, unless there are special conditions, such as insensitivity of the fingertips caused by diabetes. The specialist will adapt teaching to the interests, needs, and abilities of the child. The classroom teacher may expect some problems with assignments that require reading while the child is making the transition to braille, unless readers can be provided when materials are not immediately available in recorded form. An older beginning student of braille may never read it fast enough nor easily enough for it to be an enjoyable medium, and may always depend heavily on records, tapes, and live readers.

Electronic machines are now available that give a blind person direct access to the printed page. The Optacon (Optical-to-Tactile-Converter) is a small, portable device that converts the printed letters appearing under its miniature camera to identical tactile letters under the blind person's finger. It makes it possible for the blind person to read any ordinary printed material: books, magazines, telephone directories, typed personal and business correspondence, or instructions on packages. Since it represents only one letter at a time (though very rapidly), it does not provide a fast mode of reading. *It is not intended to supplant braille,* but to *supplement* it by providing access to many materials not available in braille. Learning to read with the Optacon requires lengthy, expert training. Attachments to the machine extend its usefulness and open some job opportunities not previously practical for blind people.

Another marvelous machine in increasing production and use is the Kurzweil Machine, which reads printed matter aloud in synthetic speech. The company that manufactures the Optacon has a working experimental model of a modified Optacon, which also reads aloud from print. These machines can be used with earphones, so that a student using one need not disturb the rest of the class. The vision specialist gives instruction in reading with these devices.

Listening.   Concepts presented orally by the teacher, a reader, or on record or tape players may go unlearned because of poor listening skills (which also hamper mobility and social interactions). Visually impaired children do not automatically use their hearing more effectively than sighted children.

Good listening skills must be taught, especially if the student uses audio-aids frequently. "Accurate auding (reading and learning by listening) is more difficult than accurate reading because listening is more transitory in nature . . . it lacks the physical activity necessary in reading" (Henderson 1973, p. 196).

Many teachers include listening lessons in the regular curriculum. Visually impaired students can benefit from these, provided that cues and responses do not depend on vision. In addition, the vision specialist should provide a *listening training program* planned specifically to satisfy the individual needs of visually impaired students.[4] This may include training in the use of compressed speech—recordings of speech at speeds faster than normal.

Writing. Blind and low-vision children usually require special training and writing materials: the blind child for braille writing, the partially seeing for handwriting. Some handwriting may be nearly illegible because of visual loss or poor muscular coordination. Written communication with the sighted is limited when the blind student relies solely on braille.

For the blind student or one with extremely low vision, instruction in braille writing begins on the braillewriter, a machine roughly the size of a portable typewriter. As the student progresses, there should be instruction in the use of the hand slate and stylus, which is easily carried in pocket or purse and is very useful for notes. Training in the use of both braille writing tools is the responsibility of the vision specialist. This teacher should also teach blind students at least enough handwriting so that they can sign their names.

For the partially seeing student, marking pens and bold-line paper, which the vision specialist can provide, may be necessary. Close supervision is important during beginning instruction in both manuscript and cursive writing. Initially, the size of the letters is not as important as correct letter formation. The specialist may supplement classroom instruction with individual help.

Both partially seeing and blind students should learn to type. The latter especially need this skill as a means of communicating with the sighted. Children's needs vary, but a general guideline is to introduce typing in the fourth grade, providing the child's motor skills are normal. Typing relieves the visually limited child of the tedious task of handwriting and the teacher of trying to decipher illegible handwriting. It can also facilitate proficiency in spelling, especially for the student who relies on braille and encounters so many words in contracted form.

Crafts. Craft projects can be frustrating to the visually impaired student when manipulation must be guided by vision, when the project must conform to certain standards, or when the finished product is only visually enjoyable. In teaching art and crafts, the emphasis should be on the process rather than the product. How the child feels about the product and the enjoyment of expression are the significant factors (Napier 1973). The finished product should bring satisfaction rather than reflect compliance with predetermined standards, especially if the student is blind and relies totally on tactile appreciation. For a project to be visually enjoyable to a partially seeing student, it

4. A number of such programs are suggested in the references following this chapter (e.g. Bischoff 1979).

may be necessary to use vivid colors and strong contrast. Projects that emphasize texture and shape can be enjoyable and beneficial to the whole class, as well as much more meaningful to the visually impaired child. Any project that requires a great deal of teacher or student help is not a good choice: for example, one that requires elaborate gluing of parts.

Color deficiency.   Color confusion or lack of color perception can create academic problems, particularly in early grades where use of crayons and color coding in texts and workbooks is common and reading instruction is just beginning. Art and craft projects may require a great deal of color discrimination.

"Color deficiency is a better term than color blindness in describing . . . abnormal color vision. Even the severely affected person sees color in nearly everything that appears colored to a normal individual. [Although] the color he sees may be quite different from that experienced by the normal individual, he nevertheless sees color" (Gregg and Heath 1964, p. 123). Most color-deficient persons adjust to their problem by learning tricks to differentiate colors or by picking up clues from the brightness or shape of an object. If color deficiency does interfere with academic progress or art activities, the classroom teacher should consult the vision specialist. Here are some suggestions.[5]

1. Eliminate, where possible, color-coded directions in favor of verbal or black-and-white directions. Inform the student of common color coding on maps: for example, water is indicated with blue.
2. Label the parts that are colored in workbooks, reading books, science books, etc. If the child cannot read yet, devise some sort of code, such as a tree for green, a pumpkin for orange.
3. Have the student use marking pens that can be distinguished by odor: for example, a "banana" pen, if an exercise requires the student to respond with colors.
4. Encourage the student to use the colors he does know, since he may be only partially color deficient. Discuss shades of dark and light, bright and dull.
5. Assign the whole class a monochromatic art project in which all contrasts are shown by different shades of one color.
6. Plan a crafts activity in which form and texture are more important than color, such as carving soap, making cloth pictures cut from prints, strips, dots, etc., fingerpainting, or texture collages.

5. Acknowledgement is made to Cornelia Benton, former Vision Resource Teacher, Salt Lake City School District, Utah, for her contributions to this list of suggestions.

Physical.   Visual impairments, especially those that are congenital or affect a child at an early age, can create a variety of problems in physical development.

1. *Coordination, balance, and posture.* Some visually impaired children may be underdeveloped or physically lethargic as a result of overprotection, lack of stimulation, or their own fear of physical involvement. Some may have a tendency to drop their heads, since there is no need for eye contact. This lack of visual orientation may lead to disturbed balance and poor posture.

   It is very important to include partially seeing and blind pupils in a good, all-around physical education program, not only to improve health and general stamina, but to help them develop the responsive body necessary for independent travel with a cane, guide dog, or electronic aid. The teacher should include them in as many game activities as possible, using a sighted partner when necessary. The vision specialist can suggest activities in which the visually impaired pupil can participate successfully with the class. When they must be left out, as in some ball games, they can be assigned some individual physical skill practice, such as rope jumping, rope climbing, or other apparatus work.

2. *Awkward movements.* An odd gait can develop in the blind child from being pushed and pulled around by people untrained in mobility techniques, or from his own untrained efforts to move about. Proper sighted guide techniques are essential for the visually impaired child to develop graceful movement. The teacher should discourage any "push" or "pull" guiding of the blind child; rather, the child's hand should be placed on the guide's elbow or arm so that he is led by the total body movements of the guide (Cratty 1971). The physical education program should also improve movement through calisthenics and corrective exercises.

3. *Tensions.* Many daily activities that are casual efforts for sighted people require full mental attention on the part of the visually impaired. Walking around school is one example. The visually impaired pupil must remain alert to sounds, air currents, textures underfoot, and other stimuli in order to keep track of the route. In class, listening must be more attentive than for other children in order to make up for the visual stimuli that are missing.

   The visually impaired pupil needs opportunities for vigorous physical activity during the day in order to release the extra nervous tension that is built up. At recess and physical education time, the teacher should include the child in group activities. The classroom teacher, the vision specialist, and the parents may need to arrange for some coaching in skills that will make the child a welcome teammate or playmate. Encourage social interaction between the visually impaired student and sighted classmates, so that the child will have friends to relax with over lunch or during class changes.

Concept development and mental functioning. "Partially seeing children either approximate or are equal in their cognitive functions to children who have no visual impairment" (Lowenfeld 1973, p. 34). Congenitally blind children and youth, on the other hand, scored four to eight years below matched sighted subjects on a battery of Piagetian reasoning assessments. Other studies have shown differences, but much less inferiority in comparing cognitive abilities of blind and sighted children. Barraga (1973) presents a helpful summary of such studies. Lowenfeld (1973, p. 34) states that blindness creates problems for the individual in the area of cognitive functions by imposing limitations "(1) in the range and variety of his experiences; (2) in his ability to get about; (3) in his interaction with the environment."

Barraga (1973) stresses the need for further study of the cognitive behavior of blind children. For the classroom teacher, it is significant that when the normal range of early childhood experiences is lacking, as it may well be with a severely visually impaired child, there is a limited mental framework to which new associations may be attached. Language may also be limited, or it may be superficially fluent but with little real meaning for the child because it is not based on actual experience. The teacher must consider these possibilities in determining readiness for reading, mathematics, and other academic subject matter. The vision specialist and school counselor or psychologist can assist in evaluating readiness. Where necessary, the classroom teacher and the specialist can strive to provide concrete experiences to fill in gaps and can encourage parents to increase the child's interaction with the family and the community.

It is important to remember that learning by touch and sound are not the same as learning by sight. The spoken word is not permanent, like the written one; the student cannot as easily go back to study a passage not clearly understood. The student relying on tactile exploration must synthesize fragmented perceptions to form a whole, which can result in a distorted mental image. After examination of a large object, such as a tractor, the blind child's mental image of it may not have the parts in proper arrangement.

There are some concepts that cannot be imparted to congenitally blind students in such a way that their understanding will be comparable to that of sighted children. Things that are very large (mountains), distant (clouds), minute (insects), fragile (soap bubbles), in motion (birds in flight), or that depend on visual perception (colors, mirrors, shadows) do not lend themselves to tactual examination or auditory perception. Verbal explanations and static models may not convey accurate perceptions, and the blind child's conception of them may be very different from reality.

To minimize the difficulties the congenitally blind child has with concepts, the teacher must impart accurate information about such material objects, and ideas dependent on them, and should realize that in most cases inaccurate concepts of them will not interfere with successful living. "In spite of all difficulties, most blind children who are free of additional handicaps learn to cope with their problems, and their intellectual, social, and often their economic achievements compare well with those of their seeing peers" (Lowenfeld 1973, pp. 40–41).

Self-Image. Limited experiences and lack of peer involvement can exclude the visually impaired child from normal opportunities to develop self-confidence. On the other hand, the child may reject his limitations and have an unrealistic view of himself. Society makes it difficult for a handicapped individual to develop a strong self-image by setting conflicting expectations. On the one hand people demand that the individual accept the handicap, and on the other they want him to become as near normal as possible. They also require the individual to sublimate feelings and meet standards of appearance that are arbitrary and often meaningless: "That doesn't look nice." They marvel at things that are really simple, like recognizing voices and familiar footsteps, but fail to appreciate the real difficulty of other tasks, such as setting up arithmetic problems on the brailler.

Many people are surprised to learn that the partially seeing child often has more difficulty with self-image and social acceptance than the blind child. He is "neither fish nor fowl," and parents, teachers, and other children may all have difficulty knowing what to expect visually; consequently, they may be inconsistent in their demands. The child is often put in the humiliating position of having to justify the inability to perform a task that a teacher or classmate thought was visually possible for him.

To help a visually impaired pupil develop assurance of integrity as a human being, with a sturdy self-image that does not deny the visual loss, the classroom teacher can use the suggestions given below.

1. Examine her own attitude toward blindness, and relate to the pupil rather than to the impairment.
2. Explain or let the child explain the impairment to the other children in a forthright and matter-of-fact manner so that they understand what is different. If the teacher feels it will not be upsetting, let the child take part in the discussion. This will help alleviate the uneasiness children feel because of inexperience with blind individuals.

Social/Emotional Problems

3. Be interested in the blind student's special equipment, and allow classmates to examine it and try it when reasonable. Have him show how it substitutes for some of the materials they use. After initial interest has been satisfied, special materials can be taken for granted.

4. Respect the child's nonvisual perceptions. Don't expect the blind student to write, for example, in the same visual terms the other children use. Encourage him to describe events in terms of his own perceptions, as does the young blind man who went on his first backpacking trip. He remembered a waterfall by "the mist in my face and the roar of the water that shook my whole body," and the ground squirrels because he could "hear them scurry over the rocks, feel them nuzzle my fingers, and jump on my shoulder" (Allen 1977). The teacher and classmates should develop new enjoyment of their other senses as each learns to appreciate how the visually impaired child uses his.

5. Try to help the child establish genuine friendships among classmates. Do not let one student help all the time. Encourage the child to accept the need for help; teach him to ask for it unself-consciously when it is needed and to refuse it gracefully when it is not. Discourage any tendency to manipulate either schoolmates or adults, who may accept it but will resent it.

6. Communicate observations of the child's strengths and weaknesses to the vision specialist. The classroom teacher spends much more time with the child than the specialist does, and feelings about progress and problems will help the specialist plan school work.

7. Help the specialist to provide experiences with visually impaired peers. These experiences allow the child to release tensions caused by the sometimes unreasonable demands made by the sighted world.

The vision specialist can best assist the visually impaired child to develop a positive self-image by teaching the special skills that allow him to achieve academically and socially in association with sighted students and that will also serve him as an adult in the sighted world. Nothing is so effective in changing traditional attitudes toward blindness as association with a successful blind person.

Emotional instability.   Inconsistent behavioral control in the home, oversolicitousness, or physical and emotional neglect are more common in relation to handicapped children than to others. Some handicapped children have been shunted from one foster home to another because the foster parents found the ramifications of the handicap overwhelming. A specialist in working with emotionally handicapped children and their parents will be needed to advise and support the teacher in working with an unstable blind child.

The appearance of the visually handicapped child's eyes may be unpleasant to classmates; unattractive physical mannerisms, such as rocking motions and head rolling, may also cause ostracism. In junior high and high school, just being noticeably different from the norm is enough to cause some schoolmates to shun him, while others may avoid him because they feel that they do not know how to relate. It is possible for the visually impaired student in an integrated program to be very much segregated from sighted classmates. Lack of recreational skills and the inability to see where a group is that he would like to join are other factors limiting interaction with sighted peers. Unsuccessful attempts to be involved with classmates may result in withdrawal, aggression, or other inappropriate behavior. The teacher may be able to help the child become truly integrated by cooperating with the specialist in correcting unattractive mannerisms and teaching social graces, skills of independence, and recreational skills.

Human sexuality. Lack of vision, or very limited vision, greatly reduces what the child learns about the human body. Distorted perceptions of sex differences result because movies, pictures, advertisements, television, and swimming party and locker room exposures—"all the informal learning experiences in which the seeing child receives information about other people's bodies" (Knappett and Wagner 1976, p. 1)—are unavailable or reduced for him. This lack of anatomical knowledge is of course only one aspect of understanding human sexuality. The possible problems of self-concept already outlined, and all the social-emotional limitations that may exist for the visually handicapped individual affect understanding of himself and others and success in human relationships.

"Ideally, parents should give their blind child information concerning anatomy and sexuality in general. A great deal can be done in this respect at an early age, before the taboos against nudity and touching come into effect" (Knappett and Wagner 1976, p. 2). Unfortunately, many parents are unwilling or unable to do this. In any case, information gained as a young child is not sufficient for the later years, and most parents become less able to communicate on sexual matters as their children become older. School programs for blind children have largely had very inadequate provisions for sex education and family life training. In day-school programs, the blind child and youth should be included in whatever provisions there are for this type of education, ideally with cooperation of an outside agency prepared to give the additional guidance that lack of vision makes indispensable.

The classroom teacher can teach the sighted students to distinguish between times to help, when the need is real, and inappropriate times, when the visually impaired child can handle a situation independently. The teacher should not put the child, nor let other students put the child, in a passive position when there could be active participation, and should be certain the child is a giver as well as a receiver. She can encourage the students to talk normally around the blind child, using *look* and *see* freely. Blind people accept these as meaning *perceive* and use them in that sense themselves. It would be helpful to the blind child and enriching to classmates if they could learn to use descriptive language in speaking. Some exercises in this would be appropriate in a language arts program.

One of the greatest material needs of the visually impaired student is that of textbooks. The classroom teacher will need to provide the vision specialist in advance with any special textbook requirements the student may have, for example the need for large-print books. The optimal time for textbook requests is before the close of one school year in preparation for the following year. The same guideline is true of individual assignments that need alterations, such as achievement tests.

The classroom teacher needs to be aware of possible format changes when a print textbook has been transcribed in braille, which the specialist can point out. Often, to save space, braille books contain two or more numbered pages on one braille book page: for example, page 23 in the print edition may end and page 24 begin all on the same page in the braille edition.

It is sometimes impossible to distinguish between a braille mistake and a spelling error, even for the vision specialist. However, the specialist can check orally with the blind student and then write the print version of the child's spelling on the braille paper for the regular teacher's benefit. As soon as the blind child is reasonably proficient on the typewriter, the regular teacher can correct the work, but in this case the teacher will need to consider the possibility of typing errors, and may sometimes want to check by having the student spell orally the word in question.

To elicit a blind student's wavering attention in the absence of eye contact,

1. Walk to the desk so the child is aware of geographical closeness.
2. Touch the child lightly on the shoulder.
3. Address the child by name.
4. Ask review questions during oral presentations.

Recently specialists in education of the visually impaired have been looking critically at themselves and their roles and realizing that more than the traditional academic tutoring and counseling is needed by visually impaired students in mainstream settings. Supplying special materials and teaching special skills to provide academic support are still seen as essential, but providing or arranging for instruction in daily living skills and career education, to name two examples, are now also considered the responsibility of the special educator. And while integrated placement is considered ideal for most visually impaired children, teachers have come to realize that placement in regular school classes, even when there is good cooperation among the classroom teacher, the parents, and the vision specialist, does not provide all that the visually impaired student needs to gain from school experiences.

In an integrated classroom there is seldom more than one visually impaired student, and in an itinerant arrangement there may be only one in a school. Such children therefore have a minority status, and "have no peers who share their vision-related probems or who understand from experience the difficulties or even the very difference of their situation" (Martin and Hoben 1977, p. 60). They are also limited by a lack of models among their peers and may have no contact with successful older blind individuals outside of school. With all the stress on how much like sighted students the visually impaired are, everyone concerned with them must remember that there *are* differences which must be dealt with (Martin and Hoben 1977).

Martin and Hoben (1977) cite examples of successful efforts to bring together groups of visually impaired young people to create peer support groups and provide opportunities for contact with success models while offering training in needed skills of independence and recreational and personal-interpersonal skills. They suggest that such efforts must be team endeavors, often going beyond school district boundaries to regional structure. After-school support groups, summer programs, workshops, and parent support groups are possible patterns for valuable nonacademic contributions to the educational process.

Special educators consider extensions of school services like these their particular challenges. However, to contribute the skills in which they alone are trained, specialists need the cooperation of regular administrators and classroom teachers, who should accept responsibility for most of the academic program and also participate in nonacademic efforts to minimize the difficulties that partially seeing and blind students experience. With this level of cooperation, the lofty goals of the Education for All Handicapped Children Act of 1975 can be reached.

References

Allen, J. L. 1977. Backpacking: more than meets the eye. *Journal of Visual Impairment and Blindness* 71:274–75.

Ashcroft, S. C. 1963. Blind and partially seeing children. In *Exceptional children in the schools,* ed. L. M. Dunn. New York: Holt.

Barraga, N. C. 1964. *Increased visual behavior in low vision children.* New York: American Foundation for the Blind.

Barraga, N. C. 1973. Utilization of sensory perceptual abilities. In *The visually handicapped child in school*, ed. B. Lowenfeld. New York: John Day.

Barraga, N. C. 1976. *Visual handicaps and learning: a developmental approach.* Belmont, Calif.: Wadsworth.

Barraga, N. C. 1978. Program to develop efficiency in visual functioning. University of Texas at Austin and American Printing House for the Blind (Final report in press). Oral reports presented at Council for Exceptional Children Annual Convention, Kansas City, May, 1978.

Bischoff, R. W. 1979. Listening: A teachable skill for visually impaired persons. *The Journal of Visual Impairment and Blindness*, no. 2, vol. 73.

Boswell, J. 1904. *Life of Johnson*, ed. G. B. Hill. New York: Harper and Brothers.

Cratty, B. J. 1971. *Movement and spatial awareness in blind children and youth.* Illinois: Charles C Thomas.

Gregg, J. R. and Heath, G. G. 1964. *The eye.* Boston: D. C. Heath.

Hatlin, P. 1978. Some highlights of the convention. *DVH Newsletter* 22:12.

Henderson, F. 1973. Communication skills. In *The visually handicapped child in school*, ed. B. Lowenfeld. New York: John Day.

Knappett, K. and Wagner, N. N. 1976. Sex education and the blind. *Education of the Visually Handicapped*, no. 1, 7:1.

Lowenfeld, B. 1973. Psychological considerations. In *The visually handicapped child in school,* ed. B. Lowenfeld. New York: John Day.

Martin, G. J. and Hoben, M. 1977. *Supporting visually impaired students in the mainstream.* Council for Exceptional Children.

Miller, J. 1976. Letter to editor. *DVH Newsletter*, no. 1, 21:15–16.

Napier, G. D. 1973. Special subject adjustment and skills. In *The visually handicapped child in school*, ed. B. Lowenfeld. New York: John Day.

Report on Research and Development Activities. 1978. Louisville: American Printing House for the Blind.

Scholl, G. T. 1978a. Current activities directed toward improvement of educational programs for visually handicapped pupils. *DVH Newsletter*, no. 3, 21:4–5.

Scholl, G. T. 1978b. *Self-study and evaluation guide for day programs for visually handicapped pupils: a guide for program improvement.* Ann Arbor, Mich.: The University of Michigan.

Spungin, S. J. 1977. *Competency-based curriculum for teachers of the visually handicapped: A National Study.* New York: American Foundation for the Blind.

Taylor, J. L. 1973. Educational programs. In *The visually handicapped child in schools,* ed. B. Lowenfeld. New York: John Day.

Taylor, J. L. 1976. Mainstreaming visually handicapped children and youth: yesterday, today and tomorrow. In *Selected papers from Association for the Education of the Visually Handicapped.* Philadelphia.

Walker, D. L. 1977a. Editorial: a striptease. *Education of the Visually Handicapped* 19:31–32.

Walker, D. L. 1977b. Editorial: teacher skills needed for new types of services. *Education of the Visually Handicapped* 9:61–62.

10 Teaching Students with Physical Disabilities and Health Impairments

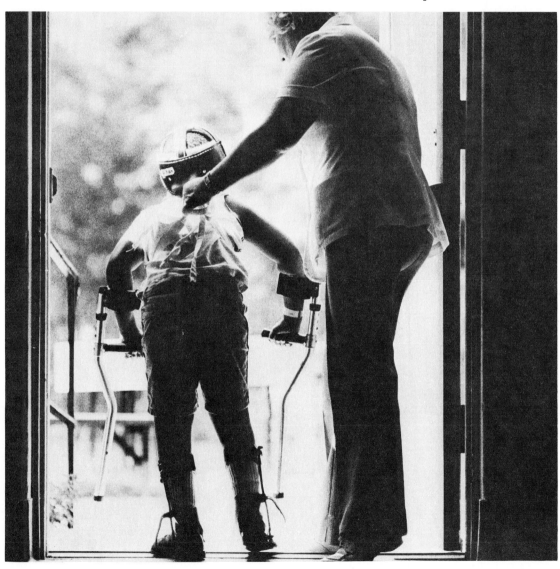

The most diverse of all the labeled populations of exceptional children are those with physically limiting conditions. The population consists of people who need special help in school with problems related to mobility, stamina, time, environment, or equipment. The child who is physically handicapped may also have unique learning needs due to retardation or giftedness, learning disabilities, emotional or social problems, language and speech difficulties, or hearing or vision impairments.

Often children with physical impairments will require no special services in school. A child may come to school in a wheelchair, or with a missing limb, or with a heart condition, but that does not mean, necessarily, that he or she will be a candidate for special education or for therapy services in addition to the regular classroom program. Each child's needs must be considered individually and the most appropriate program developed based on input from many professionals in education, medicine, and related areas. One child with cerebral palsy who uses crutches and braces may need a great deal of special help in order to succeed in school, while another who uses similar equipment and has the same diagnosis may be able to participate in all activities in the regular classroom and be identified as a leader by the other children. Attitudes of the family, previous training, age of onset, and other variables besides physical ability contribute to the nature of any one child's overall requirements for special services.

Not only is there little homogeneity within the group labeled *physically handicapped,* but there are numerous, often interchangeable, terms used to refer to children who are physically handicapped. In some states special education categories are used, such as *motor impaired* or *motor disabled,* while others include categories such as *orthopedically handicapped* or *crippled, and other health impaired* (COHI), in order to specify programs designed to meet the needs of these children. Many children who are physically impaired have difficulties in other developmental areas; therefore, the terms *physically handicapped* or *physically impaired,* and the term *multiple handicapped* are becoming linked frequently as descriptors for the population receiving special services. Although there is not a direct relationship, it is often true that the more severely physically handicapped children are, the higher the probability that they will require special help in other areas of development besides motor skills. Severely physically handicapped individuals may be intelligent, highly verbal, achieving, fully functioning people who have difficulty moving, or, on the other hand, they may demonstrate significant deficits in any or all of these areas.

Within the academic setting, many children who are physically impaired need not be considered handicapped. A handicap interferes with the skills that are expected of the individual in a specific setting. Children whose legs are paralyzed are handicapped if the tasks they are to perform require the use of legs for support or movement: they cannot perform as required. A nonvocal child who is required to give a speech is handicapped, since the physical impairment prevents the child from performing the task required. Unless the impairment keeps the individual from performing as expected, there is no handicap. The nonvocal child is not handicapped in silent reading, art, volleyball, or other activities where speech is not a requirement. "A difference is a difference only if it makes a difference" (Wolfe 1963). For many of the physically handicapped, there is little or no difference in their performance in a classroom when compared with the performance of students who are not physically impaired.

Students who require special assistance in order to be assigned to the regular program may need very different types of help. The student who has difficulty with fine motor skills may require a tape recorder or an electric typewriter to complete assignments. Other students may require help in meeting personal needs only, such as toileting or getting a tray in the cafeteria. Assistance in changing positions, moving between classes, or communicating may be required by others.

Teachers of the physically handicapped as well as physical, speech, and occupational therapists serve as resource personnel who help the regular classroom teacher meet the needs of the child in the mainstream. Teachers, therapists, or their aides, may provide direct services to the child, consult with the teacher, prepare special materials and equipment, or assist the child with self-help skills as needed and agreed upon in the team conference. Often the specialist(s) will assist the classroom teacher in discussing the progress of the child with the parents or in obtaining various community resources for the family.

Special education teachers trained in the area of the physically handicapped are competent to manage medical conditions in the classroom, and to meet the special communication, academic, physical, sensory, and social needs of the child. They also serve as a liaison between the regular classroom teacher and therapist and medical advisors or clinical staff members. The special education teacher should inform the regular classroom teacher of any unique needs, equipment, and so forth, of the student joining a class, and help to prepare the classroom environment and the student's future classmates for the successful integration of the child who is physically handicapped.

There are several major types of programs for students receiving services as physically handicapped. Most such students are served in regular elementary and secondary programs; however, there are two specialized programs through which specific needs may be met. These are the programs for pregnant students and for students who are hospitalized or homebound. Students from any of these three programs may become a part of regular educational programs when specialized services are no longer needed or when special communication systems are installed in the classrom, such as intercoms, phones, or terminals, which allow the student to become a part of regular classroom activities.

Students receiving services in the elementary and secondary programs for the physically handicapped and in regular education include those who require adaptations in programs due to neurological, muscular, skeletal, or systemic conditions or diseases. A teacher of physically handicapped children learns quickly that a condition rarely manifests itself to the same degree or in the same way in any two students with the same medical diagnosis or physical condition. There are, however, several principles to remember for all physically handicapped students regardless of the cause of the impairment.

Definitions of the Population and Implications for Teachers

1. There are more mildly handicapped children with physical conditions than those who are severely/multiply handicapped. No two individuals are involved in exactly the same way or to the same degree, even though they have the same condition or disease.
2. Children who are physically handicapped have the same needs and hopes as other children; they have feelings and desires, and aspire to achieve independence, inclusion, and autonomy.
3. Children who lack the ability to express themselves because of motor difficulties may be as capable as other persons of taking in information and producing new information. A student's inability to communicate should not lead one to the erroneous conclusion that the student is also incapable of receiving and processing information.
4. Handicaps are easily imposed on individuals who are physically impaired. If changes are made in programs, environments, and so forth, they should be based on individual needs, not just on a label, diagnosis, or category. It is not a kindness to excuse students from exhibiting social courtesies, doing homework, or taking tests just because they are physically different.

Society requires certain skills and behaviors of all members. Students should not be allowed to manipulate people or otherwise use their handicaps to avoid responsibilities and positive interaction with others.

Conditions and Diseases
Cerebral Palsy

The most frequently identified condition among children requiring services for the physically handicapped is **cerebral palsy** (CP). This condition is caused by damage to or dysfunction of the developing brain. The damage may occur before birth, at birth, or during the developmental years. Some professionals use the term *cerebral palsy-like* for disturbances in motor patterns that occur in children between the ages of three and eighteen years but were not present at birth. The condition itself is not progressive; that is, one does not get worse as a direct result of the condition. Children with cerebral palsy often require therapy to keep muscles from becoming contracted and to prevent deformities in the skeletal system. These problems are often due to muscle imbalance or energy overflow, which interfere with movement, regular exercise, or appropriate posture. The incidence of learning disabilities, hearing and vision problems, mental retardation, seizures, and language/communication disorders is greater among cerebral palsied children than among children without cerebral palsy. Nevertheless, there are many individuals with cerebral palsy who are gifted and have no other handicapping conditions. Children with spastic cerebral palsy have more seizures than those with other types of cerebral palsy. The individual with athetoid cerebral palsy has a greater chance of having a hearing loss than persons with other types of cerebral palsy (Bleck 1975).

Some children with cerebral palsy will not appear to have any different needs until they call upon their muscles to perform a physical task such as writing or walking. Spasticity or spastic cerebral palsy occurs when nerves do not get the proper message from the brain due to damage to the motor cortex area of the cerebrum. This causes some muscles to become too tight while others are too loose. When muscle groups do not work together properly, jerky movements occur, and the individual has a difficult time performing tasks requiring motor skills. Other children will be in constant motion except when they sleep. People with athetosis, or athetoid cerebral palsy, lack the ability to keep their muscles at rest and exhibit shaking, flailing motions. When specific muscles are called upon to perform a task, the purposeless motion becomes heightened.

The ataxic individual has damage in the cerebellar area of the brain and therefore has difficulty with balance. Uncoordinated movement and difficulty with position in space are characteristic of those with ataxia. The most common type of cerebral palsy reported in children is a mixed one: the individual has characteristics of athetoid, spastic, and perhaps ataxic cerebral palsy.

There are other types of cerebral palsy, but they do not occur as frequently as those that have been mentioned. Rigid and tremor types of cerebral palsy occur in less than 10 percent of cases and involve damage to the motor cortex and basal ganglia area of the brain.

Individuals with motor difficulties are often described using another type of classification system, which is based on where the damage is exhibited. A **quadriplegic** is one who has difficulty moving all four limbs. A **hemiplegic's** difficulty in motor functioning occurs on one side of the body. **Diplegia** and **paraplegia** occur when the problems in movement are primarily in the legs. The diplegic has greater paralysis in the legs than in the arms.

Spina Bifida, Meningocele, or Myelomeningocele

Spina bifida, meningocele, or myelomeningocele result when the development of the spine and spinal column is interrupted early in pregnancy and have been referred to generally as *myclodysplasia.* This condition is present at birth and may require numerous hospitalizations during the developmental years. Braces and crutches are required to help many of these children to walk; others use wheelchairs, canes, or walkers.

Myelomeningocele is the most severely debilitating of the three conditions generally referred to as **spina bifida.** The spinal cord, the membranes that surround it, and the spinal fluid protrude through the vertebral column. The child is usually paralyzed from the area of protrusion downward since nerves below this point cannot receive messages from the brain and spinal column. The lower down the column the myelomeningocele occurs, the more likely it is that the child will receive at least some sensation in the legs and feet. Among children with spina bifida, it is more frequent to find a child with myelomeningocele than with meningocele or spina bifida occulta.

A **meningocele** occurs when only the membranes and fluid surrounding the spinal column push out through the backbones or vertebrae. Children with this condition are usually not paralyzed but may exhibit some motor or sensation difficulties.

Spina bifida occulta is of least concern to educators since children with this condition are rarely in need of special services. In this condition there is a lack of bone at the lower end of the backbone. This is usually a small area and is covered with skin. The only difference that might be noted may be an increase in the number of characteristic hairs in the skin covering the area. This condition may not be identified until the student is examined by the physician for participation in high school sports. The student may be limited to noncontact sports and cautioned to protect the area from blows.

Children with myelomeningocele or meningocele may have additional conditions that require special educational services. The child may miss numerous days of school for surgery, appointments with medical personnel, and therapy sessions. Children who miss a long period of school (at least three to six weeks in most states) may be eligible for services from the homebound or hospital teacher during their absence from school.

Other conditions that may be present include hip and foot problems, a loss of pain and pressure sensations, lack of control of bowel and bladder functions, and **hydrocephalus**. Therapy, nursing, or medical staff members working with school personnel can develop toileting, mobility, or general monitoring programs needed by such children who attend regular school classes.

Many children with spina bifida are of normal intelligence although they may be handicapped by a lack of experiences due to their inability to explore their environment independently. Some parents find it difficult to take their child places since needed equipment (wheelchair, etc.) is bulky and heavy. Also, as with other handicapped children, the parents may feel a social stigma about having a handicapped child and try to protect the child and themselves from stares and comments.

Socially appropriate verbal skills may be more highly developed in the child with spina bifida than the intellectual skills of comprehension, association, memory, and so forth. Teachers need to be aware that such children may not be learning at the rate or depth that their verbal skills may indicate; therefore, assessment techniques for learning about their skills must be used on a regular basis in the classroom.

A unique problem in the classroom for children without bowel/bladder control is that of odor. It is important that this problem be referred to the appropriate person—the school nurse, special teacher, or therapist—so that steps can be taken to correct it. As a general rule, odors should not be present. They are usually a signal that something is wrong with the program or equipment being used to meet toileting needs. It is especially important that this problem be worked out immediately so that the child is not isolated or rejected by other children.

If the child with hydrocephalus seems to deviate greatly from the usual learning pattern, it may be due to a malfunction of the shunt (the mechanism used to drain fluid from the brain). Any substantial or sustained decrease in attending, memory, or expression skills may be a sign that the shunt is not working properly, and that the child is in need of medical attention.

Muscular Dystrophy Genetically based conditions that lead to (1) progressive weakening of the muscles that support the body and (2) replacement of muscle tissue with fat cells are called **muscular dystrophies.** The type that affects children and is seen usually in boys in the school age population is called Duchenne-type muscular dystrophy (MD).

Children with muscular dystrophy are generally in regular classrooms in the schools until they require special help to meet their physical needs. Frequently this process is the opposite for children with spina bifida and cerebral palsy, who often begin school in special programs and are then placed in regular classes as their academic skills, performance, and independence levels improve.

An early sign of motor problems in muscular dystrophy involves walking with the heels off the floor. This is caused by a weakness in the foot and is progressive, causing the child to begin to walk on tiptoes eventually. A sway back becomes prominent and the child begins to develop a pivot walk. If the child falls he will use his hands to "climb up himself" to regain his walking balance. Some muscles may look as though they are developing into large, strong ones; however, the opposite is true. The tissue of these muscles is being replaced by fatty tissue. The muscle looks big, but in reality it is becoming less and less useful.

Children with MD in the regular program may be helped by special staff members to learn to fall and get up, as well as to position themselves so as not to become tired. As the condition progresses, they may need to be taught how to transfer from a chair or toilet to a wheelchair and back. Adapted equipment, such as long handled scissors or graspers to extend their reach, and eating and writing equipment may be supplied as needed. Some orthopedic specialists will brace children with muscular dystrophy to help them remain independent walkers for a longer period of time.

Although no cure has been found for MD, many of these children are living much longer and are reaching adulthood. At one time, children with muscular dystrophy were not in school and spent many years at home with little to occupy them. Now children attend school as long as they are able, and when they are no longer able to come to school, they are eligible for the services of a homebound teacher. Death due to complications related to muscle weakness may occur within ten to fifteen years of when the symptoms of MD first appear (Calhoun and Hawisher 1979).

Developing and maintaining positive self-regard and mental health may be difficult for the child with muscular dystrophy. Thoughts of growing strong, leading a productive adult life, and of becoming a worker are all motivators for children; however, when these are not realistic goals, other motivators or reinforcers need to be identified to help a child find reason and purpose for continuing to work and to learn. Appropriate counseling opportunities with both adults and peers should be made available.

Skeletal Conditions There are many different conditions that prevent the growth of bones or cause them to grow in a faulty way. *Osteogenesis imperfecta* (brittle bones), *artheogryposis* (non-flexible joints and weak muscles), amputations that are from birth or from childhood accidents, and *Legg-Perthes disease* (degeneration of the hip socket and head of the bone of the upper leg), are some of the conditions that might require specialized instruction or environmental modifications for a child in school.

Children with amputations of upper limbs require unique assistance in the classroom. The child who has lost one or both limbs may use a prosthetic or artificial limb in its place. Some children find these devices to be cumbersome, hot, or inflexible and therefore do not use them. Children who do use them must learn to inspect the fitting of the prosthesis and to seek help if the connecting skin area becomes irritated.

Some children become skilled at writing using varied techniques if they do not have fingers or hands. One child may write by trapping a pencil between the short upper arm and chest, another may use a mouthpiece, while yet another may write using toes to grasp the pen. Classroom adaptations for children with amputations of arms include an appropriate seating arrangement and specialized equipment. Some children will need a higher table so they can stand to write, others a slanted desk top, and still others a low, slanted desk or flat surface for writing with their toes.

Convulsive Disorders Abnormalities in the functioning of the brain are the causes of **seizures** and **convulsions.** The term **epilepsy** is used to describe the condition in which both seizure (the sudden onset of a set of symptoms) and convulsion (spasm) are present. There are numerous causes of the disorders grouped within the generic term of *convulsive disorders.* The label *fit* is considered improper in the United States.

Convulsive disorders have had a stigma attached to them throughout history. Society has learned only in modern times that dysfunctions of the chemistry of the brain are responsible for these conditions and not spirits, the devil, or meanness in the individual. In some societies of old, persons with convulsions were worshipped as inspired by the gods, while in other cultures they were stoned or cast out as persons inhabited by evil spirits.

Each school district and each school should have a written plan for medical emergencies that includes a statement about the best practices for handling a convulsion. The Epilepsy Foundation of America has published the following procedure to follow when a major convulsion occurs:

1. Remain calm. Students will assume the same emotional reactions as their teacher. The seizure is painless to the child.
2. Do not try to restrain the child. There is nothing you can do to stop a seizure once it has begun. It must run its course.

3. Clear the area around him so that he does not injure himself on hard or sharp objects. Try not to interfere with his movements in any way.
4. Don't force anything between his teeth. If his mouth is already open, you might place a soft object like a handerkerchief between his side teeth.
5. It isn't necessary to call a doctor unless the attack is followed almost immediately by another major seizure, or if the seizure lasts more than about ten minutes.
6. When the seizure is over, let the child rest if he wants to.
7. The child's parents and physician should be informed of the seizure.
8. Turn the incident into a learning experience for the entire class. Explain what a seizure is, that it is not contagious, and that it is nothing to be afraid of. Teach understanding for the child—not pity—so that his classmates will continue to accept him as "one of the gang."

Convulsions in classrooms are not limited to just those identified as handicapped. The student who has a convulsion may never have had a seizure before and may have no known physical conditions related to convulsive disorders. The student may also have been seizure-free for many years after having had only one or two as a small child. Any child in the classroom may be the one to have a convulsion. Most individuals who experience convulsions do so before age twenty, but they may have their first seizure as they attain the age of puberty. The child who has been seizure-free as a result of medication may have the first seizure since early childhood with the onset of adolescence and the change in body chemistry. For most children, seizures can be controlled through the use of medication.

Seizures vary in their intensity and duration from localized minor seizures, previously referred to as petit mal seizures, to generalized major seizures described as tonic-clonic states in which the individual loses consciousness, previously referred to as grand mal seizures. Some seizures last a few seconds without major movement, while others may occur for several minutes with tremendous amounts of motor involvement.

The academic performance of children with convulsive disorders is widely varied. Most students should be expected to function within the normal range. As with other children, some will be gifted and others less than average in ability. As a student enters a seizure and during the "misfiring time" in the brain, he or she will not be able to take in information. It is difficult to generalize about how much impact convulsive disorders will have on the learning pattern of a specific individual. With the less obvious seizure pattern, a child may actually have ten to thirty interruptions in intake of information within a minute or two. There have been numerous instances in which children were disciplined for inattention or daydreaming when they were actually experiencing minor seizures. This is not to say that all or even very much of the lack of attending in school is caused by convulsive disorders!

Health-Related Conditions

There are many health conditions and diseases that could cause a child to require special services. This chapter will cover only the most prominent conditions that will require the teacher's attention. The conditions most frequently observed in children in programs for the physically handicapped will be discussed and reviewed. The conditions themselves are not the primary point of concern in educational programs for the physically handicapped. A major concern is the support and facilitation of the child in academic, mental health, and physical areas in which his or her needs are different from those of the child who is not physically impaired.

Problems related to the functioning of specific organs, such as heart, lungs, kidneys, and pancreas, are among those found in children in special programs. Heart defects, tuberculosis, asthma, diabetes, and cystic fibrosis may all require that the child have special routines, equipment, or programs within the school. Depending on the severity and treatment of the problem, children will require that specific programs be outlined for them. Such programs may require only that times be set aside during the day for medication or injection supervision, or they may require that rest periods as well as special procedures, such as postural drainage or suction, be carried out during the day.

As with muscular dystrophy, children with various cancers, luekemias, and anemias are in school today who were not in school in the past. For some childhood cancers and leukemias the cure rate is now over 60–75 percent if treatment is initiated early. Children with these conditions may miss school and be assigned to homebound or hospital teachers after surgery or during periods of intensive therapy. When children are in a state of remission of symptoms, they are usually in school and able to participate in most activities in the regular program.

The death or impending death of a student with a terminal condition is an especially difficult time for those who know the child. For teachers and other students in the classroom, it is a time of reflection and thought. Some children may talk openly about death, while others deny it or remain silent. The classroom teacher may seek help from the school counselor and special teacher in handling the topic of death in the classroom. It is the teacher's role to set the tone of the classroom and to provide discussion periods in which children can ask questions and express their feelings. Students should have a time to discuss their feelings and to share their emotions in a supportive environment. Teachers cannot ignore the situation during such a difficult period. The teacher's role is one of honest sharing of feelings and guidance in helping the students decide how to show their feelings of grief and participate in any services upon the death of a classmate. Several texts, such as those by Gyulay (1978) and Grollman (1969, 1974), are excellent resources for helping teachers consider the issue of death.

Special programs for students who become pregnant are provided in most states. In some areas the programs are part of the regular program and are conducted in a regular high school. In other districts, the services are provided by the school board but at a center or nonregular school facility. Advantages of both systems for services can be argued. In the first model the regular classroom teacher may be involved in helping the student to stay in school, to make special arrangements for completing assignments at home after she delivers, and to learn skills that she will need to care for herself and her baby. In some programs the father may be included in special classes or counseling programs. Day care is provided as a part of some programs. Special classes on child care, growth and development, and nutrition may be made available to mothers in school. Although these programs serve high-school students and those in secondary programs primarily, there are many younger girls eligible for such programs. There are a significant number of ten-, eleven-, and twelve-year-olds being served in these programs; therefore, it is not unlikely that a teacher of elementary-age children would be involved in providing for the needs of a returning student-mother. Problem areas in which the regular classroom teacher may be of assistance to the student include making up academic work as required, reestablishing old friendships or developing new ones, developing a positive self-image, and scheduling and establishing priorities for time and attention if the girl is raising the child.

Pregnancy Programs

The characteristics of students receiving services within hospital and home-bound programs have changed a great deal in the last ten years. No longer are children taught at home solely because they are physically handicapped, not expected to live long, or the only child "like that" in the district. The advent of state and federal legislation to ensure the rights of children to participate in an appropriate, least restrictive educational program has caused many previously excluded children to be in classrooms now.

Hospital/ Homebound Programs

Those children receiving homebound instruction today are often those recovering from accidents, diseases, or surgery who are temporarily in need of being educated at home. A second group may include children who have been so aggressive in schools that they have been removed so that others may learn. Included in this group are seriously emotionally disturbed children and youth. It may be argued whether a homebound program is appropriate for this population.

There are two groups of children receiving educational services in the hospital: (1) the short-term surgery patient or the child with an illness and (2) the child requiring long-term hospitalization, such as in a specialized service for those with orthopedic disabilities, kidney dysfunction, or severe burns. For the second population, the regular classroom teacher may not be involved until the child is ready to re-enter the school.

The regular classroom teacher's role with most homebound and hospitalized children is to provide lessons, texts, and so forth for the special teacher to present to the child. In some communities special electronic devices, such as telephones or televisions, are used to keep the child in touch with the class at school.

Establishing Positive Regard for All Individuals

When a new student is introduced, it is usual to describe or remember the child using labels related to physical appearance—the red-headed boy; the tall, black girl, and so forth. As teachers learn of individual's behaviors and positive qualities, the students become "Johnny, who always helps me after school," "Sally with the caring attitude," and so forth. Children who are physically handicapped have difficulty in getting people to know them beyond the "braces" or "wheelchair" level of superficial knowledge. Teachers, administrators, and peers need to be encouraged to talk to, tease, and generally include the child with a physical handicap just as they do anyone else.

There is a difference in the attitude behind saying "the physically handicapped child" and "the child with a physical handicap." All children have the same qualities of humanness; that is, they are children first! It can be expected that the personality, skills, and needs of a child in braces will be more like those of a child in the regular classroom than those of another child who happens to wear braces also.

Some adults who have not known persons who are physically handicapped may tend to think that anyone whose physical skills are significantly impaired will also have impaired intellectual skills. This is not necessarily so. In fact, one should assume that physically handicapped children have normal intelligence. Even when test scores are low, remember that in most environments there are only two ways for a person to indicate what he or she knows: verbally, or manually through writing or gesture. Both of these avenues may be limited for the child with a physical handicap; therefore, test scores may not reflect what the child knows.

Establishing the Least Restrictive Environment

Federal and state laws require that the appropriate educational environment be established in which children with a physical impairment can develop their potential in an optimal manner. At times this requirement is difficult to meet for several reasons: (1) many professionals involved in providing services may disagree on the needs of a child; (2) the equipment and space required by a child may severely crowd a regular classroom; (3) communications equipment or systems that allow a child to interact may not be portable, available in a specific school, or known to the regular teacher (e.g., the sign language of ETRAN—gazing at a particular point on an imaginary rectangle to indicate a letter, number, phrase, etc.); (4) transportation, therapy and classroom equipment specific to the needs of a child who is physically handicapped are unique and costly; (5) building and playground modifications must be made. Even though state building codes are followed in building or remodeling, the wheelchair-bound child may have to be in school for awhile before all needed building modifications are identified and completed.

Many of the problems presented above will not be of concern if a conscientious planning effort is made prior to initiating a program in the regular classroom and school. Special and regular education as well as therapeutic, medical, architectural, and building maintenance staff members must be included in planning. Parents are especially helpful in identifying special types of building and classroom needs.

Historically, the teacher of the physically handicapped was the homebound or hospital-based teacher; however, the role is radically different today. Although some teachers of the physically handicapped still work in homes, clinics, or hospitals, most are in special student centers or special classrooms within the public schools.

Role of the Special Teacher for the Physically Handicapped

Today the specialists not only have responsibility for the direct teaching of special subjects and academic programs to children with unique needs, but they also work as liaisons or as consultants for regular classroom teachers who are responsible for children with physical handicaps within their programs. The specialist teachers coordinate medical, therapeutic, and social services for the child and family and may serve as team leaders for program development.

Although some districts, especially larger ones, have had physical and occupational therapy services available for many years, new or comprehensive therapy programs are being established in many districts for the first time. Each **physical therapist** has specific responsibilities in meeting the needs of children; however, there are areas in which educators' and therapists' training overlap, such as behavior management, perceptual training, and language development.

Role of Therapists and Other Noneducator Professionals in the Schools

In order to be eligible for therapy, a student must be assessed appropriately for services. Since almost every child could profit from therapeutic intervention and since therapy costs are high, it is important that those children most in need of therapy be the ones who receive it. Some children's potential for mobility and independence as adults is closely tied to the amount and quality of therapy they receive during the developmental period.

The physical therapist's primary responsibilities are to improve physical strength, control, and mobility. A physical therapist (PT) frequently works in a one-to-one session of approximately thirty minutes several times a week with a child. The schedule will vary depending on the physicians' prescription for the child. A PT must have a prescription for services and, in most states, a completed IEP stating a need for physical therapy *before* any services can be provided in the schools.

Services that a specialist might provide for the regular classroom teacher are varied and depend on the needs of the individual child. Some of the services include—

1. Consulting with the classroom teacher concerning use of specialized equipment, mobility, medications, learning style, etc.
2. Conducting in-service sessions for regular classroom teachers, administrators, counselors, and paraprofessionals concerning management of the child with a physically handicapping condition.
3. Acting as a liaison between parents and regular education staff.
4. Adapting assignments, communication systems, and evaluation procedures to help the regular classroom teacher meet the specific needs of the child.
5. Providing and interpreting assessment and evaluation data related to academic programming as well as physical needs and abilities.

The *occupational therapist* (OT) provides training in many areas. In working with the physically handicapped, some areas of primary concern are (1) developing self-help skills (e.g., feeding, dressing, grooming), (2) facilitating eye-hand coordination, (3) adapting and developing equipment to help the child perform in an efficient and effective manner. In some facilities occupational therapists are required to have a physician's prescription in order to provide services as indicated in an IEP; however, the trend is toward not requiring a prescription for OT services.

A *speech therapist* may provide services in the areas of speech and language development, feeding skills, and alternate communication systems for the physically handicapped. The speech therapist conducts in-service training for other professionals working with the child so that they can learn to communicate with the child.

All therapists are consultants for the classroom teacher. Teachers need to know what the therapist is requiring of the child and how the child is being taught, so that the appropriate positions and requirements can be carried over into the rest of the child's program. Provision for frequent communications between therapists and teachers in the school must be a priority if an adequate program is to be developed.

Medical. The classroom teacher may be surprised to hear the child with a physical disability mention so many different physicians as "my doctor." Depending on the type of disability, the child may see any one or a number of the following medical specialists on a regular basis in addition to the pediatrician, family care, or primary physician: (1) *orthopedic surgeon*—concerned with prevention or correction of deformities of the musculo-skeletal system (Cooley 1976); (2) *urologist*—responsible for medical procedures and prescriptions to prevent or correct defects or disorders in the urinary system, including bowel and bladder functioning; (3) *neurologist* or *neurosurgeon*—provides evaluation and treatment to improve the child's functioning, which may be impaired by problems in the brain, spinal column, or elsewhere in the nervous system.

As for other children, medical specialists such as the *ophthalmologist* (eyes), the *otorhinolaryngologist* (ear, nose, throat), *radiologist* (treatment using X-ray or radioactive substance), and the *dermatologist* (skin) are involved in providing treatment as required. There may be professionals from other fields related to medical treatment involved in helping the child, such as a *chiropractor* (manipulates vertebrae to relieve pressure on nerves), or an *optometrist* (corrects visual defects using glasses).

The *orthotist* or *prosthetist* is responsible for making, adapting, fitting, and maintaining special equipment, such as braces, shoes, body jackets, casts, and artificial limbs. This person works closely with the physicians, especially the orthopedic physician. An orthotist or prosthetist must have a prescription from the physician before working with the child. When the brace or other device rubs the child, is outgrown, or breaks, it is the orthotist who alleviates the problem. It is helpful when teachers and parents work with the child to identify specifically what it is about the appliance that causes the child discomfort before visiting the orthotist.

Other Specialists. A *social worker* is employed by the state or by an agency to help the family through counseling or to provide services to the family or child, helping to arrange for transportation, special equipment, summer programs, and so forth. "The exact functions of the social worker are determined by the setting where the individual is employed whether it be a school, rehabilitation center, hospital, or other service organization" (Cooley 1976, p. 15).

The *vocational counselor* works to provide employment opportunities. Included in the responsibilities of the vocational counselor are job evaluation, client assessment, client training, and job placement and maintenance. Depending on the counselor's employing agency and training, the title may be vocational adjustment coordinator, rehabilitation counselor, work study specialist, or something similar.

Other Professionals Providing Services to the Child with a Physical Handicap

Prekindergarten. Educational experiences and opportunities to explore the environment are critical for preschool-age children with physical impairments. Opportunities for such children may not occur as often or be available from as many sources as for the nonimpaired child; therefore, high priority should be given to the development and implementation of systematic preschool experiences for young children with physical impairments.

> For children with disabilities these early educational experiences may prove to be useful in reducing the effects of a disability; or these years may be ones during which direct stimulation will enhance learning potential so that a disability does not result in an unnecessary handicap. What is significantly different about this educational period is the inability of those involved to take for granted the needs of the child and the various experiences that the child may obtain from random sources (Best 1978, p. 130).

A comprehensive developmental prekindergarten experience may be provided in the public schools, contracted for by the schools with another agency, or directly provided for by another agency, such as Easter Seal or United Cerebral Palsy. Programs for the young child should provide education and therapy to the child as well as support and information services for the family.

Post School. Individuals with a physical disability who lack mobility, independence, or job-related skills may also require additional services when they finish formal schooling. The state, local, community, and other agencies work in various ways to meet these needs by (1) providing specialized training in a habilitation center, sheltered workshop, or other specialized facility; (2) hiring an attendant to facilitate independent living outside the core family (driver, typist, cook or personal attendant); (3) developing opportunities for recreation and leisure; and (4) providing alternative living and transportation arrangements with the home community. In many communities, youth who are more severely impaired return to their homes after the school years and do not have opportunities for work or socialization.

School Years. The regular classroom teacher should be aware that the past opportunities provided for children with physical impairments may be limited. They may not be able to discuss certain topics that normal children do simply because they have never experienced a circus, been on a bus, played on a playground, or talked on the phone. If a child has been in a well-organized prekindergarten program, the regular classroom teacher who is receiving the child will have access to data and school records kept during the preschool period. This information can be very useful in planning the child's program in the regular classroom.

Throughout a child's education in the regular classroom, the teacher joins with parents and other staff members in developing a realistic program to help the child become as autonomous and independent as possible after school days are over. Awareness of community opportunities and possible jobs in the local community for the individual have a direct influence in establishing school program priorities and goals for the child, especially in postelementary programs.

Everyone needs a sense of purpose or mission—a reason to get up each day, to try to improve and to grow. For the individual who is physically handicapped, this may be difficult to achieve. If "nothing succeeds like success," how can educators provide the necessary opportunities to help such children achieve their best? Suggested changes in traditional secondary programs that may be helpful are (1) the inclusion of a comprehensive family life curriculum for the physically disabled (social, sexual, and emotional) such as the one proposed by Sapienza and Thornton (Bigge 1976) as a priority component of a program, and (2) a comprehensive work evaluation to determine possible jobs for which the individual could develop the needed physical and social skills and which would be intellectually stimulating. A match must be obtained between the position and the individual's physical, social and intellectual abilities.

Vocational Training and Adult Living

Prior to the 1970s, braces and cumbersome special devices to assist in mobility were used to aid individuals with physically handicapping conditions much more extensively than today. Current thought is that braces should be used to help people who have the balance and stamina required for learning to walk. Years ago it was not uncommon to find young children who could not sit up being braced in hopes that some day they would walk. Braces do not prevent deformities or contractures, or develop one's walking skills. They are for control or support and are not appropriate for many in wheelchairs due to physical or functional limitations.

Equipment

In general, the devices used today are more functional. They are lighter yet stronger, and they are also more specifically designed for the precise needs of the individual than they were previously. New metals and plastics are being used. There are many more aids available now than previously, especially in the area of self-help skills. Writing, communicating, dressing, and feeding are just a few areas in which inexpensive aids have been designed to improve the ease and speed of accomplishing a task for some persons.

Examples of specialied equipment found in a mainstream program are listed below.

Mobility aids

braces

crutches

wheelchairs (motorized, portable, or standard)

Self-help

toileting aids (portable urinals, transfer devices)

clothing design and components (velcro openers, slip-over tops)

eating aids (cup with handle, scoop plate, built-up handles on utensils)

Academic

writing (splint, frame, built-up pencil, embossed line paper, typewriter, clip board)

reading (bands to hold pages, page turners, nonslide surface for text or workbook)

math (calculator with printout tape, sturdy objects for manipulation)

Communication

speech/language (communication pictures or boards, written symbols such as Bliss board or typewriter, cassette recorder)

Strategies for Regular Classroom Teachers

Referral of a Child for Assessment of a Motor or Physical Disability

The child who may be in need of special educational services for a physical disability may or may not have an obvious disability. The disabilities of some children will be obvious, while others will present no observable patterns that indicate a problem. A child who appears to be physically normal may need special services for such hidden handicaps as convulsive disorders, cancer, asthma, cystic fibrosis, ulcers, or diabetes. Some signs to look for that may be indicative of a need for special help are listed below.

1. Inability to keep up with classwork because of lack of physical skills in mobility, writing or communication.
2. Need for special equipment and intensive training to use it.
3. Lack of independence in self-help skills.
4. Use of unique or specialized communications systems that are unknown to regular classroom teachers and peers.
5. Need for specialized services related to social and emotional growth and to self-image.
6. General inability to organize activities requiring physical skills.

7. Awkward or clumsy movement that is generalized and cannot be accounted for.
8. Inability to perform physical tasks as quickly as expected or in the same way as other children; problems in motor planning and task performance.

Upon referral to the special services staff, medical as well as educational and therapeutic evaluations should be conducted by trained professionals. The referring classroom teacher should include notes concerning specific observed behaviors in question and, when possible, should include information from the parent or guardian about medical history and past performance of physical skills. Often the parent is able to provide the most useful data related to physical abilities and past performance. It is important that this data be included in referral information so that the evaluator does not look solely for social and academic performance abilities.

There are four areas in which classroom management and programming may need to be changed or adapted to meet the needs of the child with a physical handicap. Frequently very little adaptation is required for a child with a physical disability to participate in the regular program; however, the areas discussed below include some of the most often needed changes.

Adaptations of the environment.   One of the areas which most frequently requires modification in order to meet the needs of the child with a physical handicap is the space around the child. Not only does the classroom require adaptation, but also halls, foyers, bathrooms, walks, and playgrounds must be made accessible. A comprehensive checklist of requirements for accessibility has been provided by Clelland (1978). The checklist can be used by building personnel, including administrative and maintenance staff, or by teachers prior to the arrival of children with physical handicaps to survey for potential areas in which changes will be needed. If the child with a physical disability is already in the class, he or she may serve as a committee chairperson to work with other students to identify structures that should be changed.

Some of the most frequently needed modifications in the environment are listed below.

Classroom

Lowering coat hooks, lockers, water sources

Developing or ordering specialized seating and writing surfaces

Changing current seating arrangements so that the child in a wheelchair is not always in the back of the room in order for others to see over him or her

Providing appropriate foot rests if feet don't touch the ground

Placing grab bars near chalkboards, water sources, doors, stairs, sidewalks, etc., to facilitate movement and independence

Positioning groups so as to prevent distraction of those within the group and those working on other assignments

Bathroom

Lowering towel dispenser, sinks, toilets, mirrors, urinals

Changing types and positions of faucet handles so that they can be manipulated with one hand from a sitting position

Providing storage facilities for materials for specific toileting needs

Changing stall door widths and swinging direction

Including a bathtub, changing station, and other areas that could be used to teach skills in independent living

Replacing toilets and certain types of urinals with more accessible ones

Playground and walkways

Adding flat walkways in the most direct path between two traveled points (e.g., classroom, cafeteria, bus loading area, therapy rooms)

Constructing connection walks between sidewalks and hard-surface playground areas

Making sure all equipment is sturdy and well anchored in the ground

Making slanted curb cuts as needed

Replacing door thresholds, grates, and mats that prevent accessibility

Cafeteria

Widening the line area to accommodate wheelchairs

Ordering adapted utensils, etc., as needed for independence

Lowering tray-return area so that it can be reached from a wheelchair

Using tables that are the appropriate height and that can be pulled up to a wheelchair

Adaptation of communication systems. Some frequently needed modifications in communication systems to meet the needs of the child with a physical handicap are listed below.

Using various systems—symbols, communication aids, gestures, or eye patterns—instead of verbalizations for interaction

Teaching Students with Speech, Sensory, and Orthopedic Differences

Developing a means to complete assignments (electric typewriter, writing frame, built-up pencils, etc.) for children who cannot write or are slow writers

Establishing a way for the child to sign his or her name, at least for official papers

Adaptation in academic program

Providing access for all children to needed material, groups, chalkboards, etc.

Using alternative arrangements for lessons to be completed other than by vocalization (e.g., cassette recorder, typewriter with key guard)

Providing for the unique needs of the child with a physical handicap who has problems in learning due to retardation, learning disabilities, emotional/social problems, or giftedness

Ordering talking books and recorders for children who are eligible

Working with homebound or hospital-based teachers

Including students who use bulky equipment and are not mobile in group activity by bringing the group to the child (e.g., in a standing table, litter, special chair, etc.)

Adaptation for medical problems

Changing the position of the child regularly to prevent sores and skin breakdown

Supervising medication that must be taken at school

Becoming skilled in first aid *and* cardio-pulmonary resuscitation (CPR) skills

Managing a seizure

Providing a process to control odors

Establishing specific routines unique to the child (e.g., bathroom—rest periods—school subject times—snack—art)

Ordering a special diet from the cafeteria (e.g., meeting heightened calorie or protein needs of certain children)

Developing procedures for making up work missed because of extended or frequent absence

All these suggestions may sound overwhelming to a busy teacher. However, integration of physically handicapped students is made possible by the collaborative efforts of many individuals. Support and guidance rendered by physical therapists, physicians, social workers, and other related personnel make it possible for both the child and the teacher to enjoy a mutually satisfying learning relationship. Teaming takes time, but it greatly enhances the chances for successfully meeting the needs of children with physical differences.

Recommendations

The strength of a society lies in the contributions made by its members. For years minority group members, including the handicapped, have been excluded from the mainstream of society, from participating in and contributing to it. Now that the opportunity has come for persons with a physical handicap to be included, members of society in general need to examine their attitudes, stereotypes, and prejudices toward this population. Teachers in particular need to see themselves as educators of all children—not just those who can learn in a group from one textbook. In order to accomplish this task the following recommendations are made.

Suggestions for Meeting Physical Needs

Although vision and hearing acuity scores may be within normal range, the child with a physical handicap may have difficulty gaining and interpreting information through either channel. Observations should be made quickly after the child joins the program as to whether he or she is able to follow oral directions, comprehend lectures, read pictures, or written directions, and so forth. Detailed observations of the physical skills a child does have should be made so as to indicate what the child can be expected to do with the same speed and ability as others in the class.

The classroom teacher should make it known that she or he knows what postures and positions are expected of the child during the day and that the child is to be responsible for maintaining or getting into the best position for the performance of various tasks. The physical therapist is an excellent resource for learning of these needs.

The child should be given a time to demonstrate special equipment and discuss special needs with teachers and classmates. If the child is not easily understood, or is nonvocal or nonverbal, the special teacher or a therapist should assist the child in discussing his or her needs, equipment, and condition with the class.

As for any child, personal acceptance by the regular classroom teacher is of primary importance in helping the child with a physical handicap adjust to and perform well in the regular classroom. The teacher's personal regard and acceptance are important not only for the mental well being of the child with a physical handicap but also for other children to observe as they decide on their attitudes toward and interactions with the mainstreamed student. Teachers send both verbal and nonverbal messages that indicate how they feel about children with handicaps. Those who feel positively about such children and themselves in the classroom will facilitate the creation of a positive environment for academic gain and mental health maintenance.

Suggestions for Meeting Emotional Needs

Teacher awareness, intervention, and support are crucial at times for the child with a physical handicap. The times when the child is highly vulnerable include occasions that involve teasing, ostracism, or isolation by peers. Adolescence may be a particularly hard time for coping and adjustment since it is a time of peer pressure for conformity in dress, actions, language, and leisure-time activities. The classroom teacher, counselor, and support staff need to be aware and ready to intervene when difficulty arises among classmates. Puberty or adolescence may be the first time the child with a physical handicap realizes that he or she will never be just like others in appearance or actions. Younger children tend to accept their classmates more matter-of-factly and usually choose not to isolate on the basis of differences. Younger children are usually more accommodating and tolerant of different behavior, looks, speech, and physical disabilities and may become overly protective of the exceptional child in their classroom.

If the classroom teacher is unable to understand or communicate with the child, help should be sought immediately from the speech therapist or special teacher.

Suggestions Related to Intellectual and Language Needs

Although some physically handicapped persons have lowered intellectual abilities, the teacher should expect normal learning abilities from the mainstreamed child.

There may be a significant experience deficit in the early lives of the children with physical handicaps due to delicate health, lack of child or parental mobility, or embarrassment of the family; such children may be able to obtain skills at a higher level than exhibited if they are provided appropriate opportunities. School programs can provide many experiences needed by the child. Some parents or guardians may not have allowed their children to play outside, get dirty, eat certain foods, and so forth. The teacher needs to be sure that exceptional children are included in all kinds of activities as long as basic health precautions are observed (e.g., plastic can be placed over braces or equipment and sealed before the child enters a sandbox; braces can be removed for water play). The physical therapist or special teacher should be able to provide information regarding specific needs for various activities.

Suggestions Related to Testing

Since no one can do better than his or her capabilities allow, there is no such person as an overachiever. When a child performs at a higher level than expected from test data, it is the validity of the test data that must be questioned, not the child's performance.

Tests may need to be given orally or without time limits, and may need to be marked by an adult as instructed by the child. Adaptations of tests are appropriate only if they are in keeping with the purpose of the test.

Vision and hearing acuity and perception problems are more frequent in the physically handicapped population than in the general population; therefore, care should be taken to inform examiners of any suspected dysfunctions in these areas and of the conditions in which a particular child seems to hear or see best.

Examiners should be given data relevant to communication and manipulation skills before they come to test. This information and data on general functioning level, specific information desired, previous test data, and experiential background of the child will influence the informed examiner in selecting the tests and procedures to be used.

When testing for cognitive processing ability, the examiner must be careful to select a test that does not test experiential background, which may be limited.

Suggestions for Meeting Academic Needs

Minor adaptations, such as taping paper to the desk, mounting paper on a clipboard with a non-slip backing, or turning pages with pencil eraser instead of between fingertips may be all that is required for some children to function in the regular classroom. For other children assignments will need to be spoken into a recorder and homework graded from a tape instead of the page.

Educational materials are available on differing grades of paper, print forms, audiotapes, and so forth. When ordering material, it may be advantageous to check on whether other forms of the material are available for a specific child. In general it is not a good idea to order adapted print or taped material on the assumption that sooner or later there will be a child who can use them. Materials should be ordered according to the specific skills of a child who is already known to the teacher.

In math classes, the nonverbal child and the child who is unable to write without a great deal of effort may both profit from using a calculator. A printing calculator with tape allows the child to work without the teacher, who can check the tape later. Manipulative materials that are easily grasped, such as large cubes or blocks, clothespins, or plastic animals, may be used to facilitate early skill development. An abacus with a sturdy frame and large beads may be helpful for teaching math. Card and coin holders are available to help stabilize items that the child cannot manipulate but must examine. Montessori materials, which are large, sturdy, and have handles, may be especially useful for math.

Both physical and cognitive processing deficits may cause a child with a physical handicap to have difficulty in reading. Some of the classic studies in processing deficits now associated with learning disabilities (e.g., attending, long term memory, and association skills) were conducted using children with cerebral palsy as subjects. Depending on the aptitude and processing skills of the child, some may learn better using a linguistic approach, while others learn best using a phonetics, configural, or multisensory approach to learning to read. The teacher must be aware that all questions related to matters like story comprehension or understanding directions should be presented in a format to which the child has the physical ability to respond. Some children will require that all questions be answerable with a yes/no system, as these words may be their only clearly understandable communication. Pointing to pictures, stopping the instructor when the correct answer is stated, or typing an answer are all possible ways for children to indicate their level of comprehension skills.

Writing activities may require considerable adaptation. Writing frames, built-up pencils, splinting the wrist or hand to hold a pencil, and modified grasp are all possible adaptations that can help a child to write. If a child is so slow or inadequate in writing that typing or oral communication must be used in the learning process, the child must still be taught to sign his or her name if there is any possible way. Since a signature is required for documents and checks, the ability to sign one's name is a necessary skill for independent functioning.

The sensory processing needs of a child with a physical handicap may require that many of the same adaptations be made to facilitate instruction as for a child with visual or hearing impairments. Although sensory acuity may be adequate, the presence of nonintegrated reflexes, distractability, or perceptual problems may require adaptations to enable the child to take in or use visual or auditory information.

The classroom teacher may need to control illumination of materials, reduce extraneous noises, orient or position the child in a certain direction or area, tilt materials as presented, or allow the child to get closer than normal to the material in order to provide for the best use of the senses. The special teacher as well as the therapy staff can advise the teacher about approaches that will best meet the needs of particular children.

Suggestions for Meeting Recreation and Leisure-Time Needs

People need to find pleasure in their environment and to participate in activities outside the normal, daily routine. To do so, children with physical disabilities may require adaptations in activities. Educators must be careful not to replace activities that require movement with totally sedentary ones except for students whose physical limitations permit only sedentary activity. All children enjoy being out of doors. Handcarts can be substituted for tricycles, water beds for trampolines, or trampolines for football. All across the nation leagues are forming for wheelchair basketball, baseball, and football. Swimming provides excellent exercise and recreation. Jungle gyms, chinning bars, universal machines, roller boards, foam mats, and climbing ropes may all be useful in helping the children find activities in which they can participate. Activities such as fixed-loom weaving, painting, monitoring CB radio emergency bands, ham radio operation, and music are enjoyable and require minimum physical exertion.

The needs of children with physical handicaps differ widely. Some will require little or no adaptation within the classroom, while others will require environmental and academic changes. The therapy and special education staff members should provide the classroom teacher with information and equipment related to the child's specific needs and program. Teachers who have faith in their own skills and in those of the support team members, and who learn to know the children's personalities have the rewarding experience of knowing that handicapped children are participating and learning with other children and are no longer isolated from their peers and society.

References

Best, G. A. 1978. *Individuals with physical disabilities.* St. Louis: C. V. Mosby.

Bigge, J. 1976. *Teaching individuals with physical and multiple disabilities.* Columbus, Ohio: C. E. Merrill.

Bleck, E. E., and Nagel, D. 1975. *Physically handicapped children: a medical atlas for teachers.* New York: Grune and Stratton.

Calhoun, M. L., and Hawisher, M. 1979. *Teaching and learning strategies for physically handicapped students.* Baltimore: University Park Press.

Clelland, R. 1978. *Section 504: Civil rights for the handicapped.* Arlington, Va.: American Association of School Administrators.

Cooley, K. 1976. *A resource guide for educators of physically impaired and multiply handicapped children.* West Palm Beach, Florida: School Board of Palm Beach County.

Grollman, E. A. 1969. *Explaining death to children.* Boston: Beacon Press.

Grollman, E. A., ed. 1974. *Concerning death: a practical guide for the living.* Boston: Beacon Press.

Gyulay, J. 1978. *The dying child.* New York: McGraw-Hill.

National Epilepsy League. 1974. *Teacher Tips,* Washington, D.C.

Sehler, A. B., ed. 1978. *Tips for the development of programs for the homebound and hospitalized.* Lansing, Mich.: Instructional Materials Development Center, Michigan School for the Blind. In G. A. Best, 1978, *Individuals with physical disabilities.* St. Louis: C. V. Mosby.

Wolfe, W. G. 1963. Personal communication. Austin, Texas.

Apgar, V., and Beck, J. 1972. *Is my baby all right?* New York: Simon and Schuster.

Best, G. A. 1978. *Individuals with physical disabilities.* St. Louis: C. V. Mosby.

Bigge, J., with O'Donnell, P. 1976. *Teaching individuals with physical and multiple disabilities.* Columbus, Ohio: Charles E. Merrill.

Bleck, E. E., and Nagel, D. A. 1975. *Physically handicapped children: a medical atlas for teachers.* New York: Grune and Stratton.

Finnie, N. 1975. *Handling the young cerebral palsied child at home.* New York: Dutton.

Hart, V. 1979. Crippling conditions. In *Children with exceptional needs*, ed. M. S. Lilly, pp. 195–237. New York: Holt, Rinehart, and Winston.

Holvey, D., ed. 1972. *The Merck manual.* 12th ed. Rahway, N. J.: Merck, Sharp, and Dohme Research Laboratories of Merck and Co.

Gyulay, J. 1978. *The dying child.* New York: McGraw-Hill.

Johnston, R. B., and Magrab, P. R. 1976. *Developmental disorders.* Baltimore: University Park Press.

Kubler-Ross, E. 1975. *Death, the final stage of growth.* Englewood Cliffs, N. J.: Prentice-Hall.

Mullins, J. 1979. *A teacher's guide to management of physically handicapped students.* Springfiled, Ill.: Charles C. Thomas.

Sirvis, B. The physically disabled. In E. Meyen, 1978, *Exceptional children and youth: an introduction.* Denver: Love Publishing Co., pp. 360–387.

Stedman's medical dictionary. 1972. 22d ed. Baltimore: Williams and Wilkins.

Support References for Professional Library or Teacher Reference

Accent on Living, P. O. Box 700, Bloomington, Ill. 61701. Includes one issue per year as a buyer's guide.

Beasley, M. C., ed. *On Your Own.* Continuing Education in Home Ecomomics, P. O. Box 2867, University, Alabama 35486

Disabled USA. President's Committee on Employment of the Handicapped, Washington, D.C. 20210

DPH Journal (Division on the Physically Handicapped), Council for Exceptional Children, 1920 Association Drive, Reston, Virginia 22091

Journals and Monthly Publications Related to Physical Disabilities

Easter Seal Society, 2023 W. Ogden Avenue, Chicago, Ill. 60612

Epilepsy Foundation of America, 1828 L Street N.W., Washington, D.C. 20036

March of Dimes Foundation, 200 2nd Avenue, New York, New York 10017

Muscular Dystrophy Association, 1790 Broadway, New York, New York 10019

Spina Bifida Association, 104 Festone Avenue, New Castle, Delaware 19801

United Cerebral Palsy, 321 W. 44th Street, New York, New York 10036

Some Organizations/ Societies Working Specifically for Individuals Who Are Physically Handicapped

Teaching the
Gifted and Talented

part 4

11 Learner Characteristics and Curriculum Models

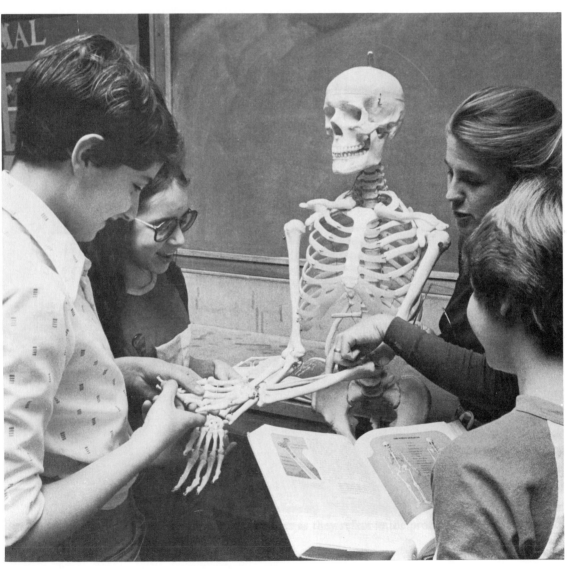

Concern for the education of gifted and talented students has been like a barometer showing the priorities and needs of the social climate of the times. Throughout history there has been documented evidence of recognition and nurturance for the gifted and talented. Plato recommended special training for children of unusual ability to maintain the Republic. The Romans provided special educators for students desiring to train in politics, law, and military strategy. The emperor Charlemagne in the late eighth century proposed education for "bright" children at State expsnse. The Turkish Empire under Suleiman the Magnificent sent "talent scouts" throughout the country seeking out the sharpest, most handsome, most intelligent youth among the Christian population. These youth were subsequently trained and educated and as a result contributed significantly to the development of the Ottoman Empire.

During the early years of the education of the exceptional population, differentiated services were regarded as an extremely low priority, and most often were completely ignored. In the last decade, however, historical events and recent litigation have considerably changed the attitude toward the education of exceptional individuals. Free, appropriate, public education is now regarded as a right of all students. Such an attitude has resulted in dramatic improvement of services for the handicapped population. Unfortunately, the impact on the education of gifted students has not been as great. Misconceptions related to the ability of gifted students to "make it on their own" and the fear of elitism add to the pressures of limited funding to impede gifted programs. The concept of free, appropriate, public education applies as much to the gifted as it does to the handicapped. All students have the right to receive education and services commensurate with their ability to learn.

Although levels of intelligence had been recognized since very early times, no one had been able to solve the problem of measuring it until the beginning of the twentieth century. The work of Alfred Binet and Theodore Simon in 1905 provided a scientific method of measuring the progress of intellectual development in children. Their intent was to screen out the "feebleminded" children from the educational system, but they found they could differentiate children along the continuum of intellectual development at various ages. Lewis Madison Terman, often hailed as the leader of the gifted-child movement, took the work of Binet and Simon and developed the now well-known Stanford-Binet Intelligence Test. It was with this test that he identified the children in his *Genetic Studies of Genius* and documented his findings in follow-up studies regarding their personality, behavior, and success in life. Many of his findings have since been confirmed by others.

John Gowan notes that, since Terman's study, tremendous changes in American life have taken place and that "In comparison with those changes in American values and life styles, it is really surprising to find only modest changes in theory and research on the academically talented during this period" (Stanley, George, and Solano 1977, p. 18). Recently, the Congress of the United States expressed interest and concern by passing an amendment to the Elementary and Secondary Education Amendments of 1969 (Public Law 91–230), regarding provisions related to gifted and talented children. It was mandated at this time that the Commissioner of Education conduct a study to—

1. Determine the extent to which special education assistance programs are necessary or useful to meet the needs of gifted and talented children;
2. Show which Federal education assistance programs are being used to meet the needs of gifted and talented children;
3. Evaluate how existing Federal educational assistance programs can be more effectively used to meet these needs;
4. Recommend new programs, if any, needed to meet these needs (Marland 1972, p. 1).

The resulting study was hailed as a landmark because the educational needs of gifted and talented students were given considerable public, professional, and Congressional attention.

The National Leadership Training Institute for the Gifted and Talented, funded through the United States Office of Education (USOE), emerged to provide the necessary training for leaders in this area at all levels—federal, state and local—and also provided for the dissemination of information regarding the education of the gifted and talented. In addition to these efforts, the contributions of various groups of parents of the gifted and talented are also recognized. They have provided an impetus from the grass roots level to get recognition, legislation, and funds for programs.

The research efforts of many scholars (Reissman 1962; Clark 1965; Fantini and Weinstein 1968; Samuda 1975; Bruch 1975; Torrance 1977; and Ellison, James, and Fox 1970) helped to identify major issues involved in identifying and nurturing giftedness in the culturally different and others. Their research findings have made inroads into areas that were formerly neglected. The work of Feldhusen and Treffinger (1977) has contributed promising materials, methods, and techniques for teaching creative thinking and problem-solving, especially for the disadvantaged children in our society. Joseph Renzulli's Enrichment Triad Model (1977) and Taylor's Multiple Talent Teaching Model (1978), which will be discussed later in the chapter, offer defensible program approaches for the gifted and talented.

This is by no means a comprehensive account of the work that has been done in the area of the gifted and talented; it does, however, give the classroom teacher a general point of reference from which to begin exploratory work in the area. Many of the findings from the above-mentioned research are incorporated in the following sections.

Public Law 91–230, section 806, directs the Commissioner of Education to define gifted and talented children for purposes of Federal education programs. The advisory panel to the Commissioner established the following definition:

Definition

> Gifted and talented children are those identified by professionally qualified persons who, by virtue of outstanding abilities, are capable of high performance. These are children who require differentiated educational programs and/or services beyond those normally provided by the regular school program in order to realize their contribution to self and society.
>
> Children capable of high performance include those with demonstrated achievement and/or potential ability in any of the following areas, singly or in combination:
>
> 1. general intellectual ability
> 2. specific academic aptitude
> 3. creative or productive thinking
> 4. leadership ability
> 5. visual and performing arts
> 6. psychomotor ability
>
> It can be assumed that utilization of these criteria for identification of the gifted and talented will encompass a minimum of 3 to 5 percent of the school population (Marland 1972, p. 2).

A recent study conducted by Karnes and Collins (1978), reported that there were presently twenty-four states using the exact terminology or a minor modification of the definition established by the Advisory Panel to the USOE. Eight states reported having no definition at all for the gifted and talented. While the USOE definition sought to delineate areas of giftedness other than intellectual ability, the study indicated that general intellectual ability is still the most widely accepted indicator in the identification of giftedness. In fact, five states reported it as their sole criterion.

Characteristics of the Gifted and Talented

From research findings a profile of the gifted emerges: "The composite impression from studies ranging from childhood to adults is of a population which values independence, which is more task- and contribution-oriented than recognition-oriented, which prizes integrity and independent judgment in decision making, which rejects conformity for its own sake, and which possesses unusually high social ideals and values" (Marland 1972, p. 16).

The report goes on to state that these are individuals who function in advance of their peers by at least two or more grade levels; have taught themselves to read before entry to school; are better adjusted and more popular than the general population (depending on the relationship between educational opportunities and adjustment). Provided their education and life experiences are what they should be, their contributions to society are greatly enhanced. These individuals like to explore ideas and issues before their age-mates. Their friends are often older than they are, and they enjoy games involving individual skills or intellectual challenges. Because of their traits, interests, capacities, and options, they are exceptionally versatile, with many talents and ways of effective expression.

The gifted child often becomes bored with routine. If the teacher does not anticipate this, the child may become a discipline problem by acting out or indulging in behaviors other than those expected in a given activity. The child may go to the other extreme and resort to "day dreaming" or resistance to completing the task at all. Many of these children will not always be willing to accept stated facts and may pursue further clarification from the teacher. Whether this is threatening or challenging will largely depend on the understanding, knowledge, and skill of the teacher regarding gifted and talented students.

For gifted students, learning quickly and finishing tasks early have not always led to more interesting levels of challenge. Instead, they have been assigned more of the same. If they do not revolt, they will soon learn to pace themselves so that they finish "on time," thus camouflaging their potential. Many of the students, with their large vocabulary and varied intellectual interests, may appear somewhat snobbish and domineering in class discussions. This has great implications in establishing good peer relations. In the regular classroom, gifted students may find it difficult to get the individual attention they need. The classroom teacher is not always able to meet their needs without some outside help. Flexibility in school programming has helped solve this problem through flexible scheduling, special classes, the use of mentors, advanced placement, and other special programs for the gifted and talented outside the public school setting. Gallagher (1975), using work completed by Rice (1970), describes some of the basic characteristics of gifted students. He also describes some of the problems teachers may experience in dealing with these characteristics (table 11.1).

Table 11.1 Characteristics of the Gifted and Concomitant Problems

Characteristic of Gifted	Possible Concomitant Problems
Critically observes, analyzes; skepticism	Teachers feel threatened; peers censure, try to silence discussion; argumentative
Emphatic response to people; leadership capabilities	Rejection causes intense reaction (e.g., depression or hostility); may seek to dominate rather than understand others
Intellectual interests; intellectuality	Snobbishness; limited recreational outlets; boring to others; intolerance for lesser capabilities
Large vocabulary; verbal facility; high retention	Inappropriate level of communication; dominates class discussion; unnecessary elaboration
Originality	Perceived as "off the subject" by others; impracticality; frequent breaks with tradition; radicalism
Scholarliness	Anti-intellectual reaction by peers; stuffiness; pedantry
Thinks with logical systems; objective, rational problem-solving	Disregard for intuitive, retrospective, or subjective solutions; rejection of belief, revelation as methods.

From *Teaching the Gifted Child* by J. J. Gallagher. Boston: Allyn & Bacon, Inc., 1975, p. 68. Adapted from J. P. Rice, *The Gifted: Developing Total Talent*, 1970. Courtesy of Charles C Thomas, Publisher, Springfield, Illinois.

The classroom teacher must keep in mind that the characteristics presented in table 11.1 may not be obvious at first. A gifted and talented child may go unrecognized. Their potential talents and gifts may never come to fruition for lack of nurturance.

Ruth Martinson (1974) suggests a series of steps that can be used to identify a gifted and talented individual. The first step is screening. This step uses multiple methods, including group tests of intelligence and achievement, creativity tests, teacher nominations, parent information, peer nominations, pupil products, and teacher and parent notations of traits and behaviors on a behavior checklist or rating scale for the characteristics of gifted children. The second step is individual testing by a qualified person who is specifically trained to administer and interpret individual intelligence tests such as the Stanford-Binet and the Wechsler Intelligence Scales for Children—Revised (WISC-R) and for Adults (WAIS). The third step is a case study, which brings all the information together and sets forth an educational plan. The crucial aspect of this identification process is the use of a multifaceted assessment procedure.

In the past it has been assumed that talents cannot be found as abundantly in certain groups; this has resulted in meager efforts to search for gifted and talented students among the handicapped, the culturally different, the disadvantaged, and females. Though no one can deny the monumental work of Terman and his associates (Terman et al. 1925; Terman and Oden 1959), researchers who are interested in expanding the concept of giftedness are studying flaws in the design of the Terman studies as related to this broadening concept. Khatena (1978a) focuses on the conceptual limitation of the IQ and

Identifying the Gifted and Talented

its correlates in instrumentation and of the selection of subjects and related variables. Children with specific abilities (e.g., music, arts, creativity) were eliminated from selection through the use of the standard IQ tests. Gowan, Khatena, and Torrance (1979) point out that Terman's study did not consider socio-economic variables or the interactive effects of heredity, environment, and self-actualization upon life success.

Individual IQ tests have been criticized for their inadequacy in identifying creative potential (Getzels and Jackson 1962; Taylor 1964) and a number of traits important to success in life (Taylor and Ellison 1968; Ellison et. al. 1969, 1971). Despite the criticisms, individual tests administered by a highly trained, qualified person yield information that is useful when combined with other information in the final assessment, especially as it relates to the identification of the intellectually superior student.

Research such as that done by Pegnato and Birch (1959) has shown that teacher nominations often overlook many gifted children that a well-designed test can identify. Teachers may often be overly influenced by obedient, hard-working youngsters and tend to overrate them. The Scales for Rating Behavioral Characteristics of Superior Students (Renzulli et al. 1976) are an attempt to provide a more objective and systematic instrument to help guide teacher judgment in the identification process. Ten scales have been developed and field tested: (1) Learning Characteristics, (2) Motivational Characteristics, (3) Creativity Characteristics, (4) Leadership Characteristics, (5) Artistic Characteristics, (6) Musical Characteristics, (7) Dramatics Characteristics, (8) Communication Characteristics—Precision, (9) Communication Characteristics—Expressiveness, and (10) Planning Characteristics.

Scales such as the Khatena-Torrance Creative Perception Inventory (Khatena and Torrance 1976) can be used by a parent or teacher to get a creative perception index of the student. In addition, the measure gives six creative orientations: Environmental Sensitivity, Initiative, Self-Strength, Intellectuality, Individuality, and Artistry. The inventory consists of two tests, "Something About Myself," and "What Kind of Person Are You?" Both measures have been designed for adolescents and adults, although the authors suggest that they may be given to younger children with the help of an adult. Khatena (1978b) reported the use of "Something About Myself," as a diagnostic tool in program development for talented and gifted children and as a screening device to see how parents perceived their children's creative development. The information gathered gives helpful clues about the relative strengths and weaknesses of these students' creative potential.

Classroom teachers should seek access to a variety of instruments and methods purporting to measure gifted and talented students. In the selection process, they should make a careful analysis of the most appropriate measures prior to using them. In addition, they should complete appropriate training in administering the instruments. Without the assistance of a trained and qualified person, many gifted and talented children are not identified. Contrary to stereotypes, these children are "normal" in most respects. They are from all socio-economic levels and of all ethnic and racial origins. We must dissolve role stereotypes, which distort our perceptions and expectations and prevent us from seeing students as individuals.

Sisk (1977, p.14) states that

> in building curriculum for gifted students, the use of various theoretical models has proven to be expedient in helping new program developers formulate philosophical standards, strategies and activities that are congruent. Models can supplement and complement one another by providing opportunities for gifted students to experience cognitive and affective growth.

One such theoretical framework makes use of the taxonomies of cognitive and affective domains. Bloom (1956) suggests, in his classification of cognitive development, that learning proceeds in a hierarchical order from low- to high-order thinking. Likewise, Krathwohl (1964), in a taxonomy of the affective domain, suggests a similar progression in the development of the affective area. Since cognitive and affective objectives of education are often difficult to separate, Williams (1979a) attempted to demonstrate the interrelationship between models of the cognitive and affective domains.

Figure 11.1 is an oversimplification of the hierarchy of the cognitive and affective domains, but it gives the teacher a quick review of what is involved when using the taxonomy models.

Theoretical Approaches to Curriculum Development for the Gifted

Figure 11.1 The interrelationship between cognitive and affective domain models. (From Frank Williams, "Models for Encouraging Creativity in the Classroom," December, 1969. Reprinted by permission of Educational Technology Magazine, Englewood Cliffs, N.J.)

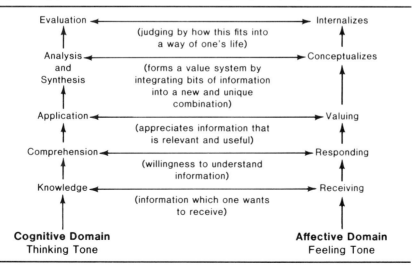

Even though this schema is one attempt to bridge the two domains, it still lacks definitive application when early grade teachers want to foster creativity because both models are taxonomies with placement of those processes which comprise this human phenomena at higher levels. There are some differing viewpoints among cognitive theorists concerning such categories arranged according to level of increasing complexity, with each category dependent on the preceding one (Williams 1979b, p. 227).

In the cognitive domain the steps include (1) the acquisition of *knowledge*, which required that we commit information to memory and to recall it at some later point in time; (2) *comprehension*, by which we understand the knowledge gained; (3) *application*, which demonstrates the use of the information in appropriate situations; (4) *analysis*, through which we "pull apart" the components of the whole to examine them and see how they relate; (5) *synthesis*, by which we take parts of previous information and combine them with other information to develop a new form or idea (this is the major step in creativity); and (6) *evaluation*, by which we make some judgment based on the evidence presented.

In the affective domain the steps are (1) *receiving*, which involves being aware of or sensitive to stimuli; (2) *responding*, which involves willingness to react to stimuli and satisfaction in reacting to them; (3) *valuing*, which occurs when there is appreciation of and commitment to a particular situation; (4) *conceptualization*, by which we begin to incorporate values into our own system . . . often modifying previous values to fit our own needs; (5) *internalization*, by which behaviors become characteristics of our identity.

The second type of model is Guilford's Structure of the Intellect (SOI), shown in figure 11.2. This model does not imply a hierarchical approach as do the taxonomy models. Instead it suggests that there are many abilities within the intellectual capacity of an individual. Guilford (1967, 1977) describes his model as a "three-way classification of known and conceivable human intellectual abilities or functions" (Guilford 1977, p. 155).

The three dimensions of Guilford's model are: (1) content, (2) products, and (3) operations. *Content* is the way information is encountered. The second dimension is *products*; it describes the forms in which information can be conceived. The categories within the third dimension—*operations*—describe the processes one uses. Guilford represents his model by a three dimensional cubic design.

According to Guilford's SOI theory, up to 5 mental operations may be performed upon 4 types of content to produce 6 kinds of products resulting in 120 possible kinds of intellectual acts. Meeker (1969) states that the SOI model implies an interrelated classification of human abilities. She has taken

Figure 11.2 Guilford's model of the structure of the intellect. (From J. P. Guilford, *Way Beyond the I.Q.*, published by the Creative Education Foundation, Buffalo, New York, 1977.)

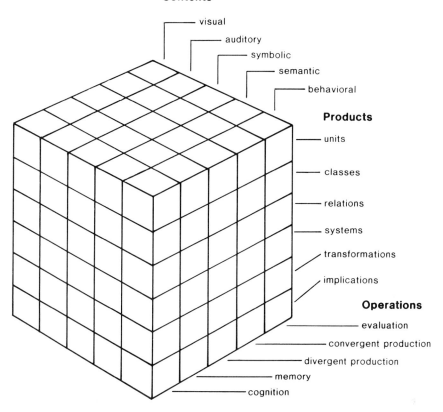

the SOI theory and pointed out the implications for education and for intelligence testing. Her research is helpful in curriculum development and in understanding learning and developmental problems. Presently, 98 high-level talents have been identified of the 120 currently estimated to exist within the intellectual abilities of humans (Taylor 1978).

Curriculum Models

Based on these theoretical models, effective curricula have been developed and are being used. Three curriculum models will be briefly discussed to give the teacher an idea of how to implement a program for the gifted and talented. It is important to note that these models were not exclusively developed for the gifted and talented; with the exception of Renzulli's model, they were designed for use with regular students.

Williams Cognitive-Affective Model. Williams (1979a), like Guilford, uses a three-dimensional cube to describe his model (figure 11.3). Dimension 1 (D1) is the elementary school program, in which all the subject matters are represented. Dimension 2 (D2) represents the eighteen strategies which the teacher employs within the content areas: paradoxes, attributes, analogies, discrepancies, provocative questions, examples of change, examples of habit, organized random search, skill of search, tolerance for ambiguity, intuitive expression, adjustment to development, study of creative people and process, evaluation of situations, creative reading skill, creative listening skill, creative writing skill, and visualization skill. Dimension 3 (D3) represents the four cognitive behaviors (fluent thinking, flexible thinking, original thinking, and elaborative thinking) and four affective behaviors (curiosity, risk taking, complexity, and imagination) elicited from the student as a result of the interaction between D1 and D2. This model is particularly helpful in the area of creativity and divergent production.

Figure 11.3 Model for implementing cognitive-affective behaviors in the classroom. (From Frank Williams, "Williams's Strategies to Orchestrate Renzulli's Triad." *G/C/T* Magazine, Sept./Oct. 1979, no. 9, p. 3.)

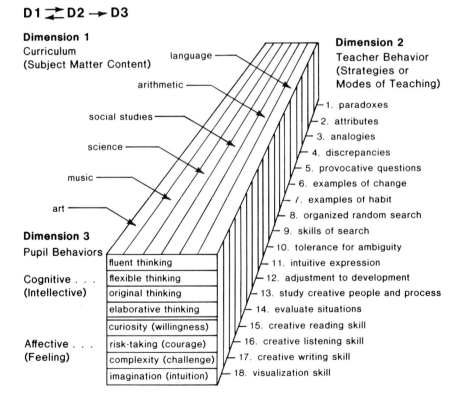

Taylor's Multiple Talent Model. Taylor's research in the area of creativity showed that the IQ score predicted only academic success in school. Once in the real world, those who were achieving and being productive in careers relied heavily on other mental abilities not represented by the IQ—abilities described by some of the higher thinking processes identified by Guilford's SOI model. Taylor identified these areas of talent as academic, creative, planning, communicating, forecasting, and decision-making. His talent totem poles (figure 11.4) are a visual means of representing the profiles of individual students across the various talents. He states that the two main features of his approach are: "(1) its convergence to only a manageable handful of major types of talent; and (2) these major talents have been selected to be ones that are meaningful to practically everyone in society" (Taylor 1978, p.102).

Figure 11.4 Multiple talent totem pole model. (From G. Stevenson, J. B. Seghini, K. Timothy, K. Brown, B. C. Lloyd, M. A. Zimmerman, S. Maxfield, and J. Buchanan, *Igniting Creative Potential*. Project IMPLODE: Bella Vista Elementary School—IBRIC, Salt Lake City, 1971.)

WHERE DO YOUR STUDENTS RATE ON THE TAYLOR TALENT TOTEM POLES?

MULTIPLE TALENT TOTEM POLES

Taylor (1978) admits that there are many specific talents that form a cluster within each of the broader talents identified by his totem poles. For example, his research indicated "that verbal communication talents involve over thirty different types of talents—not counting nonverbal communication talents" (Taylor 1978, p. 102).

Using Taylor's approach, one teaches the strategies within the content of the child's school curriculum as illustrated in the diagrams below. Figure 11.5a illustrates how it is typically done in the classroom and figure 11.5b illustrates the possibility of using his approach within the same twenty-four class hours and including talents other than academic.

Figure 11.5 The two student-centered dimensions of content and processes—two extremely different distributions of 24 class hours: (a) typical focus on academic talents; (b) inclusion of talents other than academic. (From Calvin W. Taylor, ed., *Teaching for Talents and Gifts—1978 Status*, p. 145. Salt Lake City: Utah State Board of Education, 1978.)

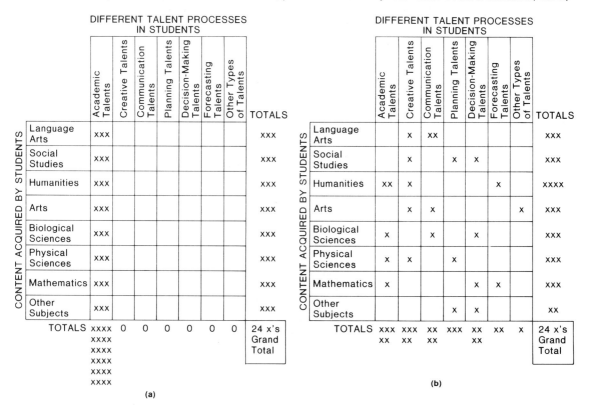

Renzulli's Enrichment Triad Model.   This model describes the use of three types of enrichment activities in which gifted children can engage (see figure 11.6).

Renzulli's Enrichment Triad Model is based on a number of assumptions: (1) students experience the most success when learning activities are tailored to their interests and abilities; (2) students must be allowed to use their unique learning styles or approaches to learning when completing learning activities; and (3) students must be allowed to pursue topics of interest to unlimited levels of inquiry.

Teacher-directed activities in types I and II can be used with most students in regular classrooms with slight deviation made for the gifted and talented. Type III activities are particularly well suited to gifted and talented students, as they heavily rely on the student's skills, motivation, and interests.

Renzulli (1977) differentiates Type III from Type I by stating that in Type III, (1) the child is active in generating the problem and methods to be used, (2) there is no set method of reaching solutions or recognizing correct answers—except perhaps an appropriate investigative technique that can be used to set criteria for judging findings and products, (3) the area of investigation is that of student choice and motivation rather than teacher selection, and (4) the student engages in the activity with a producer rather than a consumer attitude.

Figure 11.6 The enrichment triad model. (From Joseph S. Renzulli, *The Enrichment Triad Model*, p. 14. Mansfield Center, Conn.: Creative Learning Press, 1977.)

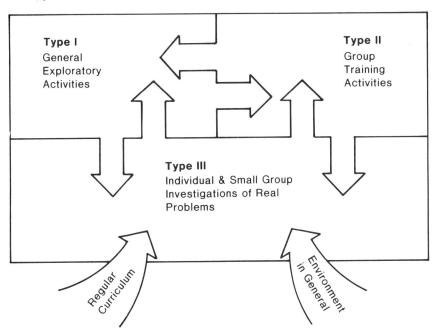

In summary, the history of education for the gifted and talented is characterized by a jagged line of ups and downs. During the past two decades, much progress has been made in identifying the gifted and talented, developing materials and programs, and serving students with exceptional abilities—but the challenge of providing differentiated education to deserving students still remains. Many students who would profit from special programs still go unserved. The challenge as stated, however, can be dealt with and successfully met if parents and teachers will work together. Many teachers are currently providing differentiated education to those with exceptional abilities without additional funding or highly specialized materials. They simply have become familiar with processes for freeing students, and allowing them to pursue their interests and questions. The following chapter introduces strategies that teachers have used successfully with the gifted and talented in regular classrooms.

References

Aschner, M. J. 1961. *The productive thinking of gifted children in the classroom.* Urbana, Ill.: University of Illinois Institute on Research on Exceptional Children (Mimeographed).

Bloom, B. S., ed. 1956. *Taxonomy of educational objectives, Handbook I: Cognitive domain.* New York: David McKay.

Bonsall, M., and Stefflre, B. 1955. The temperament of gifted children. *California Journal of Educational Research* 6:162–65.

Brandwein, P. 1955. *The gifted child as a future scientist.* New York: Harcourt Brace Jovanovich.

Bruch, C. B. 1975. Assessment of creativity in culturally different children. *Gifted Child Quarterly* 19:164–74.

Clark, K. B. 1965. *Dark ghetto.* New York: Harper and Row.

Cole, T. W. 1971. How many of you. . . ? *Teacher Magazine*, November.

Ellison, R. L., James, L. R., and Fox, D. G. 1970. The identification of talent among negro and white students from biographical data. Grant No. OEG 8-9-54003-2026 (058) Project No. 9H-033, U.S. Office of Education, U.S. Department of Health, Education and Welfare.

Ellison, R. L., James, L. R., Fox D. G., and Taylor, C. W. 1969. The prediction of high-level nursing performance. Contract No. PH 10866-02, National Institute of Health.

———. 1971. The identification and selection of creative artistic talent by means of biographical information. Grant No. OEG 8-9-540215-4004 (010) Project No. 9-0215, U. S. Office of Education, Department of Health, Education and Welfare.

Fantini, M. D., and Weinstein, G. 1968. *The disadvantaged: challenge to education.* New York: Harper and Row.

Feldhusen, J. F., and Treffinger, D. J. 1977. *Teaching creative thinking and problem solving.* Dubuque, Iowa: Kendall-Hunt.

Gallagher, J. J. 1975. *Teaching the gifted child.* 2 ed. Boston: Allyn and Bacon.

Getzels, J. W., and Jackson, P. W. 1962. *Creativity and intelligence.* New York: Wiley.

Gibson, J., and Chennells, P., eds. 1976. *Gifted children: looking to their future.* London: Latimer New Dimensions Ltd., with The National Association for Gifted Children.

Goldberg, M., and Passow, A. H. 1959. A study of underachieving gifted. *Educational Leadership* 16:121–25.

Gowan, J. C., Khatena, J., and Torrance, E. P., eds. 1979. *Educating the Ablest.* 2d ed. Itasca, Ill.: F. E. Peacock Publishers.

Guilford, J. P. 1967. *The nature of human intelligence.* New York: McGraw-Hill.

———. 1977. *Way beyond the IQ.* Buffalo, New York: The Creative Education Foundation, in association with Creative Synergetic Associates.

Karnes, F. A., and Collins, E. C. 1978. State definitions on the gifted and talented: a report and analysis. *Journal for the Education of the Gifted,* no. 1, 1: 44–62.

Keating, D. P., ed. 1976. *Intellectual talent: research and development.* In *Proceedings of the 6th Annual Hyman Blumberg Symposium on Research in Early Childhood Education.* Baltimore: The John Hopkins University Press.

Khatena, J. 1978a. Some advances in thought on the gifted. *Gifted Child Quarterly,* no. 1, 22:55–61.

———. 1978b. *The creatively gifted child: suggestions for parents and teachers.* New York: Vantage Press.

Khatena, J., and Torrance, E. P. 1976. *Khatena-Torrance Creative Perception Inventory: Norms-Technical Manual.* Research ed. Chicago, Illinois: Stoelting.

Krathwohl, D. R., Bloom, B. S., and Masia, B. B. 1964. *Taxonomy of educational objectives, Handbook II: affective domain.* New York: David McKay.

Marland, S. P. 1972. Education of the Gifted and Talented. Report to the Congress of the United States by the U. S. Commissioner of Education and background papers submitted to the U. S. Office of Education, Washington, D. C., U. S. Government Printing Office.

Martinson, R. A. 1974. *The identification of the gifted and talented.* California: Office of the Ventura County Superintendent of Schools.

Meeker, M. N. 1969. *The structure of intellect.* Columbus, Ohio: Charles E. Merrill.

Newland, T. E. 1976. *The gifted in socio-educational perspective.* Englewood Cliffs, New Jersey: Prentice-Hall.

Pegnato, C. C. and Birch, J. W. 1959. Locating gifted children in junior high school. *Exceptional Children* 25:300–304.

Renzulli, J. S. 1975. *A guidebook for evaluating programs for the gifted and talented.* Bureau of Educational Research, University of Connecticut.

———. 1977. *The enrichment triad model: A guide for developing defensible programs for the gifted and talented.* Wethersfield, Conn.: Creative Learning Press.

Renzulli, J. S., Smith, L. H., White, A. J., Callahan, C. M., and Hartman, R. K. 1976. *Scales for rating the behavioral characteristics of superior students.* Wethersfield, Conn.: Creative Learning Press.

Rice, J. 1970. *The gifted: developing total talent.* Springfield, Illinois: Charles C Thomas.

Riessman, F. 1962. *The culturally deprived child.* New York: Harper and Row.

Samuda, R. 1975. From ethnocentrism to a multicultural perspective in educational testing. *Journal of Afro-American Issues,* no. 1, 3:4–18.

Sisk, D. 1977. *Teaching gifted children.* South Carolina State Department of Education.

Stanley, J. C. 1976. The case for extreme educational acceleration of intellectually brilliant youths. *Gifted Child Quarterly,* no. 1, 20:66–75.

Stanley, J. C., George, W. C., and Solano, C. H., eds. 1977. *The gifted and the creative: a fifty year perspective.* Baltimore: The John Hopkins University Press.

Stanley, J. C., Keating, D. P., and Fox, L. H., eds. 1974. *Mathematical talent: discovery, description and development.* Baltimore, Maryland: The John Hopkins University Press.

Stevenson, G., Seghini, J. B., Timothy, K., Brown, K., Lloyd, B. C., Zimmerman, M. A., Maxfield, S., and Buchanan, J. 1971. *Igniting creative potential.* Salt Lake City, Utah: PROJECT IMPLODE, BELLA VISTA—IBRIC.

Taylor, C. W., ed. 1964. *Creativity: Progress and potential.* New York: McGraw-Hill.

———, ed. 1978. *Teaching for talents and gifts—1978 status.* Salt Lake City: Utah State Board of Education.

Taylor, C. W., and Ellison, R. L. 1966. *Manual for alpha biographical inventory.* Salt Lake City: Institute for Behavioral Research in Creativity. (Revised 1968.)

Terman, L. M., et al. 1925-1957. *Genetic studies of genius,* vols. I-V. Stanford, California: Stanford University Press.

Terman, L. M. 1975. *Genius and stupidity.* New York: Arno Press. (reprint edition.)

Terman, L. M., and Oden, M. H. 1959. *The gifted group at midlife.* In *Genetic Studies of Genius,* vol. V. Stanford, California: Stanford University Press.

Torrance, E. P. 1962. *Guiding creative talent.* Englewood Cliffs, New Jersey: Prentice-Hall.

———. 1965. *Rewarding creative behavior.* Englewood Cliffs, New Jersey: Prentice-Hall.

———. 1969. *Gifted children in the classroom.* Riverside, New Jersey: MacMillan.

———. 1977. *Discovery and nurturance of giftedness in the culturally different.* Reston, Va.: The Council for Exceptional Children.

Treffinger, D. J., and Curl, C. 1976. *Self-directed study guide on the education of the gifted and the talented.* Ventura County, California, Superintendent of Schools Office.

Williams, F. 1979a. William's strategies to orchestrate Renzulli's triad. *G/T/C Magazine,* September/October no. 9, vol.3

Williams, F. 1979b. *Models for encouraging creativity in the classroom.* In J. C. Gowan, J. Khatena, and E. P. Torrance, eds., *Educating the ablest.* 2d ed. Itasca, Illinois: F. E. Peacock Publishers, pp. 143–44.

12 Strategies in Academic Programming

While there are many ways in which gifted and talented children can be and are being served, including acceleration and homogeneous grouping, "it remains true that the greatest number of gifted children will continue to be educated within regular classrooms. The success of such programs will depend to a large extent upon how effectively the classroom teacher can enrich the curriculum" (Barbe 1961, p. 5). This statement is as true today as it was in 1961. In education we sometimes mistake activity for accomplishment. In the case of the gifted and talented, we may accept the effort to provide an enriched curriculum as the actual provision of one. But if our efforts result in assigning "more of the same," or even in stressing only the need for extra materials as a means of serving the gifted, then we may have recognized the problem, but we have not met it adequately.

The literature abounds with excellent ideas, materials, and activities. Too often missing are the teaching strategies that focus this material on the needs of the gifted, for the essence of a program for the gifted lies not in the materials themselves, but in how the materials are used, and in what happens to the student as a result. What "happens" can begin with something as ordinary as the bulletin board, a designated area with a question mark, and space for constantly changing math, word, and logic puzzles, as well as problems, provocative questions, and tangrams.

Puzzles and Problems

While puzzles requiring clear thinking appeal to most children, this type of class activity is one in which a self-selecting process takes place. It will be the gifted child who most often persists in seeing a challenging puzzle through—who will want to talk about it, analyze it verbally, and offer logical solutions that don't fit the "answer book." Puzzles may be used purposefully to initiate this type of discussion among students. The "odd one out" type of question is an obvious example. The value here may not lie in the question itself, but in the discussion that follows assigning it to a number of small groups with the stipulation that each group must discuss the options and agree as a group on their answer, with reasons to support it. "Which is the odd one out among cricket, football, billiards, and hockey?" Would a group decide it is football because it is the only game in which the ball is not struck by an implement, or cricket because in all the other games the object is to put the ball into a net (goal), or billiards because it is the only game that could be played in a home?

Inviting the class to solve the math puzzle attributed to Karl Friedrich Gauss offers everyone the challenge of arriving at the correct answer, given enough time and effort. To those who accept the challenge to find an easier way, the puzzle offers opportunity for much divergent thinking.

Can you add all the numbers from 1 to 100? (1 + 2 + 3 + . . . + 100.)

Can you find a way to determine the total without adding all of the numbers?

Pair them up:	1 plus	100
	2 plus	99
	3 plus	98
	50 plus	51
There are 50 pairs, so		101
		×50
		5,050

Is it possible to indicate all the dates in the month by placing digits on the faces of two cubes? This type of question and the different approaches children used to find a justifiable answer contributed to Lewis Terman's (1975) determination to study gifted children. The problem is purposely left unanswered as an incentive for readers to gain some insight into their own problem-solving methods before using the problem with students.

At first glance, finding the next appropriate letter in this sequence-completion puzzle depends only on convergent thinking—finding the logical pattern by which to supply the missing letter:

O T T F F S S E N __

To extend this type of puzzle, students could keep track of the stages and processes involved in their search for a solution. Seen only as simple letters, they suggest no logical pattern that can be extended to supply the missing letter. At some point the stimuli must be transformed to more meaningful information, i.e., the first letters of whole words (the first nine numerals to be exact). Awareness of this process of transformation can add to students' problem-solving ability (Fletcher 1969).

Puzzles like these are available in a wide variety of common sources: math books, magazines, game and puzzle books, newspapers, or the classroom. Providing students with blanks for crossword puzzles can result in puzzles that use the vocabulary of all areas of the curriculum. A list of class names can result in acrostics to exchange with other class members.

A very positive step toward challenging the gifted child while serving the needs of all children in the regular classroom can be made with a realistic look at existing materials. Using materials that give the basic practice needed in varying degrees by all the students, yet which have an "open-ended" quality built in, can serve well.

Open-ended Curriculum

The example shown in figure 12.1 is from the material designed by Wirtz, Botel, and Nunley (1963). It offers practice in adding, subtracting, multiplying, and dividing, yet because of the challenge of discovering the "rule," it is removed from the realm of pure practice and appeals to the quick mind of the gifted student. Each succeeding box has a more elusive "rule." Children can extend the principle by making up their own "rules" and setting up boxes to challenge the rest of the class, or the teacher can adapt this idea to fit the specific needs of class members.

Almost all areas of curriculum can be approached in an open-ended way. For example, in presenting a unit on economics, or consumerism, there is no real need to maintain the study in a lock-step fashion with pages to read, questions to answer, and tests to take. The unit could be introduced when new pencils are being distributed in grade school (or reference is made to pencils used by students in a secondary school). A class discussion and listing of "what do we collectively know about the pencil?" (Paul S. Amidon and Associates 1974) serves a number of purposes:

1. removing the inhibiting concept that only teachers are knowledgeable
2. gaining an awareness that as a group we know more than any one of us does as an individual
3. listing all possible areas in which further study could be made
4. creating interest and involvement that only such individual contribution can elicit
5. involving children in the curriculum planning process

Figure 12.1 What's My Rule? (From R. W. Wirtz, M. Botel, and B. G. Nunley, *Discovery in Elementary School Mathematics*, p. 5 Chicago: Encyclopaedia Britannica Press, 1963. Used with permission of Encyclopaedia Britannica Educational Corporation.)

WHAT'S MY RULE?

In each box, numbers have been selected because they all have something in common. Our concern is about the number named by each expression.

In each group, there are three numbers named that don't belong. Cross them out. Then add two names that do belong.

A
23 + 7   Twenty   15
70   82 − 28   10 − 1   ×8
4 × 5
X   10 × 4 × 0 + 1
14 + 56
20 + 0
91 + 19   0
40 ÷ 2   60   90   30

B
18 − 1   18 + 9   18 − 11
51 − 4   21 ÷ 3   77 ÷ 11
3 × 9   63 ÷ 9   4 × 10 − 3
39 + 18   57 × 47   106 − 9
7 × 0   3 × 13 × 3   3 × 3 × 3
7 × 7 + 1
1,287

C
3   25 + 2   60   90   30
XXI   73 + 3   46   100   6   −28   1   0
3 × 11 − 6   IX   87   43   117   12
1 × 2 × 3 × 4 × 5   36
57
102   120
3 × 5 × 17   24
2 × 3,000   7 × 8 + 1   31 + 13   60
2 × 5 − 1   85 − 4   33

D
100   1,000   56 − 4   18 − 6
100 − 48
0   100 ÷ 25   52 ÷ 13   1 × 2 × 3 × 4
12   96 − 4   68
36   90 − 4   4 × 0 + 14
120   41 + 43
24
60   1 × 3 × 5 × 7
0   4   16   36   64   100   144

E
7   2 × 5 − 1   85 − 4   33
5   101   3 × 19   5 × 5   13
5 × 9   14 + 15   29   31   1
50 + 15   7 × 7   9
4 × 5 + 1   25
3 × 7   49
403   81
1   3 × 11   121

F
0   4   16   36   64   100   144
1 × 2 × 3 × 4 + 1   44   30 − 5
1   3 × 3 × 3   19 × 19   7 × 6 + 7
9   16 + 9
25   39 + 42   1,000
49   100 − 19
81   43 + 57
121   32 + 32
3 × 27

The list may look something like this (depending on the sophistication of the group):

1. The pencil is made of graphite and wood.
2. Almost everyone uses a pencil.
3. If we lose a pencil we can always buy another one.
4. People usually buy the ones they see advertised.
5. Pencils are made by many different companies.
6. Pencils don't cost very much.
7. Pencils are made in factories.
8. If no one would pay a dime for the pencil the price might go down.

Again depending on the background of the students, matching proper vocabulary with the list can also be an exciting activity for the group:

1. Pencils are manufactured from . . . *raw materials*
2. Using the pencil is . . . *consumption*
3. Purchasing the pencil causes more to be produced . . . *production*
4. Selection of pencils influenced by T.V. . . . *advertisement*
5. All pencil companies want theirs to be purchased . . . *competition*
6. The price of a pencil the result of . . . *mass production*
7. Factories built to produce pencils . . . *investment*
8. If no one buys pencils, the price comes down or pencils are not manufactured . . . *supply and demand*

Another way to bring students into the curriculum planning process is through "webbing" (Raskin 1974). The method applies brainstorming to any curriculum problem, beginning with a single experience, word, phrase, or topic. Connecting ideas are added through an expanding web. To develop the connections, the group asks the questions, "Who? What? Why? When? Where? and How?" and weaves the answers into the web (see figure 12.2). With such class-generated options, avenues for research, production, and demonstration have been developed for all levels of ability, creativity, and commitment.

Another open-ended approach can be illustrated with social studies. The required reading for a particular period in history could form the background for an issue of a current magazine (such as *Newsweek* or *Time*) created by students as if published at that time in history. All of the sections generally found in the magazine could be represented. For example, the *Time* format includes sections on Art, Books, Cinema, Economy and Business, Education Forum (letters to the editor), Law, Milestones (obituaries of famous people), Music, The Nation, People, Press, Religion, Show Business, Sports, Theater,

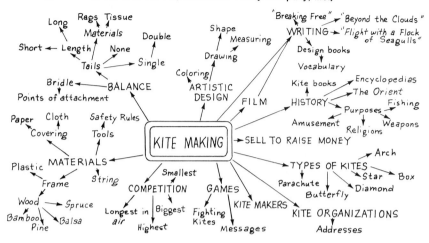

Figure 12.2 Webbing chart. (From "Let the Kids Spin Their Own Curriculum," by Bruce Raskin. Reprinted by special permission of *LEARNING, The Magazine for Creative Teaching*, February, 1974. © 1974 by Education Today Company, Inc.)

and The World. Such a project invites extensive reading and research in a wide variety of directions, and the actual depth and breadth of the study in each area can be commensurate with individual talents and abilities.

Allowing children to pursue individual or small-group interests within the framework of a content area provides for the development of such independent behaviors as organization of work and planning of time. As they become more skillful, their learning need not be restricted by subject-matter boundaries; they can be encouraged to engage in independent study of their own choosing.

Independent Study

Independent study should be an integral part of the gifted student's school schedule. Too often the reverse occurs. When recognition of giftedness in a curriculum area results in quantitative rather than qualitative adjustment for the students, the control they exercise over their own educational experiences is lessened. All children should have experiences in selecting and developing goals and learning activities that fit their own interests and needs. For the gifted, independent study offers the opportunity to pursue their interests to an extent not desired by (or necessarily recommended for) students with less motivation, sustained interest, and commitment to a specific task or topic.

Basic to Renzulli's "Enrichment Triad Model" (1977), are ways to elevate the skills of retrieving, managing, and using information that make independent study truly differentiated learning (see figure 11.6).

Type I—General Exploratory Activities. These activities extend from the regular curriculum to bring the learner in touch with areas of personal or potential interest. The activities emphasize "how to" projects that allow students to find out what it means to be, for example, a historian, writer, or geologist. Field trips, learning centers, and visiting experts are useful for Type I activities.

Type II—Group Training Activities. Group training activities are designed to provide students with skills that will enhance their ability to share feelings, to organize and prioritize learning ventures, and to solve problems. Training in these and other skills makes it possible for gifted students to pool their interests and expertise in selecting, investigating, and solving a broad variety of problems.

Type III—Individual and Small-Group Investigation of Real Problems. Type III activities emphasize the solving of real problems. In fact, the techniques used in this part of Renzulli's Triad are a blend of the skills mastered in the other two areas. Type III activities allow a student (or group of students) to investigate in depth a contemporary question or issue. In doing so, the student becomes, for example, a practicing botanist, farmer, engineer, or author. Type III activities are uniquely focused on the gifted child. They demand the general excellence in thinking and feeling processes needed to work independently through a complex set of tasks so as to solve a problem or develop a product. These tasks include:

1. identifying and structuring solvable problems
2. investigating problems, using proper methods of inquiry as an actual investigator
3. producing results that can be communicated to appropriate (rather than captive) audiences (Clasen 1978)

An example from Renzulli's guide illustrates the process.

> Students used a stop watch and diagram to record the number of automobiles that failed to come to a complete halt at a stop sign during given periods of time. They analyzed the data and submitted a report to the commissioner of public safety. Their purpose was to convince the commissioner that a traffic light and/or crossing guard was necessary to improve the safety of school children who make frequent use of the intersection (Renzulli 1977, p. 63).

Because the triad model includes general exploratory activities and group training activities that are excellent for *all* students and especially helpful in encouraging the gifted in independent investigation of real problems, it is an ideal model for the regular classroom teacher.

Independent study should not preclude interaction among students or between student and teacher. The role of teachers changes only to the extent that they are seen as counselors and facilitators, rather than as "dispensers of knowledge." They can help students to focus on problems, provide opportunities to develop the skills or techniques for valid inquiry, and encourage the effective use of available resources. The freedom of choice underlying independent study should include the options of working with another student or within a small group. Two excellent resources for promoting independent study are *Building Independent Learning Skills* (Atwood 1977) and *Independent Study at Seven* (Winn 1970).

Teaching/ Learning Models

Teaching gifted children can involve a greater emphasis on the processes of learning and thinking as well as the content of the curriculum itself. To this end the teaching/learning models described in the previous chapter, including the Renzulli model, provide a structure for developing curriculum so as to use both cognitive and affective experiences, and elicit specific levels of thinking from students. The following activity, "Free Money," is one way in which the classroom teacher can use existing materials within the present curriculum to elevate the quality of instruction for all children, while appealing to the imagination and intellect of the gifted. It is based on material that has been used successfully to provide stimulation for creative writing, both in a learning center on an individual basis, and as a class assignment. The activity has resulted in some very interesting writing, usually based on what would be done by the writer with "free money." In contrast, by following Williams's strategies (Williams 1970) with the same material, an almost unlimited number of avenues are opened to students, including research, creative thinking, problem solving, and discussion—learning activities that provide for individual differences, capabilities, and preferences.

Free Money

STRATEGY	QUESTION OR PROBLEM
PARADOXES	What is your reaction to the paradox: "Money is the root of all evil."
ATTRIBUTES	Make a list of all of the properties that something must have to be considered "money." Which of these characteristics would "free" money lack?
ANALOGIES	List all of the things you can that would have the same value as "free" money.
	In what ways is having a credit card like having "free" money?
DISCREPANCIES	Consider why money with a high monetary value in one country is almost "free" in another country.
PROVOCATIVE QUESTIONS	What would you do if you were the only one in the world with access to free money?
EXAMPLES OF CHANGE	Consider the social changes that would result in our society if there was suddenly an abundance of free money.
EXAMPLES OF HABIT	Consider the effects on our country if we had not been willing to trust banks with our money after the "Crash of 1929."
ORGANIZED RANDOM SEARCH	If you had been a leader of the Confederate States of America, how would you have kept the value of confederate currency?
	If you were to replace gold as a back-up for our currency, what would you replace it with?
SKILLS OF SEARCH	Search for ways that have been used by different societies to get along economically that have not included our form of money.
	Search for the stories behind all of the paper monetary documents that we use other than "greenbacks," i.e., checks, money orders.
	Search for the stories of coins that would have been considered almost free at the time they were commonly used, and now have great monetary value as collector's items.
	What systems of money were used in the U.S. before our present monetary system was set up?
TOLERANCE FOR AMBIGUITY	Consider the effects of our economics if we had accepted the Indian's monetary system when our country was being settled.
	A jar filled with dimes will be yours if you can guess how many there are. How many ways can you list for finding the correct number of dimes?
INTUITIVE EXPRESSION	If you were a hermit in the mountains how would you feel about money?
	Describe your feelings if you were to walk past a bank and see this sign in the window:

FREE MONEY

ADJUSTMENT TO DEVELOPMENT	Design a monetary system based on the base 5 number system.
	Consider what Supreme Court decision concerning money you would be willing to support to solve the problem of poverty.
STUDY CREATIVE PEOPLE AND PROCESS	Choose one of the men whose picture is on any of our currency who was not a president, and find out what he accomplished that warranted such an honor.
EVALUATE SITUATIONS	If you had access to free money and wanted to equalize the distribution of wealth without negatively affecting the economy, what would you do?
	What do you think would happen if we attempted to change our monetary system here in the U.S. as is being done with our change to the metric system of measurement?
CREATIVE READING SKILL	Read about a famous financier, and predict what his childhood was like.
CREATIVE LISTENING SKILL	Listen to this story (Aesop's Fable, "Gold in the Garden,") through the first half, and make a prediction about the last half.
CREATIVE WRITING SKILL	Write a story about an imaginary country that uses salt (or something else that we would consider almost free) as its currency.
VISUALIZATION SKILL	Draw the monetary units of a new form of currency.
	Change the design of our coins (they can be changed every 25 years without the approval of Congress).
	Design a new seal that is used as the official stamp on our paper money.

Bloom's Taxonomy (Bloom 1956), as described in chapter 11, is also excellent as a means of eliciting higher levels of thinking from children. Kovalic (1978) suggests using it as the basis for having gifted students write their own curriculum (see figure 12.3). Using "Curriculum in Bloom" (Arizona Department of Education 1977) as a guide to the basic vocabulary, including the process verbs that can be used for stating the learning objectives, children can write a curriculum that suggests activities and projects on each level. Pictures are gathered and glued to the fronts of file folders. Inside the file folder, questions or activities relating to the picture are posed, beginning with the area of knowledge (recall) and extending through the area of evaluation. The following example provided by Kovalic (1978 p. 92) would be titled and have a picture of a balloon on the front of a colored file folder.

Knowledge:	How did ballooning come to be? Recall the early days of ballooning through a newspaper reporter's eyes.
Comprehension:	Describe how the first balloons were made and inflated.
Application:	Illustrate at least five different types of balloons—start as far back as you can find.

Figure 12.3 Curriculum in Bloom. (From *Unicornicopia*, p. 6. Kyrene School District, Tempe, Arizona, 1977.)

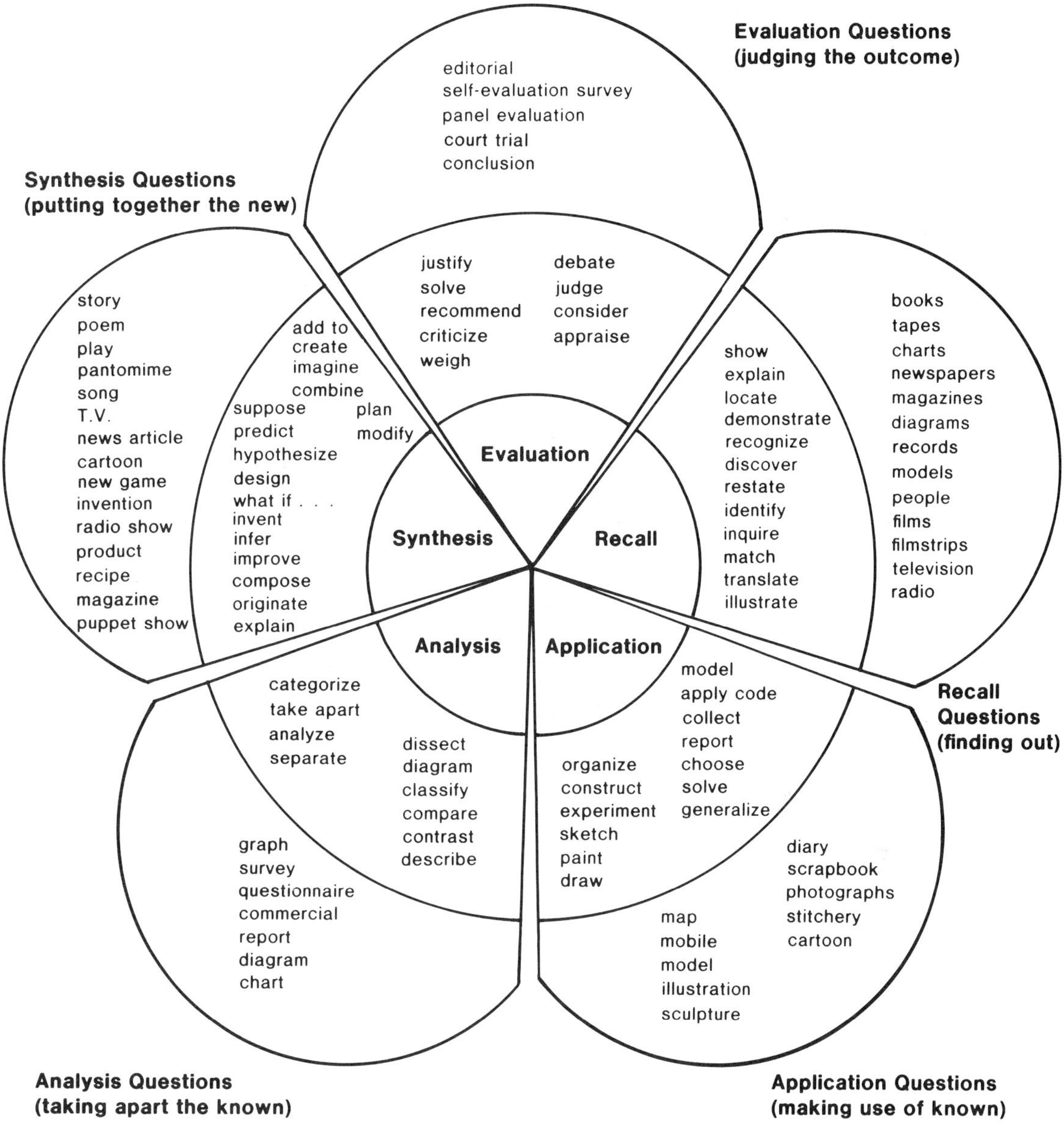

**Evaluation Questions
(judging the outcome)**

editorial
self-evaluation survey
panel evaluation
court trial
conclusion

**Synthesis Questions
(putting together the new)**

story
poem
play
pantomime
song
T.V.
news article
cartoon
new game
invention
radio show
product
recipe
magazine
puppet show

add to
create
imagine
combine
suppose   plan
predict   modify
hypothesize
design
what if . . .
invent
infer
improve
compose
originate
explain

justify   debate
solve   judge
recommend   consider
criticize   appraise
weigh

show
explain
locate
demonstrate
recognize
discover
restate
identify
inquire
match
translate
illustrate

Evaluation

Synthesis   **Recall**

Analysis   **Application**

books
tapes
charts
newspapers
magazines
diagrams
records
models
people
films
filmstrips
television
radio

**Recall
Questions
(finding out)**

categorize
take apart
analyze
separate

dissect
diagram
classify
compare
contrast
describe

organize   model
construct   apply code
experiment collect
sketch   report
paint   choose
draw   solve
            generalize

graph
survey
questionnaire
commercial
report
diagram
chart

map
mobile
model
illustration
sculpture

diary
scrapbook
photographs
stitchery
cartoon

**Analysis Questions
(taking apart the known)**

**Application Questions
(making use of known)**

Analysis: Experiment with some of the materials used in the early days of ballooning. What other materials might have been considered?

Synthesis: Design a balloon of an unusual material (a space age balloon) and launch it.

Evaluation: Bring a real live balloonist to class to discuss what it is like to "float." If the balloonist convinces you of this experience, plan to go up, up and away.

The Talents Unlimited Project is a structured method of integrating Calvin Taylor's Multiple Talent Model (Taylor 1978) into all curriculum content areas. "Kid talk" (Talents Unlimited Project 1974) helps teachers to recognize and teach for talents in the areas of productive thinking, planning, communication, forecasting, and decision making, as well as in the academic area.

Kid Talk

Productive Thinking
1. Think of many ideas.
2. Think of varied ideas.
3. Think of unusual ideas.
4. Add to the ideas.

Planning
1. Tell what you are going to plan so someone else will know what your project is.
2. Tell all of the materials and equipment you will need for your project.
3. Tell all of the steps in order needed to complete the project.
4. Tell the many, varied problems that could keep you from completing the project.

Communication
1. Give many, varied single words to describe something.
2. Give many, varied single words to describe feelings.
3. Think of many, varied things that are like another thing in a special way.
4. Let others know that you understand how they feel.
5. Make a network of ideas using many, varied complete thoughts.
6. Tell your feelings and needs without using words.

Forecasting
1. Make many varied predictions about a situation.

Decision making
1. Think of many, varied things you could do.
2. Think more carefully about each alternative.
3. Choose one alternative that you think is best.
4. Give many, varied reasons for your choice.

The following example was created by a kindergarten teacher.

Talent Lesson Plan

Title: Footprints to Friendship
Talent Area: Productive Thinking
Curriculum Application: Language Arts, Social Studies
Grade Level: Kindergarten

Motivation	As part of Friendship Week, show the children several open-ended films and filmstrips about friendship. With the use of open-ended media materials, children can discuss the best ways to solve friendship problems.
Teacher Talk	"We all like to have friends. The films we have seen and talked about this week have helped us to learn more about being a good friend. Today we are going to outline our feet on colored paper and cut them out like this." (Show them how.) "Then each of us will think of many varied and unusual things we can do to be a good friend. I will write your ideas on the foot outlines you make."
Student Response	Each child will choose a colored piece of paper, put his foot on the paper and trace around it with a black crayon, and then cut it out. The child will take it to the teacher who will write the child's ideas on it. (Examples: by smiling, sharing my swing, asking them to eat with me, etc.)
Reinforcement	Praise children for effort as well as the quality of their ideas. A large footprint could be hung in the hall with "Footprints to Friendship" written on it. Each child's footprint is attached to the wall around it. Read with the children the ideas each of them has thought of. Let them show the display to brothers and sisters and friends in other classes. *

We hope these examples have given some insight as to how models suggest structure for logical and comprehensive teaching of skills and development of curriculum and, even more, that they offer some incentive to explore these and other such models as a way of offering the differentiated learning experiences required by the gifted.

*Special thanks to Janice Thomas, Educator in the Granite School District, Salt Lake City, Utah.

Gifted children's ability not only to absorb abstract concepts but to organize and apply them effectively sets them apart from the average child. It allows them to extend beyond the acquisition of information to activities related to "higher mental processes." To help them make this extension, they should deliberately be taught the educational objectives of the learning activities they participate in, including the use of proper terms. This can be done by helping them to analyze or evaluate an activity in terms of the process goals. For example, this is done when a group problem-solving activity is followed with a discussion of whether the four steps in problem-solving have been met (recognition of the problem, fact finding, hypothesizing, and selecting a solution). Further discussion could focus on whether synthesis (ability to combine and test related ideas) or flexibility (willingness to consider alternative solutions to problems) was used. Discussion of the affective areas could center on how individuals felt about contributing ideas, or on their reaction to others' response to their input.

There are numerous ways to stimulate thinking behaviors. One such activity is the M & M game, an activity related to the thinking behaviors of fluency, flexibility, originality, and elaboration, which are recognized as qualities of creativity. Directions to students:

1. Write down all the different ways M & M candies can be used. You have _____ minutes. Total these.
2. Now categorize them into lists according to what you would use them for (eating, games, etc.). Total these.
3. Now determine how many uses you listed that no one else had (will invoke discussion among the group). Total these.
4. Now can you add to or elaborate on any single use as suggested by you or others in the group? Total these.

The totals represent your individual scores in:

1. Fluency—being able to think of *many* alternatives, ideas, questions, answers, solutions
2. Flexible Thinking—being able to think of a *variety* of alternatives, ideas, questions, answers, solutions
3. Original Thinking—being able to think of *unique,* less obvious alternatives, ideas, questions, answers, solutions
4. Elaborative Thinking—being able to *add to* or enhance alternatives, ideas, questions, answers, solutions

Gifted students could develop this into a discussion of the learning models that describe these qualities as they relate to the processes of learning. These qualities of creativity form the cognitive area of dimension 3 of Williams's Model (Williams 1970), Type II of Renzulli's Model (Renzulli 1977), and the productive thinking area of Taylor's Multiple Talent Model (Taylor 1978). Such a discussion can add structure for students that can be satisfying and motivating, helping them to develop and value these abilities. *The Almost Whole Earth Catalogue of Process Oriented Enrichment Activities* (Stewart and Howard 1977) lists descriptive information about a great variety of resources available to teachers.

Using Questions in the Classroom

It has been said that questions rather than answers form the beginning of learning. This may not be as true as it should be if too little attention has been given either to the purpose of questioning or to the proper techniques for questioning. Certainly an awareness of how we use questions in the classroom and how we respond to our students' questions can be a big step in learning to deal more effectively with the gifted. Posing the proper questions can encourage higher levels of thinking in the gifted child.

An excellent way to focus on the form and phrasing of questions for the task intended, and to become comfortable with the teaching/learning models, is in using these models to structure questions for discussion that cover the many levels of thinking and provide a means to explore values, insights, and attitudes. This can be illustrated rather simply with "Jack and the Beanstalk," using the Taxonomy of Educational Objectives (Krathwohl, Bloom, and Masia 1964), Guilford's Structure of the Intellect (Guilford 1977), and Williams's Strategies (1970).

1. The Taxonomy of Educational Objectives—Affective Domain
   a. *Receiving* (directing of attention): Did you find the story interesting?
   b. *Responding* (behavior accompanied by feeling of satisfaction): What part of the story touched you the most, emotionally?
   c. *Valuing* (ascribing worth or emotional acceptance): Do you feel there was any worthwhile moral to this story?
   d. *Organization* (ordered relationship of complex of values): Does this moral have present day application? How?
   e. *Characterization* (generalized sets consistent with total philosophy or beliefs): Can you relate this story to any feelings you have had about events in your own life?
2. Guilford's Structure of Intellect—Operations
   a. *Cognition* (understanding, discovery, rediscovery, awareness and comprehension): Why was Jack trying to sell the cow?
   b. *Memory* (retention and recall of knowledge): What was the cow's name?

c. *Convergent Thinking* (reorganization of information): What made the Giant's wife and Jack friends?

d. *Divergent Thinking* (imaginative, spontaneous and fluent self-expression): What do you think might have happened if the Giant's wife had not befriended Jack?

e. *Evaluation* (judgment, assessment, evaluation): Do you think Jack's Mother's attitude was appropriate toward Jack? Why?

3. Williams's Strategies—Teacher Behavior

a. *Strategy #4, Discrepancies*: Do you think the old man really knew the beans were magic when he traded them for the cow?

b. *Strategy #5, Provocative Questions* (inquiry to bring forth meaning): What do you think would have happened if Jack had left the beans in his pocket?

c. *Strategy #6, Examples of Change* (consider all things dynamic rather than static): Should the events of the story have changed Jack's Mother's attitude toward him? Why or why not?

Questioning is also related to the indirect teaching method that has been found to result in higher student spontaneity, initiative, and contribution to problem-solving situations (Renzulli 1975). This method, one of acceptance, encouragement, and questioning as opposed to lecturing, directing, and criticizing, is seen as offering the learning conditions that lead to student-directed rather than teacher-directed learning, an environment in which the child's own questions can be heard and assistance given in seeking an answer.

Self-Evaluation

Self-evaluation is an important part of the learning process. Gifted children should use it to manage their own efforts. It should be encouraged from the beginning of the student's school experience, in a form consistent with ability. This may be as informal as an oral evaluation shared with the teacher or as structured as recording evaluative information relative to the cognitive and affective objectives of an independent project.

One way to involve students in self-evaluation as a new process is to have them brainstorm a list of items that they see as important in evaluation. A number of items can be selected from the list to form the basis for a general self-evaluation form. Individual students may identify additional items that they may want to include in their own evaluation. The actual evaluation remains an individual matter, helping to clarify for each student what can be regarded as strengths and what are perceived as areas requiring self-improvement.

Self-evaluation can also be part of an independent study contract in which students state the learning problem or ideas they intend to explore, describe the process or source of information that will facilitate the study, and describe the form of the product(s) they hope to produce. Although the self-evaluation part of the contract is based on student-determined criteria, a class list of evaluation criteria offers a basis for selection that helps students to focus on the specific objectives of their individual projects.

If our goal for gifted children is to help them learn to organize, conduct and evaluate their own learning, the process of "learning how to learn" should involve more than the use of the card catalog and the Dewey Decimal System, or an awareness of the encyclopedia as a reference. Research and study skills must be taught with integrity. Special attention should be given to the skills involved in finding information in all fields of knowledge. This requires a working knowledge of references such as anthologies, bibliographies, concordances, abstracts, reader's guides, catalogues, periodicals, histories, and even chronicles of particular fields and organizations.

Research and Study Skills

Equally important are the nonbook reference materials, including films, film loops, records, slides, charts, kits, transparencies, models, maps, and video tapes. The "media center" concept of the school library has changed the function of the library and increased the variety of materials offered to teachers and students. The same kinds of changes have occurred in community libraries, which also offer extensive aids and services that can lend support to a gifted program.

Individual research can actually begin in the early grades with reading material by one author and telling what is read. Such activity can quickly proceed to reading from several sources and first making comparisons, then analyzing and evaluating the readings.

Children's research efforts can be exciting if encouraged by educators, and media coordinators can be particularly helpful. Their efforts to help teachers expand the research and study skills of their gifted students can result in a simple, yet classic integration of many programming elements in a superior program. One media coordinator invited a group of gifted third graders to write and tape narration for silent super-8 film loops. A gifted sixth grader interested in the same subject was selected to act as a mentor for each student.

This research activity precluded the "straight from the encyclopedia" type of reporting so common in the grade school setting. It necessitated the use of such pertinent study skills as reading for specific purposes, notetaking, outlining, as well as the writing and editing necessary to correlate with the film loop. The selection of appropriate musical background for the taping provided an added dimension to the project.

The results are a fine addition to the school media center that encourages individual use of media materials in listening centers, preview centers, etc. The programs are also available for presentation to classrooms in the school.*

Becoming a "library helper" has long been one answer for a gifted child who finishes classroom assignments quickly and needs to be kept busy. Too often the experience is limited to shelving books. A better way is to view such children as "interns" who, with proper training in media and materials, can serve as assistant media coordinators. The benefit to themselves and the school is great if they are allowed to participate in such activities as—

Preparing and presenting readings to primary grade groups to acquaint them with books on their level

Teaching younger children basic library skills, such as the use of the card catalog

Helping younger children begin researching (selecting two books on the same subject and making comparisons between the two)

Writing (and gathering from other children) annotations on available books appealing to various ages and interests

Acting as a resource for teachers using media equipment

Gathering all available books and media materials on a specific subject for teachers

Setting up learning centers on various topics, using books, periodicals, media (to be available for use in the center or checked out to a teacher).

Reading   The high correlation of reading ability to giftedness reinforces the idea that the gifted students can learn by themselves, but to assume that gifted children need no instruction in reading can be a serious mistake. Even these students need to develop specific skills. Their similarity to others of their own mental age does not preclude the individual deficiencies, proficiencies, interests, and learning rates that characterize all children. Reading proficiency should be stressed because of the high degree of independence in learning it offers the child—actually a major source of learning throughout life. Reading skills should be presented to children as early and as rapidly as they can assimilate them, for they are the skills that aid the most in other learning. Reading instruction should also be constantly motivational as well as instructional, with the greatest emphasis being placed on comprehension and critical reading (Cushenbery and Howell 1974).

*Special thanks to Mr. Gaylen Wycherly, Media Coordinator, Granite District, Salt Lake City, Utah.

Books such as *Developing Skills in Critical Reading* (Atwood 1975) can take the gifted child "beyond and behind the printed word" through creative activities and projects. One example is the use of folk tales, plays, and stories in which there is a villain (such as the wolf in "Little Red Riding Hood") to introduce students to stress, pitch, and juncture on the oral level in preparation for recognition that they can also be applied in silent reading. Each reader's interpretation of certain words and phrases in repeating the wolf's speech will affect or color the meaning of the message.

Encouragement of critical reading can be enhanced by creating an awareness that words themselves color meaning, perhaps by collecting and classifying pictures of vehicles by their names. These could include fast-moving animals, (Pinto, Rabbit, Cougar); "jet-set" names (Monte Carlo, Continental Mark III); and names of astronomical elements (Comet, Satellite, Vega, Galaxy). Questions that might be discussed include—

Can buyers be influenced by the image the name of the car evokes?

Are facts about a car conveyed by its name?

Does a car's name affect its performance?

Could you discourage the purchase of a car by naming it "The Snail?"

Could you rename cars to appeal to certain groups, such as musicians or athletes?

Interest centers with a great variety of types and levels of books, materials, and objects, can provide for children of all abilities, while offering the gifted the opportunity for more extensive and intensive reading experiences. Providing these students with enough challenging material commensurate with their instructional level can help prevent the cycle of underachievement that too often begins early in the school setting. You might—

Combine a book on cyphers with Edgar Allan Poe's famous story, *The Gold-Bug*

Gather some of the Arco Publications (Arco Publications, 219 Park Avenue S., N.Y., N.Y. 10003) that would interest gifted students:
Mechanical Aptitude and Spacial Relations Test
Miller Analogies Test
Triple Your Reading Speed
Typing for Everyone

Gather an abundance of books on one subject—on every reading level (kindergarten through college)

Include appropriate books not generally found in the school media center:

Design Yourself (Hanks, Belliston, and Edwards 1977)
The Memory Book (Lorayne and Lukas 1974)
The Book of Think (Burns 1978)
30 Days to a More Powerful Vocabulary (Funk and Lewis 1971)

Create a learning center around any idea or object with which your children have contact (apples, rocks, eggs, etc.). Then use any of the following in creating your learning center: books, models, songs, projects, recipes, stories, questions, poetry, activities.

One answer for students is the *Junior Great Books* program (Dennis and Moldof 1975), a sequence of courses in interpretive reading and discussion for students in elementary, junior, and senior high school. It is based on a method of learning called shared inquiry, with discussions led by two adult volunteers, or by one teacher in a regular class. The discussion centers on problems of interpretation to which there are no sure answers. For the classroom teacher, the training in how to ask questions that encourage thinking can extend beyond the reading program to facilitate invoking higher levels of thinking in all areas of the curriculum. When used with cluster grouping of gifted children, it provides the opportunity for them to meet with their mental peers and to interact on a high cognitive level. This type of program also constitutes a wise use of capable parent volunteers. The following poem, while not from the program, can be used to illustrate the type of questions that can be asked, and the type of discussion that can result.

Street Scene

A helicopter in the sky
　　Observed the traffic down below,
Establishing the where and why
　　Of anything that stopped the flow.
A motorist in a crawling queue,
　　Distracted by the whirring rotor,
Looked up to get a better view
　　And rammed (of course) another motor.
Policemen worked for half the day
　　To clear things, and at last succeeded.
The helicopter whirled away
　　To see where else it might be needed.

Peter Suffolk (1971, p. 158)

Types of factual questions (simple recall of what the author said)—

"What was the motorist doing when he rammed the next car?"

"Why was the helicopter hovering over traffic?"

Types of interpretive questions (asking for opinion about the author's meaning)—

"What is the author telling us about helicopters in the last line?"

"What kind of attitude toward the use of helicopters in traffic control does the author present?"

"Who should assume responsibility for the accident?"

Types of evaluative questions (your consideration of whether you agree or disagree on the basis of your own experience)—

"In your opinion, how serious was the accident?"

Expose your students to the accomplishments of other young people through magazine articles and newspaper clippings. Back this up with a collection of books and other reference materials that let your students add to their own knowledge, and encourages their own involvement in areas of interest in which their age-mates are successful.

Seek ways of introducing your gifted students to books that might at first seem formidable because of the title, size, subject, etc. Again, newspaper clippings and magazine articles can provide the motivation that opens up a whole new world to a child. For example, Jules Verne, acknowledged as the father of science fiction is often the subject of articles. Have students locate an article that discusses his anticipation of such scientific advances as the airplane, television, and space travel. This could serve well to motivate a child to be carried vicariously over the earth by balloon, under it by submarine, and above it through interplanetary travel.

An awareness that most libraries now belong to an interlibrary loan system that extends throughout the nation, including university libraries, can assure accessibility of virtually any book desired by student or teacher. Securing lists of books such as the minimum reading lists required of English majors in any university may be incentive to some children to begin early contact with adult books. Many of these same books appear on other lists very appropriate for reading between seven and twelve years of age, including Swift's *Gulliver's Travels,* Defoe's *Robinson Crusoe,* and Bunyan's *Pilgrim's Progress.* To have read the book yourself as a teacher and to be willing to discuss it on a one-to-one basis, can be the highest motivation for a gifted student's own reading.

Simulation   Activities and games that simulate real-life situations can offer excitement and satisfying opportunities for learning on all grade levels. Simulation is usually based on a problem related to a real-life situation or event that requires involvement in the facts, processes, and key concepts related to the problem. The higher levels of creative, critical, and logical thinking that should be part of a differentiated education for gifted children can be simulated in such a setting.

In addition, social values related to competiton, cooperation, and interaction with peers can be discussed. Simulation games can be very effective in motivating students because the learning is immediately purposeful. Situations that can be used in simulation are as available as life itself, and are a natural way of learning even in the classroom.

Simulation games are published commercially on a variety of subjects for all grade levels. An excellent reference is *The Guide to Simulation Games for Education and Training* (Zuckerman and Horn 1977). They can also be devised in the classroom by the teacher or students.

As with all activities of a gaming nature, there should be objectives beyond the activity itself. These should include the specific learning outcomes desired as well as an effort to make it possible for students to transfer their learning to real-life situations. Discussing the instructional objectives before the activity and following it with some group analysis of its value is an excellent means for accomplishing this goal. It may be as simple as telling children why they are doing what they are doing.

Career Education   Making a wise career choice should be a major concern of all young people. For many gifted students there can be unique problems related to the selection of a career. While some may seem almost "programmed" in a certain direction, the multiple competencies and interests of many gifted children make it hard for them to focus their efforts on one area. On the other hand the expectations of others interested in their achievement can act to restrict their choices to certain professions. No less a dilemma can be present when students make a distinction between fulfillment and success, and see them as an either/or kind of choice (Hoyt and Hebeler 1974).

A teacher can lend support to such students by exposing them to as many career fields as possible. This should begin in grade school, and can be done through reading, inviting resource people to the classroom, and seeking mentors for students who exhibit special interest and involvement in a specific area. It can also be accomplished by projecting a program beyond the school setting. The community offers experiences with people, places, and processes that can be useful only if a program can extend into the community itself, with children learning from the reality of their everyday lives. This has particular importance for minority and rural students (Marland 1972). An ideal way to do this with gifted students is to plan for two to six or eight students, rather than for the traditional "whole-group" field trips, depending on the interests of the students and facilities of places to be visited. A look into the possibility of "shadowing" (actually participating in the function of the company or place visited) can provide the kind of enrichment activity discussed in Renzulli's Model (Renzulli 1977). This might be done for two hours a week for an extended period of time. Parents or other volunteers could provide transportation or chaperoning if necessary. Prearranged commitment to projects, reports, demonstrations, and so forth, can focus student learning in the field, and involve the class in the experience on their return. An excellent reference to help teachers focus on learning resources outside the classroom is *The Yellow Pages of Learning Resources* (Wurman 1972). The book is an invitation to discover the city as a learning resource—an invitation in three parts:

1. A selection of seventy typical firsthand learning resources that can be found in almost any city. For example: "Look around at the multiplicity of signs, information and directions for pedestrians and vehicles, each vying for attention but often lost in the collage. How many different kinds of information are offered there and to whom? How effective do you think it is?" (p. 29)
2. An outline of the avenues to follow in order to make these resources available (the where and how of converting people, places, and processes into sources of learning).
3. A directory of schools or programs that are making direct use of environments other than the classroom as a learning resource and setting.

One of the common difficulties in education has to do with relating the academic world to the "real" world outside the classroom. Also, young people are often isolated from much of the working community and commonly end up in a career by chance rather than as a result of an informed and systematic choice. In response to these concerns, educators and community leaders in

Utah have established BICEP (Business—Industry—Community—Education—Partnership). BICEP operates as a central clearinghouse to arrange for resource people from the community who will provide students with first-hand career exploratory experiences in a variety of ways, including classroom speakers on career fields, "shadowing" (on-site experiences for students), and internships (participation in work experience). Approximately five hundred communities throughout the nation have some similar form of interaction between the schools and business, industry, and community. It is an area worth checking into.

The affective area should also be considered in preparing gifted children to choose careers and life goals because of the subjective significance they place on them. Helping them to develop insight into their own attitudes and values can be of benefit. The importance of developing independence through experience in selecting and controlling their own educational experiences should not be underestimated. Being able to identify and set their own priorities at an age when attitudes and patterns are being determined is a very important option.

Hobbies, Collections, and Special Interest Clubs

Gifted children are recognized as avid collectors and hobbyists. They should be encouraged to join or help organize clubs related to subjects in which they have a special interest or aptitude. This is one way of assuring them of contact with others who share a need to expand their horizons in similar directions. An excellent example is the Benjamin Franklin Stamp Club, which is sponsored by the United States Post Office and is available throughout the nation. The Post Office is represented by a knowledgeable stamp collector with films, books, materials, and instructions for organizing a club in the classroom. There is no charge for the books and materials or for the additional material that is sent to the club each month. The collection of used stamps is emphasized so there need be no expense involved for the teacher or students.

The serious attempt in the past few years to design games that relate to real-life situations has resulted in simulation games that reflect almost every conceivable interest. Rather than the abstract and the elements of luck, they emphasize skill, decision making, and judgment. This, coupled with the authentic representation of the subject they reflect, makes many of them excellent resources for special-interest groups or clubs in a school setting.

An awareness of groups or associations in the community that welcome young people with common interests, such as astronomy clubs, solar energy associations, and other hobby-related groups can open avenues beyond the school setting for gifted students with aptitude in particular areas. The association with adults who are experts in areas that interest them is invaluable.

"Most teachers have always recognized that every child is an individual. But even with this recognition, students, by and large, have been forced to fit into an existing system without regard for their individual differences" (Barbe 1961, p. 5).

Involving students in activities in which they can be seen and heard as individuals can help insure against doing this. The more we understand students and see them as people, the less inclined we are to group them arbitrarily, for whatever purposes. In addition, we offer children the opportunity to see themselves and others as individuals, helping them to be more accepting and more accepted—no small problem for many gifted children who are often "set apart" because of vocabulary or interests.

One such activity that is easy to facilitate in the classroom is "Boundary Breaking." This group interaction technique offers students an informal yet structured setting that can create self-awareness and "other awareness" through questions that reveal more than ordinary conversation and provide the teacher with insight into the needs, interests, and motivations of the group members. The children, seated in a circle, respond one at a time to a question posed by the leader. Saying "pass" allows a child more time to think, with an opportunity to answer after the question has gone full-circle, including a response from the leader. It is wise to begin with simple questions ("What is your favorite color?") before proceeding to ones that require more thought and produce greater insight ("When do you feel best?"). *Teaching Gifted Children* (Sisk 1977) is a good resource for additional information on breaking the boundaries that prevent children from learning about themselves and others in the classroom.

Self-introductions on the first day of school are standard. A variation of this activity can better serve the purpose of helping students see themselves and others as individuals. Rather than self-introductions, each student talks to another student on a one-to-one basis for a specified length of time, and then the two introduce each other to the group. Gifted children need opportunities to find areas of common interest with other students, even though the depth of interest may vary.

The advantages of small-group activities can be "added upon" when students are grouped for specific roles in discussing, listening, responding, and writing. Four rows of three desks each face center (like spokes in a wagon wheel). The students facing each other in the center four desks are asked a provocative, open-ended question to initiate discussion. After a determined amount of time, the second row of students, who have acted only as listeners to this point, are given time to respond to what has been said. The last four listeners respond only in writing to the entire proceeding. This activity is especially suited to grouping gifted students who ordinarily lack the stimulation of working with equally advanced peers.

Using the "How many of you . . . ?" (Cole 1971) type of voting list is also a way of tuning in to what children think and feel. It is a simple technique using a list of questions prepared by the teacher, which deal with the concerns of the students. They can range from such factual questions as, "How many of you have a hobby?" to such value questions as, "How many of you are proud of your family?" The students are made aware that this technique is a way of learning how others think and feel, and that they can vote in three different ways—raising one hand if in agreement (two if strongly so), sitting on hands if disagreeing or objecting to the question, and doing nothing if preferring not to vote. The complexity of feelings, attitudes, and personalities becomes even more apparent as the stage is reached when class members can contribute lists of their own.

The Classroom Teacher

A teacher can begin to focus on the gifted and talented without the necessity of having all the answers. Perhaps Syphers (1972, p. 23) is correct when she states that "Planning for teaching the gifted must be done in an endless corridor with numberless doors." But there has to be more than a grab bag of activities to provide qualitatively differentiated education for these students. This requires a measure of planning in terms of time, space, and materials in conjunction with appropriate program practice. Whether the teacher's efforts are directed toward initiating an enrichment program within her own classroom or participating in an institutional program, *Providing Programs for the Gifted and Talented* (Kaplan 1974) provides a structure within which models, curriculum development, and the various prototypes are seen in proper perspective. It is an excellent resource.

Perhaps the key phrase in terms of time, space, and materials is "planned flexibility." Gifted students need time to pursue their own interests, time to extend their learning in one area until they have plumbed its contents to their satisfaction, time to interact with others who function on the same mental level, time to talk to the teacher on a one-to-one basis, time to ponder, to think, even some time to do nothing. Gifted children need space to meet with a mentor or a small group, space to carry out an experiment, space to set up research material that won't have to be put away when it's time for spelling, space that extends beyond the classroom door and even beyond the school doors. Gifted children need materials to extend their learning, to motivate them, to play around with, to question, to send for.

But with all of this, gifted children need a measure of structure, a philosophical base for what happens to them in the classroom. They need a teacher who is willing to act as a resource for learning rather than a dispenser of knowledge, one who can initiate a program that will offer experiences and challenges, even an opportunity for developing expertise that may exceed the teacher's.

The following is an excellent account from a seventh-grade teacher who successfully served as a resource to a gifted student in one of her classes.

> I viewed Chad as a gifted child. He was at the top of math class from the very beginning of the year. He was questioning, interested, and motivated. I was aware that his curiosity could be dampened if I did not make some attempt to stimulate him further in an area of interest to him. Because of this, I spoke with Mike Harris, the Computer Science teacher at Bountiful High School, about the possibility of my teaching Chad computer programming. He was extremely accommodating and Chad showed enthusiasm towards learning how to write programs.
>
> Mr. Harris gave me a book on the basic computer language and supplemented it with his Master's thesis on the same subject. Chad completed a chapter in his own seventh-grade math book on flow charts in order to prepare him for writing programs. He then completed several chapters and related exercises in Mr. Harris' book. As a review, I assigned him a simple program to write. The program was to find the area of a rectangle. He wrote it and simulated it. When he completed this I introduced him to Mr. Harris and observed while Chad was shown how to punch his own cards out. His program was run and sent back to me. I went over it with Chad, as did Mr. Harris, and it was perfected by him. Chad is now running a more complicated program and spends time working in his own math book in addition to working with computers. He spends about half of his time with computer work and half with his regular math work.[*]

With the teacher in the regular classroom in mind, perhaps the most encouraging way to end this chapter is with a quote from Sylvia Rimm (1978, p. 11), "Encouraging giftedness develops an environment of excellence which benefits all children."

References

Amidon, P. S., and Associates. 1974. *Mod money management*. St. Paul, Minnesota: Paul S. Amidon and Associates.

Arizona Department of Education. 1977. *Unicornicopia—a guide book for gifted and talented*. Tempe, Arizona: Kyrene School District.

Atwood, B. S. 1975. *Developing skills in critical reading*. Palo Alto, Calif.: Education Today Co., Inc.

——. 1977. *Building independent learning skills*. Palo Alto, California: Education Today.

Barbe, W., and Stephens, T. 1961. *Educating tomorrow's leaders*. Ohio Department of Education.

Burns, M. 1976. *The book of think*. Boston, Mass.: Little, Brown.

Bloom, B. S., ed. 1956. *Taxonomy of educational objectives, Handbook I: cognitive domain*. New York: David McKay.

[*]Special thanks to Judy Hurd, educator in the Davis School District, Farmington, Utah.

Cole, T. 1971. How many of you. . . ? *Grade Teacher,* no. 3, 8:28–40.

Cushenbery, B. C., and Howell, H. 1974. *Reading and the gifted child: a guide for teachers.* Springfield, Illinois: Charles C Thomas.

Dennis, R. P., and Moldof, E. P., eds. 1975. *Junior great books.* Chicago, Illinois.

Fletcher, H. 1969. *Toward a general model for describing cognitive processes.* Madison, Wisconsin: Wisconsin Research and Development Center for Cognitive Learning.

Funk, W., and Lewis, N. 1971. *30 days to a more powerful vocabulary.* New York, N.Y.: Simon and Schuster.

Guilford, J. P. 1977. *Way beyond the IQ.* Buffalo, N.Y.: The Creative Education Foundation, in association with Creative Synergetic Associates.

Hanks, K., Belliston, L., and Edwards, D. 1977. *Design yourself.* Los Altos, California.

Hoyt, K. B., and Hebeler, J. R. 1974. *Career education for the gifted and talented students.* Salt Lake City, Utah: Olympus.

Kaplan, S. N. 1974. *Providing programs for the gifted and talented: a handbook.* Ventura, California: Ventura County Superintendent of Schools.

Kovalik, S. 1978. *Teaching the gifted and talented.* Englewood, Colorado: Educational Consulting Assoc.

Krathwohl, D. R., Bloom, B. S., and Masia, B. B. 1964. *Taxonomy of educational objectives, Handbook II: affective domain.* New York: David McKay.

Lorayne, H., and Lukas, J. 1974. *Memory book.* New York, N.Y.: Ballantine Books, Division of Random House.

Marland, S. P., Jr. 1972. *Education of the gifted and talented.* Congress of the United States by the U.S. Comm. of Education and background papers submitted to the U.S. Office of Education, Washington, D.C.: U.S. Government Printing Office.

Raskin, B. 1974. Let the kids spin their own curriculum. *Learning* 2 (no. 6):61.

Renzulli, J. S. 1975. *A guidebook for evaluating programs for the gifted and talented.* Ventura, California: Office of Ventura County Superintendent of Schools.

Renzulli, J. S. 1977. *The enrichment triad model: a guide for defensible programs for the gifted and talented.* Creative Learning Press.

Rimm, S. 1978. *The exceptional educational needs of the gifted.* In R. E. Clasen and B. Robinson, eds. *Simple gifts: Book of readings.* Madison, Wisconsin: University of Wisconsin, Extension Programs in Education.

Sisk, D. 1977. *Teaching gifted students.* Columbia, South Carolina: South Carolina State Department of Education.

Stewart, E. D., and Howard, H. R. 1977. *The almost whole earth catalogue of process oriented enrichment activities.* Wethersfield, Conn.: Creative Learning Press.

Suffolk, P. 1971. Street scene. In *The poet's tales: A new book of story poems,* W. Cole, ed. New York: World Publishing, (Times Mirror).

Syphers, D. F. 1972. *Gifted and talented children: practical programming for teachers and principals.* Reston, Va.: The Council for Exceptional Children.

Talents Unlimited Project. 1974. Unpublished material developed by the project. Mobile County Public Schools, Mobile, Alabama.

Taylor, C. W. ed. 1978. *Teaching for talents and gifts—1978 status report.* Salt Lake City, Utah: Utah State Board of Education.

Terman, L. 1975. *Genius and stupidity.* New York: Arno Press, reprint edition.

Williams, F. E. 1970. *Classroom ideas for encouraging thinking and feeling.* Buffalo, New York: D. O. K. Publishers.

Winn, M. 1970. Independent study at seven. *Childhood Education,* November, pp.72–74.

Wirtz, R. W., Botel, M., and Nunley, B. G. 1963. *Discovery in elementary school mathematics.* Chicago, Illinois: Encyclopedia Britannica Press.

Wurman, R. S., ed. 1972. *Yellow pages of learning resources.* Cambridge, Mass.: MIT Press.

Zuckerman, D., and Horn, R. 1977. *The guide to simulation games for education and training.* Cranford, New Jersey: Didactic Systems.

The Team
Effectiveness Scale Appendix A

You are being asked to respond to a series of ten statements that relate to the functions of an interdisciplinary team. These functions may be viewed as being *actually* or presently performed by you and other team members or viewed as *ideal* functions expected to be performed by team members.

For your present or *actual* team situations, please rate first the degree of effectiveness you see yourself as having on each of the ten team functions. Next, rate yourself on the degree of effectiveness you would expect (*ideal*) yourself to have on the same functions. Indicate your ratings on the 1 to 5 scale shown under *actual* and *ideal* by circling the appropriate number. (1 represents lack of effectiveness; 2 represents slight effectiveness; 3 represents average effectiveness; 4 represents above average effectiveness; and 5 represents extremely high effectiveness.)

Once you have completed your own *actual* and *ideal* ratings, *do the same for each of the other team members.* If you are a school psychologist, for example, and have already rated yourself, now rate the special education teacher on the degree of effectiveness you feel this person has in *actual* team situations and *ideally* how you would expect this person to perform on each of the ten team functions. Your ratings, as indicated above, may vary from 1 to 5.

The following completed example is provided to help you understand how to use the rating scale.

Example: Rate your newspaper boy's effectiveness as you see his *actual* **newspaper deliveries; next rate his effectiveness as you would expect it to be in** *ideal* **delivery situations.**

Newspaper Boy	Actual	Ideal
1. Delivers the paper on the front porch.	1 ②️ 3 4 5	1 2 3 4 ⑤
2. Gets to know the people on his route.	1 2 ③ 4 5	1 2 ③ 4 5
3. Delivers paper in good condition.	1 2 3 ④ 5	1 2 3 4 ⑤
4. Collects for the paper monthly.	1 2 3 4 ⑤	1 2 ③ 4 5

From J. M. Leininger and V. H. Rhode. "An investigation of actual and ideal teaming effectiveness as perceived by members of the interdisciplinary team." An unpublished thesis, University of Utah, 1978. Reprinted with permission of authors.

Team Functions

Regular Classroom Teacher	Actual	Ideal
1. Participates in referral and evaluation processes of the student, as appropriate for the team member's role.	1 2 3 4 5	1 2 3 4 5
2. Carries through the parts of the individualized instructional plan (IIP) of the student for which team member is responsible.	1 2 3 4 5	1 2 3 4 5
3. Contributes to placement decision which will best meet the student's needs.	1 2 3 4 5	1 2 3 4 5
4. Develops abilities to communicate with other team members, including utilization of problem-solving approach when differences arise.	1 2 3 4 5	1 2 3 4 5
5. Seeks out and utilizes outside resources for the student, if needed.	1 2 3 4 5	1 2 3 4 5
6. Takes part in the team meeting in which diagnostic data is reviewed and tentative placement decision is made.	1 2 3 4 5	1 2 3 4 5
7. Communicates diagnostic information used to determine suggested placement to parents.	1 2 3 4 5	1 2 3 4 5
8. Contributes to development of student's overall educational plan (IEP), based on his needs.	1 2 3 4 5	1 2 3 4 5
9. Monitors and records the student's progress toward educational goals for which team member is responsible.	1 2 3 4 5	1 2 3 4 5
10. Contributes to the use of fair procedures according to law (due process), for each student and his/her family.	1 2 3 4 5	1 2 3 4 5

Pupil Services Specialist	Actual	Ideal
1. Participates in referral and evaluation processes of the student, as appropriate for the team member's role.	1 2 3 4 5	1 2 3 4 5
2. Carries through the parts of the individualized instructional plan (IIP) of the student for which team member is responsible.	1 2 3 4 5	1 2 3 4 5
3. Contributes to placement decision which will best meet the student's needs.	1 2 3 4 5	1 2 3 4 5
4. Develops abilities to communicate with other team members, including utilization of problem-solving approach when differences arise.	1 2 3 4 5	1 2 3 4 5
5. Seeks out and utilizes outside resources for the student, if needed.	1 2 3 4 5	1 2 3 4 5
6. Takes part in the team meeting in which diagnostic data is reviewed and tentative placement decision is made.	1 2 3 4 5	1 2 3 4 5
7. Communicates diagnostic information used to determine suggested placement to parents.	1 2 3 4 5	1 2 3 4 5
8. Contributes to development of student's overall educational plan (IEP), based on his needs.	1 2 3 4 5	1 2 3 4 5
9. Monitors and records the student's progress toward educational goals for which team member is responsible.	1 2 3 4 5	1 2 3 4 5
10. Contributes to the use of fair procedures according to law (due process), for each student and his/her family.	1 2 3 4 5	1 2 3 4 5

Team Functions

Special Education Teacher	Actual	Ideal
1. Participates in referral and evaluation processes of the student, as appropriate for the team member's role.	1 2 3 4 5	1 2 3 4 5
2. Carries through the parts of the individualized instructional plan (IIP) of the student for which team member is responsible.	1 2 3 4 5	1 2 3 4 5
3. Contributes to placement decision which will best meet the student's needs.	1 2 3 4 5	1 2 3 4 5
4. Develops abilities to communicate with other team members, including utilization of problem-solving approach when differences arise.	1 2 3 4 5	1 2 3 4 5
5. Seeks out and utilizes outside resources for the student, if needed.	1 2 3 4 5	1 2 3 4 5
6. Takes part in the team meeting in which diagnostic data is reviewed and tentative placement decision is made.	1 2 3 4 5	1 2 3 4 5
7. Communicates diagnostic information used to determine suggested placement to parents.	1 2 3 4 5	1 2 3 4 5
8. Contributes to development of student's overall educational plan (IEP), based on his needs.	1 2 3 4 5	1 2 3 4 5
9. Monitors and records the student's progress toward educational goals for which team member is responsible.	1 2 3 4 5	1 2 3 4 5
10. Contributes to the use of fair procedures according to law (due process), for each student and his/her family.	1 2 3 4 5	1 2 3 4 5

Team Functions

Speech Therapist	Actual	Ideal
1. Participates in referral and evaluation processes of the student, as appropriate for the team member's role.	1 2 3 4 5	1 2 3 4 5
2. Carries through the parts of the individualized instructional plan (IIP) of the student for which team member is responsible.	1 2 3 4 5	1 2 3 4 5
3. Contributes to placement decision which will best meet the student's needs.	1 2 3 4 5	1 2 3 4 5
4. Develops abilities to communicate with other team members, including utilization of problem-solving approach when differences arise.	1 2 3 4 5	1 2 3 4 5
5. Seeks out and utilizes outside resources for the student, if needed.	1 2 3 4 5	1 2 3 4 5
6. Takes part in the team meeting in which diagnostic data is reviewed and tentative placement decision is made.	1 2 3 4 5	1 2 3 4 5
7. Communicates diagnostic information used to determine suggested placement to parents.	1 2 3 4 5	1 2 3 4 5
8. Contributes to development of student's overall educational plan (IEP), based on his needs.	1 2 3 4 5	1 2 3 4 5
9. Monitors and records the student's progress toward educational goals for which team member is responsible.	1 2 3 4 5	1 2 3 4 5
10. Contributes to the use of fair procedures according to law (due process), for each student and his/her family.	1 2 3 4 5	1 2 3 4 5

Team Functions

Principal	Actual	Ideal
1. Participates in referral and evaluation processes of the student, as appropriate for the team member's role.	1 2 3 4 5	1 2 3 4 5
2. Carries through the parts of the individualized instructional plan (IIP) of the student for which team member is responsible.	1 2 3 4 5	1 2 3 4 5
3. Contributes to placement decision which will best meet the student's needs.	1 2 3 4 5	1 2 3 4 5
4. Develops abilities to communicate with other team members, including utilization of problem-solving approach when differences arise.	1 2 3 4 5	1 2 3 4 5
5. Seeks out and utilizes outside resources for the student, if needed.	1 2 3 4 5	1 2 3 4 5
6. Takes part in the team meeting in which diagnostic data is reviewed and tentative placement decision is made.	1 2 3 4 5	1 2 3 4 5
7. Communicates diagnostic information used to determine suggested placement to parents.	1 2 3 4 5	1 2 3 4 5
8. Contributes to development of student's overall educational plan (IEP), based on his needs.	1 2 3 4 5	1 2 3 4 5
9. Monitors and records the student's progress toward educational goals for which team member is responsible.	1 2 3 4 5	1 2 3 4 5
10. Contributes to the use of fair procedures according to law (due process), for each student and his/her family.	1 2 3 4 5	1 2 3 4 5

Team Functions

School Nurse	Actual	Ideal
1. Participates in referral and evaluation processes of the student, as appropriate for the team member's role.	1 2 3 4 5	1 2 3 4 5
2. Carries through the parts of the individualized instructional plan (IIP) of the student for which team member is responsible.	1 2 3 4 5	1 2 3 4 5
3. Contributes to placement decision which will best meet the student's needs.	1 2 3 4 5	1 2 3 4 5
4. Develops abilities to communicate with other team members, including utilization of problem-solving approach when differences arise.	1 2 3 4 5	1 2 3 4 5
5. Seeks out and utilizes outside resources for the student, if needed.	1 2 3 4 5	1 2 3 4 5
6. Takes part in the team meeting in which diagnostic data is reviewed and tentative placement decision is made.	1 2 3 4 5	1 2 3 4 5
7. Communicates diagnostic information used to determine suggested placement to parents.	1 2 3 4 5	1 2 3 4 5
8. Contributes to development of student's overall educational plan (IEP), based on his needs.	1 2 3 4 5	1 2 3 4 5
9. Monitors and records the student's progress toward educational goals for which team member is responsible.	1 2 3 4 5	1 2 3 4 5
10. Contributes to the use of fair procedures according to law (due process), for each student and his/her family.	1 2 3 4 5	1 2 3 4 5

Forms to Facilitate the
Multidisciplinary Team Process Appendix B

The first section of appendix B provides the reader with forms to facilitate communication related to the multidisciplinary team (figures B.1 to B.3). Not only must team members communicate effectively during the meetings, but a permanent record of the discussion, including any decisions made and programs developed, should be maintained. A current and accessible tracking system is then available for future reference.

The second section of appendix B contains forms designed to facilitate communication between team members regarding an individual student's progress (figures B.4 to B.7). These forms may also assist team members in reporting at follow-up team meetings.

Figure B.1 Team meeting agenda form

Date:_____

Time:_____

Place:_____

The following students will be discussed at the meeting scheduled for the date noted above. All members of the team should come prepared to discuss strengths and weaknesses of each child and to provide input relative to each student's current performance.

Time	Student	Meeting Purpose	Team Members to be in Attendance

Figure B.2 Team meeting record form

Student: _____   Teacher: _____

Grade: _____   Date: _____

Purpose of Team Meeting: _____

_____

_____

Team Members Present:

Name   Title

_____   _____

_____   _____

_____   _____

_____   _____

Problem / Need / Concern: _____

_____

_____

_____

_____

Alternative(s) discussed: _____

_____

_____

_____

Recommendations: _____

_____

_____

_____

Persons responsible: _____

_____

_____

_____

Re-evaluation date: _____

Figure B.3 Team meeting log

Student: _____

Date of first team meeting: _____

Date of last team meeting: _____

(Formal or Informal) Meeting Date	Purpose	Members Present	Information Discussed	Recommendations

Figure B.4 Record of daily student work completed

Student _____

Week of:

_____ to _____

Day	Task / Assignment	Location and Signature Indicating Completion			Comments
		Classroom	Resource Room	Other	

Figure B.5 Teacher record of student progress

(Enter significant incidents concerning student's program, progress, and parent-teacher contacts)

Student: _____ Grade:_____ Phone:_____

Teacher: _____ Parent:_____

Date	Summary Notes	Date	Summary Notes

Figure B.6 Teacher record of student behavior

Name: _____ Date: _____

	Monday			Tuesday			Wednesday			Thursday			Friday		
	G	A	P	G	A	P	G	A	P	G	A	P	G	A	P
1. On time															
2. Courteous to teacher and classmates															
3. Actively listened and followed directions															
4. Participated in class activities															
5. Verbally responded appropriately															
6. Completed assignments or worked consistently the entire period															
7. Behaved appropriately in hallway															
Daily Total															

2—Good   Comments:
1—Average
0—Poor

Figure B.7 Summary of student progress

Student: _____   Date: _____

Teacher: _____   Class: _____

Attendance: Absences (unexcused) _____

              Tardies _____

Goals/Objectives working on:

Completion of assignments:

   Number of assignments assigned: _____

   Number of assignments completed by student: _____

Has student mastered objectives as seen through assignments and quizzes or tests?

Participation in class: Does this student show an understanding of the concepts being discussed in class through oral
   discussion of ideas concerning these concepts, or through answers given to questions asked in class?

Is extra help needed through resource, and if so, what help is required?

Grade to date in class?

Selection and Use
of Instructional Materials Appendix C

This resource section is designed to assist regular educators in selecting the most appropriate and effective instructional materials for the exceptional students in their classrooms. Given the vast amount of materials available, it is not surprising that teachers experience considerable frustration in the decision-making procedure. The process of selecting materials begins after the exceptional student's present academic and behavioral functioning levels have been assessed. Generally, the formal assessment of the exceptional student is conducted by the special educator in conjunction with the school psychologist. After the assessment has been completed, the individuals involved in programming for the exceptional student have a better understanding of the student's academic levels, intellectual capacity, social/emotional status, general functioning level compared to peers, and preferred learning approaches. All of this information is used in selecting appropriate instructional materials. When possible, the materials selected should be closely matched to the learning characteristics and achievement level of the exceptional student. Unfortunately, many teachers do not always have the variety and quantity of materials necessary to meet all the instructional needs of their students.

The first step is to check the instructional materials bank for both exceptional and regular students and develop a resource list detailing the characteristics of all the basic learning materials in the school. In many cases this resource list will already be available through the school or district-level media/materials specialist. The following format is provided for people interested in creating such a list on their own.

Media and Material Location and Characteristics

1. Curriculum area (i.e., math, reading, science, etc.):

2. Grade level(s) of the material:

3. Age level of students for whom the material was prepared:

4. Delivery system (i.e., self-instructional, small group, individual, etc.):

5. Location of the material (i.e., media center, resource room, regular classroom, etc.):

If current commitments and time constraints prohibit the creation of such a resource file or catalogue, the best source for acquiring specialized instructional materials is the exceptional student's special education teacher. In acquiring materials from the special education teacher or the resource materials bank, the following questions need to be addressed:

1. What does the student need to learn?
2. Where does the student need to start?
3. How does the student generally learn best?
4. How can I determine whether the student has learned from the material and procedures used?

Likewise, questions regarding specific instructional materials also need to be addressed:

1. What does this material or program teach?
2. At what level does this material or program begin?
3. How does the material or program make provision for particular learning preferences of the student?
4. How does the material or program present information to be learned?
5. Does the program or material provide a means for assessing student progress?

If the special education teacher or the school media and materials facility do not have appropriate materials for the exceptional student, they can be secured from district, regional, or state instructional media centers, some of which are equipped to loan materials for extended periods of time. In addition to loaning materials, many states and regions employ a media and materials coordinator who can provide very specific information on material for exceptional students.

In making an appropriate match between instructional materials and the learning characteristics of the exceptional student, the following form (figure C.1) has been successfully used by regular teachers in a number of school districts.

When student learning characteristics and material characteristics have been identified, matched, and coordinated, successful learning is much more likely. Following is a brief description of an exceptional student accompanied by a completed *Student/Material Planning Form* (figure C.2).

David, age seven, speaks in isolated words and not in complete sentences. He reads in a limited fashion, a few isolated words, but seems to forget these words from one situation to another. He forgets things easily, but he always seems to try very hard. David can spell and write his own name; however, he has problems in drawing, connecting lines, and ending a line. He gets along well with his peers; he is chosen for many group activities, and tries hard to be part of these functions. David appears motivated when he is in a nonacademic situation; however, when interacting with the curriculum, he displays a lack of interest.

Figure C.1 Student / material planning form

Student name: _____

Curriculum area: _____   Publisher: _____

Material / Program: _____   Location: _____

I. Student learning characteristics

   A. Chronological age: _____

   B. Grade level as determined by appropriate

      testing: _____

   C. Primary interests: _____

      _____

      _____

II. Student-preferred approaches to processing new information:

   A. Multisensory _____

   B. Visual _____

   C. Auditory _____

   D. Tactile-kinesthetic _____

   E. Olfactory _____

I. Material characteristics

   A. Age for which material was intended: _____

   B. Grade level: _____

   C. Type of interest areas portrayed in the material:

      _____

      _____

II. Material input modes:

   A. Combination of inputs _____

   B. Worksheets, posters, printed material, charts and pictures

      _____

      _____

   C. Tapes, records, cassettes, etc. _____

      _____

   D. Beaded surfaces, sandpaper, etc. _____

      _____

   E. Scented paper, scented marking pens, etc. ____

      _____

Figure C.1 (cont.)

III. Student-preferred approaches to expressing new information:

    A. Writing _____

    B. Speaking _____

    C. Drawing _____

    D. Acting _____

    E. Reading _____

    F. Combination of approaches _____

    _____

III. Material output modes required

    A. Motor (writing, drawing, acting, etc.)

        1. Fine _____

        2. Gross _____

    B. Verbal (reading, speaking, etc.)

        1. Answer questions _____

        2. Repeat modeled information _____

        _____

        3. Make spontaneous response _____

        _____

    C. Visual (reading, writing, etc.)

        1. Observe _____

        2. Matching _____

        3. Other _____

IV. Student-preferred delivery system

    A. Individual _____

    B. Small group _____

    C. Independent _____

    D. Large group _____

    E. Peer tutoring _____

    F. _____ (etc.)

    G. _____ (etc.)

IV. Material delivery system

    A. Tutorial (one-to-one) _____

    B. Small group (teacher directed)

    _____

    C. Self-instruction/programmed

    _____

    D. Large group (teacher directed)

    _____

    E. Peer tutoring _____

    F. _____

    G. _____

Figure C.1 (cont.)

V. Other Information: V. Misc.

_____

_____

_____

_____

_____

_____

_____

Figure C.2 Student / material planning form—completed

Student name: *David*

Curriculum area: _____

Material/Program: *Children Playing*

I. Student learning characteristics

   A. Chronological age: *7 yrs. 2 mos.*

   B. Grade level as determined by appropriate

      testing: *pre primer*

   C. Primary interests: *younger friends, group activities etc.*

II. Student-preferred approaches to processing new information:

   A. Multisensory ____✓_____

   B. Visual _____

   C. Auditory _____

   D. Tactile-kinesthetic _____

   E. Olfactory _____

Publisher: *Non-applicable-teacher made*

Location: *regular classroom, teacher files*

I. Material characteristics

   A. Age for which material was intended: *5-7 yrs.*

   B. Grade level: *pre primer for which material was intended.*

   C. Type of interest areas portrayed in the material: *Small groups, clubs, etc.*

II. Material input modes:

   A. Combination of inputs _____

   B. Worksheets, posters, printed material, charts and pictures

      _____✓_____

   C. Tapes, records, cassettes, etc. _____

   D. Beaded surfaces, sandpaper, etc. _____

   E. Scented paper, scented marking pens, etc. _____

Figure C.2 (cont.)

III. Student-preferred approaches to expressing new information:

A. Writing _____

B. Speaking _____

C. Drawing _____

D. Acting _____

E. Reading _____

F. Combination of approaches ___✔_____

_____

III. Material output modes required

A. Motor (writing, drawing, acting, etc.)

1. Fine _____

2. Gross _____

B. Verbal (reading, speaking, etc.)

1. Answer questions _____✔_____

2. Repeat modeled information ___✔_____

_____

3. Make spontaneous response ___✔_____

_____

C. Visual (reading, writing, etc.)

1. Observe _____✔_____

2. Matching _____

3. Other _____

IV. Student-preferred delivery system

A. Individual _____

B. Small group ___✔_____

C. Independent _____

D. Large group _____

E. Peer tutoring ___✔_____

F. _____ (etc.)

G. _____ (etc.)

IV. Material delivery system

A. Tutorial (one-to-one) _____

B. Small group (teacher directed)

_____✔_____

C. Self-instruction / programmed

_____

D. Large group (teacher directed)

_____

E. Peer tutoring _____✔_____

F. _____

G. _____

Figure C.2 (cont.)

V. Other Information: V. Misc.

In addition to peer tutoring,
David should be involved in
direct teaching techniques in order
to develop the skills necessary for
partial involvement in the regular
Class reading activities.

Biographies

Grant B. Bitter

Grant B. Bitter is Coordinator of Teacher Education, Area of the Deaf, Department of Special Education, at the University of Utah. He completed his B.A. degree at the University of Utah, his M.A. degree at Columbia University, and his doctorate at Wayne State University. During his twenty-one years of experience, he has been active in a variety of educational settings. He has served as a regular class teacher, a special educator, and an administrator of special education programs. As a consultant, he has been very active nationally in providing workshops and training related to mainstreaming hearing-impaired children.

Dr. Bitter is the immediate past president and a member of the board of the International Parents' Organization of the Alexander Graham Bell Association for the Deaf, Inc. He also serves as an advisor to many national parent advocacy organizations. His publications include manuals and materials for parents and families of hearing-impaired children, audiovisual materials on mainstreaming, and articles on issues and concerns in the field of the education of the deaf.

Mary L. Buchanan

Mary Buchanan is an Assistant Professor in the Department of Special Education at the University of Utah. While at the University of Utah, she has served as a coordinator of programs in learning disabilities, and Acting Department Chairperson (1976–77). She earned a B.A. degree in education from Weber State College, and an M.Ed. in Special Education from the University of Texas at Austin. Dr. Buchanan received her Ph.D. degree in Educational Administration from the University of Utah.

Dr. Buchanan taught English at the junior high level for three years, and has also taught in elementary special education programs. Additional experiences include workshop and consultant activities in Utah and the Intermountain region.

Margot Butler

Margot Butler earned her B.A. in English from the University of Utah, and her M.A. in Special Education from Teacher's College, Columbia University. She has taught the hearing-impaired at every level from preschool to adult classes. She has also taught in elementary classroom settings. As an integration specialist for the Utah School for the Deaf, she was actively involved for several years in facilitating the mainstreaming of hearing-impaired students in regular classrooms. Ms. Butler has also supervised a number of day-school programs for deaf children. She is currently a coordinator of special education and has taught graduate courses in the teacher preparation program in the Department of Special Education at the University of Utah.

Ruth Craig

Ruth Craig is an emeritus faculty member of the Department of Educational Psychology at the Brigham Young University. She received her B.A. from Hunter College in New York City in 1937. She completed her M.A. at Teacher's College, Columbia University in 1939. During her tenure at Brigham Young University, she was responsible for developing a teacher education program for the visually handicapped. She served as the Supervisor/Director of the Visually Handicapped Program until 1977.

Mrs. Craig began her teaching career in a large residential school for blind children and youth. Later in her professional career, she was responsible for developing a program for multiply-handicapped persons at the Utah State Training School. She has also published a number of articles related to the teaching of braille.

Mary K. Dykes

Mary K. Dykes is a professor in the Department of Special Education at the University of Florida. She completed her doctorate at The University of Texas at Austin in the area of the physically and multiply handicapped. She has served as a regular class teacher, a special educator in a center for children with cerebral palsy, and has taught preschool and elementary-aged children in gifted, regular, and handicapped programs.

Her primary responsibilities are educational leadership preparation and research in the area of the severely and multiply handicapped. In addition she serves as a member of the interdisciplinary team in cerebral palsy in the medical center at the University of Florida. Dr. Dykes is involved in numerous activities and has published in an array of professional volumes. At the present time, she is President of the Teacher Education Division of the Council for Exceptional Children. She serves on several policy boards for the state of Florida and for local education agencies. Each year she provides in-service training sessions for university and field-based special educators in various states. She is an associate editor and reader for several journals and publishing firms.

M. Winston Egan

M. Winston Egan is a faculty member and Area Coodinator of Behavioral Disorders of the Department of Special Education at the University of Utah. He completed his Ph.D at the University of Florida with an emphasis in special education and early childhood education. His Master's degree in Early Childhood Education was completed at Oakland University in Rochester, Michigan. Dr. Egan has served in a variety of educational positions. For three years he was an elementary teacher. He subsequently worked at the Utah Boys' Ranch. During his graduate education, he taught preschool and kindergarten, and served as a tutoring coordinator for the Reading and Study Skills Center of the University of Florida. From 1974–1977, he served as the director of Headstart training for the State of Utah. As a researcher, Dr. Egan has been very involved with work related to multidisciplinary teams, reconstituted families, juvenile delinquency, and child guidance. He has also taught a variety of graduate and undergraduate courses in special education and provided consultation to a number of school districts and agencies.

Joanne Gilles

Joanne Gilles is an Instructional Media Specialist for the Special Education Area of the Utah State Office of Education, and the Director of the Utah Learning Resource Center. She also serves as an Adjunct Clinical Instructor in the Department of Special Education at the University of Utah. Ms. Gilles graduated from Buena Vista College at Tulane University, the University of Utah, and Westminister College.

She taught elementary education and special education for eighteen years. She has conducted workshops for various special education agencies and organizations, including The National Inservice Network, Regional Resource Centers, and Indian Educational Programs. Ms. Gilles has also been honored by her colleagues as the Utah Special Educator of the Year in 1979.

Her publications and media productions include materials related to learning disabilities and multicultural education. She is the editor for the Idea Sparkers column in the Childhood Education Publication of ACEI. She also is the author of the Preferred Picks, a regular feature of the Pointer publication.

Michael L. Hardman

Michael Hardman is an Assistant Professor and Director of Graduate Programs in the Department of Special Education at the University of Utah. He completed a Bachelor of Science degree in Psychology, M.Ed. degree in Special Education, and a Ph.D. in Educational Administration from the University of Utah. Dr. Hardman has several publications in the field of special education, including the text, *Mental Retardation: Social and Educational Perspectives* (co-authored with C. J. Drew and H. P. Bluhm). He has published in *Mental Retardation, Journal of Applied Behavior Analysis,* and *Education and Training of the Mentally Retarded.*

Dr. Hardman is active in several professional associations, including the Association for the Severely Handicapped (TASH), American Association on Mental Deficiency (AAMD), and the Council for Exceptional Children (CEC). He is currently President of the Utah Council for Exceptional Children and Chairman of the Utah State AAMD Chapter.

Claudia Howard

Claudia Howard is an itinerant teacher of the visually impaired with the Salt Lake City School District. She received her Bachelor of Science degree in elementary and special education from the University of Texas at Austin. She completed her Master of Education degree in special education from East Texas State University. Her graduate work prepared her for the role of educational diagnostician in special education.

Ms. Howard's teaching experience includes working with the learning-disabled in Texas and the visually impaired in the State of Utah. Additional experiences include consultive work for the University of Utah and workshops specifically designed for regular classroom teachers.

Elliott D. Landau

Elliott D. Landau is Professor of Child Growth and Development in the Department of Education at the University of Utah. He holds a Ph.D. degree in Child Development from New York University. He has written the following books: *Just a Minute, You and Your Child's World, Raising Fine Families, Today's Family, Child Development Through Literature,* (1972); *A Teaching Experience: An Introduction to Education Through Literature,* (1975); and *The Exceptional Child Through Literature* (1978).

Dr. Landau has been active in community and national committees. He was chairman of the Second District Juvenile Court Advisory Committee from 1967–71. For several years he was a member of the Board of Directors at large of Odyssey House of New York, a drug treatment facility with therapeutic centers in seven states. He is a Fellow of the American Orthopsychiatric Association and a member of the American Psychological Association.

Dr. Landau was the founder and director of the Intermountain Conference on Children's Literature from 1960–1974. He has been an advisor to the Scott-Foresman Company, McGraw-Hill, and numerous other publishing houses. In 1968, Dr. Landau was awarded the Distinguished Teaching Award at the University of Utah. He is the author of many articles, monographs, and research materials in the field of children's literature and child development.

Dr. Landau has done postdoctoral work in Family Therapy, and is a licensed marriage and family therapist. He is also a clinical member of the American Association for Marriage and Family Therapy.

Jeanette M. Misaka

Jeanette M. Misaka is a Clinical Instructor in the Department of Special Education at the University of Utah. She earned her B.S. degree in elementary education and her M.S. degree in educational psychology with an emphasis in special education. She holds teaching certificates in the areas of elementary education, behavioral disorders, and learning disabilities. Ms. Misaka taught five years in regular education and seven years with the emotionally handicapped. She has conducted and participated in many workshops concerning the gifted and talented, and has also served on numerous state and national committees concerned with educating the gifted and talented.

Ms. Misaka has also been active in many professional and community organizations and commitees, such as the Council for Exceptional Children (CEC), The Council for Children with Behavioral Disorders, Delta Kappa Gamma, American Association of University Women, and the Utah PL 94-142 Advisory Committee on the Handicapped. She is presently representing Utah as a member of the CEC National Board of Governors.

Gloria Rupp

Gloria Rupp is Project Demonstrator for the Gifted and Talented Programs in Granite School District, Salt Lake City, Utah. She earned her B.S. and M.Ed. degrees in education from the University of Utah.

Ms. Rupp taught fifth and sixth grade for seven years. Other professional experiences include acting as Gifted Consultant, University of Utah Dean's Curriculum Revision Project, 1977–1980; and instructional participant in gifted education workshops for the University of Utah.

Susan Ryberg

Susan Ryberg is a professional consultant for a number of professional and private organizations. She attended Arizona State University for three years and graduated from the University of Utah with a Bachelor's degree in education. In 1971, she graduated with a Master's degree in special education with an emphasis in teaching the learning-disabled. Following the completion of her Master's program, she served as an elementary resource room teacher. Ms. Ryberg was a Clinical Instructor in the Department of Special Education at the University of Utah from 1973 to 1978.

Ms. Ryberg's active involvement in educational consulting has been directly related to writing and implementing curricula for persons responsible for mainstreaming exceptional students. Her publications include *Bag of Tricks: Instructional Games and Activities* (with J. Blake and J. Sebastian, Love Publishing Co., 1976), and *Personalizing the Educational Program for Handicapped and Special Needs Students in the Classroom* (Utah State Board of Education, 1978).

Joan P. Sebastian

Joan Sebastian is currently working as an independent educational consultant. In this capacity she has been extensively involved in the development of in-service training for regular educators throughout the State of Utah. Mrs. Sebastian received her Bachelor of Science degree in elementary education and her Master of Education degree in special education from the University of Utah. She has taught in special education classrooms in the public schools and served as a Clinical Instructor in the Department of Special Education at the University of Utah. Her publications include *Bag of Tricks: Instructional Games and Activities* (with J. Blake and S. Ryberg, Love Publishing Co., 1976), and *Personalizing the Educational Program for Handicapped and Special Needs Students in the Classroom* (Utah State Board of Education 1978).

Bill R. Wagonseller

Bill R. Wagonseller is Professor and Coordinator of the Emotional Disturbance Program at the University of Nevada, Las Vegas. He received his B.A. from Wichita State University in 1959, and his M.S. from Kansas in 1971. He began his special education teaching career in the Wichita Public Schools, where he was named Outstanding Young Educator in 1965. He has served as a consultant to several school districts and has been very active in parent training. He is codirector of the annual Western Regional Conference on Humanistic Approaches in Behavior Modification.

Dr. Wagonseller is presently National President of Teacher Educators for Children with Behavior Disorders and Chairman of the Nevada Special Education Advisory Committee. He has held several offices in the Nevada State Council for Exceptional Children and has been a member of the State of Nevada Governor's Advisory Committee on Rehabilitation and the Nevada State Department Advisory Committee on Exceptional Pupil Education.

In addition to being the author of a number of professional papers and articles, he conducts many regional and national level workshops. Dr. Wagonseller is also coauthor of a multimedia kit for parent training called *The Art of Parenting*.

Carol Weller

Carol Weller is an Assistant Professor and Director of Clinical Practice in the Department of Special Education at the University of Utah. Dr. Weller received her Ed.D. degree in learning disabilities from the University of Florida. She graduated with minors in the areas of language and applied psychology.

Dr. Weller has been on the faculty of Purdue University and Indiana University-Purdue University at Fort Wayne. She has also been the Director of the Northeast Indiana Instructional Resource Center for Handicapped Children and Youth. Her previous publications have included articles in the *Journal of Learning Disabilities* and *Learning Disabilities Quarterly*. She is currently an Executive Board member of the Teacher Education Division, Council for Exceptional Children.

Joan S. Wolf

Joan S. Wolf is a Clinical Assistant Professor in the Department of Special Education at the University of Utah. A native of Boston, Massachusetts, she began her career as an elementary school teacher. She completed her B.S. degree in elementary education at the University of Utah, an M.A. in School Psychology, and a Ph.D. in Exceptional Children at the Ohio State University in Columbus, Ohio. Dr. Wolf is certified as a teacher, a school psychologist, and a supervisor in the area of learning disabilities.

Her experiences include working with learning and behavior disordered children in a variety of settings as well as work with the gifted. She has worked as a research associate with the Ohio State University and the Ohio Department of Education in developing programs for gifted/talented children. She has taught courses in learning disabilities, behavior modification, parent counseling, and gifted education.

Glossary

Attending behavior   On-task behavior marked by appropriate responses to the specific situation (e.g., listening and looking at a teacher during an instructional period).

Audiogram   A graph on which the hearing test is recorded. The horizontal axis represents the pitch; the vertical axis represents the intensity.

Auditory deficit   A disability in listening, hearing, recognizing, interpreting, and responding to spoken language.

Auditory modality   The channel through which individuals receive and process auditory stimuli.

Blending   The ability to synthesize the phonemes of a word and produce an integrated whole.

Cause-and-effect comprehension skills   The ability to understand cause-effect relationships in reading, listening, and experiential situations.

Central nervous system   That part of the nervous system consisting of the brain and spinal cord, to which sensory impulses are transmitted and from which motor impulses pass out.

Cerebral palsy   A condition characterized by motor impairment caused by brain damage during the prenatal period or at birth.

Contract   Refers to a verbal or written agreement between two or more individuals, which stipulates responsibilities of each of the individuals and identifies rewards that can be earned by successfully fulfilling the responsibilities or tasks.

Convergent thinking   The act of bringing disjointed thoughts together towards one central point or focus.

Convulsion   A violent and involuntary contraction or series of contractions of the muscles.

Cross categorical   Refers to more than one category of exceptionality (e.g., behavior disorders, learning disabilities, mental retardation).

Decibel   The unit in which sound is measured and recorded.

Diplegia   A paralysis of corresponding parts of the body on both sides.

Divergent thinking   Thinking that is characterized by moving from one focal point to many points or ideas.

Epilepsy   A disorder characterized by a variety of seizures; can be controlled in many instances with appropriate anticonvulsant medication.

Error analysis   An examination of student errors in order to determine the nature of the error pattern.

Etiology   Cause or origin; a branch of knowledge dealing with causes.

Extinction   Refers to a process in which a specific behavior is eliminated by no longer following the behavior with a reward.

Fingerspelling   Refers to specific configuration/placement/movement of the hand to represent the letters of the alphabet. Any word can, in this way, be spelled out on the hand as specifically as a word can be spelled out on paper.

Hemiplegia   Paralysis of one side of the body.

Hydrocephalus   A condition in which fluid within the brain does not drain or circulate as it should; the most common cause of an enlarged head. A shunt may be used to help circulate the fluid.

Hyperkinetic   Abnormally increased and usually purposeless and uncontrollable muscle movement.

Impulse control   The act of exercising restraint over impetuous or thoughtless behavior.

Inferential skills   The ability to arrive at a conclusion from facts or premises.

Language-experience approach to reading   The child's own language and experiences are the basis for reading lessons.

Lipreading   Refers to the manner in which a hearing-impaired person may receive information from another person. The hearing-impaired person watches the speaker and uses the placement of the tongue and teeth and the movement of the lips, along with general facial expression and body movement to understand the speaker's message.

Mainstream   Refers to the functional integration and participation of exceptional students in the social and instructional programs of regular classrooms.

Meningocele   A condition in which the membrane covering the spinal column protrudes through the vertebral column forming a sac-like mass under the skin.

Muscular dystrophy   A disorder in which the muscle tissue of the body gradually weakens and atrophies. The condition is usually genetically determined and is characterized by difficulty in walking and performing self-help skills.

Myelomeningocele   A sac of nerve tissue that protrudes from the back through a cleft in the spine.

Negative feedback   Responses characterized by unpleasant or aversive messages.

Neurological impress   A system of teaching reading designed to repattern the reading habits of a student through overlearning and repetition.

Normative-referenced assessment   Assessment that compares the individual with some population of persons who have also been assessed on the same instrument; e.g., average IQ is 100. An individual with an IQ of 50 is significantly below the average of the general population taking the test.

Paraplegia   Paralysis of the lower back half of the back or body on both sides.

Perceptual-motor   Refers to functions that involve coordination of the various senses (hearing, seeing, feeling) with the movement of various muscles (e.g., copying words from a blackboard, catching a ball, or throwing a basketball through a hoop).

Peripheral nervous system   That part of the nervous system consisting of the receptor organs of the eye, ear, skin, joints, and muscles. It transmits sensations to the central nervous system.

Physical therapist   Professionally trained person who helps people to obtain optimal performance in motor skills. A registered physical therapist may use many techniques to facilitate change once a prescription for services is written by a physician.

Positive reinforcer   A reward that maintains or increases a specified behavior.

Premack principle   Refers to the utilization of a high-frequency behavior to reinforce a low-frequency behavior.

Psycholinguist   A specialist in the study of language behavior.

Punishment   Refers to the application of an aversive stimulus following a specified behavior.

Quadriplegic   A person who is paralyzed in both arms and both legs.

Recall   The ability to remember.

Reinforcement menu   Refers to a list of items, activities, and edibles that can be utilized to reinforce behaviors.

Residential classroom   A class located within a residential school wherein exceptional students are enrolled according to specific disabilities (deaf, blind, mentally retarded, etc.). Residential schools provide live-in facilities (dormitories) for students twenty-four hours a day. Some residential schools, however, admit day students who live at home but attend the school for instructional services.

Resource program   An educational setting that provides assessment and remedial services on a regular basis for part of each school day.

Resource room   A room in the regular school that is equipped with specialized materials wherein exceptional students receive instruction for a portion of their school day from a special educator.

Response cost   Refers to the withdrawing of a reward as a consequence of some inappropriate behavior.

Self-contained classroom   A classroom usually located within regular school facilities wherein instructional services are provided by a special education teacher for small numbers of exceptional students by designated disability areas (deaf, blind, and others). Some students may spend the whole day in the self-contained classroom, while others may experience some degree of social and instructional involvement in regular classes and other school activities.

Seizure   The sudden onset of symptoms that are characterized by involuntary and violent movement of the muscles.

Sequencing   The ability to reproduce from memory a sequence of stimuli presented visually or aurally.

Shaping   Refers to a series of progressive steps to be followed in helping a child master a certain behavior.

Sign language   Refers to a representation of words and phrases by bodily movement—mostly the hands, but the arms and body are also used—supplemented with facial expression. Fingerspelling is used with sign language to supplement names or words that are special or unknown. There are a number of sign systems.

Sight word skills   The ability to recognize words by shape or configuration.

Sociogram   A method for assessing the nature of the interpersonal relationships in a classroom.

Special school   A day school for handicapped students wherein they are provided segregated instructional services according to designated disability areas. The students return to their homes during non-school hours.

Spina bifida   Refers to a congenital malformation of the spine.

Temporal lobe   A large lobe of each hemisphere of the brain that contains a sensory area associated with the organ of hearing.

Time-out   A procedure for removing students from reinforcing conditions or taking away their opportunity to earn rewards for a specified period of time.

Visual modality The channel through which individuals receive and process visual stimuli.

Visual sequencing tasks The ability to reproduce a sequence of visually perceived items from memory.

Wide Range Achievement Test (WRAT) An individually administered norm reference test that measures performance in reading, spelling, and arithmetic.

Word attack skills The use of contextual, phonic, and structural analysis skills to identify unknown words.

Author Index

A

Affleck, J., 121, 138
Allen, J. L., 204, 207
Amidon, P. S., 261, 285
Anderson, K. E., 41, 43
Aschcroft, S. C., 183, 207
Atwood, B. S., 266, 277, 285

B

Bakwin, H., 50, 63
Bakwin, R. M., 50, 62
Barbe, W., 259, 283, 285
Barclay, J. R., 14, 29
Barraga, N. C., 181, 202, 207, 208
Barrie-Blackey, S., 153, 163
Bateman, B. D., 58, 62
Becker, W. C., 31, 44, 100, 107, 109, 116, 117
Belliston, L., 278, 286
Berry, M. F., 150, 163
Best, G., 226, 236
Bigge, J., 227, 236
Birch, J. W., 246, 255
Bleck, E. E., 214, 236
Bloom, B. S., 247, 254, 268, 273, 285, 286
Blount, W. R., 150, 163
Boswell, J., 183, 208
Botel, M., 261, 262, 287
Brown, K., 251, 256
Brown, L., 107, 116
Bruch, C. B., 242, 254
Buchanan, J., 251, 256
Buckholdt, D. R., 90, 91, 93, 98, 99, 104, 116
Bullock, L., 52, 63
Burch, N., 72–75, 78–83, 106, 116

Burns, M., 278, 285
Bush, W. J., 136, 137
Butz, G., 100, 105, 116

C

Caccamise, F. C., 169, 179
Calhoun, M. L., 217, 236
Callahan, C. M., 246, 255
Calvert, D., 170, 179
Charles, C. M., 107, 116
Chinn, P. C., 61, 62
Clarizio, H. F., 51, 62, 94, 95, 97, 100, 109, 116
Clark, K. B., 242, 254
Clelland, R., 229, 236
Clements, S. D., 56, 61, 62
Cole, T., 284, 286
Collins, E. C., 243, 255
Cooley, K., 225, 236
Cooper, J., 131, 137
Cratty, B. J., 201, 208
Cushenberry, B. C., 276, 286

D

Della-Piana, G. M., 90, 91, 93, 98, 99, 104, 116
Delquadri, J., 116
Dembinski, R. J., 33, 44
Dennis, R. P., 278, 286
DeRisi, W. J., 100, 105, 116
Dreikurs, R., 83–85, 107, 116
Drew, C. J., 61, 62
Drury, A. M., 169, 179
Dunn, L. M., 57, 59, 63
Dykes, M., 52, 63

E

Edwards, D., 278, 286
Ellison, R. L., 242, 246, 254, 256
Engelmann, S., 100, 109, 116
Eyman, R. K., 63

F

Fagen, S. A., 86, 87, 89, 90, 100, 116
Fantini, M. D., 242, 254
Feldhusen, J. F., 242, 254
Ferritor, D. E., 90, 91, 93, 98, 99, 104, 116
Fletcher, H., 260, 286
Fox, D. G., 242, 246, 254
Freisen, W. V., 114, 117
Funk, W., 278, 286

G

Gallagher, J. J., 244–45, 254
Gallagher, P. A., 34, 44
Galloway, C., 39, 44
Galloway, K. C., 39, 44
Gattengno, C., 124, 137
Gearheart, B. R., 57, 58, 63, 123, 136, 137
Gearheart, D. K., 58, 63
George, W. C., 242, 256
Getzels, J. W., 246, 254
Giles, M. T., 136
Glasser, W., 67, 71, 109, 116
Glidewell, J., 50, 63
Gordon, T., 25–29, 42, 44, 72–75, 78–83, 106, 107, 116
Gorham, K. A. A., 32, 44
Greenwood, C. R., 109, 116
Gregg, J. R., 200, 208

325

Grollman, E. A., 220, 236
Gross, N. C., 14, 29
Grossman, H. J., 53, 61–63
Grunwald, B. R., 83–85, 107, 116
Guilford, J. P., 248–49, 255, 273, 286
Gyulay, J., 220, 236

H

Hallahan, D. P., 55, 60, 63
Hammill, D. D., 57, 59, 61, 63
Hankins, W. E., 123, 138
Hanks, K., 278, 286
Haring, N., 52, 63, 120, 132, 138
Hartman, R. K., 246, 255
Hatlin, P., 186, 208
Hawisher, M., 217, 236
Heath, G. G., 200, 208
Hebeler, J. R., 280, 286
Heber, R., 53, 63
Henderson, F., 195, 198, 208
Hill, J. M., 86, 87, 89, 90, 100, 116
Hirsh, I. J., 169, 179
Hobbs, N., 32, 43, 44
Hoben, M., 207, 208
Homme, L., 100, 101, 104, 116
Hops, H., 116
Horn, R., 280, 287
Howard, H. R., 273, 286
Howell, H., 276, 286
Hoyt, K. B., 280, 286

J

Jackson, P. W., 246, 254
James, L. R., 242, 246, 254
Jensen, A. R., 153, 163
Junkala, J., 122, 138

K

Kaplan, S. N., 284, 286
Karnes, F. A., 243, 255
Karnes, M. B., 37, 45
Kauffman, J. P., 55, 60, 62, 63
Keeran, C. V., 63
Kelly, T., 53, 63
Kephart, N. C., 56, 63
Khatena, J., 245, 255
Kirk, S. A., 56, 61, 63, 136, 138
Kleibhan, J. M., 136, 138
Knappett, K., 205, 208

Kounin, J. S., 114–15, 117
Kovalic, S., 268, 286
Krathwohl, D. R., 247, 273, 286
Kroth, R. L., 34, 35, 38, 40, 45
Krumboltz, H. B., 92, 96, 117
Krumboltz, J. D., 92, 96, 117

L

Lehtinen, L. E., 56, 63
Lerner, J. W., 14, 29, 56, 63, 121–22, 136, 138
Levin, J. R., 153, 163
Lewis, J. F., 54, 63
Lewis, N., 278, 286
Lillie, D. L., 31, 45
Ling, D., 170, 179
Lloyd, B. C., 251, 256
Logan, D., 61, 62
Long, A., 33, 45
Long, N. J., 110–14, 117
Lorayne, H., 278, 286
Lovitt, T. C., 120, 138
Lowenbraun, S., 121, 138
Lowenfeld, B., 202, 203, 208
Lukas, J., 278, 286

M

McCabe, A. E., 153, 163
McCory, G., 51, 62
McDowell, R. L., 39, 41, 42, 45
MacEachern, A. W., 14, 29
MacMillan, D. L., 53, 54, 63
Madsen, C., 108, 117
Madsen, C. H., 107, 108, 117
Marland, S. P., 243–44, 255, 281, 286
Marsh, G. E., 58, 63
Martin, G. J., 207, 208
Martinson, R. A., 245, 255
Masia, B. B., 273, 286
Mason, W. S., 14, 29
Mauser, A. J., 34, 44
Maxfield, S., 251, 256
Mayer, G., 123, 138
Meeker, M. N., 248, 255
Mercer, J., 53, 54, 63
Miller, J., 185, 208
Moldof, E. P., 278, 286
Morse, W. C., 110

N

Napier, G. D., 187, 199, 208
Newman, R. G., 110–14, 117
Norton, A. E., 114, 117
Nunley, B. G., 261–62, 287

O

Obradovic, S., 114–15, 117
Oden, M. H., 245

P

Pate, J. E., 51, 63
Pegnato, C. C., 246, 255
Pepper, F. C., 83–85, 107, 116
Philips, L., 52, 63
Polsgrove, L., 100, 117
Premack, D., 113, 117

R

Raskin, B., 263–64, 286
Reissman, F., 242, 255
Renzulli, J. S., 243, 246, 249, 253, 255, 265, 273–74, 281, 286
Rice, J., 244, 255
Rimm, S., 285, 286
Ring, B., 125, 138
Rovner, W. D., 153, 163

S

Samuda, R., 242, 255
Scholl, G. T., 184, 208
Seghini, J. B., 251, 256
Shea, T. M., 100–103, 117
Silverman, S. R., 170, 179
Simpson, R. L., 34, 35, 45
Sisk, D., 247, 255, 283, 286
Sloan, H. N., 80, 91, 93, 98, 99, 104, 116
Smith, D., 107, 117
Smith, J. M., 107, 117
Smith, L. H., 246, 255
Solano, C. H., 242, 256
Stanley, J. C., 242, 256
Stennett, R. G., 50, 63
Stephens, T. M., 121, 138
Stevenson, G., 251, 256
Stewart, E. D., 273, 286
Strauss, A. A., 56, 63

Suffolk, P., 278, 286
Sulzer, B., 123, 138
Susser, P., 37, 46
Swallow, C., 50, 63
Syphers, D. F., 284, 286

T

Taba, H., 14, 28, 29
Tarjan, G., 53, 63
Taylor, C. W., 243, 246, 249,
    251–52, 254, 256, 270, 273,
    287
Taylor, J. L., 181, 185, 208
Terman, L. J., 245, 256, 260, 287
Thomas, D. R., 100, 107, 109,
    116, 117
Timothy, K., 251, 256
Torrance, E. P., 242, 246, 255–56
Treffinger, D. J., 242, 254

V

Vance, H. B., 125, 138
VanRiper, C., 143, 163

W

Wagner, N. N., 205, 208
Wagonseller, B. R., 41, 42, 46
Walker, D. L., 185, 186, 208
Walker, H. M., 116
Walker, J. E., 100–103, 117
Weinstein, G., 242, 254
Weishahn, M. W., 57, 63, 136,
    137
Wender, P., 124, 138
White, A. J., 246, 255
Wickman, E. K., 50, 63

Williams, F. E., 247–48, 250,
    256, 266, 273, 287
Wirtz, R. W., 261–62, 287
Wolf, B., 179
Wolfe, W. G., 212, 236
Wolff, P., 153, 163
Woody, R. H., 14, 29
Wright, S. W., 63
Wurman, R. S., 283, 287

Z

Zehrbach, R. R., 37, 45
Zifferblatt, S. M., 100, 117
Zimmerman, M. A., 251, 256
Zuckerman, D., 280, 287

Subject Index

Convulsive disorders, 218–19, 319
  epilepsy, 218, 320
  seizures, 218–19, 322
Counselor
  as member of multidisciplinary team, 16, 21–23
  in parent eduation and training, 33
Crafts, for the visually impaired, 199–200
Cranmer abacus, 185, 196

D

Deafness. *See* Hearing impairments
Death, 220
Delayed language, 149–50
Deviant language, 150–52
Dialectical differences, 145, 149
Diplegia, 215, 319
Disability, as goal of misbehavior, 84
Divergent thinking, 154, 274, 319
Dreiker's model, 83–85
  attention, 83–84
  disability, 83–84
  power, 83–84
  recognition reflex, 84–85
  revenge, 83–84
Dyslexia, 55, 58

E

Echolalia, 151
Educable mentally retarded, 53
Education of All Handicapped Children Act (Public Law 94-142), 3–8, 13, 28, 32, 43, 57–59, 141, 186
  annual review, 8
  free and appropriate education, 6
  individualized education plan (IEP), 5–7, 20–21, 32, 33, 36
  least restrictive environment, 6–7, 141, 185, 222
  nonbiased assessment, 6
  personnel development, 7
  procedural safeguards, 8
Elementary and Secondary Education Act (Public Law 91-230), 242, 243

Emotional needs
  of physically handicapped and health-impaired, 233
  of visually impaired, 203–5
Environment, adaptations of
  for physically handicapped, 229
  for visually impaired, 191–93
Epilepsy. *See* Convulsive disorders
Epilepsy Foundation of America, 218
Error analysis. *See* Reading
Exceptional students
  attitudes toward, 8–10
  definition of, 3
Extinction. *See* Behavior modification strategies

F

Federal Rules and Regulations (guidelines for classification of learning disabilities), 58
Feedback
  in hearing aids, 168
  internal, in speech, 151
  negative, 119, 321
Fingerspelling. *See* Hearing impairments
Flexibility, in placement, 185, 244
Free and appropriate education, 4
  as defined in PL 94-142, 6

G

Gifted and talented, 242–87
  academic programming, 259–74
  career education, 281
  characteristics, 244
  definition, 243
  identification, 245
  independent study, 264–66
  open-ended curriculum, 261–63
  questioning techniques, 273–74
  reading, 276–80
  research and study skills, 275–76
  self-evaluation, 274–75
  simulation, 280
  teaching/learning models, 266–70
  theoretical approaches, 247–53
Guilford's SOI theory, 248

H

Handicapped children, definition of, 3
Health impairments, 211–36
Hearing aids. *See* Hearing impairments
Hearing impairments, 165–78
  degrees of impairment, 165–67
  fingerspelling, 169, 320
  hearing aids, 167–68
  involving classmates, 174–77
  involving parents, 176
  language deficits, 172–74
  lipreading, 169, 175–76, 178, 320
  roles of professionals, 169–70
  sign language, 169, 322
  teaching methodology, 169–70
Hemiplegia, 215, 320
Hospital/homebound programs, 221
Hydrocephalus, 216, 320
Hyperactivity, 124. *See also* Hyperkinetic
Hyperkinetic, 55, 320

I

I messages, 78–81, 83
Impulse control, 130, 320
Independent study, for gifted and talented, 264–66
Individualized education plan (IEP). *See* Education of All Handicapped Children Act
Inferential skills, 123, 320
Intelligence tests, 53–54, 60–61, 246, 251
  Stanford-Binet, 242, 245
  Wechsler Intelligence Scale for Children—Revised, 53, 245

J

Jargon speech, 150–51

K

Khatena-Torrance Creative Perception Inventory, 246
Kounin's strategies, 114

legal blindness, 182
placement, 184
prevocational training, 186
Visual modality, 120, 323
Visual sequencing tasks, 134, 323
Vocational Rehabilitation Act
(Section 504 of Public Law
93-112), 4–5, 43
Vocational training, 186
for the blind, 186
for the physically handicapped,
227
Voice disorder, 145

W

Wechsler Intelligence Scale for
Children—Revised, 53, 245
Wide Range Achievement Test,
131, 323
Williams's cognitive-affective
model, 250
Word attack skills, 121, 158, 323
WRAT. *See* Wide Range
Achievement Test
Writing
and the gifted and talented,
266
and physical handicaps, 222,
235
and visual impairments, 199